Why I Love Hawai'i, the Big Island

By Luci Yamamoto, Writer

Growing up in Hilo, I took my island home for granted. Didn't everyone wake to birdsong, homegrown bananas for breakfast and the unmistakable silhouette of Mauna Kea in the distance? Didn't everyone gaze at an unobstructed blue horizon and fall asleep to the rat-a-tat of pounding rain on metal rooftops? It wasn't until I explored Hawai'i as a writer that I finally appreciated the island's uniqueness. The power of Pele and nature is phenomenal here, from fiery volcanic eruptions to otherworldly lava deserts – and the unpretentious nature of the local people is palpable. I love the Big Island for its small-town heart.

For more about our writers, see p320.

Above: View from the summit of Mauna Kea (p170)

Hawai'i, the Big Island

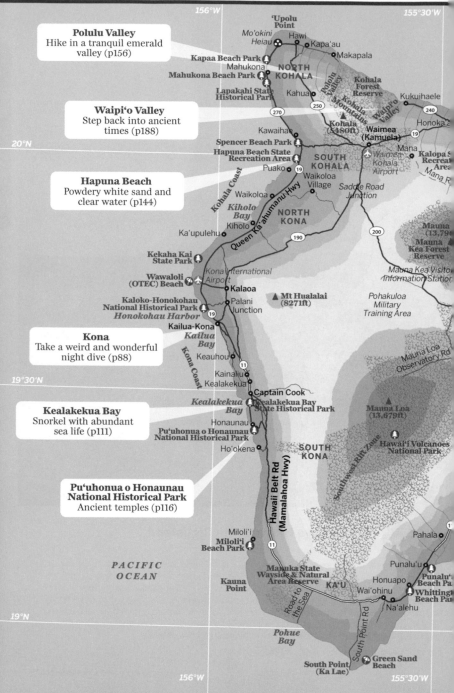

Polulu Valley
Hike in a tranquil emerald valley (p156)

Waipi'o Valley
Step back into ancient times (p188)

Hapuna Beach
Powdery white sand and clear water (p144)

Kona
Take a weird and wonderful night dive (p88)

Kealakekua Bay
Snorkel with abundant sea life (p111)

Pu'uhonua o Honaunau National Historical Park
Ancient temples (p116)

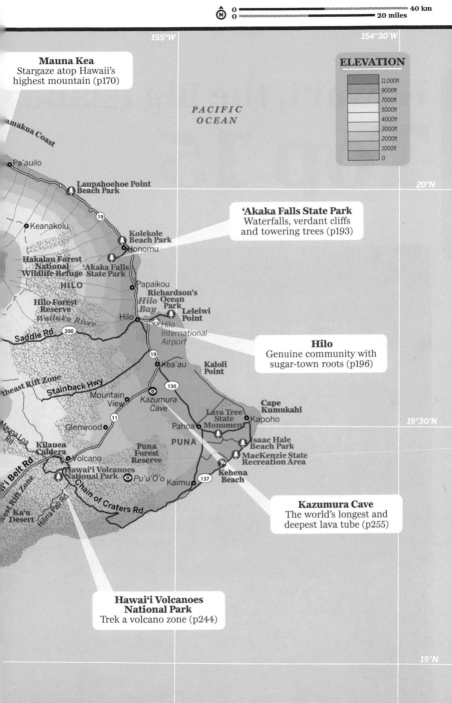

N 0 ———————— 40 km
0 ———————— 20 miles

155°W 154°30'W

Mauna Kea
Stargaze atop Hawaii's
highest mountain (p170)

PACIFIC
OCEAN

ELEVATION

11,000ft
9000ft
7000ft
5000ft
4000ft
3000ft
2000ft
1000ft
0

amakua Coast

Pa'auilo

Laupahoehoe Point
Beach Park

20°N

Keanakolu

'Akaka Falls State Park
Waterfalls, verdant cliffs
and towering trees (p193)

Kolekole
Beach Park
Honomu

Hakalau Forest
National
Wildlife Refuge

'Akaka Falls
State Park

HILO

Papaikou

Hilo Forest
Reserve

Richardson's
Ocean
Park

Leleiwi
Point

Hilo
Bay

Wailuku River

Hilo

Saddle Rd 200

Hilo
International
Airport

Hilo
Genuine community with
sugar-town roots (p196)

theast Rift Zone

Kea'au

Kaloli
Point

Stainback Hwy

19

130

Mountain
View

Kazumura
Cave

Cape
Kumukahi

Glenwood

11

Lava Tree
State
Monument

Kapoho

Mauna Loa Rd

Pahoa

19°30'N

Kilauea
Caldera

PUNA

Isaac Hale
Beach Park

Volcano

Puna
Forest
Reserve

MacKenzie State
Recreation Area

est Rift Zone

Hawai'i Volcanoes
National Park

Pu'u'O'o

137

Kehena
Beach

Kaimu

Kazumura Cave
The world's longest and
deepest lava tube (p255)

Ka'u
Desert

Hilina Pali Rd

Chain of Craters Rd

i Belt Rd

**Hawai'i Volcanoes
National Park**
Trek a volcano zone (p244)

19°N

155°W 154°30'W

Hawai'i, the Big Island's
Top 15

Hawai'i, the Big Island

Kohala & Waimea
p128

Hamakua Coast
p176

Kailua-Kona & the Kona Coast
p78

Mauna Kea & Saddle Road
p162

Hilo
p196

Puna
p222

Hawai'i Volcanoes National Park
p236

Ka'u
p258

Contents

HONU (GREEN SEA TURTLE)

WAIPI'O VALLEY P188

FINE ART PHOTOS/SHUTTERSTOCK ©

PNG STUDIO PHOTOGRAPHY/SHUTTERSTOCK ©

Contents

SURVIVAL GUIDE

SPECIAL FEATURES

4

Welcome to Hawai'i, the Big Island

Indulge your spirit of adventure on the biggest Hawaiian island. It's still a vast frontier, full of unexpected wonders.

Island Diversity

We doubt that it's possible to get 'island fever' on Hawai'i. The aptly named Big Island is fantastically diverse, with miles of highways – and, better yet, byways – to explore. Eight of the world's 13 climate zones exist here, adding sensory variety as you circumnavigate the island. Gaze at vivid emerald cliffs, swaths of black-, white- and even green-sand beaches, majestic volcanic mountains (possibly snowcapped!), stark lava desert, rolling pastureland and misty valleys, weathered by rain, waves and time. Hawai'i is twice as big as the other Hawaiian Islands combined, and its dramatic terrain is ever-fascinating.

Volcanic Wonders

Less than a million years old, Hawai'i is a baby in geological terms. Here you'll find the Hawaiian Islands' tallest, largest and only active volcanic mountains. Kilauea, on the eastern side, is the world's most active volcano. If you see glowing, red-hot lava, you are witnessing Earth in the making, a thrilling and humbling experience. At 33,000ft tall when measured from the ocean floor, Mauna Kea is the world's tallest mountain, and its significance cannot be overstated – as a sacred place to Hawaiians and a top astronomical site to scientists.

Ancient History & Modern Multiculturalism

Ancient history looms large on Hawai'i, a place of powerful mana (spiritual essence). The first Polynesians landed at Ka Lae, the windswept southern tip. Kamehameha the Great, who unified the Hawaiian Islands, was born in Kohala and died in Kailua-Kona. Hula and *oli* (chant) are deep-rooted here, and Miloli'i on the Kona Coast is perhaps the last Hawaiian fishing village. During the sugarcane era, traditional ways became intertwined with those of immigrant cultures: Chinese, Japanese, Filipino, Portuguese and more. This legacy is palpable in the mix of languages, foods and festivals.

Roads Less Traveled

Thanks to its sheer size, Hawai'i has lots of legroom. Enjoy the freedom of the open road, where the journey becomes the main attraction. From east to west, the island has multiple personalities, and it's worthwhile experiencing them all. While the 'Gold Coast' caters to travelers en masse, most island towns exist primarily for residents. Even the capital seat, Hilo, is a former plantation town that's still slow-paced and populated by *kama'aina* (people born and raised here). Ultimately this down-home localness marks the real Hawai'i. Don't miss it.

Hawai'i Volcanoes National Park

1 The eerie glow of a lava lake, secluded palm-fringed beaches, ancient petroglyphs pecked into hardened lava, and miles of hiking trails through smoking craters, rainforest and desert – you'll never run out of fascinating wonders at Hawai'i's number-one attraction. The park (p244) is also one of the island's top spots to experience traditional Hawaiian culture at hula dance performances, annual festivals, concerts and talks. After dark, warm up by the fireplace inside the landmark Volcano House lodge, perched right on the rim of Kilauea Caldera.

Mauna Kea Stargazing

2 It's breathless *and* breathtaking to be in the rarefied air of Mauna Kea (p170), Hawaii's highest mountain and most sacred spot. Once the sun goes down, the stars come out – and so do the telescopes. Mauna Kea is one the world's best astronomical sites, and the clear skies make for good amateur stargazing as well. What you see through visitor telescopes, whether at the visitor center or on a tour, you won't soon forget. For a trophy experience, be here during a meteor shower.

ALEXEY KAMENSKIY/SHUTTERSTOCK ©

LAURASLENS/SHUTTERSTOCK ©

AVPROPHOTO/SHUTTERSTOCK ©

Kona (& Ka'u) Coffee Farms

3 When Christian missionaries planted Kona's first coffee trees, they were only a floral fad. Eventually, thanks to ideal conditions along South Kona's rain-kissed 'coffee belt,' Kona coffee (p38) became a successful gourmet crop. Today rural byways wind past small, often family-owned plantations, some of which let visitors drop by. Since the late 2000s, Ka'u coffee growers have won awards in major contests, becoming the Cinderella story of Hawai'i coffee. Look for 100% locally grown labeling on bags of beans and menus.

Above left: Kona coffee beans

Pu'uhonua O Honaunau National Historical Park

4 Imposing *ki'i* (deity statues) watch over ancient temples at this historic site (p116), which is a visceral introduction to traditional Hawaiian culture. There's no better place to gain an understanding of the *kapu* (taboo) system that once governed life across the Hawaiian Islands. Breaking a *kapu* often meant death – unless you made it to a *pu'uhonua*. The bones of ancient chiefs are interred in a thatched-roof *hale* (house), emanating protective *mana* (spiritual essence).

Waipi'o Valley

5 You can linger at the scenic viewpoint overlooking this lush green valley (p188), but the waterfalls, wild horses and wilder black-sand beach beckon. But first you must reckon with the dauntingly steep access road. Then you can explore the valley on foot, on horseback or even in an old-fashioned mule-drawn wagon. Intrepid hikers can proceed along the King's Trail or reach for the most spectacular panoramas along the grueling Muliwai Trail – head up, up and up even higher for the money shot.

JAMES R.D. SCOTT/GETTY IMAGES ©

Snorkeling in Kealakekua Bay

6 It's all true – Kealakekua Bay (p111) is a giant real-life aquarium of abundant tropical fish, *honu* (Hawaiian green sea turtles) and spinner dolphins. Tourist brochures hype this as the best snorkeling in the state, and you'd better believe it. Eco-conscious regulations, such as restrictions on kayaks, are helping to preserve this underwater paradise. If you're a confirmed landlubber, it's still worth hiking down to this historically significant spot, where Captain Cook perished.

Chasing Lava

7 Pele, the Hawaiian goddess of fire and volcanoes, is notoriously fickle. But if you're lucky, you may get the chance to see live lava crawling over and under newly birthed land. Lava usually flows inside or around Hawai'i Volcanoes National Park (p244), sometimes plunging into the sea, sending a steam plume over a mile skyward as hot lava mixes with roiling surf. Feel the heat on a walking or boat tour out of Puna. Guided tours are recommended. Don't mess with Pele. Below: Lava flowing into the sea, Hawai'i Volcanoes National Park

Hapuna Beach

8 Stake out a spot on this half-mile stretch (p144) of powdery white sand, hire an umbrella and a boogie board and make this iconic beach your personal playground. Whatever your pleasure – surfboard, lounge chair or water wings – this beach is ideal for the whole family. While the basic A-frame camping cabins are not for the finicky, sleeping here means having a legendary beach in your front yard. For more magic, detour just north to tranquil Mauna Kea Beach, sitting on crescent-shaped Kauna'oa Bay.

OCEAN IMAGE PHOTOGRAPHY/SHUTTERSTOCK ©

WILDNERDPIX/SHUTTERSTOCK ©

Merrie Monarch Festival

9 Remember what you saw at that resort luau? That's to hula what Velveeta is to cheese. If you want to see how an authentic hula *halau* (school) invokes the gods and legends through Hawaiian chants and dance, attend this prestigious hula competition (p210) held in Hilo every Easter week. Book festival tickets, flights and accommodations a year in advance – people fly in from around the world for this one. In addition to the intense competitions, there's a parade, craft fair and a free exhibition of hula and pan-Pacific dances.

Diving in Kona

10 With glassy waters, thriving coral and teeming marine life, Kona waters make for phenomenal diving (p88). Due to the Big Island's 'youth' (relative to the other Hawaiian Islands), its less-eroded dive sites feature both shallow reefs and deep dropoffs, showcasing a variety of underwater terrain. There are many reliable dive companies along the Kona Coast, catering to both novices and experts. For a bucket-list experience, go deep on a Black Water night dive and see glowing, bioluminescent pelagic creatures in their inky element.

'Akaka Falls State Park

11 Shimmering like a jewel in a rainforest of towering trees and fragrant ginger, this 420ft-high waterfall (p193) is no less spectacular for its easy access. Drive up alongside constant tour buses, stroll a half mile through a Disney-esque nature trail and there you are. Like all waterfalls on Hawai'i's windward coast, the park's two falls are most impressive during seasonal rains when they pour copiously over the verdant cliffs. On your way out, poke around the tiny plantation village of Honomu for local color.

Hiking into Pololu Valley

12 Which is superior, Waipi'o Valley or Pololu Valley? It's a tough call to choose between Hawai'i's most prominent emerald valleys, each threaded with waterfalls and blessed with a formidable black-sand beach. But remote Pololu (p156) retains a tranquility lost to Waipi'o thanks to SUVs and monster trucks. It takes a 10-minute hike to descend into the valley, and that's the only way in. Combine your visit with lunch and a stroll around diminutive Hawi, Kohala's charming arts hub. In this northernmost thumb of land, find old Hawai'i at its most evocative.

Hilo

13 If one word describes Hilo (p196), that word would be 'real.' This former sugar town had a life before tourism and remains refreshingly unpretentious and normal – if normalcy includes tropical flora growing wild, drive-up beaches, farmers markets brimming with local edibles, unique museums, historic storefronts and sublime views from Mauna Kea to the horizon. Here you'll rarely find tourist traps, but instead be immersed in Hilo's diverse mix of residents, including multigenerational locals whose ancestors arrived as plantation workers. The pace is leisurely here, so slow down and smell the plumerias.

12

PETER CAREY/ALAMY ©

HANS GEEL/SHUTTERSTOCK ©

Kazumura Cave

14 In Hawai'i, what you see on the surface is never the whole story. Beneath the forests and volcanic flows lie elaborate systems of lava tubes, caves and caverns, multiplying by miles your exploration possibilities. The world's longest and deepest lava tube, Kazumura Cave (p255), near Volcano, is astounding in size, darkness and deafening silence. Also impressive are the newer Kula Kai Caverns in Ka'u. For a DIY experience, there's also Kaumana Caves in Hilo, while the family-friendly Thurston Lava Tube is roadside adventure doable for the whole family.

Local Food

15 What is local food (p34)? First there's locally grown produce, locally caught fish and locally raised meat. Hawai'i, with its vast acreage of fertile land, deftly transitioned from large-scale sugarcane to diverse small-scale crops, while fresh ahi (yellowfin tuna) is the fish of choice. Then there's traditional Hawaiian cuisine, such as smoked *kalua* pig and *laulau* (meat and fish wrapped in *ti* leaf and cooked). And finally there's 'local kine grinds' – comfort food: *loco moco*, plate lunches and Spam *musubi* (rice balls). Surprise your taste buds and try them all.
Bottom right: *Poke* (raw fish mixed with condiments)

Need to Know

For more information, see Survival Guide (p299)

Currency
US dollar ($)

Language
English, Hawaiian, Pidgin

Visas
Generally not required for Canadians or for citizens of Visa Waiver Program countries for stays of 90 days or less with ESTA pre-approval.

Money
Credit cards are widely accepted (except by some lodgings) and often required for reservations. Traveler's checks (US dollars) are occasionally used.

Cell Phones
International travelers need a multiband GSM phone to make calls in the USA. Popping in a US prepaid recharge-able SIM card is usually cheaper than using your home network.

Time
Hawaii-Aleutian Standard Time is GMT/UTC minus 10 hours. Hawaii doesn't observe Daylight Saving Time.

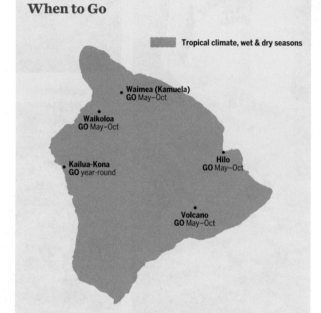

When to Go

Tropical climate, wet & dry seasons

Waimea (Kamuela)
GO May–Oct

Waikoloa
GO May–Oct

Kailua-Kona
GO year-round

Hilo
GO May–Oct

Volcano
GO May–Oct

High Season
(Dec–Mar & Jun–Aug)

➡ Accommodations up 50% to 100%.

➡ Especially busy around Christmas and New Year; in Hilo, Easter is jammed during the Merrie Monarch Festival.

➡ Winter is rainier and cooler on windward side.

Shoulder
(Oct & Nov)

➡ Decent prices on airfares and accommodations.

➡ Kona fully booked during Ironman World Championship (October) and Kona Coffee Cultural Festival (November).

➡ Increased crowds and business closures around Thanksgiving Day.

Low Season
(Apr–May & Sep)

➡ Mild temperatures and generally sunny days in spring and fall.

➡ Crowds and prices slightly drop before and after summer vacation.

➡ Memorial Day weekend is busy with local travelers.

Useful Websites

Big Island Visitors Bureau
(www.gohawaii.com/big-island) A good primer on sights, regions, weather, accommodations and other Big Island basics.

Big Island Hikes (www.big islandhikes.com) Dozens of hikes are reviewed, with first-hand accounts and helpful tips.

Konaweb (www.konaweb.com) Handy all-island events calendar and forums.

Andy Bumatai's the Daily Pidgin (www.youtube.com/user/ToolinAroundHI) Island insights and lol hilarity from this favorite island comedian.

NigaHiga on YouTube (www.youtube.com/user/nigahiga) Twenty-something Hilo native Ryan Higa, a YouTube sensation, exemplifies the humor of today's youth.

Lonely Planet (www.lonely planet.com/usa/hawaii/hawaii-the-big-island) Destination information, hotel bookings, traveler forum and more.

Important Numbers

Emergency (police, fire, ambulance)	☏911
Local directory assistance	☏411
Long-distance directory assistance	☏1-(area code)-555-1212
Toll-free directory assistance	☏1-800-555-1212
Operator	☏0

Exchange Rates

Australia	A$1	$0.76
Canada	C$1	$0.75
Euro zone	€1	$1.07
Japan	¥100	$0.90
New Zealand	NZ$1	$0.70
UK	£1	$1.24

For current exchange rates see www.xe.com.

Daily Costs

Budget: Less than $100

➡ Hostel dorm bed: $25–35

➡ Hostel room with shared bath: $75

➡ Plate lunch or *poke* bowl: $6–10

➡ Bus fare (one way): $2

➡ Stargazing on Mauna Kea: free

Midrange: $100–250

➡ Room with private bath at midrange hotel or B&B: $120–200

➡ Rental car (excluding insurance and gas): from $35/175 per day/week

➡ Dinner at informal sit-down restaurant: $20–40

➡ Snorkeling tour: $100–150

Top End: More than $250

➡ Luxury B&B or resort room: over $250

➡ Three-course meal and cocktail: $75–100

➡ Guided outdoor adventure tour: $80–200

➡ Helicopter tour: $200–500

Opening Hours

Banks 8:30am–4pm Monday–Friday, some to 6pm Friday; 9am–noon or 1pm Saturday.

Bars and clubs Noon–midnight daily, some to 2am Friday and Saturday. Bars may close early if business is slow.

Businesses (general) and government offices 8:30am–4:30pm Monday–Friday, some post offices also 9am–noon Saturday.

Restaurants Breakfast 6–10am, lunch 11:30am–2pm, dinner 5–9:30pm. Smaller restaurants may have more flexible hours.

Shops 9am–5pm Monday–Saturday, some also noon to 5pm Sunday; major shopping areas and malls keep extended hours.

Arriving in Hawai'i, the Big Island

Car rental booths for major agencies line the road outside the arrivals area at both airports. Taxis are curbside. Shuttle-bus services typically cost as much as taxis.

Hilo International Airport (p305) The approximate taxi fare from the airport to downtown is $20. Shuttle-bus services typically cost as much as taxis.

Kona International Airport (p305) From the airport to Kailua-Kona a taxi costs $30 and to Waikoloa it's $55. **Speedi Shuttle** (p305) will get you to destinations up and down the Kona Coast; it costs $34/100 for a shared/private shuttle to Kailua-Kona and $55/170 to the Waikoloa resort area. Book in advance.

For much more on **getting around**, see p306.

What's New

Hilo Bayfront Trails

A concrete path for pedestrians and bicyclists now circumnavigates Hilo's bayfront, Lili'uokalani Park, Banyan Dr and Wailoa River State Park. (p206)

Halema'uma'u Crater's Lava Lake

Pele, the Hawaiian goddess of fire and volcanoes, continues to display her power, sending lava flows into Puna. In October 2016, a lava lake in Halema'uma'u Crater overflowed onto the crater floor, adding an approximately 30ft layer of fresh lava. If the lake level remains high, molten lava is visible from the Jaggar Museum overlook. (p244)

Ka'u coffee

The small-scale upstart plantations in Ka'u continue to hold their own against established Kona growers, proving that their superior quality is no fluke. In the 2016 Hawaii Coffee Association Cupping Competition, Ka'u farms placed in the top five in two divisions: creative and commercial. (p258)

Hamakua Harvest Farmers Market

In 2016 a new farmers market launched in Honoka'a, featuring local produce and products. (p185)

Flumin' Kohala

In North Kohala, the 'Kohala Ditch' irrigated 10,000 acres of sugarcane. Today you can kayak on remaining flumes with this latest company to offer tours. (Two tour operators have folded in the past decade due to natural disasters that damaged the ditch.)

Real Estate Boom

Big Island home sales have recovered since the crash of 2008, with Puna as the busiest (and lowest priced after Ka'u) region.

Health food trends

Fruit salad is nothing new on Hawai'i, but trendy acai bowls have finally arrived and become ubiquitous at healthy cafes – *pitaya* (dragon fruit) is first runner-up. Local versions might include *poi,* coconut or cacao nibs. Vegetarian, vegan and gluten-free options abound, as do fermented products (kombucha and kimchi).

Pana'ewa Rainforest Zoo

Since 2016, the stars of Hilo's zoo are two Bengal tiger cubs, a playful orange female and a cool white male. (p201)

Saddle Road (Hwy 200) renovation

Improvement continues on this formerly death-defying roller coaster of a road. The county is currently working realigning sections of the eastern end near Hilo. (p162)

Merrie Monarch Festival

Tickets for the Merrie Monarch Festival can be reserved from applications mailed from December 1. Don't wait for December 26 as before, else lose your preferred seats! (p210)

For more recommendations and reviews, see lonelyplanet.com/usa/hawaii/hawaii-the-big-island

If You Like...

Beaches

Mention Hawai'i and most people immediately imagine sun, sand and surf. For Hollywood-worthy examples, head to Kona and Kohala. Elsewhere, beaches might be rugged and windswept, but are stunning nevertheless.

Mauna Kea Beach Arguably the island's loveliest beach, with powdery sand, gentle waters and a perfect crescent shape. (p146)

Hapuna Beach State Recreation Area Ever popular, this gorgeous expanse of white sand and jaunty surf is convenient, if crowded. (p144)

Kiholo State Park Reserve Less crowded, this black-sand beauty will likely reveal sea turtles, a swimmable lava tube and glorious sunsets. (p123)

Anaeho'omalu Beach Park Find lively ambience and lots of water-sports lessons and equipment rentals at this family-friendly beach. (p134)

Kekaha Kai State Park Those with 4WD can beach hop from one sandy gem to another (sun protection is imperative). (p126)

Richardson's Ocean Park This family-friendly, easy-access, multi-sport beach in Hilo is known as a *honu* (green sea turtle) habitat. (p200)

Kahalu'u Beach Park This multipurpose, drive-up favorite is always jammed, but convivial and remarkably full of marine life. (p98)

Honoli'i Beach Park Surfers, this is East Hawai'i's go-to surf spot, with reliable breaks and a steadfast local contingent (be respectful). (p205)

Extreme Adventures

Need some video for your GoPro or simply bragging rights? There's no shortage of excitement, with Hawai'i's inherent natural wonders.

Night diving with manta rays Gliding underwater with these graceful giant creatures is an unforgettable thrill. (p88)

Lava viewing in Puna Hike or, more thrillingly, go by boat to witness glowing lava at night, if your timing is right.(p231)

Mauna Kea Summit Trail Ascend the island's tallest mountain by foot – for the brave and hearty. (p171)

Lava caving Descend into the fantastic underworld of the Kazumura Cave in Puna or Kula Kai Caverns in Ka'u. (p41)

Ziplining For aerial thrills and a bird's-eye view of verdant North Kohala (p149) or Hamakua (p193) forest.

Scenic Drives

Hankering for the freedom of the open road? The Big Island's diverse geography and sheer size guarantees fascinating, visually striking drives. Up the ante on a motorcycle or bicycle.

Kohala Mountain Road Take in breathtaking vistas of bucolic pastureland and an immense backdrop of mountains and ocean. (p133)

Pepe'ekeo 4-mile Scenic Drive Wind through a lush tangle of greenery, across weathered bridges, past sparkling little waterfalls. (p182)

Hwy 132 to Hwy 137 Experience Puna's sultry tropical splendor on these mesmerizing roads. (p224)

Chain of Craters Road Journey across an active volcano zone to where – stop! – lava has buried the road. (p242)

Mauna Kea Access Road With 4WD and excellent driving ability, ascend to the top of this sacred mountain. (p168)

Saddle Road It's an honor to navigate between the island's tallest mountain and its largest. (p162)

Akoni Pule Highway For an 'edge of the world' sensation, this drive offers sweeping horizon views with zero obstructions. (p152)

Local Street Food

Don't miss the variety of local street food, influenced by the island's longstanding multicultural population. Inexpensive and readily available, these eats pack a powerful punch of flavor.

Cafe 100 Famous for *loco moco* (rice, fried egg and hamburger patty or fish/veg substitutes), which they have trademarked. (p215)

Suisan Fish Market Ah, a heaping bowl of fresh *poke* (cubed, marinated raw fish) hits the spot. (p214)

Super J's Go here for your first taste of Hawaiian *laulau, kalua* pig and lots of genuine aloha. (p113)

Anuenue Hit this counter for fantastic shave ice in almost incongruously gourmet flavors. (p148)

Tex Drive-In One whiff of freshly made *malasadas* (Portuguese doughnuts) and there goes the diet. (p185)

Two Ladies Kitchen Japanese *mochi* (sticky rice cake) meets island flavors like *liliko'i* (passion fruit) in this tiny Hilo gem. (p214)

Maku'u Farmers Market Come not only for fresh produce and wacky local characters, but also for fantastic food from various cultures. (p228)

Top: 'Anaeho'omalu Beach Park (p134)
Bottom: *Loco moco* (p36)

Month by Month

January

Although typically the rainiest and coolest month, January bursts into tourist high season, when snowbirds migrate to escape winter elsewhere.

🎊 Waimea Ocean Film Festival

Watch eco documentaries, high-adrenaline sports footage and films about Hawaiian culture in Waimea, South Kohala and Kona. (www.waimeaoceanfilm.org)

March

Weather improves and tourist traffic remains high, especially when students go on 'spring break' at the end of the month.

🍷 Kona Brewers Festival

This beer fest on the second Saturday of March just keeps getting bigger. Sip dozens of handcrafted brews from across Hawaii, the western USA and elsewhere. (p92)

April

Tourist high season winds down, just as rainstorms decrease. But Hilo's busiest week starts on Easter, when the Merrie Monarch Festival opens.

🎊 Merrie Monarch Festival

Hilo's most important event is a weeklong celebration of Hawaiian arts and culture, starting on Easter Sunday. This Olympics of hula competitions draws premier *halau* (schools) statewide and worldwide. (p210)

⭐ Laupahoehoe Music Festival

In late April, this all-day event at Laupahoehoe Point Beach Park features authentic Hawaiian music and hula, plus traditional handicrafts and lots to eat. (p192)

May

Crowds thin and prices drop between spring break and summer vacation. Temperatures are mild and sunny. Hotels sell out for the Memorial Day holiday weekend in late May.

🎊 May Day Lei Day Festival

This statewide cultural festival kicks off on May 1 (Lei Day) at Kalakaua Park in downtown Hilo, with plenty of masterful lei on display, and continues with live music and hula at Hilo's beautiful Palace Theater. (p210)

June

Beat the summer rush by arriving in early June, when visitors can expect warm, dry weather and good deals on hotels and flights.

🎊 North Kohala Kamehameha Day Celebration

On June 11, a state holiday, join the crowds at King Kamehameha's birthplace in North Kohala for a flowery parade, arts-and-crafts fair, live music and food booths. More events take place on Mokuola (Coconut Island) in Hilo. (p201)

✨ Hawai'i Volcanoes National Park Cultural Festival

This one-day festival draws crowds to Hawai'i Volcanoes National Park to celebrate Hawaiian culture with lei and basket-making demonstrations, hula dancing and even nose-flute jam sessions. (p253)

July

Temperatures soar and showers are less frequent. School summer vacations and the Independence Day holiday make this a busy travel month. Book early and expect steeper prices.

✨ Fourth of July Rodeo

Held on the Parker Ranch, this annual event packs in *paniolo* (Hawaiian cowboys) and their fans for team roping, horse racing and other yee-haw fun. (p159)

August

Families on vacation keep things busy. Expect hot, sunny weather, especially on the Kona side. Statehood Day observed on the third Friday of the month.

🎣 Hawaiian International Billfish Tournament

Kailua-Kona is the epicenter of big-game fishing, and this is the granddaddy of tournaments, held in late July or early August. Watch the weighing of the catch at Kailua Pier. (p92)

September

After a hectic Labor Day weekend in early September, crowds dwindle as families and students bid farewell to summer. Weather remains hot and relatively dry.

🏃 Queen Lili'uokalani Canoe Race

Traditional outrigger canoeing is a favorite local sport, and fall is the season for long-distance events. Labor Day weekend kicks off a series of races along the Kona Coast. (p92)

🍴 A Taste of the Hawaiian Range

This popular gala in Waikoloa is your ticket to sample gourmet bites of local meats and produce prepared by notable island chefs. Held in late September or early October. (p136)

October

The Kona Coast is booked solid with Ironman visitors. But elsewhere around the island, tourist traffic is moderate.

🏃 Ironman Triathlon World Championship

This triathlon is the ultimate endurance contest, combining a 2.4-mile ocean swim, 112-mile bike race and 26.2-mile marathon in Kailua-Kona on the second Saturday of October. (p90)

☆ Hawaii International Film Festival

Although the hot spot for the state's film festival (www.hiff.org) is Honolulu, highlights among the 200-plus Asian, Polynesian and Hawaii produced films are shown at theaters around the Big Island.

November

Prices are reasonable at the start of November, but Thanksgiving on the fourth Thursday of the month is a busy and pricey time to visit. Rainfall increases.

✨ Black & White Night

Go downtown wearing your best black-and-white outfit to Hilo's biggest multi-block party on the first Friday of November. (p210)

🍴 Kona Coffee Cultural Festival

Celebrate Kona's signature brew during the harvest season with 10 days of tastings, farm tours, cultural events and competition in early November. (p91)

☆ Waimea Ukulele & Slack Key Guitar Institute Concert

Aspiring musicians can study with Hawaii's foremost musicians during three days of workshops, while everyone can enjoy their concerts and *kanikapila* (jam sessions).

December

Peak tourist season kicks off in mid-December, as does the rainy season. The Christmas to New Year holiday period is booming. Book well in advance and expect to pay top dollar.

Itineraries

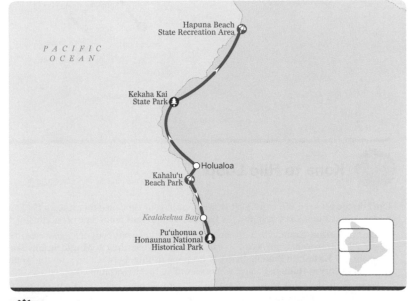

Gold Coast

If your idea of Hawai'i is sun, sand and surf, focus on the famous Gold Coast. Here you'll find a variety of beaches, from convivial drive-up favorites to remote gems accessible only by 4WD. Between beach trips, explore ancient Hawaiian sites and the world-renowned Kona Coffee Belt.

After landing in Kailua-Kona, beat jet lag at easy-access **Kahalu'u Beach Park**, where you might be rewarded with a sighting of *honu* (Hawaiian green sea turtles). Later, explore **Pu'uhonua O Honaunau National Historical Park**, an ancient 'Place of Refuge,' and gaze at your first island sunset. The next day, book a cruise or a kayaking permit to snorkel in **Kealakekua Bay**, a veritable aquarium of fascinating marine life. Cool off in upcountry **Holualoa**, a former coffee village now thriving as an arts community.

If you're then hankering for a more off-road experience, hire a 4WD (and bring lots of sunscreen) to reach **Kekaha Kai State Park**, a string of once-remote beaches. Alternatively, bask in the rays at **Hapuna Beach State Recreation Area** or treat yourself to a round of golf or luxury spa treatment at one of South Kohala's resorts.

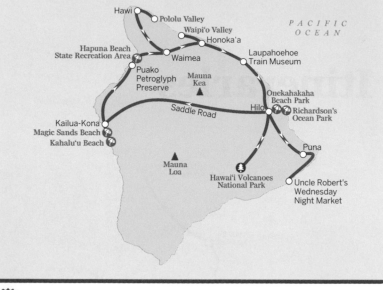

10 DAYS Kona to Hilo Loop

Can't decide between West and East Hawai'i? Split your time on either side, in the gloriously verdant Hamakua Coast and the barren mountainous landscape of Saddle Road.

Start in **Kailua-Kona**, where the sunshine will switch your body clock to local time. Spend a day or two enjoying ocean sports, such as bodyboarding at **Magic Sands Beach**, snorkeling at **Kahalu'u Beach**, diving or deep-sea fishing. Between dips, ground yourself in island history at Hulihe'e Palace, where Hawaiian royalty vacationed.

Meander up the South Kohala Coast, stopping for a walk to the **Puako Petroglyph Preserve** and to **Hapuna Beach State Recreation Area** for an archetypal beach day.

Next, enjoy the island's bucolic side in **Waimea**, a *paniolo* (Hawaiian cowboy) town, and **Hawi**, surrounded by rolling hills. Eating is excellent in these towns, where you'll find acclaimed Hawaii Regional Cuisine and innovative sushi. Make your way into **Pololu Valley**, where each little switchback presents another stupendous view.

Now it's time to head east. First stop: **Honoka'a**, a historic town now known for niche crops, a strong local community and irresistible *malasadas* (Portuguese doughnuts) at Tex Drive-In. Work off those doughnuts by walking down the steep road into **Waipi'o Valley**. Along the Hamakua Coast, stop at the **Laupahoehoe Train Museum**, a mini gallery highlighting the magnificent railroads that once chugged over the gigantic gulches.

Settle now in **Hilo**, the untouristy capital seat, with a charming historic downtown. Splash with the tots at **Onekahakaha Beach Park** or look for *honu* (Hawaiian green sea turtles) at **Richardson's Ocean Park**. From Hilo, take a day trip or two to **Puna**, cruising through sultry tropical jungles and, if your timing's right, trekking to see molten lava at night. Don't miss **Uncle Robert's Wednesday Night Market** for a truly local experience.

End your visit with the island's prize: **Hawai'i Volcanoes National Park**, a veritable jackpot for hikers and nature lovers. Check with the rangers at the visitor center first. Don't miss the impressive collection at Volcano Art Center and the farmers market on Sunday. Finally return to Kona via **Saddle Road**, which snakes its way between Mauna Kea and Mauna Loa.

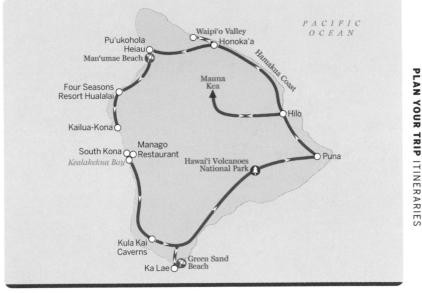

 2 WEEKS Circle Island Tour

To get your arms around Hawai'i, you need at least two weeks. You need enough time not only for driving, but also for absorbing the sheer diversity of terrain, climate and culture.

Stay a couple of nights in **South Kona**, where the easygoing village pace and lush scenery make for a relaxing tonic. Reserve a kayak permit to explore the breathtaking marine life in **Kealakekua Bay**. For an extraordinarily retro experience, feast on pork chops or fried *'opelu* (mackerel scad) at **Manago Restaurant**.

Go south into Ka'u, stopping to explore the stunning **Kula Kai Caverns** with expert guides. Stop at **Ka Lae**, the southernmost point in the USA, and, if undeterred by whipping winds and rugged terrain, trek to **Green Sand Beach**, where the 'reward' is not the actual beach (which is not swimmable), but the striking scene (and spirit of adventure).

Enter new territory as you approach **Hawai'i Volcanoes National Park**. Avid hikers should find accommodations in Volcano village and start all-day hikes bright and early. To see molten lava, go to **Puna**, where you most likely have to hoof it over punishing terrain or sail across choppy waters to a viewing site. Recover by kicking back amid lush tree canopies and tide pools, enjoying the anything-goes attitude.

Continue circling the island to **Hilo**, a convenient home base with a multitude of restaurants, shops and things to do. Cobble together a picnic lunch and find a shady spot at Lili'uokalani Park, and visit the Bengal tigers at the well-tended Pana'ewa Rainforest Zoo. Ascend **Mauna Kea** to witness an unforgettable sunset and stargaze.

After a few days in Hilo, head west along the **Hamakua Coast**, arguably the most scenic route along the highway. Take the short, steep hike into **Waipi'o Valley**. For an interesting *paniolo* (cowboy) plantation town, stay in **Honoka'a**, where nearby niche farms are thriving.

Finally head south along the Kohala Coast, stopping for a dip at picturesque **Mau'umae Beach**. Pay homage to Kamehameha I at the ruins of his **Pu'ukohola Heiau**. Splurge on a couple of nights at the **Four Seasons Resort Hualalai**. For variety, check out **Kailua-Kona's** burgeoning restaurant scene for dinner.

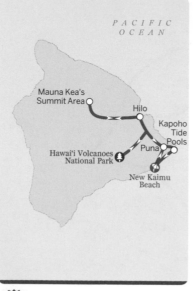

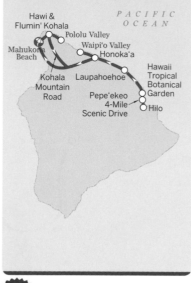

5 DAYS Volcano Watching

Only on Hawai'i can you fully appreciate the power of Pele, goddess of fire and volcanoes. Here, drive past lava deserts, hike across huge craters and glimpse red-hot molten lava, if you're lucky. Stay in Hilo, Puna or Volcano and reserve one day for Mauna Kea.

To explore Hawai'i's volcanoes, **Hilo**, the island capital, is an ideal starting point. Go to 'Imiloa Astronomy Center to ground yourself in volcanology, astronomy and ancient voyaging. Picnic at Lili'uokalani Park, Japanese gardens with a view of Mauna Kea. Next head to **Hawai'i Volcanoes National Park** and make a beeline for the museum and kid-favorite lava tube. Hiking in the national park is a must; choose from all-day treks to short nature walks.

Spend at least a day in **Puna**, the epicenter of lava activity and alternative lifestyles (welcome hippies!). Drive the jungly back roads, and you'll find lava attractions, from the **Kapoho Tide Pools** to the island's newest black sand at **New Kaimu Beach**. Lava sighting typically requires an arduous hike or choppy boat tour. Finally make your way to **Mauna Kea's Summit Area**, either by 4WD, by tour or, for the extremely fit and intrepid, by foot.

4 DAYS Small Town Retreat

To escape high-rises, traffic, big-box stores and crowds, target the Hamakua Coast and North Kohala. Here former plantation towns are remarkably unchanged, and you'll revel in silence and small-town pace.

From **Hilo** cross the 'Singing Bridge' and suddenly you're in the country. Veer onto the **Pepe'ekeo 4-mile Scenic Drive** for a visual extravaganza of tropical flora, which you can see close-up at **Hawaii Tropical Botanical Garden**. In **Laupahoehoe**, wind your way down to the windswept coast.

Honoka'a is tiny, but it's a rustic charmer with indie eats and sleeps. Spend one day exploring **Waipi'o Valley**, either walking the steep path to the beach or joining a guided tour into the valley. Along the entire coast, try touring a boutique farm: mushrooms, vanilla, tea or coffee.

Next drive up the windswept North Kohala coast, stopping to snorkel at **Mahukona Beach**, which has zero beach appeal but boasts colorful marine life. Stay in **Hawi**, where you'll find standout dining. On your last day, hike down into **Pololu Valley** and kayak with **Flumin' Kohala** in historic irrigation ditches. Drive down **Kohala Mountain Road** for a final visual treat.

Top: Waipi'o Valley
(p188)
Bottom: Hapuna Beach
(p144)

Hawai'i, the Big Island: Off the Beaten Track

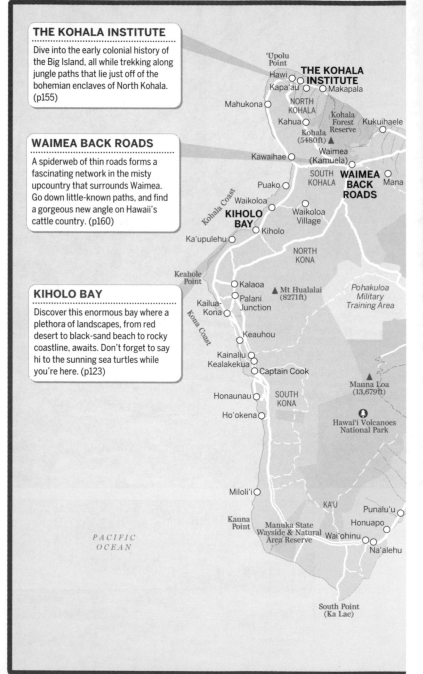

THE KOHALA INSTITUTE

Dive into the early colonial history of the Big Island, all while trekking along jungle paths that lie just off of the bohemian enclaves of North Kohala. (p155)

WAIMEA BACK ROADS

A spiderweb of thin roads forms a fascinating network in the misty upcountry that surrounds Waimea. Go down little-known paths, and find a gorgeous new angle on Hawaii's cattle country. (p160)

KIHOLO BAY

Discover this enormous bay where a plethora of landscapes, from red desert to black-sand beach to rocky coastline, awaits. Don't forget to say hi to the sunning sea turtles while you're here. (p123)

'Upolu Point

Hawi
THE KOHALA
INSTITUTE
Kapa'au   Makapala
NORTH
Mahukona   KOHALA
Kohala
Kahua   Forest   Kukuihaele
Reserve
Kohala
(5480ft)▲
Waimea
Kawaihae   (Kamuela)
SOUTH   WAIMEA
KOHALA   BACK   Mana
Puako   ROADS
Kohala Coast
Waikoloa
KIHOLO   Waikoloa
BAY   Village
Kiholo
Ka'upulehu

NORTH
KONA

Keahole
Point   Kalaoa   ▲ Mt Hualalai   Pohakuloa
Palani   (8271ft)   Military
Kailua-   Junction   Training Area
Kona

Keauhou
Kona Coast
Kainaliu
Kealakekua
Captain Cook

▲
Mauna Loa
Honaunau   SOUTH   (13,679ft)
KONA
Ho'okena   ⓐ
Hawai'i Volcanoes
National Park

Miloli'i
KA'U   Punalu'u
Kauna   Honuapo
Point   Manuka State
Wayside & Natural Wai'ohinu
Area Reserve   Na'alehu

PACIFIC
OCEAN

South Point
(Ka Lae)

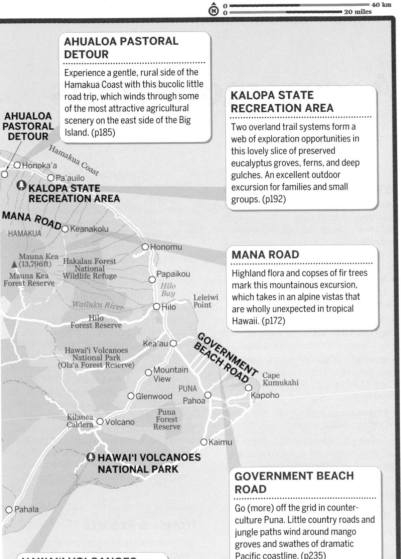

0 ——— 40 km
0 ——— 20 miles

AHUALOA PASTORAL DETOUR

Experience a gentle, rural side of the Hamakua Coast with this bucolic little road trip, which winds through some of the most attractive agricultural scenery on the east side of the Big Island. (p185)

KALOPA STATE RECREATION AREA

Two overland trail systems form a web of exploration opportunities in this lovely slice of preserved eucalyptus groves, ferns, and deep gulches. An excellent outdoor excursion for families and small groups. (p192)

MANA ROAD

Highland flora and copses of fir trees mark this mountainous excursion, which takes in an alpine vistas that are wholly unexpected in tropical Hawaii. (p172)

GOVERNMENT BEACH ROAD

Go (more) off the grid in counter-culture Puna. Little country roads and jungle paths wind around mango groves and swathes of dramatic Pacific coastline. (p235)

HAWAI'I VOLCANOES NATIONAL PARK

Witness the primal engine of creation churning out actual lava, which bubbles in dramatic flows across the Mordor-esque slatescape of Volcanoes National Park. When else will you get a chance to see creation in action? (p253)

Accommodations

Types of Accommodations

Availability is scarcer during high season (mid-December through March or April, and June through August) and around major holidays and special events. Book months in advance for peak periods, when room rates rise.

➡ **Hotels & resorts** Prevalent on South Kohala and Kona Coasts; top-end resorts offer the best beaches and splashy pools.

➡ **Condos** Mainly south of Kailua-Kona; ideal for independent travelers who prefer apartment-style amenities; discounted weekly rates.

➡ **B&Bs & inns** Generally reliable, with more space and amenities than comparably priced hotels; B&Bs provide breakfast. Multinight stays often required.

➡ **Hostels** Simple private rooms and dormitory beds at rock-bottom prices.

➡ **Camping & cabins** Low-cost campsites and budget cabins at national, state and county parks; bring your own camping gear.

Camping

Hawai'i has enough good campgrounds to mean you can enjoyably circumnavigate the island with a tent, plus there are several highly memorable backcountry camping opportunities. Some parks also offer simple cabins and DIYers can rent camper vans.

Hawai'i Volcanoes National Park has two drive-up campgrounds (one fee-paying with cabins, the other free) and several great backcountry sites. Only backcountry sites require permits available at the Backcountry Office (p252).

State parks require camping permits for tent sites ($12/18 residents/non-residents) and cabins. The easiest way to make a reservation and obtain a permit for state park cabins and campgrounds (plus those in Waimanu Valley) is using the online reservation system of the State of Hawaii Department of Land and Resources (https://camping.ehawaii.gov); reservations must be made seven days prior to check-in. The maximum stay per permit is five consecutive nights.

County park facilities and upkeep range from good to minimal. Some parks are isolated. Camping permits are required for county parks, and can be obtained (up to a year in advance) online from the Department of Parks & Recreation (☑808-961-8311, 808-323-4322; http://hawaiicounty.ehawaii.gov/camping; Suite 6, 101 Pauahi St, Hilo; ☺7:45am-4:30pm Mon-Fri). Daily camping fees are $6/3/1 for adults/teens/children 12 years and under, with the exception of Ho'okena Beach Park (p118). Details about facilities at each county park are available at www.hawaiicounty.gov/parks-and-recreation.

Hotels & Resorts

Ranging from no-frills motels to mega beach resorts, hotels typically offer full-time staff, housekeeping and amenities such as swimming pools, bars and restaurants.

'Rack rates' refer to the the highest published rates. Hotels often hugely undercut rack rates to book as close to capacity as possible. Reserve ahead online for discounts, which can often be enormous, even during high season. There's a sweet spot (around three months in advance, in our experience) when it comes to reserving online – too far out and you may miss promotions; too close in and there won't be anything available.

At some hotels, rates depend mainly on the view. Even partial ocean views cost 50% to 100% more than garden or mountain views.Most large resorts charge 'resort fees,' which cover a wide range of incidentals that are normally just part of the rate at other properties.

Note that all beaches are public access in Hawaii. Resorts maintain parking lots for non-guest access to their beaches.

Booking Services

➡ **Hawaii Vacation Rentals** (www.hawaiianbeachrentals.com) Reliable source of good rentals across the state.

➡ **Kona Coast Vacations** (www.konacoastvacations.com) Lists properties across the island.

➡ **Affordable Paradise** (www.affordable-paradise.com) Statewide rental and condo listings.

➡ **Two Papayas** (www.2papayas.com) Comprehensive list of Puako rentals.

➡ **Boundless Hawaii** (http://boundlesshawaii.com) Well-designed database of island-wide accommodations.

➡ **Waikoloa Vacation Rentals** (www.waikoloahawaiivacations.com) Rentals for the Waikoloa area in South Kohala.

➡ **Lonely Planet** (lonelyplanet.com) Recommendations and bookings.

Top Choices

Best Splurge

➡ **Hale Kawehi**, Hilo (apt $125; www.halekawehi.com)

➡ **Kohala Lodge**, Hawi (per night $300; www.vacationhi.com)

➡ **Volcano Rainforest Retreat**, Volcano (cottage incl breakfast $195-350; www.volcanoretreat.com)

➡ **Kalaekilohana**, South Point (Ka Lae; d incl breakfast $369; www.kau-hawaii.com)

➡ **Cliff House Hawaii**, Waipi'o Valley (house $200, additional person $35; www.cliffhousehawaii.com)

A resort swimming pool

Best B&Bs

➡ **Ka'awa Loa Plantation & Guesthouse**, Captain Cook (r $129-149, cottage/ste $159/199; www.kaawaloaplantation.com)

➡ **Hilo Bay Hale**, Hilo (r incl breakfast $130-160; www.hilobayhalebnb.com)

➡ **Honu Kai B&B**, Kailua-Kona (d incl breakfast $220-255; www.honukaibnb.com)

➡ **Holualoa Inn**, Holualoa (r/ste/cottage from $365/405/525; www.holualoainn.com)

➡ **Kane Plantation**, Honaunau (d $300; http://kaneplantationhawaii.com)

Best on a Budget

➡ **Hedonisia**, Pahoa (tent site $25, dm from $30, cottages $95; www.hedonisiahawaii.com)

➡ **Arnott's Lodge**, Hilo (camping per person $16, dm from $30, r with/without bath $90/70, ste from $100; www.arnottslodge.com)

➡ **My Hawaii Hostel**, Kailua-Kona (dm/rm $40/80; www.myhawaiihostel.com)

➡ **Pineapple Park**, Captain Cook (dm $30, r shared/private bath from $79/89; www.pineapple-park.com)

➡ **Kama'aina Inn**, Hilo (r from $105; www.kamaainainn.com)

Getting Around

How to Get Around

➡ **Car Rental** Having your own set of wheels is the best way to see all of the Big Island. If you're planning off-the-beaten-track adventures then consider a 4WD vehicle, but for basic sightseeing it's unnecessary.

➡ **Bike** Although getting around the island by bicycle is possible for very fit, enthusiastic cyclists, riding between towns is no casual cruise. Weather conditions can be challenging, and roads with no shoulder for bicycles can be risky. In towns, however, bikes can be an efficient, green option.

➡ **Bus** Public transit by bus is available, but service is limited and you'll probably find it way too time-consuming.

➡ **Resort Shuttle** Some hotels and resorts run complimentary shuttles to major sights.

➡ **Taxi** Most cab companies serve only a limited area, and won't drive islandwide.

Car Rental

➡ Most agencies require you to be at least 25 years old, to possess a valid driver's license and to have a major credit card (not a debit card).

➡ A few companies will rent to drivers between the ages of 21 and 24, typically for an underage surcharge of about $25 per day; call ahead for details.

➡ Without a credit card, many agencies simply won't rent a vehicle to you. Others might require prepayment by cash,

---

BEST ROAD TRIPS

➡ **Mauna Kea Access Road** (p168) A high-altitude climb through cinder cones to a lunar landscape.

➡ **South Puna Triangle** (p224) Cruise the coastline with stops for snorkeling, sun-basking and lava hikes.

➡ **Kohala Mountain Road** (p132) A new scene around every bend, each more photogenic than the last.

➡ **Chain of Craters Road** (p242) A man-versus-nature trail through fantastic lava formations.

➡ **South Point Road** (p262) A windswept drive to the southernmost point of the USA.

➡ **Hamakua Highlights** (p182) Wind through lush foliage to discover gardens and waterfalls.

traveler's check or debit card, with an additional refundable deposit of $500 per week, proof of return airfare and possibly more.

→ When picking up your vehicle, most agencies will request the name and phone number of the place where you're staying. Some will refuse to rent to those who list a campground as their address.

→ For more flexibility on rules, independent car rental agencies are your best bet. Only an indie company, such as **Harper Car & Truck Rentals** (☎800-852-9993, 808-969-1478; www.harpershawaii.com), will let you drive your 4WD rental vehicle to the summit of Mauna Kea. That said, Harper will require a high deductible, charge top dollar and very thoroughly inspect the condition of your vehicle when you return it.

For more on driving in the Big Island, see p48 and p308.

No Car?

Bus

The island-wide **Hele-On Bus** (☎808-961-8744; www.heleonbus.org; per trip adult/senior & student $2/1, 10-ride ticket $15, monthly pass $60) will get you to major destinations on the Big Island, but service is limited, especially on Sunday and holidays. Be sure to check the website for current routes, schedules and fares. Most buses originate from the Mo'oheau Bus Terminal in downtown Hilo.

A one-way adult fare includes a free two-hour transfer. You cannot board with a surfboard or boogie board; luggage, backpacks, skateboards and bicycles are charged $1 each. Children under four years old ride free with fare-paying passenger.

Bicycle

The Big Island is a good training ground for adventurous, avid and very fit cyclists, but pedaling around as a primary form of transportation is not recommended. While doable, it's a big challenge. The sun, rain and wind can be brutal, and the Hamakua Coast has absolutely no shoulder for bicycles. And on this car-dominated island, drivers can be oblivious to cyclists.

Within towns, however, a bicycle can be a pleasant, green option. If you're staying in Hilo or Kailua-Kona for a week or more, renting a bike might be worthwhile. Bike rental and repair shops can be found around the island. Go-to shops include Bike Works in Kailua-Kona and Mid-Pacific Wheels in Hilo.

For more on cycling in the Big Island, see p43 and p311.

PLAN YOUR TRIP GETTING AROUND

FAST FACTS: DRIVING

→ Drive on the right-hand side of the road.

→ Slow, courteous driving is the rule.

→ It's illegal to carry open containers of alcohol (even if they're empty) inside a vehicle.

→ You may hear the words *makai* (seaward) or *mauka* (inland) in directions.

→ Child safety seats are required for children aged three and under. Those aged four to seven must sit in a booster seat.

Road Distances (miles)

	Kailua-Kona	Hilo	Naalehu	Captain Cook
Hilo	76			
Naalehu	59	65		
Captain Cook	12	87	48	
Waimea	40	58	98	50

Poke (cubed raw fish mixed with condiments)

Plan Your Trip
Eat & Drink Like a Local

Food is a vehicle of celebration and bonding on the Big island, a means of connecting to family, friends, and the Earth and ocean from which said food derives. The Big Island has big appetites, and local plate lunches and dinners will usually leave visitors in need of a nap.

The Year in Food

Mild, tropical weather year-round means it's always a good time to eat on the Big Island.

Winter (December to February)

Winter on the Big Island is about as cold as...well, a sunny day in Hawai'i. Still, there are hearty meals for you to ward off any (wrongly) perceived chill, such as steak at the Panaewa rodeo in Hilo (http://hawaiirodeo stampede.com).

Spring (March to May)

Toss back some brew at the Kona Brewers Festival (p92) or indulge your sweet tooth at the Big Island Chocolate Festival (p146). if the above doesn't put you in a food coma, caffeinate yourself at the Ka'u Coffee Festival (p264).

Summer (June to August)

It's hot, so cool off with a Mai Tai at Don's Mai Tai Festival (p91). Parker Ranch (p158) holds a rodeo on the 4th of July.

Autumn (September to November)

This is premier foodie season: you can hit up the Kona Coffee Cultural Festival (p91), plus A Taste of the Hawaiian Range (p136).

Eat Local

Many Big Islanders are backyard farmers, growing more apple bananas, star fruit and avocados than they can consume themselves. Still, a whopping 85% to 90% of Hawaii's food is imported, and food security (aka 'food sovereignty') is a hot topic. Small-scale family farmers are trying to shift the agriculture industry away from corporate-scale monocropping (as seen in sugar or pineapple) enabled by chemical fertilizers, pesticides, herbicides and genetically modified organisms (GMOs).

Diversified agriculture and agrotourism are booming on the Big Island. It's not just about Hawai'i's signature macadamia nuts and Kona coffee anymore, but a delicious range of locally grown edibles: Hamakua Coast mushrooms, vanilla, tomatoes and salad greens; lobsters, abalone (sea snails) and *kampachi* (yellowtail) from the Kona coast; grass-fed beef and lamb from Waimea; Kona chocolate; organic tea from Volcano and the Hamakua Coast; Ka'u oranges and coffee; yellow-flesh Kapoho Solo papayas from Puna; and local honey. While the Big Island's egg and poultry farms are long gone, the state's two biggest cattle dairies still operate here.

Despite the popularity of Hawai'i's farmers markets, supermarkets still typically stock blemish-free Sunkist oranges and California grapes. An exception is the Big Island's KTA Superstores, a minichain that carries 200 products – including milk, beef, produce and coffee – from dozens of local vendors under its Mountain Apple Brand. For what it's worth, KTAs usually have a fantastic range of local hot plates and takeout lunches, including trays of delicious *poke* (raw fish salad, which is way better than it sounds).

Native Hawaiian Food

With its earthy flavors and Polynesian ingredients, Native Hawaiian cooking is a genre unique unto the culinary world. But it's not necessarily easy for visitors to find – look for it at roadside markets, plate-lunch kitchens, old-school delis and island diners.

Kalua pig is traditionally roasted whole underground in an *imu,* a pit of red-hot stones layered with banana and *ti* leaves. Cooked this way, the pork is smoky, salty and succulent. Nowadays *kalua* pork is typically oven-roasted and seasoned with salt and liquid smoke. At a commercial luau, a pig placed in an *imu* is usually only for show (it couldn't feed 300-plus guests anyway).

Poi – a purplish paste made of taro root, often steamed and fermented – was sacred to ancient Hawaiians. Taro is highly nutritious, low in calories, easily digestible and versatile to prepare. Tasting bland to mildly tart or even sour, *poi* is usually not eaten by itself, but as a starchy counterpoint to strongly flavored dishes such as *lomilomi* salmon (minced, salted salmon with diced tomato and green onion). Fried or baked taro chips are sold at grocery stores, gas stations and the like.

A popular main dish is *laulau,* a bundle of pork or chicken and salted butterfish wrapped in taro or *ti* leaves and steamed until it has a soft spinach-like texture. We find it a little bland, but locals swear by the stuff. Other traditional Hawaiian fare includes baked *'ulu* (breadfruit), with a mouthfeel similar to potato; *'opihi* (limpet), tiny mollusks picked off reefs at low tide; and *haupia,* a coconut-cream custard thickened with arrowroot or cornstarch.

In general, we'd characterize Native Hawaiian cuisine as extremely filling, if not the most flavorful. There's a lot of emphasis on starch and meat. If you've dined elsewhere in Polynesia, it has a very similar ingredient and flavor profile to sister cuisines located across the ocean.

Hawaii Regional Cuisine

Hawaii was considered a culinary backwater until the early 1990s, when a handful of island chefs – including Alan Wong, Roy Yamaguchi, Sam Choy and Peter Merriman, all of whom still have restaurants on the Big Island – created a new cuisine, borrowing liberally from Hawaii's multiethnic heritage.

These chefs partnered with island farmers, ranchers and fishers to highlight fresh, local ingredients, and in doing so transformed childhood favorites into gourmet Pacific Rim masterpieces. Suddenly macadamia nut-crusted mahimahi, miso-glazed butterfish and *liliko'i* (passion fruit) anything were all the rage.

This culinary movement was dubbed 'Hawaii Regional Cuisine' and its 12 pioneering chefs became celebrities. At first, Hawaii Regional Cuisine was rather exclusive, found only at high-end dining rooms. Its hallmarks included Eurasian fusion flavors and gastronomic techniques with elaborate plating.

Upscale restaurants are still the mainstay for Hawaii's star chefs, but now you'll find neighborhood bistros and even platelunch food trucks serving dishes inspired by Hawaii Regional Cuisine, with island farms lauded like designer brands on menus.

Local Specialties

Cheap, tasty and filling, local 'grinds' (food) is the stuff of cravings and comfort. There's no better example than that classic plate lunch: a fixed-plate meal of 'two scoop' rice, macaroni or potato salad and a hot protein dish, such as fried mahimahi, teriyaki chicken or *kalbi* short ribs. Often eaten with disposable chopsticks on disposable plates, these meals pack a flavor (and caloric) punch: fried, salty and meaty. Nowadays healthier plates come with brown rice and salad greens, but in general, the backbone of the plate lunch are those two scoops of rice and potato/macaroni salad, a heaping mountain of carbohydrates that are Mauna Kea-esque in their proportions.

Sticky white rice is more than a side dish in Hawaii – it's a culinary building block, and an integral partner in everyday meals. Without rice, Spam *musubi* (rice balls) would just be a slice of canned meat. *Loco moco* would be nothing more than an egg-and-gravy covered hamburger patty. Just so you know, sticky white rice means exactly that. Not fluffy rice. Not wild rice. And definitely not instant.

One must-try local *pupu* (snack or appetizer) is *poke* (pronounced *'poh*-keh'), a savory dish of bite-sized raw fish (typically ahi), seasoned with *shōyu,* sesame oil, green onion, chili-pepper flakes, sea salt, *ogo* (crunchy seaweed) and *'inamona* (a condiment made of roasted, ground *kukui* – candlenut tree – nuts). Few foodstuffs we've tried short of a raw oyster can match *poke* when it comes to evoking the flavors of the ocean.

Another favorite local food is saimin, a soup of chewy Chinese egg noodles swimming in Japanese broth, garnished with green onion, dried nori (Japanese dried seaweed), *kamaboko* (steamed fish cake) and *char siu* (Chinese barbecued pork).

The traditional local sweet treat is Chinese crack seed. It's preserved fruit (typically plum, cherry, mango or lemon) that, like Coca-Cola or curry, is impossible to describe – it can be sweet, sour, salty or spicy. Sold prepackaged at supermarkets and Longs Drugs or scooped by the pound at specialty shops, crack seed is truly addictive.

They grow avocados here that look to be the size of your head, their size only

Luau food

outstripped by their tastiness. With that said, don't measure an avocado strictly by its size; smaller ones can be just as delicious. Many avocado trees are marked with 'no spray' signs, especially in, shall we say, the 'crunchier' corners of the island (Puna, North Kohala and the South Kona Coast come to mind). The 'no spray' request is aimed at those spraying pesticides – there's a muscular no-pesticide, no-GMO movement (p66) on the island, and while Big Island folks are generally laid-back, the issue can provoke incredibly heated discussions.

There's beef, and then there's Big Island beef. The northern valleys of Hawai'i are carpeted in mile upon mile of grassy pastureland, all dotted with roaming herds of cattle. This enormous well of beef is often exported, but head to the right restaurants and you'll be dining on finely marbled steaks and juicy, locally sourced burgers that would be the envy of any Texas table. We're not sure what it is about the grasses these cows are dining on, but the beef here has a richness that is hard to both describe and match.

In parts of the Big Island, particularly Hilo and the South Kona Coast, a version of Japanese cuisine that has taken on island elements has become its own subgenre of native cuisine. In diners run by Japanese Americans, you may see hot dogs served alongside rice and *furikake* (a seasoning of dried fish, seaweed and other goodies), while most meals are preceded by a complimentary bowl of *edamame* (soybeans) and come with a bowl of miso soup.

Luau

In ancient Hawaii, a luau commemorated auspicious occasions, such as births, war victories or successful harvests. Modern luau to celebrate weddings or a baby's first birthday are often large banquet-hall or outdoor gatherings with the *'ohana* (extended family and friends). Although the menu might be daring – including Hawaiian delicacies such as raw *'a'ama* (black crab) and *'opihi* – the entertainment is low-key.

Hawaii's commercial luau started in the 1970s. Today these shows offer the elaborate pseudo-Hawaiian feast and Polynesian dancing and fire eaters that many visitors expect. But the all-you-can-eat buffet of luau standards is usually toned down for the mainland palate, with steamed mahi-mahi and teriyaki chicken. Most commercial luau are overpriced and overly touristy, but they're fun for all that – it's one of those experiences you check off the list and probably don't need to repeat again.

Coffee, Tea & Traditional Drinks

Hawaii was the first US state to grow coffee. World-famous Kona coffee wins raves for its mellow flavor with no bitter aftertaste. The upland slopes of Mauna Loa and Hualalai volcanoes in the Kona district offer an ideal climate (sunny mornings and afternoon clouds with light seasonal showers) for coffee cultivation.

While 100% Kona coffee has the most cachet, commanding $20 to $40 per pound, in recent years crops from the island's southernmost district of Ka'u have won accolades and impressed aficionados. Small coffee farms have also fruited in Puna and Honoka'a on the island's windward side. It's worth noting that the '100%' designation on real Kona coffee is more than marketing language; a lot of the 'Kona' coffee you see sold in larger chain grocery stores consists of cheaper beans laced with a smattering of the real stuff. True, 100% Kona coffee has an incredibly complex, multinote flavor, balancing bitterness with dark, caffeinated depths.

Ancient Hawaiians never got buzzed on coffee beans, which were first imported in the early 19th century. Hawaii's original intoxicants were plant-based Polynesian elixirs: 'awa (a mild, mouth-numbing sedative made from the kava plant's roots) and noni (Indian mulberry), which some consider a cure-all. Both of these drinks are pungent in smell and taste, so they're often mixed with other juices, but it's not terribly tough to find drinkable kava. It pretty much tastes like the earth; some people think this speaks to kava's deep connections to Hawaiian *terroir,* and some people say, 'Hey, this stuff tastes like dirt. Yech.'

Tea-growing was introduced to Hawaii in the late 19th century, but never took hold as a commercial crop due to high labor and production costs. In 1999 University of Hawai'i researchers discovered that a particular cultivar of tea would thrive in volcanic soil and tropical climates, especially at higher elevations. Small, often organic, tea farms are now spreading around Volcano and along the Hamakua Coast.

Fruit trees also thrive here. Alas, most supermarket cartons contain imported purees or sugary 'juice drinks' like POG (passion fruit, orange and guava). Don't get us wrong, it's tasty, but it's also just fruity enough to fool you into thinking you're drinking something healthy – you're not. Look for real, freshly squeezed and blended juices at health food stores, farmers markets and roadside fruit stands. Don't assume that the fruit is local, though.

Beer, Wine & Cocktails

Once a novelty, a handful of micro-breweries are now firmly established on the Big Island. Brewmasters claim that the mineral content and purity of Hawai'i's water makes for excellent-tasting beer. Another hallmark of local craft beers is the addition of a hint of tropical flavors, such as Kona coffee, honey or liliko'i.

Lively brewpubs and tasting rooms where you can sample popular pours include eco-conscious Kona Brewing Company (p91) in Kailua-Kona, the Big Island Brewhaus (p160) in Waimea and Hawai'i Nui Brewing (p217) (which also owns the Mehana Brewing Company label) in Hilo. The island's sole winery, **Volcano Winery** (☏808-967-7772; www.volcanowinery.com; 35 Pi'i Mauna Dr; tasting flight $5; ⊙10am-5:30pm), is untraditional in its guava-grape and macadamia-honey concoctions – they're not to everyone's taste.

Every beachfront and hotel bar mixes tropical cocktails topped with fruit garnish and a toothpick umbrella. Hawaii's legendary mai tai is a mix of dark and light rum, orange curaçao, orgeat and simple syrup with orange, lemon, lime and/or pineapple juices. There are plenty of tropical drinks to be had here, but you have to order at least one from Don's (p95) in Kaliua-Kona for sheer retro charm.

Top: A classic plate lunch including *poke*, *lomilomi* salmon, *laulau* and *kalua* pig

Bottom: Kona coffee beans

PRAWEENA STYLE/SHUTTERSTOCK ©

Caving in Hawai'i Volcanoes National Park (p244)

Plan Your Trip
On the Land

Hawai'i is a true micro-continent, boasting 8 of the world's 13 eco-systems. The island's unique geology makes for incredible hiking and trekking that encompasses some true Pacific wilderness destinations. Travelers should pack a good LED flashlight for cave explorations, a rainproof jacket and binoculars for lava viewing and wildlife watching.

Caving

Being the youngest Hawaiian Island and still volcanically active, Hawai'i is a caving hot spot, claiming six of the world's 10 longest lava tubes. No visit to the island is complete without exploring their dark, mysterious (and often very dry) depths. In Puna you can tour parts of the Kazumura Cave (p255), the world's longest and deepest lava tube. In Ka'u, the Kula Kai Caverns (p269) are geological wonders. Even within the unlikeliest of destinations one can find lava caves that were once the shelter and home of Native Hawaiians.

Golf

While playing on a championship course at a Kona or Kohala beach resort in the 'Golf Capital of Hawaii' can cost over $200 a round, Hawai'i's much more affordable municipal courses still boast scenery you probably can't get back home. Afternoon 'twilight' tee times are usually heavily discounted. Club rentals are sometimes available.

As you might guess, premium country club-style courses are concentrated on the western side of the island, within the big all-inclusive resorts. On the plus side, you're almost guaranteed sunshine in this dry atmosphere; on the down side, you'll be teeing off under a sun that gets downright broiling come afternoon. Keep in mind that Kohala, where larger resorts are located, can often be quite windy.

Helicopter & Air Tours

Flying over the world's most active volcano and gushing waterfalls provides unforgettable vantages you simply can't get any other way. That said, 'flightseeing' tours do negatively impact Hawai'i's natural environment, both in noise generated and fuel burned.

Expensive helicopter tours are all the hype, but fixed-wing planes offer a smoother, quieter ride. Questions you should ask before booking either include:

Do all passengers have a 360-degree view? Are noise-cancelling headsets provided? For the best views, sit up front.

Helicopter tours fly if it's cloudy, but not if it's raining – wait for a clear day, which is more likely during summer. Most tour companies offer online discounts (book in advance).

Recommended flightseeing outfitters include the following:

Blue Hawaiian Helicopters (☑800-745-2583; www.bluehawaiian.com; tours $230-580) Reliable, dependable and high-volume company; departures from Waikoloa and Hilo.

Iolani Air (☑800-538-7590, Hilo 808-961-5140, Kona 808-329-0018; www.iolaniair.com; tours $150-700) Flightseeing tours in small prop planes take off from Kona and Hilo.

Paradise Helicopters (☑866-876-7422, 808-969-7392; www.paradisecopters.com; tours $300-800) More personalized helicopter tours leave from Kona and Hilo.

Safari Helicopters (☑808-969-1259, 800-326-3356; www.safarihelicopters.com; tours from $150) Tours of East Hawai'i's volcanoes and coastline depart from Hilo.

Sunshine Helicopters (☑808-882-1851, 866-501-7738; www.sunshinehelicopters.com; Hapuna Heliport, 62-100 Kaunaoa Dr, Kamuela; tours $170-600) Provides tours of the Kohala mountains and the volcano that leave from the heliport in Hapuna.

Hey, you may be thinking to yourself – why should I be a passenger in a helicopter when I could fly my own *powered hang glider*? We feel your need for speed, Maverick: get in touch with the friendly folks at Kona Coast by Air (p86), who can provide you with an FAA Certified Flight Instructor to train you in the basics of piloting a Weight Shift Control (WSC) trike – ie a hang glider with an engine.

Horseback Riding

In Hawai'i's hilly green pastures, *paniolo* (Hawaiian cowboys) wrangle cattle and ride the range. Up in North Kohala and Waimea especially, as well as around Waipi'o Valley, you can arrange trail and pony rides and customized horseback tours. Book ahead!

An aside: there's a particular utility to using a horse to explore Hawai'i. Much of the Big Island is simply so rugged that you need a high degree of physical fitness to explore it, yet many of the areas that can only be accessed by the physically fit are wilderness spaces. Entering a wilderness space in an ATV or similar vehicle can feel intrusive; a horse provides a similar level of all-terrain access, minus the noise of an engine and stink of petroleum.

Spas

Healing and wellness are virtually synonymous with Hawai'i, where *lomilomi* (traditional Hawaiian massage using a rhythmic elbow action combined with prayer), reiki and herbal scrubs, plus more intense treatments, including sweat baths and ayurvedic medicine, are available.

For an array of traditional treatments, try Hale Ho'ōla Spa (p255) in Volcano, especially after a grueling hike. Stargazing from one of the soaking tubs at Kealakekua's Mamalahoa Hot Tubs & Massage (p109) is absolutely divine. Of course, the top Kohala Coast resorts also have fabulous on-site spas, especially Spa Without Walls (p140) at the Fairmont Orchard and Mauna Lani Spa (p141).

Stargazing

While the presence of all those observatories is controversial, from an optical perspective, there may simply be no better spot in the world for stargazing than the top of Mauna Kea. Here you will find a glut of international superpowered telescopes trained on the heavens, operated by scientists exploring our universe. You can too – on Mauna Kea itself, with the eye-opening nightly stargazing program at the visitor information station. Kids under 16 can participate, but it's recommended they don't go to the summit.

An outdoor yoga class

Yoga

A centering place to practice your downward dog and *pranayama* (breath control), the Big Island has everything from drop-in yoga classes to week-long retreats. We especially like Yoga Centered (p208) and Balancing Monkey (p207) in Hilo, and Hawaii Beach Yoga (p86) in Kailua-Kona. Yoga lessons and a studio space almost feel par for the course at crunchier Big Island guesthouses and B&Bs.

Ziplining

If you're keen to zoom along suspended cables while the landscape whizzes by far below, several zipline outfitters now dot the island. Tours offer a totally different perspective on the island's forests, waterfalls and coastline. Plan on spending half a day on an adrenaline-pumping tour (minimum age and weight requirements apply).

Biking the Chain of Craters Road in Hawai'i Volcanoes National Park (p244)

Plan Your Trip
Hiking & Biking

The Big Island is rife with excellent hiking options that take in every shade of its varying topography and diverse ecosystems. If you prefer getting around on two wheels, there are bicycle routes that range from ocean shores to the slopes of Mauna Kea.

Hiking

From an afternoon stroll through a lava tube to a multiday summit trek, the Big Island has a ton of wild walks. Hawai'i Volcanoes National Park (p244) boasts the most varied trails, but you can also hike to secluded Kona Coast beaches or easily explore petroglyph fields without leaving West Hawai'i. In fact, some of the best beaches and snorkeling spots in the island are, barring access to a boat, *only* accessible via a hike (or at the very least, a strenuous walk). In general, you'll find more desert- and beach-oriented treks around Kailua-Kona and more jungle walking on the east side of the island. Hikes into the Pololu and Waipi'o valleys count as some of the most beautiful treks in the state.

Camping permits are required for all overnight hikes, including in Hawai'i Volcanoes National Park and Waimanu Valley. It's best to bring your own backpacking gear from home. For anything else you need (or forgot to pack), try the Hawaii Forest & Trail (p122) headquarters in Kailua-Kona.

Both Hawaii Forest & Trail and Hawaiian Walkways (p190) offer recommendable guided hiking tours. Helpful resources for independent hikers include the following:

Na Ala Hele (www.hawaiitrails.org/trails) Online maps and directions for public-access trails, including the long-distance Ala Kahakai National Historic Trail.

Sierra Club – Moku Loa Group (☏808-965-9695; http://sierraclubhawaii.org/MokuLoa) Island-wide group day hikes and volunteer opportunities doing trail maintenance and ecological restoration.

Safe & Responsible Hiking

You don't have to worry about snakes, wild animals or poison ivy on Hawai'i. What you *do* have to worry about is lava – from ankle-twisting '*a'a* (slow-flowing rough and jagged lava) and toxic fumes to collapsing lava benches and hellishly hot conditions. Heed all posted warnings and hike with a buddy. Observe '*kapu*' (no trespassing) signs (residents of Waipi'o Valley are particularly territorial). If you're ever hiking to an active lava flow site, or across the lava fields that emanate from Puna, we highly recommend going with a guide.

Note the two types of lava you can walk on: smooth and rope-y *pahoehoe*, and '*a'a,* which was invented by the devil on a particularly slow day in Hell. '*A'a* is rough, spiky, spiny, and makes a very satisfying 'clink' noise when you throw it. When you walk on it, it feels like treading your feet over a field of blunt razors. Note that many paths to some of the Big Island's prettiest beaches cross over '*a'a* flows; if you're going to walk over this stuff, you may want to bring sneakers or at the least, reef shoes. Flip-flops (thongs) will leave your feet uncomfortably exposed to the basalt.

To be fair, if you plan to hike anywhere here, sturdy, ankle-high footwear with good traction is a must. Flash floods are a real danger in many of the steep, narrow valleys that require stream crossings (yes, including Waipi'o Valley). You'll need to come prepared for winter mountaineering conditions if hiking to the summit of Mauna Loa or Mauna Kea is in your sights.

Please keep away from anything that resembles a sacred site; it's not uncommon to find the crumbling remnants of Native Hawaiian heiau (temples), and these should not be climbed on. Also note that many Big Island residents love their home for the considerable isolation it affords them, which can be difficult to discover in smaller islands. If you see 'No Trespassing' signs, its best to take those warnings seriously.

You can experience a ton of elevation gain and loss in the course of a trek on the Big Island, so be prepared for rapid shifts to temperature, precipitation and even air quality.

Bicycling & Mountain Biking

Also known as 'triathlon's most iconic event,' the Kailua-Kona Ironman World Championship (p90) is one of the largest public events in the state and a a a blue chip addition to the Big Island calendar. And said event is anchored, in part, by a cycling route that takes in 112 miles of hills and lava desert, all the way up to Hawi and back.

What we're saying is: cycling is great on the Big Island, but outside of Hilo, this isn't the place for chilled-out, relaxed pedaling on a fixed gear. Alright, alright, we hear you protesting this characterization, fixed-gear cyclists on the west coast, but c'mon. You know we're right about this: Big Island cycling is more geared toward the neon-colored, lycra-clad, drop-bars crowd.

Road cycling is tricky here, with narrow, winding roads light on shoulders. The Ironman route on Hwy 19 north of Kailua-Kona is an exception, and bike rentals are most readily available in Kailua-Kona. Peoples Advocacy for Trails Hawaii (p97) has a good database of information on island trails. Kona-based outfitter Bike Works (p97) organizes daily cycling tours and multiday vacations. Kailua-Kona also boasts a bike-sharing program, which is just fine for exploring the town and Keahou, although you'll want something with more gears if you plan to cycle further afield.

South Kona is full of huge drops and lifts in elevation, as well as frequent rain and narrow road shoulders. With that said, if you've got the stamina to deal with large altitude drops, Middle Ke'ei Road and Painted Church Road can be gorgeous spots for a rural ride through the best of coffee country.

South Kohala roads have shoulders for cyclists, but if you're pedaling by day, you'll be dealing with scorching heat roasting you as you wind through miles of lava desert. This sunny spin on a moonscape can be quite attractive, but remember to bring a lot of water. in North Kohala, the shoulders tend to thin out to the point of non-existence, and the winds pick up as well. There is some truly gorgeous scenery for an intrepid cyclist to appreciate, but be aware of these inimical road and weather conditions. Out in Waimea, the folks at Mountain Road Cycles (p159) are friendly, knowledgeable and very helpful. The ride from the town of Hawi to Pololu is one of our favorite activities on the island. You can also access the saddle road from this area.

Over on the east coast, Mid-Pacific Wheels (p221) in Hilo is a good resource. In general, you'll find that east side cycling is a bit more casual than the Ironman-ish routes and trails that are prevalent on the west side. Cycling around downtown Hilo is about as close as the Big Island gets to laid-back urban biking. The Hamakua Coast has some prime cycling scenery,

Waipi'o Valley (p188)

especially if you pedal out to the Hawaiian Vanilla Company. South of Hilo, the 10-mile long Old Mamalahoa Hwy is simply world class; if you're an avid cyclist, it's a must-do trip.

While Puna is relatively (we stress, *relatively*) more topographically flat than the rest of the island, it still has its hills, and the area's most attractive feature – its surreal, magical forests – also tends to crowd road shoulders.

Biking in Volcanoes National Park will get you up close and personal with some of the most rugged, gorgeous terrain in the archipelago, but as you may expect, such beauty is contained within a park that contains incredible variations in altitude. On the plus side, strictly enforced slow speed limits within the park reduce the dangers of vehicular traffic.

Ka'u is another place to appreciate jaw dropping Big island vistas of wide horizons, dried lava flows and wind swept oceanfront, but we have to put an emphasis on *windswept*. Just as in North Kohala, the gusts here are no joke. You also need to bring plenty of water, as towns are few and far between.

Hawai'i, the Big Island: Hiking

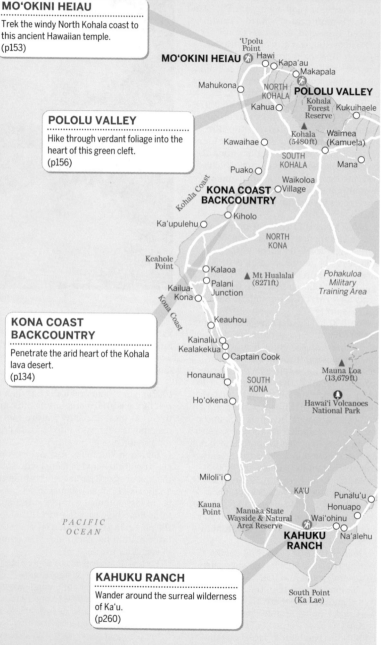

MO'OKINI HEIAU
Trek the windy North Kohala coast to this ancient Hawaiian temple.
(p153)

POLOLU VALLEY
Hike through verdant foliage into the heart of this green cleft.
(p156)

KONA COAST BACKCOUNTRY
Penetrate the arid heart of the Kohala lava desert.
(p134)

KAHUKU RANCH
Wander around the surreal wilderness of Ka'u.
(p260)

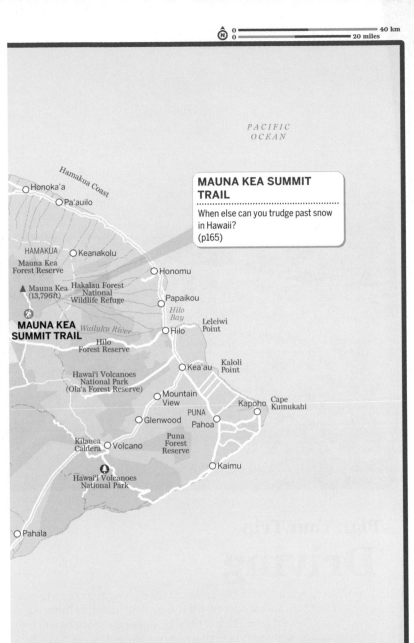

N 0 ━━━━━━━━━━ 40 km
0 ━━━━━━━━━━ 20 miles

PACIFIC
OCEAN

MAUNA KEA SUMMIT TRAIL

When else can you trudge past snow in Hawaii?
(p165)

Hamakua Coast

○ Honoka'a
○ Pa'auilo

HAMAKUA   ○ Keanakolu
Mauna Kea
Forest Reserve
▲ Mauna Kea   Hakalau Forest
(13,796ft)   National
            Wildlife Refuge   ○ Honomu

                              ○ Papaikou
                              Hilo
                              Bay   Leleiwi
MAUNA KEA   Wailuku River   Point
SUMMIT TRAIL   ○ Hilo
            Hilo
            Forest Reserve
                              Kaloli
                              Point
      Hawai'i Volcanoes   ○ Kea'au
      National Park
      (Ola'a Forest Reserve)   ○ Mountain
                              View   Kapoho   Cape
                       PUNA   Kumukahi
            ○ Glenwood   ○ Pahoa
Kilauea   Puna
Caldera ○ Volcano   Forest
                  Reserve
      Hawai'i Volcanoes   ○ Kaimu
      National Park

○ Pahala

Chain of Craters Road (p242)

Plan Your Trip
Driving

There's only one island in the state of Hawaii where you can take a proper road trip, and of course, it's the biggest island in the state. The Hawaii Belt Rd (Hwy 11 and Hwy 19, depending where you are), also known as Mamalahoa Highway, rings the entire shebang. If you're just making a circuit around the island, it takes about four hours in normal traffic. For detailed information on driving in the Big Island, see p32 and p308.

Kailua-Kona & Around

The main town on the west side of the island is better for cycling than driving, but it's almost inevitable that you'll end up driving through it at some point. Traffic in town can actually be a major headache, especially around Ali'i Dr, which is also often closed for special events. A major bottleneck tends to hit at the lights that lead off the main highway (Queen Ka'ahumanu Hwy, or Hwy 19) to the airport. During rush hours (around 7am to 9am and 4pm to 6pm on weekdays), driving around Kailua-Kona can be pretty painful.

Need altitude? Consider driving up the mountain along the cool, forested, winding lanes of Hwy 180, which winds past the artsy enclave of Holualoa.

The Costco that sits across the highway near Kaloko-Honokohau National Historical Park has the cheapest gas on the island, but you have to be a Costco member to use it.

South Kohala

Driving north from Kailua-Kona, you first come to South Kohala. This is classic west side lava desert country, the fields of ochre, black and gray extending to the mountains on the one hand, and the deep blue ocean on the other. With high winds and sunny skies, this is a great spot to crack your windows open and feel the salt breeze in your hair. As you drive along you'll pass the entrance to some of the Big Island's largest resorts. You can gas up in Waikoloa Village.

North Kohala & Waimea

One of the finest parts of the island for road tripping, North Kohala alternates between the barren, red dirt and lava desert that extends along Hwy 270, and the wet cliffs and vines of the north coast heading toward the Pololu Valley. There are some intense crosswinds on Hwy 270 climbing out of Kawaihae. Small pull-offs are common, affording the opportunity to poke around the North Kohala coast by foot, but we've noticed broken glass – signs of a break-in – at some of these parking areas.

Do not attempt to drive local side roads in anything less than a well-lifted 4WD.

Kohala Mountain Road – Hwy 250 – connects Hawi to Waimea and traces some 22 miles of undulating emerald green ranch land peppered with impressive views of the ocean along the way. It's one of the most beautiful roads on the Big Island, and shouldn't be missed.

Dense, pea-soup fog can sometimes descend upon Waimea – drive carefully!

Saddle Road

You can connect from Kohala to Hilo via the Belt Road, but if you like narrow tracks cutting through rugged alpine countryside, take the Saddle Rd and skirt the edges of Mauna Kea. Who knew you'd see mountain prairie and scads of snow in Hawaii? While much of the road is two lane, there are single lane portions that feel like they've crept out of another era.

Hamakua Coast

You feel as if you've really entered the wet side of the island along the Hamakua Coast. Enormous emerald trees soar into the air while the road dips and ascends through sheer valleys, all the while overlooking the ocean. This is as good as road tripping on the Big Island gets. Be on the lookout for tight hairpin curves.

Hilo to Volcano

Hilo's waterfront area makes for a pretty urban interruption to your Big Island exploration. As in Kailua-Kona, beware of traffic during rush hours.

Hop back on the highway and the Belt Rd changes from Hwy 19 to Hwy 11. While the subdivisions just outside of Hilo may not be the most memorable, the road soon climbs through acres of misty forests to the surreal jungle-and-lava-flow landscape of Volcano and Hawai'i Volcanoes National Park. The park is filled with many unforgettable miles of scenery, with the Chain of Craters Road to the sea constituting one of the island's great drives.

Road through an orchard, Kona Coast (p104)

Puna

Puna district is known as a wild and wet corner of the island, a land where fertility and a vibrant life force are practically palpable. The fecundity of the land is evidenced by great groves of albizia, papaya, ginger, monkeypod and guava forests that form enormous 'tree tunnels' that line many of the roads and back roads that cut across the eastern corner of the island.

A trio of roads form a triangle that could easily eat a lazy Sunday of scenic driving: Hwy 132, Red Rd (Hwy 137) and the Kalapana Hwy (Hwy 130). All of these roads pass under green tree tunnels and climbing vines, while Hwy 137 also hugs rugged black cliffs that shred the restless Pacific.

Ka'u

The wide, windswept stretches of Ka'u include some of the most raw landscapes on the Big Island, from serrated rows of misty forest to lava cliffs tumbling toward grassy peninsulas that extend into the furious ocean. The Kahuku Unit of Volcanoes National Park is an odd mix of Big Island wilderness and ranch pastureland, while the road to south point – also known as Ka Le, the southernmost point in the USA – is simply stunning.

Kona Coast

Coming back up along the west coast of the island, Hwy 11 threads along cliffs and through green forests and coffee plantations. Every now and then, you'll catch glimpses of the ocean, and the often dry scrub desert that forms the coastal plain of the Kona Coast. Beware of serious traffic jams at the split of Hwy 11 and Hwy 180.

For a gorgeous side road drive, head down Middle Ke'ei Rd, which leads to Painted Church Rd. Both of these roads plunge and dip amid scads of jungle, rustic coffee farms and bright green avocado groves.

Honu (green sea turtle)

Plan Your Trip

Diving & Snorkeling

The Big Island is stunning enough when you're traveling across its surface, but an entire alien – and utterly enticing – realm lays below the turquoise waves that lap at local beaches.

Snorkeling

The Big Island is ringed with crystal tropical waters teeming with electric-colored coral canyons and rainbow clouds of reef fish. Playing amateur marine biologist and discovering this sea life is a highlight for many visitors to Hawai'i. Unusually for such a rugged place, where so much beauty is accessed via a lengthy trek, climb or bicycle ride, snorkeling here is often just a matter of strapping on fins and a mask and slipping into the cool ocean.

The majority of the best snorkel spots on the island are located on the drier west coast. Why is that? Well, the fresh water pouring off of Mauna Kea and Loa flows east, and fresh water makes for cloudier conditions (you can often see a cloudier, colder layer of fresh water over-laying a warmer, clearer 'base' of denser, heavier saltwater at east coast snorkel spots).

Popular West Hawai'i snorkeling areas – like Kealakekua Bay (p111) and Kahalu'u Beach Park (p98) – are also often teeming with tourists. To escape the crowds, go in the early morning (when conditions are best anyway), drive further up or down the coast to places like Beach 69 (p144), Two-Step (p117) or Puako (p145)), or hike or kayak to more remote spots. In East Hawai'i,

snorkelers can drive right up to Hilo's Richardson's Ocean Park (p200) or detour down to the magnificent Kapoho Tide Pools (p235) in Puna. If you want to truly escape the crowds, get yourself to North Kohala (p149), where there are a couple of snorkeling areas that only at-tract locals and a smattering of visitors (a description that also kind of applies to North Kohala as a whole).

Always follow coral-reef etiquette when you're in the water: don't touch any coral, which are living organisms; watch your fins to avoid stirring up sand and breaking off pieces of coral; and don't feed the fish. Snorkel gear rental typically costs around $10/25 per day/week, de-pending on the quality of the gear. Most places rent out prescription masks, which are essential for the myopic. Reef shoes are recommended for shores lined with lava and urchins. If you want to teach your kids how to snorkel, it's hard to do better than the tide pools at Wawaloli Beach (p125), just a few miles north of Kailua-Kona.

Catamaran and Zodiac raft tours will transport you to prime spots and provide gear and food. On the Kona Coast, tours leaving from Keauhou Bay (instead of in-town Kailua Pier or Honokohau Harbor north nearer the airport) have shorter rides to Kealakekua Bay, meaning more snorkel time for you. Book in advance, especially during high season and for nighttime snorkeling with manta rays.

SEA URCHIN STINGS

Be careful where you place your hands and feet while snorkeling and diving around Hawai'i. Sea urchins, which have venomous spikes, are incredibly common in Big Island waters, even in the shallowest tide pools. If you get stung, use tweezers to extract the spine, then shave the area with shaving cream and a razor (this removes the pedicellaria, a sort of tiny pincer that carries a kind of venom). Wash the wound and soak your skin in hot water or a vinegar-water solution, and don't seal (ie bandage) the wound – you want to let spine fragments work their way out of your body.

Diving

Hawai'i's underwater scenery is every bit the equal of what's on land. Ocean temperatures are perfect for diving, av-eraging 72°F to 80°F (22°C to 27°C) at the surface year-round. Even better is the visibility, especially in the calm waters along the Kona Coast. While September and October are traditionally considered the best months for diving visibility, there's never really a bad month for div-ing around the Big Island.

About 700 fish species call these wa-ters home, as do spinner dolphins, sea turtles and moray eels, so you won't want for variety – even during on-shore dives. If you've dreamed of diving, this is a per-fect spot to learn, with a smorgasbord of

RESPONSIBLE & SAFE DIVING

The popularity of diving places immense pressure on many sites. Help preserve Hawai'i's reef and marine ecosystems by following these tips:

➡ Respect Native Hawaiian cultural practices and sacred places, including fishing grounds.

➡ Do not use reef anchors or ground boats on coral. Encourage dive operators to establish permanent moorings at popular sites.

➡ Never touch living marine organisms or drag equipment across the reef. Even the gentlest contact can damage polyps. Never stand on coral. If you must hold on to the reef, touch only exposed rock or dead coral.

➡ Be fin conscious. Heavy fin strokes and kicking up clouds of sand near the reef can damage delicate organisms.

➡ Spend as little time in underwater caves as possible – your air bubbles may get trapped against the roof, leaving previously submerged organisms high and dry.

➡ Do not collect live coral or rock – it is illegal!

➡ Resist the temptation to buy coral or shells. It's ecologically damaging and depletes the beauty of a site.

➡ Carry out all trash, including found litter and abandoned fishing gear. Plastics, especially, are a serious threat to marine life.

➡ Don't feed the wildlife or disturb marine animals. It is illegal to come within 50yd of turtles and 100yd of whales, dolphins and Hawaiian monk seals. Do not ride on the backs of turtles; this causes them great anxiety.

dive operators offering open-water certification courses and beginner dive experiences. As far as prices go, the Big Island falls around the middle of the pack, but put it this way: if you're going to shell out hundreds of dollars to learn to dive, do you want to learn in the local public pool, or while surrounded by a panoply of wildlife?

The combination of sheer visibility, healthy coral and underwater lava formations makes the west coast of the island simply brilliant for diving. Among the many fantastic West Hawai'i dive sites are Honokohau (p122), Turtle Pinnacle (p122) and Suck 'Em Up (p122) along the Kona Coast, plus Puako Point (p144), further north in Kohala. The manta ray night dive, which is conducted

out of Kailua-Kona, is very popular, so book early. In Kohala, you'll find decent dive training and infrastructure around Kawaihae, which tends to be a little off the tourist trail.

River runoff on the Hilo side can often make for cloudy visibility, but Pohoiki (Isaac Hale Beach Park (p230)) in Puna – East Hawai'i's best site – teems with marine life. While dive tourism isn't as developed on the east coast as the Kona side, there's still plenty to be seen.

Night dives, also known as Black Water dives, are increasingly popular excursions on the Big Island that will bring you face to glowing, bio-luminescent face with an extraordinary bevy of surreal fauna that only come out under the cover of a thick, midnight curtain.

Hawai'i, the Big Island: Diving & Snorkeling

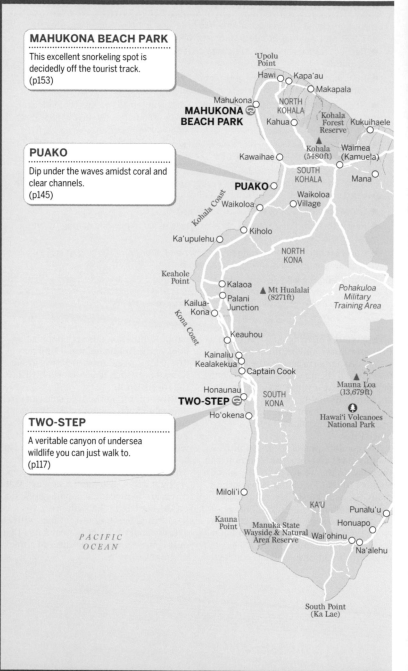

MAHUKONA BEACH PARK

This excellent snorkeling spot is decidedly off the tourist track. (p153)

PUAKO

Dip under the waves amidst coral and clear channels. (p145)

TWO-STEP

A veritable canyon of undersea wildlife you can just walk to. (p117)

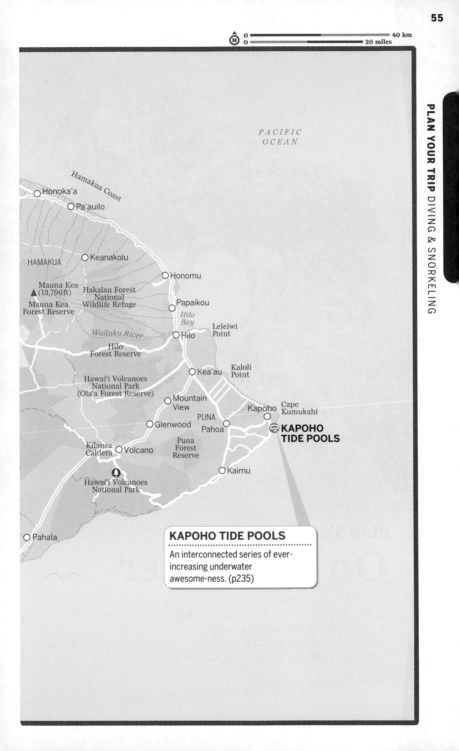

PACIFIC
OCEAN

Hamakua Coast

Honoka'a
Pa'auilo

HAMAKUA

Keanakolu

Honomu

Mauna Kea
▲ (13,796ft)
Mauna Kea
Forest Reserve

Hakalau Forest
National
Wildlife Refuge

Papaikou

Hilo
Bay

Leleiwi
Point

Wailuku River

Hilo

Hilo
Forest Reserve

Kea'au

Kaloli
Point

Hawai'i Volcanoes
National Park
(Ola'a Forest Reserve)

Mountain
View

PUNA

Glenwood

Pahoa

Kapoho

Cape
Kumukahi

Kilauea
Caldera

Volcano

Puna
Forest
Reserve

**KAPOHO
TIDE POOLS**

Hawai'i Volcanoes
National Park

Kaimu

Pahala

KAPOHO TIDE POOLS

An interconnected series of ever-
increasing underwater
awesome-ness. (p235)

Kayaking off the Kona Coast

Plan Your Trip

On the Water

With Hawai'i's long and strong tradition of communing with the ocean, you're sure to get wet on your Big Island vacation. Even if you've never snorkeled or surfed, this is a great place to start, with experienced outfitters on both sides of the island. Not much advance planning is required, save checking the weather.

Know Your Tides

Being on the Big Island awakens a sense of adventure, and a closer connection with nature. How bad is the vog (volcano fog)? Will our helicopter tour be grounded by rain? What's the swell like? Smart travelers continually ask such climate-related questions to ensure proper conditions for the day's adventures. Calling a local surf, kayak or dive shop to get current information on wind, wave and water conditions before setting out is a good idea.

Another tip is to know your tides. While it may seem tangential, think again: what the wildlife is doing and what the landscape looks like are inexorably influenced by the tides. At low tide, for example, Green Sands and Magic Sands beaches will be bigger; there will be more secluded black-sand coves to explore at Kiholo; and the tide pools will be exposed at Old Kona Airport Beach Park. High tide, meanwhile, means more marine wildlife at Two-Step and the Kapoho Tide Pools; more turtles at Punalu'u; and snorkeling in the brackish pool behind Keawaiki Beach.

Know before you go by consulting the tide charts at www.hawaiitides.com.

Beaches & Swimming

On Hawai'i, coastal strands come in a rainbow of hues and infinite textures – with sand sparkling white, tawny, black, charcoal or green, and scattered with sea-glass, pebbles and boulders or cratered with lava-rock tide pools.

By law, all beaches in Hawaii are open to the public below the high-tide line. Private landowners can prevent access to their shoreline over land, but not by water. Resort hotels often provide public beach access with limited parking spots, occasionally charging a small fee for the privilege. The trick is getting to the resort early enough to snatch a coveted parking space – on weekdays you can usually be casual about it, but on weekends and holidays, it's best to get yourself out of bed by 7am if you want to snag a spot.

West Hawai'i is most inviting for swimming, including crescent-shaped Mauna Kea Beach (p146) and white-sand Manini'owali Beach (p126) with its brilliant turquoise waters, or try a short lap of the lava tube in Kiholo Bay (p123). East Hawai'i is generally rougher and mostly only for strong swimmers, although local families can be found at Hilo's beaches. With that said, rough waters and strong currents can be present anywhere you go.

Stand Up Paddle Surfing

Back in 2000, Hawaiian-born surfer Rick Thomas took a paddle, stood on a board and introduced this traditional Hawaiian sport known as *hoe he'e nalu* to the mainland masses. Many surfers aren't too happy about it, though, since it means sharing the waves.

What's so cool about SUP is that it's relatively easy (the paddling part anyway, the surfing is a wee bit trickier) and it's versatile (any body of water will do). For water babies, there's nothing like paddling along and catching a whale breach or a baby dolphin learning to leap.

Outfitters renting gear and giving lessons are easy to find around Kailua-Kona and Hilo.

Fishing

The Kona Coast is a deep-sea fishing fantasy: at least one 'grander' (1000lb or more) marlin is reeled in every year. With over 100 boat and kayak fishing charter companies leaving from Honokohau Harbor (p122), the next one could be yours. These waters are also rich with ahi (yellowfin tuna) and *aku* (bonito or skipjack tuna), swordfish and mahimahi (dolphin-fish). If you keep your catch, find a harborside restaurant that will cook it for you.

Bodyboarding

Boogie boarding (aka bodyboarding) rivals surfing and stand up paddle surfing as the most popular way to ride

Humpback whale breaching off the Big Island

Hawai'i's waves. Winter brings the best action to West Hawai'i at Hapuna Beach (p144), Magic Sands (p85), Honoli'i Beach (p205) and Kekaha Kai (p126), particularly Manini'owali (p126). If you really know what you're doing, venture to Puna's Isaac Hale Beach Park (p230) or Hilo's Honoli'i Beach Park (p205), both in East Hawai'i.

Kayaking

The warm, calm seas hugging the Kona Coast, combined with hidden coves and turquoise, fish-filled waters, make Hawai'i prime sea-kayaking turf. (Forget rivers – there are none.) Variants on the sport – fishing, surfing and sailing – are all possibilities, with guides and outfitters along the Kona and Kohala Coasts offering rentals and tours.

Kealakekua Bay (p112), with its smooth waters and abundance of fish and spinner dolphins, is one of the state's most popular kayaking spots. Up north, the pristine coastline around Kiholo Bay (p123) offers solitude, while the reefs around Puako (p144) beckon paddlers to don their masks.

Whale Watching

During their annual 6000-mile round-trip between Alaska and Hawaii – one of the longest migration journeys of any mammal – humpback whales breed, calve and nurse in the Big Island's nearshore waters between December and April.

Over 60% of the North Pacific humpback population winters in the Hawaiian Islands, so you'll have a good chance of seeing their acrobatics on a cruise, while kayaking, or even from shore – don't forget your binoculars. Tours also run year-round from Kailua-Kona to view sperm, melon-headed, pilot and pygmy killer whales and, of course, dolphins.

Surfing the Big Island

Plan Your Trip
Surfing

On Hawai'i today, surfing is its own intense subculture as well as part of everyday island life. Generally, winter northern swells are bigger and leeward breaks are cleaner. Along the Kona Coast, surf at Kahalu'u Beach Park, Banyans and Lymans, all south of Kailua-Kona, and Pine Trees near Wawaloli (OTEC) Beach. Down south in Ka'u, Kawa Bay has a left break that locals love. Consistent east-side spots are Honoli'i Cove in Hilo and Waipi'o Bay. Puna's Pohoiki Bay is much hairier, but experienced surfers will dig the reef breaks at Isaac Hale Beach Park.

Surf Beaches & Breaks

Because Hawai'i the Big Island is the youngest of Hawaii's islands and its coastline is still quite rugged, it's often assumed there isn't much in the way of surfable waves. As a result, places like O'ahu and Kaua'i have stolen the surf spotlight, but archaeologists and researchers believe that Kealakekua Bay (p111) is probably where ancient Polynesians started riding waves. With all of that said, it is not possible for visitors to follow in the footsteps of the ancient Hawaiians and surf at Kealakekua Bay, due to a moratorium on unlicensed visitors.

Unlike neighboring islands, whose north and south shores are the primary centers of swell activity, the Big Island's east and west shores are its focal points. Because swells are shadowed by the other islands, as a general rule the surf doesn't get as big here. The Kona Coast offers the best opportunities, with north and south swell exposures, as well as offshore trade winds. Kawaihae Harbor (p148) is surrounded by several fun, introductory reefs near the breakwall, while further south, near Kekaha Kai State Park (p126), is a considerably more advanced break that challenges even the most seasoned surfers.

If you have a 4WD vehicle or don't mind an hour-long hike through searing lava desert while carrying a board, be sure to check out heavy reef breaks such as Mahai'ula (p126) and Makalawena (p126). They break best on northwest swells, making the later winter months the prime season. A hike or 4WD is also necessary to reach popular Pine Trees (p125) at Keahole Point, near Kailua-Kona's airport.

On East Hawai'i, just outside of Hilo, there are several good intermediate waves. Richardson's Ocean Park (p200) is a good option within Hilo, and just west of town is Honoli'i (p205), a fast left and right peak breaking into a river mouth.

Further up the Hamakua Coast is Waipi'o Bay (p188) – access to the beach requires a long walk or a 4WD vehicle, but the waves are worth the effort. But do be careful; the north shore of the island has notoriously temperamental waters. Puna's Pohoiki Bay (p230), meanwhile, boasts three breaks and offers the island's best surfing, according to many. This is decidedly not a beginner's break – the waves crash right up on some rough rocks.

In Ka'u, locals brace a rough paddle out to catch long rides on the nearly perfect left-break at Kawa Bay (p265) and South Point.

In Kailua-Kona, newbies take lessons and test the waves at Kahalu'u Beach Park (p98).

Top bodyboarding and bodysurfing spots include Hapuna Beach (p144), Magic Sands Beach (p85), Honl's Beach (p86) near Kailua-Kona, and the beaches at Kekaha Kai State Park (p126).

Surf Spots for Beginners

Locals are usually willing to share surf spots that have become popular tourist destinations, but they reserve the right to protect other 'secret' surf grounds. As a newbie in the line-up, don't expect to get every wave that comes your way. There's a definite pecking order and tourists are at the bottom.

ONLINE RESOURCES

Besides the below, you can always check with ocean sports professionals like Kona Boys (p108), as well as Hawai'i County Parks and Recreation, to assess surfing conditions.

Surf News Network (www.surfnewsnetwork.com) Check local tides, weather and swells.

Surfline (www.surfline.com) A nicely designed website that includes useful maps, tide charts, surf charts and wind predictions.

The Big Island's waves, shore breaks and rocky coastline favor more experienced riders, but there are still some perfect spots for those just starting out.

There are a glut of both beginner beaches and expert instruction baked into the tourism landscape of Kailua-Kona and nearby Keahou. Both Hawaii Lifeguard Surf Instructors (p90) and HYPR Nalu (p88) are great places to get surfing lessons. Kahulu'u Beach Park (p98) is a good spot for novice riders.

The waters off of Hapuna Beach (p144) in South Kohala can be a bit temperamental, but on calmer days this wide bay is good for surfers who are starting out. In North Kohala the harbor (p148) in Kawaihae can have a tricky entry, but by mere dint of it being a harbor, this is a protected surfing space.

Surf Spots for Experienced Riders

Advanced riders will be more at home surfing the Big Island. Note that locals can be pretty proprietary; surf with this attitude in mind. Because of the remoteness of many Big Island beaches, lifeguards are a rarity. Always practice the buddy system when surfing here – even locals who have surfed these waters their entire lives are sometimes claimed as casualties.

➡ **Kailua-Kona & Keahou** If you head south on Ali'i Dr, Banyans (Map p99; marked by, what a surprise, a Banyan tree) is near the spot Kamehameha himself surfed. Honl's (p86) is great for bodyboarding (which makes sense, considering its history).

➡ **North Kona Coast** Although some may tell you that remote Pine Trees (p125) is good for beginners, we believe this is a break for moderate to advanced surfers. The same goes for any surfing done in the beaches along Kekaha Kai State Park (p126).

➡ **Hamakua Coast** Getting to the bottom of the Waipi'o Valley (p189) is an effort enough; doing so with a board is just punishment. But the waves here can be some of the best on the island. That said, locals are *very* protective of this spot.

➡ **Hilo** The waves at Honoli'i (p205) are awesome, but the break is deceptively tricky.

➡ **Puna** At Isaac Hale Beach Park (p230), locals surf in Pohoiki Bay and ride the waves almost right into to the rocky shoreline. It's thrilling, to be sure (or is that to be shore? Ha ha), but don't attempt unless you know what you're doing.

➡ **Ka'u** The windy conditions at South Point should ward off all but advanced surfers.

Surfing: A Brief History

Native Hawaiians invented surfing, calling it *he'e nalu,* or 'wave sliding,' but it may not be as ancient as some may have you believe. While there is no reliable timeline on the history of surfing, it is likely just a few hundred years old – a tradition, to be sure, but in the scope of Polynesian history, perhaps a relatively recent one. It is likely Tahitians and other Polynesians were catching waves on outrigger canoes (James Cook described seeing such a practice); later, in the Hawaiian islands, this canoe riding evolved into the forerunner of modern surfing. It is likely canoe surfing and board surfing existed side by side when Europeans first made contact with Native Hawaiians.

Boards were shaped from *wiliwili, koa* and *'ulu* wood; the best boards, and the best waves, were reserved for the *ali'i* (nobility). Just south of Kailua-Kona, largely overgrown Keolonahihi State Historical Park (p83) preserves the area around Kamoa Point, where Kamehameha the Great learned and practiced surfing. This legacy has led surfing to be deemed 'the sport of kings,' but 'sport' may be too reductive a term – surfing, scholars argue, was practiced for enjoyment, but was also integrated into religion, culture and even politics.

By the late 19th and early 20th centuries, surfing began migrating out of the Hawaiian islands into the world, but the Big Island can lay claim to one more significant milestone in surfing history: in 1971, at Honl's Beach (p86), barely 2 miles from Keolonahihi, Tom Morey tested what was to become the modern boogie board.

Hawai'i, the Big Island: Surfing

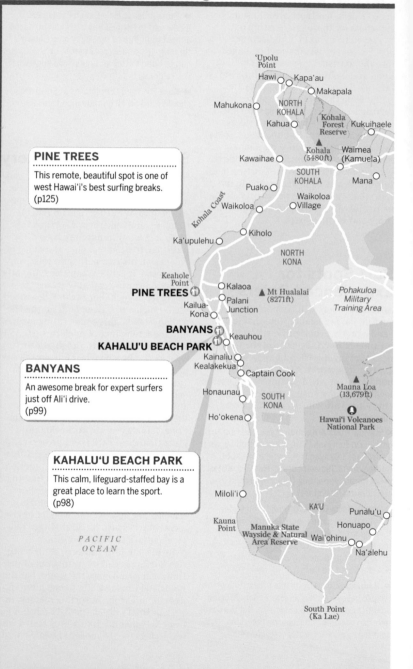

PINE TREES

This remote, beautiful spot is one of west Hawai'i's best surfing breaks. (p125)

BANYANS

An awesome break for expert surfers just off Ali'i drive. (p99)

KAHALU'U BEACH PARK

This calm, lifeguard-staffed bay is a great place to learn the sport. (p98)

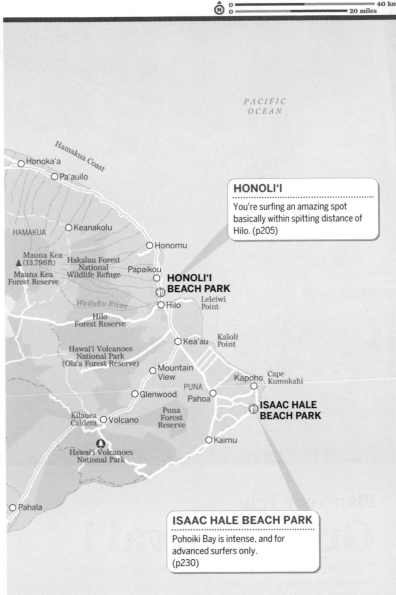

Windmills near Hawi (p149)

Plan Your Trip

Green Hawai'i

If you've been to other Hawaiian Islands, you'll notice an immediate difference on Hawai'i: rows of windmills stand sentry along the coast, roadside signs clamor for Hawaiian sovereignty, and people who would rather be tucked up in bed skulk around in the dark hunting invasive coqui frogs. Being green is an active, participatory process, and everyone on the island – the people, businesses and government – is engaged.

The Green Traveler

Going 'green' is easier said than done, especially as a traveler. The good news is that the Big Island's conscientious local population works hard to ensure it is possible for you to make sustainable choices during your stay. Listed here are a few simple but effective ways you can make your trip a more environmentally friendly one.

➡ Consider carbon offsetting your flight and rental car. Enterprise, National, Hertz and Alamo all have programs, although sadly they tend not to advertise them. Alternatively, calculate your own carbon costs (www.sustainabletravel.org/utilities/carbon-calculator/) and donate that to a worthy cause.

➡ Patronize local businesses that employ responsible practices as a greener way to spend your green. Look for the 'sustainable' symbol in our listings.

➡ The trash dumps on Hawai'i are full to overflowing, so it's important to minimize your waste production; consider carrying a reusable storage container for leftovers or takeout, and bring a reusable water bottle.

➡ Look for biodegradable 'Sustainable Island Products' at restaurants and food retailers, and use reusable bags for purchases.

➡ In grocery stores, products labeled 'Island Fresh,' 'Hawaii Seal of Quality' and 'Made in Hawaii with Aloha' are locally sourced or manufactured.

➡ KTA Super Stores carry Mountain Apple Brand, which denotes local products; fish sold at KTA is usually locally caught.

➡ Where you buy is as important as what you buy. According to a 2008 study by Civic Economics, for every $100 spent at a non-local chain store, $43 stays in the community, as opposed to $68 if that same money is spent at a locally owned store. It makes a difference.

➡ Choose tour companies that promote environmentally friendly practices. Support Hawaiian guides.

➡ Volunteer a day of your vacation – it's a great way to do some good and meet other cool people like you.

Of course, being 'green' for Hawaiians is about more than just reducing waste; it includes respect for the land and culture on many levels. It all starts and ends with aloha – the spirit-philosophy of love and

SUSTAINABLE ICON

It seems like everyone's going 'green' these days, but how can you really know which Big Island businesses are genuinely ecofriendly and which are simply jumping on the sustainability bandwagon?

Our 'sustainable' icon ✔ indicates listings that we are highlighting because they demonstrate an active sustainable-tourism policy. Some are involved in conservation or environmental education, while others maintain and preserve Hawaiian identity and culture, and many are owned and operated by local and indigenous operators.

compassion; a humanistic, harmonic way of being.

Visitors can participate in that self-perpetuating, good karma cycle by yielding to other drivers, sharing waves and staying off private property. Make the effort to seek out and participate in cultural programs and activities, and respectfully engage with Native Hawaiians to gain a better understanding of their unique and deep connection with the island.

On the Ground

Tourism on Hawai'i is, not surprisingly, a hot green topic. While it is the island's economic engine, it also chafes against ecological fundamentals like land and fossil-fuel use, resource allocation, waste creation, and erosion of natural and cultural features. But what's so inspiring is that Big Islanders are doing something about it.

Innovative protection initiatives like 'conservation easements' are keeping developments at bay. For example, tireless antidevelopment groups in Ka'u have managed to steadily purchase and protect the Big Island's southern coastline with the help of the Trust for Public Land. Currently they hope to outdo their 550-acre $3.9 million purchase of Kawa Bay in 2011 with a 1363-acre purchase south of Naʻalehu. The land is listed for $11.5 million.

Meanwhile, the Slow Food Movement is championed by gourmands and grocers alike. Many restaurants can tell you the names of the guy who caught your fish, and the cow that became your burger. 'Locally Sourced' is so frequently printed in menus that it has almost lost its impact – almost.

On a much larger scale, Hawaii passed landmark legislation in 2016 allocating $2 million in state money to assist farmers with fees for organic certification applications and inspections (that process is neither cheap nor easy). This should help small operations overcome the barriers to entry preventing them from getting fair market value for their produce.

Hawaii is also the first state to eliminate single-use plastic bags from all of its counties, starting with an ordinance that went into effect on the Big Island in January 2014. Meanwhile Hawaii increased its renewable energy commitment, pledging to source 100% of its electricity from renewable sources by 2045. It is the first state in the union to make that commitment.

In this area, the Big Island is already ahead of the game. It is the highest renewable energy user in the state, with geothermal and solar power generating over 20% of the island's energy. In 2016 a biodiesel plant in Keaʻau, which produces 13,000 gallons a day from waste cooking oil and fast-growing non-food sources, received the US first-ever sustainability certification for biofuel.

GMO-Free Hawaiʻi

Genetically modified organisms (GMOs) are a tinderbox issue pitting farmers and activists against politicians and business interests. The Big Island's *kalo* (taro) farmers have historically been center stage in this drama, arguing against GMOs for both scientific and cultural reasons. *Kalo* is a sacred plant central to the Hawaiian creation narrative and has grown here for over a millennium (and continues to grow in Waipiʻo Valley). Using traditional techniques, including

hand pollination, Hawaiian taro farmers cultivate over 300 varieties of this staple food. Introducing GMO taro, they argue, threatens the biodiversity of the plant while compromising its genetic integrity.

Since the GMO Free Hawaii initiative started, other genetically engineered plants have cropped up, most notoriously papaya. In 1998 the first genetically modified papaya was released in Puna. It proved resistant against the devastating ringspot virus as intended, but also cross-contaminated 50% of the island's non-GMO varieties, according to one scientific study. Organic varieties were also contaminated, as was the University of Hawaii's non-GMO seed supply, and as a result, exports of Big Island papaya plummeted to places like Japan that had strict policies against modified foods. The Japanese ban was lifted in 2012, and today over 85% of papaya exported from the island are GMO.

Activists have successfully ushered a number bills through the state legislature imposing restrictions on GMO cultivation, including a moratorium on GMO taro in 2013. However, a federal judge ruled in late 2016 that local and county laws regarding GMOs could not supersede state laws. This major win for industrial agriculture effectively crushes the burgeoning bans on several islands.

Red-Hot Green Issues

Understanding the issues that impassion locals – invasive species, resort developments, renewable energy and sovereignty – provides insight into what makes this island tick. It seems everyone is involved, but they don't necessarily agree on what's best for the land. You'll see placards, squatters, DIY projects and graffiti addressing many of these hot topics in your travels.

➡ **10% Kona coffee blends** These cheaper blends using foreign beans threaten local farmers who are fighting to get Kona coffee recognized as a Product of Designated Origin. This would protect the name and origin of Kona coffee à la Napa Valley wines and Parmigiano-Reggiano cheese.

Top: Organic fruit stand

Bottom: The invasive coqui frog (p68)

DESIGN PICS/DAVID PONTON/GETTY IMAGES ©

➡ **Dolphin encounters** Whether in captivity or the wild, human–dolphin encounters carry potential risks for the latter. If disturbed by swimmers or boats, wild dolphins may become too tired to feed. Captive 'show' dolphins can suffer from stress, infections and damaged dorsal fins. Proposed laws may ban swimming with dolphins altogether, which certain business owners fear will harm the tourist economy.

➡ **Marine reserves** A 10-year ban on fishing along Kaupulehu Bay, enacted in 2016 to replenish fisheries, has angered some Hawaiians who believe their rights to the land are being violated to protect the interests of the mega-resorts nearby.

➡ **Kealakekua Bay** This popular bay where pods of spinner dolphins sleep has been a source of controversy since the government temporarily banned kayaks in 2013. Locals and biologists have claimed that the dolphins are being disturbed by the hordes of snorkelers and boaters, and a ban on activities during certain periods of time is being considered.

➡ **Thirty Meter Telescope** Mauna Kea, Hawaii's most sacred spot, may become home to the TMT, slated for construction in 2018. The community is divided over this project, which will be bigger than all of the mountain's current observatories combined.

➡ **Geothermal energy** The island's only geothermal power plant (p231) has antagonized the very demographic you think would be in favor of it by venting toxic hydrogen sulfide over Puna. Some Native Hawaiians feel that the plant is a desecration of the Earth and violates Pele, the goddess of fire.

➡ **Solar energy** Hawaii's high electricity costs and a blazing sun, coupled with government incentives, have catapulted its rooftop solar uptake well past other states. However, energy companies are now fighting to reduce the amount they pay for the electricity customers feed back into the grid, claiming they can no longer afford to maintain the power infrastructure.

➡ **Coqui frog** The county government reprioritized their focus on invasives in 2016, shuffling money and resources to species that are an immediate threat to human health. Alas, the high-decibel coqui (p228) does not directly fall in that category, leaving sleepless landowners to deal with the issue as best they can.

➡ **Ungulate control** Despite their ability to cause millions of dollars in damage and to

WEBPHOTOGRAPHER/GETTY IMAGES ©

A solar power station

VOLUNTEER OPPORTUNITIES

Instead of just visiting Hawai'i, consider engaging with the land, its people and its environment through a volunteer experience. Short-term opportunities can cap off a vacation nicely, while long-term programs allow you to dive deep into this diverse landscape.

➡ **Sanctuary Ocean Count** (www.sanctuaryoceancount.org) Help count humpback whales with the National Marine Sanctuary in January through March.

➡ **Friends of Hawai'i Volcanoes National Park** (p252) Conducts an assortment of projects and hikes at the national park.

➡ **Kalani Retreat** (☑808-965-7828, 800-800-6886; www.kalani.com; 12-6860 Hwy 137; r with shared bath $95, r with private bath $140-245; 🛜💱) Pay-to-volunteer programs support activities at Kalani yoga retreat center.

➡ **Hawai'i Volcanoes National Park** (p244) Sporadic short- and long-term volunteer opportunities within the park.

➡ **WWOOF Hawaii** (www.wwoofhawaii.org) World Wide Opportunities on Organic Farms lists short- and long-term farming opportunities.

➡ **Hawai'i Wildlife Fund** (www.wildhawaii.org/volunteer.html) Turtle support, seal watching and marine conservation programs.

➡ **Mauna Kea Volunteer Program** (p173) Volunteers clean up trash, lead stargazing programs and staff the visitor center.

➡ **USGS Hawaiian Volcano Observatory** (http://hvo.wr.usgs.gov/volunteer) Three-month-long, full-time volunteer positions to help monitor Hawai'i's volcanoes.

decimate native plant populations, government efforts to remove deer, pigs, goats and other invasive grazers have angered hunters and sovereignty activists who see this as an attack on their traditional way of life.

Keeping It Green

Being green means protecting Hawai'i's native species from outside threats. Although there are too many invasive species to list (many of which are impossible to control), these two relatively new arrivals to the Big Island have the potential to do great damage, but can still be successfully controlled.

➡ **Axis deer** Someone dropped a few Axis deer from a helicopter in 2009 (possibly to diversify the Big Island's hunting) and they quickly multiplied to almost 100 in less than three years. Officials removed them all – they hope – before the deer could repeat the millions of dollars in damage they have already caused in Maui.

➡ **Molucca raspberry** This thorny bush has the potential to create impenetrable thickets and crowd out native plants. The bottom of its leaves are covered in yellowish hair, which distinguishes it from the endemic varieties that do play nice with their neighbors. Crews have removed known infestations around Hawai'i Volcanoes National Park, but fear it may still be growing elsewhere.

Report sightings of either of these species to the **Big Island Invasive Species Committee** (☑808-961-3299; www.biisc.org/report-a-pest).

Plan Your Trip

Travel with Children

With its phenomenal natural beauty, Hawai'i is perfect for a family vacation. *Nā keiki* (kids) can play on sandy beaches galore, snorkel amid tropical fish, zipline in forest canopies and even watch lava flow. Then get them out of the sun (or rain) for a spell at family-friendly museums.

Best Regions for Kids

Kailua-Kona
Has the shopping goodness of Ali'i Dr, plus good intro beaches for bodysurfing, stand-up paddling and snorkeling. Up the mountain, the Donkey Mill Arts Center has tons of children's programming.

South Kohala
The resorts of this area all include family-friendly amenities and infrastructure. Kids have access to pools in case the water in the ocean is too rough.

North Kohala
There are lots of educational programs, like the Kohala Institute and Kohala Mountain Educational Farm, aimed at children.

Hilo
Many of the parks, museums and educational centers in this town are either aimed at kids, or accommodate their needs.

Puna
Some of the markets and weekly events in Puna are kid-friendly; the general hippie vibe is in line with the 'it takes a village' approach.

Volcano & Around
The sheer natural beauty of the national park, plus many ranger-led activities, should wow older kids.

Activities

Mixing up natural and cultural sites and activities, as well as managing expectations, helps to maximize children's fun. The latter is especially important when it comes to lava: kids may be sorely disappointed, expecting the fiery fountains dramatically seen on the Discovery Channel. Check current lava flows with the Hawaiian Volcano Observatory (http://hvo.wr.usgs.gov/activity/kilaueastatus.php) before booking an expensive helicopter or boat tour.

Commercial luau might seem like cheesy Vegas dinner shows to adults, but many kids love the flashy dances and fire tricks. Children typically get discounted tickets (and sometimes free admission when accompanied by a paying adult).

Food & Drink

Hawai'i has to be one of the most food-friendly places for kids on the planet. Not only are all the favorites readily available but there are also tempting exotic tidbits like crack seed and Spam *masubi*. Wrinkly passion fruit, spiky rambutan and downright strange soursop are just some of the odd duck fruits you can find

Little hikers in 'Akaka Falls State Park (p193)

at farmers markets, which are a fun introduction for kids to Hawai'i's tropical bounty.

You'd be surprised how many restaurants – including upscale places like Brown's Beach House – warmly welcome children, and even have specific *keiki* menus. However, children are expected to behave – one screech and you'll be getting the 'stink eye' from other diners. One of our top picks for white tablecloth kiddie dining is **Jackie Rey's Ohana Grill** (☑808-327-0209; www.jackiereys.com; 75-5995 Kuakini Hwy; mains lunch $13-19, dinner $16-35; ☉11am-9pm Mon-Fri, 5-9pm Sat & Sun; P 🚹) in Kailua-Kona, where the tablecloths can be colored in and kids are invited to check out 300lb fish hanging from hooks in the freezer. Aloha, Big Island style.

The island's many small-to-medium-size diners and plate-lunch joints are all sustained by repeat, family-oriented clientele; if you're ever in need of a spot where the food is clean, the portions are enormous and the price is right, you really can't go wrong with a plate-lunch establishment.

Children's Highlights

Animal Encounters

Three Ring Ranch Exotic Animal Sanctuary (p87), Kailua-Kona More mature kids will be wowed by this incredible wildlife sanctuary.

Ocean Rider Seahorse Farm (p125), Keahole Point Seahorses (which are always cute) are raised and reared at this conservation facility.

Pana'ewa Rainforest Zoo & Gardens (p201), Hilo The only zoo in the USA located within an actual rainforest.

Beginner Snorkeling, Island-wide Spots like Kahaluu Beach (p98), Mahukona (p153) and Wawaloli Beach (p125) are perfect for young snorkelers.

Sea Turtles, Kiholo Bay There are areas on the northern side of this beach where sea turtles regularly bask.

Education & Exploration

'Imiloa Astronomy Center of Hawai'i (p201), **Hilo** A brilliant, immersive exploration of the universe and Polynesian culture.

Hawai'i Volcanoes National Park Junior Ranger Program (p244), Volcanoes National Park Learn about the raw power of nature – by an actual volcano!

The Kohala Institute (p155), Kapa'au Hosts programs that focus on sustainability and environmental education.

Donkey Mill Art Center (p102), Holualoa A brilliant spot for Big Island arts education.

Kona Coffee Living History Farm (p109), Captain Cook Older kids will appreciate this outdoor exhibition.

Planning

Accommodations

Choose accommodations based on your family's sightseeing and activity priorities. Resorts offer spectacular swimming pools, along with kids' activity day camps and on-call babysitting services. But some parents prefer the convenience and cost savings of having a full kitchen and washer/dryer, which many condominiums and vacation rentals offer. Smaller B&Bs

may have a more familial vibe – and on that note, many Big Islanders have a big soft spot for kids – but you run the risk of limited kid-friendly amenities.

Children often stay free when sharing a hotel or resort room with their parents, but only if they use existing bedding. Otherwise roll-away beds may be available – sometimes free, but usually for a surcharge of up to $40 per night. At condos, kids above a certain age might count as extra guests and entail an additional nightly surcharge.

Because long drive times can make kids antsy, you may not want to base yourself in just one place on the Big Island. On the other hand, for that very reason you may want to find one area that has everything you need within quick tripping distance.

When to Go

When deciding when and where to visit, know that most families choose the sunny leeward side of the island, staying around Kailua-Kona or on the South Kohala coast. The windward side of the Big Island gets more rain year-round

IS MY CHILD OLD ENOUGH?

Although parents will find plenty of outdoor family fun for all ages on Hawai'i, some activities require that children be of a certain age, height or weight to participate. Always ask about restrictions when making reservations to avoid disappointment – and tears.

To learn to surf Kids who can swim comfortably in the ocean are candidates for lessons. Teens can usually join group lessons; younger kids may be required to take private lessons.

To take a boat tour Depending on the outfit and type of watercraft, tours sometimes set minimum ages, usually from four to eight years. Larger boats might allow tots as young as two to ride along.

To summit Mauna Kea Not advised for children under 16 years due to high-altitude health hazards.

To ride in a helicopter Most tour companies set minimum ages (eg two to 12 years) and sometimes also minimum body weights (eg 35lb). Toddlers must be strapped into their own seat and pay full fare.

To go ziplining Minimum age requirements range from five to 12 years, depending on the company. Participants must also meet weight minimums (usually 50lb to 80lb).

To ride a horse For trail rides the minimum age ranges from seven to 10 years, depending on the outfitter and if your child has riding experience. Short pony rides may be offered for younger kids.

and higher waves in winter, which can nix swimming. Year-round, vog (volcanic smog) can be a factor island-wide. Sometimes the air pollution is negligible, but at other times its health effects can be hazardous, especially for young children and pregnant women.

What to Pack

Hawai'i's small-town vibe means that there's almost no place – apart from star chef's restaurants and five-star resorts – that is formal, whether in attitude or attire. You can let your kids wear T-shirts, shorts and *rubbah slippah* (flip-flops) just about anywhere. When visiting Hawai'i Volcanoes National Park and the island's windward side, rain gear and a sweater or fleece jacket will come in handy – those areas experience some wacky weather.

At tourist convenience shops, such as the ABC Store, you can buy inexpensive water-sports equipment (eg floaties, snorkel sets and boogie boards). In Kailua-Kona, Snorkel Bob's (p90) rents and sells all kinds of water sports gear for kids, from reef shoes to snorkel masks. If you do forget some critical item from home, services like Big Island Baby Rentals (p220) rent cribs, strollers, car seats, backpacks, beach toys and more.

Resources

➡ **Travel with Children** (Lonely Planet) This book is loaded with valuable tips and amusing tales, especially for first-time parents.

➡ **Lonely Planet** (www.lonelyplanet.com) Ask questions and get advice from other travelers in the Thorn Tree's online 'Kids to Go' forum.

➡ **Go Hawaii** (www.gohawaii.com) The state's official tourism site lists family-friendly activities, special events and more – just search the site using terms like 'kids' or 'family.'

Need to Know

➡ **Baby food and formula** Sold at supermarkets and pharmacies.

➡ **Babysitting** Ask your hotel concierge; some resorts offer day-care programs and kids' activity clubs.

Swimming in a shallow tide pool

➡ **Breastfeeding** Done discreetly (cover up) or in private.

➡ **Car seats** Reserve in advance through car-rental companies.

➡ **Changing facilities** Ubiquitous in public restrooms except at beaches.

➡ **Diapers (nappies)** Sold everywhere (eg supermarkets, pharmacies and convenience stores).

➡ **Dining out** High chairs and kids' menus are available at most sit-down restaurants, except top-end dining rooms.

➡ **Hiking** Keep hydrated and wear sunscreen. Be careful when hiking over sharp *a'a* lava, which can be painful even through rubber soles. Be on the lookout for *kiawe* thorns, which can pierce rubber soles.

➡ **Strollers** Bring from home or reserve via Big Island Baby Rentals (p220).

➡ **Swimming** The waters off of Hawai'i have incredibly strong currents and undertows. Tide pools are the safest spot for novice swimmers.

Regions at a Glance

Kailua-Kona & the Kona Coast

Activities
Beaches
Nature

Plunge Right In

Daredevil surfer? Novice diver? Occasional snorkeler? Whatever your experience level, you'll revel in your ocean sport of choice. Kona waters are famous for their clarity, making for first-rate snorkeling and diving.

Beaches Galore

From compact drive-up strips to seemingly endless stretches of sand, Kona offers a diverse array of beaches. Decide what's top priority – glassy waters or vigorous waves, solitude or animated company – to ensure a fantastic beach day.

Real-Life Aquarium

Oh! Is a *honu* (Hawaiian green sea turtle) really swimming near me? Seeing marine creatures in their habitat is a profound experience. Kona waters are home to tropical fish, dolphins, manta rays, *honu* and much more. Honor them by keeping your distance while in their fascinating underwater world.

p78

Kohala & Waimea

Beaches
Resorts
Food

Picture Perfect

Flaunting silky white sand, lapped by gentle waves and ringed by palms, South Kohala's 'Gold Coast' beaches live up to the Hollywood archetype. Some are located on public parks, while others are adjacent to resorts (but still accessible).

Pure R&R

If you're seeking a pampering resort vacation, South Kohala offers a range of them, with on-site spas, golf course and beaches. Resorts are a convenient option for those who want a one-stop place to eat, play and stay.

Locavore Dining

Foodies, you're in luck. Waimea and Hawi are mighty little hubs for destination restaurants featuring locally grown, raised and caught ingredients prepared with flair. For added viewing pleasure, oceanfront dining at South Kohala's resorts promises spectacular sunsets.

p128

Mauna Kea & Saddle Road

Landscapes
Remoteness
Hiking

Explore the Extraordinary

After the first few miles along Saddle Road, you'll know you're entering unfamiliar territory. By the time you ascend to the 9000ft elevation, the novelty transforms to wonder. The utter foreignness of Mauna Kea makes for unforgettable memories.

Above the Clouds

To Native Hawaiians, Mauna Kea was absolutely sacred, and off-limits to commoners. To scientists, the mountain is a precious astronomy site, with immaculately dark skies. Ascending the nearly 13,800ft summit of Mauna Kea is not only challenging – it's an honor.

Diehards Only

If 'climb every mountain' is your motto, Mauna Kea and Mauna Loa majestically await. Be prepared for high altitudes, relentless lava-rock terrain, freezing temperatures and a singular, otherworldly experience.

p162

Hamakua Coast

Culture
History
Landscapes

Small-Town Folk

The biggest town along the coast is Honoka'a, with only one commercial street, no hotels and no stoplights. Here you'll find traditional taro fields in Waipi'o Valley, small-scale farmers growing specialty crops, descendants of plantation immigrants and others living close to nature.

Plantation Legacy

Many towns in Hamakua arose due to King Sugar, and memories of ol' plantation days remain strong – as do old-fashioned values of neighborliness and hard work. Small museums along the coast help locals to remember – and visitors to imagine.

Green Oases

In ceaseless waterfalls hidden in foliage and wild tropical rainforest, in thriving tea plantations and in three immense gulches, admire Hamakua's verdant beauty. Most impressive is the emerald panorama of Waipi'o Valley.

p176

Hilo

Food
Culture
History

Broke Da Mouth

For the gustatorily adventurous, Hilo's edible variety offers endless delights. Eat your way from fresh ahi *poke* (cubed, marinated fish) to heaping plates of comfort food, from succulent papayas and sweet-tart mini bananas to locavore menus by creative chefs.

Merrie Monarch Festival

Home of the world-famous Merrie Monarch Festival, Hilo is home to many revered *kumu* hula: master teachers of this ancient practice. More than a dance, hula was a means of communication and storytelling – and a disciplined way of life.

Tsunami Survivor

Why do Hilo residents live upland, far from the beautiful bay? Learn about the two 20th-century tsunamis that destroyed the town – and you'll glimpse Hiloans' resilience and pragmatism. For starters, visit the Hawaii Tsunami Museum.

p196

Puna

Activities
Culture
Landscapes

Surf & Turf

It's hard to stay indoors in sultry Puna. Go tide pool exploring or watch daredevils face Pohoiki's daunting surf. Hike to the fresh air of Cape Kumukahi – or double down to view molten lava. Or cycle the fantastic yet underrated back roads.

Counterculture Central

Puna has always beckoned the proudly independent (or, let's face it, the fringe). You might find sovereignty activists, nouveau hippies, off-the-grid minimalists, organic farmers, *pakalolo* (marijuana) growers and anyone preferring to skirt conventionality.

Land of Pele

So close to Kilauea Volcano, Puna has long borne witness to Pele's fiery theatrics. See 'lava trees' remaining from long-ago eruptions, explore a thrilling lava-cave underworld, splash in lava-rock tide pools, hike to a baby black-sand beach or trek toward a live lava flow.

p222

Hawai'i Volcanoes National Park

Hiking
Culture
Nature

Volcanic Treks

Miles of trails – from easy scenic loops to grinding alpine treks – let all levels explore Hawai'i's two active volcanoes, Mauna Loa and Kilauea. The lava terrain ranges from barren swaths to pristine forests of native species.

Authentic Arts

Misty Volcano is home to many artists who thrive in solitude and proximity to raw nature. Halema'uma'u Crater, Pele's home, is a sacred site, and *kahiko* (ancient style of hula) performances here are stirring spiritual offerings.

Native Species

Those nene (native Hawaiian goose) crossing signs posted throughout the park are cute – and also deadly serious. Nene are endangered. The park is a fragile ecosystem for many native species, including honeycreepers and other songbirds, *i'o* (Hawaiian hawk) and Mauna Loa silversword.

p236

Ka'u

Remoteness
History
Landscapes

Rural Solitude

To cross the island, most people take the northern Hamakua route or the central Saddle Rd. Less traveled is the southern Ka'u route. On this lengthy stretch, you'll find scrubby lava plains, wind-whipped cliffs and little else.

Sugar to Coffee

When the Ka'u Sugar Company closed in 1996, locals were left adrift. In this rural spot, there were no alternative industries. But several entrepreneurial farmers decided to try coffee. More than a decade later, this region is producing award-winning beans; tour a coffee mill and try them for yourself.

Windswept Beaches

With rough surf, cold water and often daunting access over rugged terrain, Ka'u's beaches aren't the stuff of typical tropical fantasies. But in these wild and formidable beaches, there is unmistakable mana (spiritual essence).

p258

On the Road

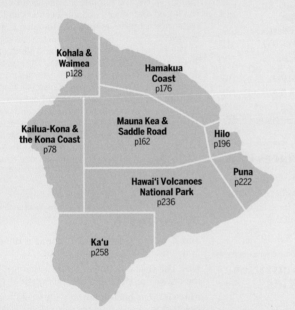

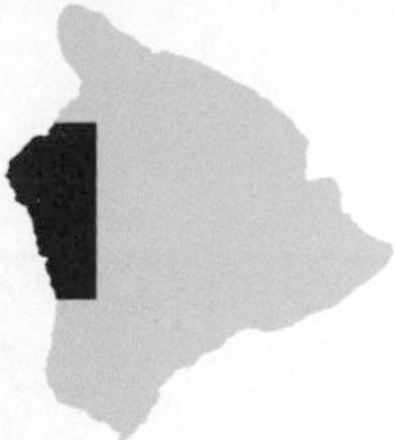

Kailua-Kona &
the Kona Coast

📞 808

Best Places to Eat

➡ Umekes (p92)

➡ Da Poke Shack (p92)

➡ Annie's Island Fresh Burgers (p105)

➡ Sushi Shiono (p94)

Best Activities with Kids

➡ Learning to splash around at Kikaua Beach (p126)

➡ Swimming and beach-combing at Kiholo Bay (p123)

➡ Snorkeling in Ka'awaloa Cove (p112) or Two-Step (p117)

➡ Learning to paint at Donkey Mill Art Center (p102)

Why Go?

The main access point to the Big Island presents visitors with multiple destinations possessed of very distinct identities. Kailua-Kona is the urban heart of the west side, although you're free to place air quotes around 'urban.' Here you'll find tour offices, shopping centers and some very fine restaurants. Up the mountain, Holualoa is a breezy artists' enclave.

The Kona coast extends north and south of Kailua 'town.' To the north you'll find the edges of the great Hawaiian lava deserts, as well as hidden coves, Hawaiian ruins and resort communities. The South Kona Coast is a fascinating microcosm of Big Island ecosystems and cultural groups. Coffee farms tended by mainland transplants and generations-deep Japanese families stud the jungle hills, which smooth down to a coast studded with superlative snorkeling opportunities. Connecting the South Kona Coast to Kailua is Keauhou, a slice of mainland condo-country carved out of the Big Island.

When to Go

Jun A two-day festival at Pu'uhonua o Honaunau celebrates traditional Hawaiian culture.

Nov The Holualoa Village Coffee & Art Stroll showcases the region's produce and artistic output.

Mar Get your microbrew on with a cold beer on the beach at the Kona Brewers Festival.

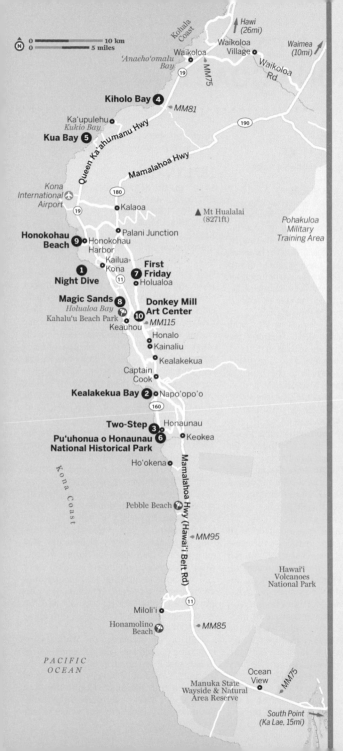

Kailua-Kona & the Kona Coast Highlights

❶ Night Dive (p88) Plunging into the water with an otherworldly cast of angelic manta rays.

❷ Kealakekua Bay (p111) Hiking from the highway or kayaking to the cliffs.

❸ Two-Step (p117) Dipping into the coral canyons and multicolored reef panorama.

❹ Kiholo Bay (p123) Walking through the desert to sea turtles and crashing waves.

❺ Kua Bay (p126) Bodyboarding or snorkeling into teal waters that wash up on white sand.

❻ Pu'uhonua o Honaunau National Historical Park (p117) Finding sanctuary and exploring Native Hawaiian history at the Place of Refuge.

❼ First Friday (p103) Soaking up the arts on a stroll through Holualoa.

❽ Magic Sands (p85) Bodysurfing as the sun sets over the beach.

❾ Honokohau Beach (p119) Trekking past lava rock and Hawaiian ruins to this sweep of sand.

❿ Donkey Mill Art Center (p102) Finding the perfect hand-crafted souvenir.

HIKING & CYCLING
THE KONA COAST

KONA COAST BACKCOUNTRY HIKE

START 'ANAEHO'OMALU BEACH PARK
END KEAWAIKI BEACH
LENGTH 4 MILES, 2–3 HOURS

Walking across miles of 'a'a (rough, jagged lava) under the beating sun is like stumbling over sharp Cap'n Crunch in an oven. But once you plunge into the turquoise depths of the Kona Coast's remote beaches, you'll realize all that ankle-wrenching was worth it. If you're not up for a grueling hike, opt for the 20-minute walk to Keawaiki, accessed from a small parking area off Hwy 11 between the 78- and 79-mile markers.

This first section travels south from **'Anaeho'omalu Beach** (p134). Hugging the coastline, the trail is relatively well marked, crossing varying beaches and lava fields. Start by heading south from the beach at the **Waikoloa Beach Marriott** (Map p136; ☑ 808-886-6789; www.waikoloabeachmarriott. com; 69-275 Waikoloa Beach Dr). Adding increased solitude with each forward step, the protected coves and outer reefs at **Kapalaoa Beach** provide good possibilities for swimming, snorkeling and surfing.

Look for the Pu'uanahulu Homesteads after the first point and, a mile beyond, a lone palm at Akahu Kaimu. Continue for another 2 miles over rugged 'a'a flows, and past swimming holes and hidden snorkeling gems. The trail is occasionally marked by white coral, but mainly follows the coast until the beach at **Keawaiki** (p127). You'll know you've arrived when you reach the former estate of Francis I'i Brown, an influential 20th-century Hawaiian businessman. Passing the well-fortified house, look for the lava trail through a grove of mesquite trees. This leads 1.5 miles back to the highway. Note that the ocean does not play nicely at this beach, so if you're going to swim, do so at your own risk and be very aware of the tides and currents.

Bring at least 2L of water per person for this hike. The sun is intense because of the reflection off the lava and sea, and there is almost no shade, so bring a wide-brimmed hat, sunglasses and lots of sunscreen.

1871 TRAIL

START PU'UHONUA O HONAUNAU NATIONAL HISTORICAL PARK
END HO'OKENA BEACH PARK
LENGTH 3.5 MILES, 2 HOURS

At the southern end of the parking lot in the **national park** (p117), you'll find a dirt road which leads to the beginning of the trail (there's an information kiosk to let you know you're on the way). As you walk along the trail, you'll be framed by an enviable bracket of fascinating beauty; clear shallow water extending to the blue ocean on one side, and archaeological sites on the other. Those latter sites are strictly *kapu* (forbidden). Confident snorkelers will be tempted by the numerous looking-glass coves that indent the trail; by all means, take a dip and cool off, but always be aware of the strength of the currents and the tides.

The visitor center stocks trail guides describing the ancient Hawaiian history and natural wonders you'll see along the way, which include a collapsed lava tube and a tremendous, if overgrown, *holua* (lava-sledding course) that *ali'i* (chiefs) raced down. Watch out for feral goats. They're usually benign. Usually.

After about a mile you'll see a little detour that leads to lovely **Alahaka Bay.** Past here is the steep Alahaka Ramp, which... well, it's a ramp, obviously human-made, and it's both fascinating and incongruous given the solitude that surrounds you. This clever bit of engineering once allowed riders on horseback to travel to the now abandoned village of Ki'ilae.

Halfway up the ramp, the Waiu o Hina lava tube (closed for safety reasons) opens to the sea. From the top of the ramp, the incredible vista of ocean coves and ragged cliffs is a trail highlight. Continuing, you reach a gate that once marked the park's boundary; this is the current Ki'ilae Village

From hiking trails that trace Kona's history and the Big Island coast to cycling paths that wind past altars to surfing, there's a glut of outdoor exploration options along the Kona Coast.

site – the ruins are pretty, well, ruined, with almost nothing to see.

The trail turns inland after the Ala-haka Ramp and becomes increasingly rough and humid. Keep pushing on, and eventually, the trail will turn back toward the coast, passing some housing developments along the way. Keep tight to the coast until you reach **Ho'okena Beach Park** (p118) – congrats!

CYCLING TWOUR: KAILUA TO KEAUHOU

START ROYAL KONA RESORT
END KAHALU'U BEACH PARK
LENGTH 4.2 MILES, 2 HOURS

Head south on Ali'i Dr and you'll pass a long, thin coast of condos, vacation homes and residential streets, with views out onto the water. The parts of Ali'i that connect Kailua-Kona to the resorts at Keauhou are an odd duck mix of timeshares, 20th-century suburban development and traces of Hawaiian archaeological heritage.

You can rent a bicycle from **Bikeshare Kona Hawaii Island** (p97) or **Bike Works** (p97) – take your pick, proceed south, and if you stop anywhere, always securely lock your bike up. Ali'i Dr is a narrow road, and it is popular with cyclists, so be sure to keep to your right. Barely a mile south of the Royal Kona Resort is **Honl's Beach** (p86), where Boogie Board developer Tom Morey tested his invention in the strong surf.

Keep cycling south, and on your left (*mauka,* or inland), you'll see signs for **Ali'i Gardens Marketplace** (p95), an outdoor shopping bazaar that's a nice spot to wander around. You can grab some food here, or get back on your bicycle and roll half a mile south to **Da Poke Shack** (p92), purveyors of fine *poke* (raw fish salad).

As you continue south, the road passes through Keolonahihi State Historical Park, a historical area that is largely overgrown today, but once contained a heiau (temple)

for surfers. About half a mile south, you can end your tour at **Magic Sands Beach** (p85), if you're into bodysurfing, or head 1.3 miles further on to **Kahalu'u Beach Park** (p98), the best spot for easy snorkeling access in the Kailua-Kona area.

ℹ️ Getting There & Away

Kona International Airport is the main access point not only to this region, but the Big Island itself. From here, Hwy 19, also known as the Belt Rd and Mamalahoa Hwy, extends south to Kailua-Kona and the South Kona Coast, and north to Kohala. The **Hele-On** (📞 808-961-8744; www.heleonbus.org; adult one-way $2, 10-ride ticket $15, monthly pass $60) bus service is the only public transportation link across the region (indeed, across the island); it's reliable, but is primarily used by commuters working at local resorts, and may not leave at times that are convenient for travelers. At the end of the day, by far the easiest way around is with your own set of wheels.

KAILUA-KONA

📞 808 / POP 12,000

Kailua-Kona, also known as 'Kailua,' 'Kona Town' and sometimes just 'Town,' is a love-it-or-leave-it kind of place. On the main drag of Ali'i Dr, along the shoreline, Kailua works hard to evoke the nonchalance of a sun-drenched tropical getaway, but in an injection-molded, bargain-priced way.

But we like it. Spend enough time here and you'll scratch past the souvenirs to an oddball identity built from a collision of two seemingly at-odds forces: mainlanders who want to wind down to Hawaiian time, and ambitious Big Islanders who want to make it in one of the few local towns worthy of the title. Somehow, this marriage works. Kailua-Kona can be tacky, but it's got character.

At the end of the day, Kailua is a convenient base from which to enjoy the Kona Coast's beaches, snorkeling, water sports and ancient Hawaiian sites, so you'll likely spend at least a day here.

History

For all its tourist-trap vibe, Kailua-Kona holds a significant place in Hawaiian history. Kamehameha the Great lived his last years here, worshipping at **Ahu'ena Heiau** (p83), his own temple. Soon after his death in 1819, his son Liholiho broke an important *kapu* (taboo) by dining with women. He suffered no godly wrath, so when the first missionaries sailed into Kailua Bay in 1820 they easily converted the Hawaiians to Christianity.

In the 19th century, the town was a leisure retreat for Hawaiian royalty. **Hulihe'e Palace** (p83) was a favorite getaway for King David Kalakaua, a talented patron of the arts, including hula, music and literature.

Since the 1970s Kailua-Kona has been the Big Island's economic powerhouse, fueled by tourism, retail and real estate.

👁️ Sights

Ali'i Dr bombards you with surf shops and ABC Stores, but amid the tourist kitsch are a handful of historic buildings and landmarks worth seeking out.

Old Kona Airport State Recreation Area   BEACH

(Map p120; www.hawaiistateparks.org; Kuakini Hwy; ⏲7am-8pm; 🅿️♿) 🏖️ Visitors often overlook this quiet park, located a mile from downtown. The swimming isn't great but it's a grand spot for a picnic. The beach area is studded with lava rock and tide pools, the latter occasionally occupied by napping sea turtles. Jogging and fishing are the main activities, but scuba divers and confident snorkelers can make for Garden Eel Cove, a short walk from the north end of the beach. To get here, follow Kuakini Hwy to its end.

Just inside the southern entrance gate is one tidal pool large and sandy enough to be the perfect *keiki* (child) pool. When the surf's up, local surfers flock to an offshore break.

Facilities include restrooms, showers and covered picnic tables on a lawn dotted with beach heliotrope and short coconut palms. Oh, and you know what makes getting to the beach better? Barreling down an unused airport runway. There's still a tarmac at Old Airport Park, which was the area's airport until it was deemed too small.

Herb Kane Paintings   GALLERY

(75-5660 Palani Rd) FREE Step inside King Kamehameha's Kona Beach Hotel, just next to to Ahu'ena Heiau (p83), to view historical paintings and a mural by legendary artist and Hawaiian historian Herb Kawainui Kane. Each image depicts an element of indigenous Hawaiian history or culture – fishing, the hula, farming etc. Also on display are a rare feathered helmet and cloak once worn by *ali'i* (royalty), Hawaiian war weapons and musical instruments, and a whale's-tooth pendant strung on a braided cord made of human hair.

Moku'aikaua Church   CHURCH

(📞 808-329-1589, 808-329-0655; www.mokuaikaua.org; 75-5713 Ali'i Dr; ⏲7:30am-5:30pm) Completed in 1836, this church is a handsome building with walls of lava rock held together by sand and coral-lime mortar. The posts and beams, hewn with stone adzes and smoothed with chunks of coral, are made from ohia, and the pews and pulpit are made of koa, the most prized native hardwood. The steeple tops out at 112ft, making this the tallest structure in Kailua. Contemporary services are held at 9am on Sundays, with traditional services at 11am.

Often referred to as 'the big stone church on Ali'i,' Moku'aikaua is the gestation point of Hawaiian Christianity. On April 4, 1820, the first Christian missionaries to the Hawaiian Islands sailed into Kailua Bay. When they landed they were unaware that Hawai'i's *kapu* system had been abolished on that very spot just a few months before.

The church is popular for weddings, and inside is a dusty model of the missionaries' ship, *Thaddeus,* and a history of their arrival.

Hulihe'e Palace   HISTORIC BUILDING
(☑808-329-1877; http://daughtersofhawaii.org; 75-5718 Ali'i Dr; adult/child \$10/1; ⊙9am-4pm Mon-Sat, 10am-3pm Sun) 🏖 This palace is a fascinating study in the rapid shift the Hawaiian royal family made from Polynesian god-kings to Westernized monarchs. Here's the skinny: Hawai'i's second governor, 'John Adams' Kuakini, built a simple two-story, lava-rock house as his private residence in 1838. After Kuakini's death, the house became the favorite vacation getaway for Hawaiian royalty. The palace contains Western antiques collected on royal jaunts to Europe and ancient Hawaiian artifacts, most notably several of Kamehameha the Great's war spears.

Hard times befell the monarchy in the early 20th century, and the house was sold and the furnishings and artifacts auctioned off by Prince Kuhio. Luckily his wife and other royalty numbered each piece and recorded the names of bidders.

In 1925 the Territory of Hawaii purchased the house to be a museum run by the Daughters of Hawai'i, a women's group dedicated to the preservation of Hawaiian culture and language. This group tracked down the furnishings and royal memorabilia, such as a table inlaid with 25 kinds of native woods, several of Kamehameha the Great's war spears and the (surprisingly small) bed of 6ft, 440lb Princess Ke'elikolani.

DON'T MISS

KAILUA-KONA SUNSET SPOTS
....

Kailua Pier (p85)

Magic Sands Beach (p85)

Huggo's on the Rocks (p95)

Don's Mai Tai Bar (p95)

Kona International Airport (p97), while touching down.

You'll learn these and other stories on 40-minute guided tours (\$2 extra charged on adult tickets only) given by Daughters of Hawai'i docents. The free concert series, held at 4pm on the third Sunday of each month, is a treat, with Hawaiian music and hula performed on the grass facing sparkling Kailua Bay.

Ahu'ena Heiau   TEMPLE
(http://ahuenaheiau.org; 75-5660 Palani Rd; 🚶) After uniting the Hawaiian Islands in 1810, Kamehameha the Great established the kingdom's royal court in Lahaina on Maui, but he continued to return to the Big Island. After a couple of years, he restored this sacred site as his personal retreat and temple (which now sits adjacent to a hotel). Notice the towering carved *ki'i* (deity) image with a golden plover atop its helmet: these long-distance flying birds may have helped guide the first Polynesians to Hawaii.

When Kamehameha I died at Ahu'ena Heiau on May 8, 1819, his body was prepared for burial here. In keeping with ancient Hawaiian tradition, the king's bones were secreted elsewhere, hidden so securely no one has ever found them (though some theorists point to a cave near Kaloko Fishpond).

Keolonahihi State
Historical Park   ARCHAEOLOGICAL SITE
(off Ali'i Dr; ⊙sunrise-sunset) 🏖 While largely overgrown with jungle and scrub brush today, this was once a major religious complex for Native Hawaiians. A heiau (temple) here was once dedicated to surfers, and tradition holds Kamehameha the Great learned to ride waves nearby. Public access is limited, although there was a small shoreline access path at time of research which led to a beach of coral rubble and the debris of ancient Hawaiian buildings. Per normal, you are not allowed to disturb any archaeological remains.

Kailua-Kona

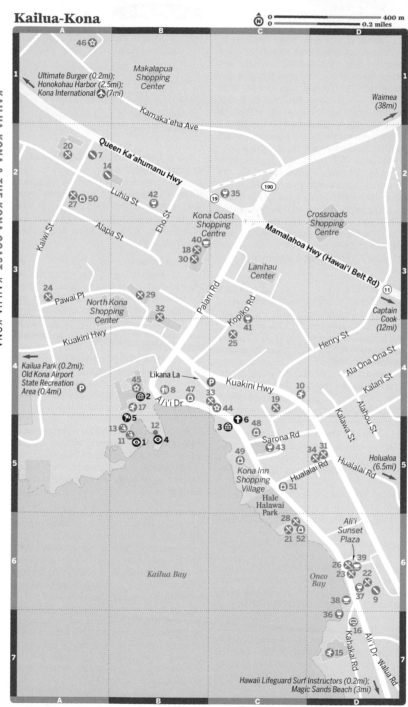

0 — 400 m
0 — 0.2 miles

Ultimate Burger (0.2mi);
Honokohau Harbor (2.5mi);
Kona International ✈ (7mi)

Makalapua
Shopping
Center

Waimea
(38mi)

Kamaka'eha Ave

Queen Ka'ahumanu Hwy

Luhia St

Eho St

Alapa St

Kaiwi St

Pawai Pl

North Kona
Shopping
Center

Kuakini Hwy

Kona Coast
Shopping
Centre

Mamalahoa Hwy (Hawai'i Belt Rd)

Crossroads
Shopping
Centre

Lanihau
Center

Palani Rd

Kopiko Rd

Captain
Cook
(12mi)

Henry St

Ala Ona Ona St

Kālani St

Kailua Park (0.2mi);
Old Kona Airport
State Recreation
Area (0.4mi)

Likana La

Kuakini Hwy

Ali'i Dr

Sarona Rd

Kalawa St

Alahou St

Holualoa
(6.5mi)

Hualalai Rd

Kona Inn
Shopping
Village

Hale
Halawai
Park

Oneo
Bay

Ali'i
Sunset
Plaza

Kailua Bay

Kanakai Rd

Ali'i Dr

Walua Rd

Hawaii Lifeguard Surf Instructors (0.2mi);
Magic Sands Beach (3mi)

Kailua-Kona

Kailua Pier   LANDMARK

Kailua Bay was once a major cattle-shipping area, where animals were stampeded into the water and forced to swim to steamers waiting to transport them to Honolulu slaughterhouses. Now locals come to swim at lunchtime and canoe clubs launch their vessels. The Hawaiian International Billfish Tournament (p92) kicks off here, continuing a sportfishing tradition begun in 1915, when the pier was built.

Beaches

Kailua-Kona might act like a beach town, but most of its in-town beaches don't rank among the Kona Coast's showstoppers.

★ **Magic Sands Beach**   BEACH

(La'aloa Beach Park; Ali'i Dr; ☉ sunrise-sunset; P ⊞) This small but gorgeous beach (also called White Sands and, officially, La'aloa Beach) has turquoise water, great sunsets, little shade and possibly the best bodysurf-

ing and bodyboarding on the Big Island. Waves are consistent and just powerful enough to shoot you across the water into a sandy bay (beware: the north side of the bay has more rocks). During high winter surf the beach can vanish literally overnight, earning the nickname 'Magic Sands.' The park is about 4 miles south of central Kailua-Kona.

When the rocks and coral located past the disappearing sands are exposed, the beach becomes too treacherous for most swimmers. Gradually the sand returns, transforming the shore back into its former beachy self. Facilities include restrooms, showers, picnic tables and a volleyball court; a lifeguard is on duty.

White Sands is almost always packed but there's little proprietary attitude from locals. Sunsets here will get you all the likes on social media.

Honl's Beach
BEACH

(Wai'aha Beach Park; Map p120; Ali'i Dr) If you're an avid bodyboarder, Honl's, also known as Wai'aha ('Gathering Water'), may feel like a historical pilgrimage. It was here, in 1971, that Tom Morey tested the Boogie Board (the brand-name version of the most popular type of bodyboard). The sandy beach here is small, and sharp rocks make the water unfriendly to casual swimmers, but as you may guess, the area is quite popular with local bodyboarders. Limited parallel parking available.

Kamakahonu Beach
BEACH

(King Kam Beach; ⊛) Kailua-Kona's only swimmable in-town beach is this teeny-tiny strand between Kailua Pier and Ahu'ena Heiau, where ocean waters are calm and usually safe for kids. Concession stands rent all kinds of beach gear. This is a pretty perfect spot for learning stand up paddle surfing, given the proximity of a) gear vendors and b) calm water. If you paddle (or swim) out past the heiau, waters get a little choppier. This is also a good spot to teach kids snorkeling basics.

🏃 Activities

Many activity outfitters and tour companies are based either here or in Keauhou, about 5 miles south of Kailua-Kona.

Paradise Sailing
BOATING

(Map p120; www.paradisesailinghawaii.com; Honokohau Marina; $94) The beauty of the Big Island can be hard to appreciate when you're screaming past it with an outboard motor ringing in your ears, and as such, Paradise Sailing offers a nice alternative: true wind-powered sailing aboard a 36ft catamaran, with a small number of passengers as your companions. Guests are given the chance to operate the boat themselves.

Kona Coast by Air
SCENIC FLIGHTS

(Map p120; ☑808-646-0231; http://konacoast byair.com; 73-200 Kupipi St, Airport; 45/75min flight $230/330; ⊙6:30am-11am & 5-6:30pm) You can see the Big Island while hiking, and you can see it underwater, but what about seeing it from the sky? That's the promise of Kona Coast by Air, which leads powered hang glider trips through the clouds. You get to operate the flying tri-cycle (yup, that's what you're piloting), which is pretty damn exhilarating.

Hawaii Beach Yoga
YOGA

(http://hawaiibeachyoga.webplus.net/) 🖋 FREE Nothing helps achieve inner yogic balance quite like engaging your pranas in the cool sea breeze. That's the promise at Hawaii Beach Yoga, which leads free yoga classes (no registration required) at various beach parks across the Big Island (when we were in town, most were conducted around Pahoehoe Beach Park). Check the website or Facebook page (www.facebook.com/HawaiiBeachYoga) for more details.

Ka Lima Hana Kukui
MASSAGE

(☑808-345-7542; www.lomilomihawaii.net; 75-5706 Kuakini Hwy, Suite 105; 1hr massage from $80; ⊙9am-5pm Tue-Sat) Friendly Teresa runs this massage therapy spa, where she offers traditional Hawaiian massage treatments (lomilomi), deep tissue, Swedish, prenatal, hot stones and other services that will loosen you up after a hard day's vacationing. Also conducts outcalls if you don't feel like trekking downtown – either way, call ahead to sort out your appointment.

UFO Parasailing
PARAGLIDING

(☑800-359-4836; www.ufoparasail.net; 75-5660 Palani Rd, Suite 111; from $76) Harness the wind and the water and parasail your way through paradise via trips with UFO, which operates out of the King Kamehameha hotel. You can opt for single or tandem 'flights.'

Kailua Park
PARK

(Map p120; Kuakini Hwy; ⊙6:30am-7:30pm Mon-Fri, 8:30am-5:30pm Sat & Sun; ⊛) Adjacent to the Old Kona Airport State Recreation Area, this county park contains extensive facilities aimed at the community, including a toddler playground, an attractive Olympic-size lap pool and kids' pool, soccer and softball fields, night-lit tennis courts and a gym. As you might expect, the area is very busy on weekends, plus during after school hours and early evening.

Lotus Center
SPA

(☑808-334-0445; www.konaspa.com; 75-5852 Ali'i Dr; 90min massage & 1hr facial from $255; ⊙8am-8pm) Located within the Royal Kona Resort, there's a long menu of spa services, including massage, acupuncture and chiropractic services. The facilities here are in need of an update, but the staff tends to be on point when it comes to providing some mind, body and soul relief.

Outrigger Canoeing & Kayaking

Kona Boys Beach Shack   KAYAKING
(☑ 808-329-2345; www.konaboys.com; Kamakahonu Beach; kayak tours $140-190, rentals per hr/day from $19/54; ☺ 8am-5pm) Experience what the original Polynesian settlers must have felt with the water rushing under their hull as they approached the volcanic shores of the Big Island. Paddle an outrigger canoe around Kamakahonu Bay or all the way from Keauhou to snorkel in Kealakekua Bay. Sea-kayaking tours often stop to snorkel too.

Kai 'Opua Canoe Club   CANOEING
(www.kaiopua.org; Kamakahonu Beach; ☺ Mon-Sat) 🏄 This local club is dedicated to traditional Hawaiian outrigger canoeing; visitors are welcome to join paddling excursions that leave every morning except Sunday, usually around 6am or 7am. There is no club office, so check its website or Facebook page for schedules. Trips launch next to Ahu'ena Heiau.

Fishing

Kailua-Kona is legendary for its big-game fishing, especially Pacific blue marlin (June to August are the best months), which can grow into one-ton 'granders.' It's also home to ahi (yellowfin tuna), aku (bonito or skipjack tuna), swordfish, spearfish and mahimahi (white-fleshed fish also called 'dolphin'). Most of the world records for catches of these fish belong to Kona fishers.

On average, charter boats run around $600/750/900 for a four/six/eight-hour excursion, not including tax (note that depending on the boat, these rates can increase substantially). That cost is for the whole boat and can be split among individuals. Ask whether the captain shares the catch.

Agencies book for so many boats that it's impossible to guarantee quality or consistency, but Charter Desk (p122) is reputable and can match you with 60 boats.

Top Shot Spearfishing   FISHING
(Map p120; ☑ 808-205-8585; http://topshotspearfishing.com; 75-6129 Ali'i Dr; from $189 per person) 🏄 If fishing turns you off because sitting on a boat feels too passive, why not get underwater and hunt down your dinner in the deep blue sea? That's the pitch at Top Shot, which offers tours around the island

KAILUA-KONA & THE KONA COAST KAILUA-KONA

WORTH A TRIP

THREE RING RANCH EXOTIC ANIMAL SANCTUARY

Dr Ann Goody is as close to a real-life Dr Dolittle as you'll ever be lucky to meet. She doesn't just talk to the animals, she also fixes their broken bones and psyches. When she can, she then sets them free, but if they can't cut it in the wild they become residents of the **Three Ring Ranch Exotic Animal Sanctuary** (☑ 808-331-8778; www.threeringranch.org; 75-809 Keaolani Sbd; minimum donation $50 per person; tours by reservation), located on five lovely acres in upland Kona.

Visiting the ranch is one of the most fascinating animal encounters you can experience...well, anywhere. It's hard to explain how *natural* Dr Goody is with her animals – we're not kidding, she seems to truly communicate with them in a way that is almost as eerie as it is enchanting. On the flip side of that equation, the animals seem as comfortable around her as they would in the wild, although Dr Goody might criticize us for making that observation. That's because she is both smart and unsentimental; honestly, a visit to the sanctuary can be quite challenging, even for those who consider themselves hardcore animal lovers. Dr Goody will quickly dismantle any romantic anthropomorphizing you may be projecting onto the animal world. With that in mind, children are welcome here, but they shouldn't consider this a visit to the zoo.

Licensed by the US Department of Agriculture and accredited by the American Association of Sanctuaries, Three Ring currently hosts zebras, South African crowned cranes, lesser flamingos, giant tortoises and much more, including native endangered species such as the Hawaiian owl.

Dr Goody – who, incredibly, has been struck by lightning, tossed by a shark and is a breast cancer survivor – is as good with people as she is with animals. This has led to enormously successful educational initiatives, including an after-school program, a resident-intern program and a residency placement program for pre-veterinarian students. Since the sanctuary's primary commitment is to the animals and their welfare, it leads two-hour tours by prior arrangement only; email to arrange a tour. See the website for details.

for newbies and experienced 'Spearos' alike. This company admirably targets invasive species, so you'll feel extra good about spearing that peacock grouper.

Captain Jeff's Charters FISHING

(☑ 808-895-1852; http://fishinkona.com) Long-time Captain Jeff is a straight shooter who offers tailored trips, insider advice and a share of the catch. Not for nothing, he has maintained a very high catch record for more than 15 years – the guy puts in an extra effort to net your fish. Rates vary; expect around $500 for a day trip, but contact the captain for a quote.

High Noon Sport Fishing Charters FISHING

(Map p120; ☑ 808-895-3868; http://fishingchart erskona.com/; Honokohau Harbor) Captain Dee takes guests – including plenty of repeat visitors – out on these well-regarded fishing charters, run out of Honokohau Harbor. Offers full-, three-quarter- and half-day expeditions; contact them for rates.

Diving

The Kona Coast is known for calm, clear waters, unique lava formations and coral reefs. Near shore, divers can see steep drop-offs with lava tubes, caves and diverse marine life. In deeper waters there are dozens of popular boat-dive areas, including an airplane wreck off Keahole Point.

Most dive boats launch from Honokohau Harbor but have bricks-and-mortar offices in Kailua-Kona. Including all gear, the cost of a standard two-tank morning dive or one-tank night dive to see manta rays ranges from $110 to $150. Multiday PADI Open Water certification programs cost around $500 or more.

Big Island Divers DIVING

(☑ 808-329-6068; www.bigislanddivers.com; 74-5467 Kaiwi St; manta dive/snorkel $150/105; ⊙ 8am-6pm) Personable staff, an expansive shop and boat dives that are open to snorkelers all score this spot big points. This outfit specializes in night and manta-ray dives. Black-water boat trips ($170, or $250 if you combine with a manta ray excursion) are for experienced divers only. It also offers advanced long-range dives ($209).

Sandwich Isle Divers DIVING

(☑ 808-329-9188; www.sandwichisledivers.com; dives with/without gear from $120/140; 🖪) 🖉 This small charter dive-boat outfit run by a husband-and-wife team organizes person-

alized trips (six-person maximum). These folks have decades of experience in Kona waters, Captain Steve has a marine-biology degree, and the pair are particularly wonderful with new divers. Contact them for boat and launch location. A great spot to get open-water certified ($550).

Jack's Diving Locker DIVING

(☑ 808-329-7585; www.jacksdivinglocker.com; 75-5813 Ali'i Dr, Coconut Grove Marketplace, Bldg H; manta snorkel/dive from $105/155; ⊙ 8am-8pm Mon-Sat, 8am-6pm Sun; 🖪) 🖉 With top-notch introductory dives and courses, plus extensive programs for kids, this eco-conscious dive outfitter has a 5000-sq-ft facility with a store, classrooms, tank room and Hawaii's only 12ft-deep indoor dive pool. Sign up for a boat or shore dive, as well as a night manta-ray dive. Snorkelers are welcome on many dive-boat trips.

Kona Honu Divers DIVING

(☑ 808-324-4668; www.konahonudivers.com; 74-5583 Luhia St; ⊙ 7:30am-5pm) Well-reviewed dive company that schedules diverse boat trips, including manta-ray night dives, black-water dives and Nitrox trips.

Bodyboarding, Surfing & SUP

Magic Sands Beach (p85) is a favorite spot for bodyboarding and bodysurfing. Local experts surf at Banyans, north of White Sands, and Pine Trees (p125), south of the airport near Wawaloli (OTEC) Beach. Newbies can surf at Lymans, south of Banyans.

It's hard to explain the appeal of stand up paddle surfing (SUP) to someone who's completely new to the concept. Initially the sport consisted of people standing balanced on surfboards, paddling them about. This might appear to make surfing slower and paddling more difficult but, in fact, it's a sweet blend of intense exercise, aquatic adventure and marine biology lesson. SUP delivers a core workout accompanied by dolphins, turtles, tropical fish and very meditative, Zen-like paddling techniques.

It's the perfect way to slow down and drink up the mana (spiritual essence) of the Big Island although, be warned, your first day on a board may be less about relaxing and more about tumbling into the drink. Give it a spin in Kailua Bay or Kahalu'u Bay.

HYPR Nalu Hawaii SURFING

(☑ 808-960-4667; www.hyprnalu.com; 75-5663A Palanai Rd; semi-private/private surfing lessons $120/175) While this is primarily a surf and

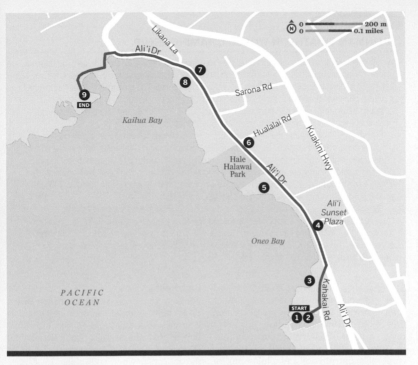

City Walk
Kailua Town Tour

START ROYAL KONA RESORT
END AHU'ENA HEIAU
LENGTH 1 MILE; TWO HOURS

On this tour, you'll get a taste of Ali'i Dr in all its waterfront, beachy and (let's be honest) commercialized glory. There are a bunch of good spots on this walk to stop and enjoy a meal, and indeed, we get this walking tour started the right way: with a drink.

We get rolling at the ❶**Royal Kona Resort**, home of ❷**Don's Mai Tai Bar** (p95), where bartenders do great justice to the genre of tropical drinks with fruit slices and little paper umbrellas. Thus fortified (or not), head north on Ali'i Dr. You'll pass ❸**Huggo's** (p95) on your left, and shortly after, on your right, Sunset Plaza. Taken together, these two spots are the major nexus of nightlife in Kailua-Kona.

Continue north and you'll swing by ❹**Island Lava Java** (p93) on your right. If it's breakfast time, or you just need some fuel to carry on after that pre-walk mai tai (we're not judging), pop in here for some

coffee, watch the waves crash on the sea wall across the street, and sigh, you lucky thing.

Further on, you'll pass on your left a large shopping center that houses ❺**Wyland Kona Oceanfront Gallery** (p96), home of many neon-chic marine-themed paintings. Just across the street, a little further north, the ❻**Kona Farmers Market** (p96) operates during the day from Wednesday to Sunday.

Keep walking for a half mile or so north and you'll pass by numerous shopping centers selling clothes, art and souvenirs on one side, and the blue ocean on the other. Eventually on your right you'll see the stone walls of the ❼**Moku'aikaua Church** (p82), and on the sea side, the wide lawn and airy windows of ❽**Hulihe'e Palace** (p83). Both locations speak deeply to the Big Island's history of Western colonization.

Finally, you'll reach ❾**Ahu'ena Heiau** (p83), once a seat of indigenous Hawaiian power. While the surrounding cove is full of tourists, the heiau itself remains apart from the activity on Ali'i, straddling the line between its protected cove and the deep ocean.

DON'T MISS

IRONMAN TRIATHLON WORLD CHAMPIONSHIP

When thousands of athletes and fans swoop into Kailua-Kona each October, locals gripe about traffic and crowds. But nobody can deny the thrilling spectacle of the **Ironman Triathlon World Championship** (www.ironman.com). The granddaddy of triathlons is a brutal combination of a 2.4-mile ocean swim, 112-mile bike race and 26.2-mile run. And it has to be done in under 17 hours. Australian Craig Alexander set the current course record at eight hours, three minutes and 56 seconds in 2011.

Harsh conditions make the event the ultimate endurance test. Heat bouncing off the lava commonly exceeds 100°F, making dehydration and heat exhaustion major challenges. Many contenders arrive on the island weeks before to acclimatize. On race day, the world's toughest athletes are pushed to the max – in the past, they've included a 75-year-old nun, an Iraq war veteran amputee, and father–son Team Hoyt, with Rick pushing son Dick in a wheelchair (they're six-time finishers).

Begun in 1978 by a US Navy man on a dare, the Ironman was labeled 'lunatic' by *Sports Illustrated*. Only 15 people competed the first year, and three didn't even cross the finish line. With that kind of crazy drama, the sports world was hooked. Today the event draws up to 2000 athletes from more than 50 countries, everyone seeking the rights to 'Brag for the rest of your life!'

SUP gear shop, the folks at HYPR Nalu also offer respectable surfing lessons. Rather than throwing you right onto the water, they're big on prior preparation: this outfit makes a point of observing your technique in store, all while giving feedback that incorporates the physics and philosophy of surfing.

SUP at Kona Boys Beach Shack SUP
(Kona Boys; ☑ 808-329-2345; www.konaboys.com; Kamakahonu Beach; surfboard/SUP rental from $29, SUP lesson & tours per person group/private $99/150; ⊙ 8am-5pm) The Kona Boys Beach Shack organizes SUP lessons as well as more ambitious coastal paddling tours, and rents SUP sets and surfboards right on Kamakahonu Beach – which, sheltered as it is, is perfect for learning SUP basics. Call in advance to arrange group or private surfing or SUP lessons. You can also book through the shop in Kealakekua (p108).

Hawaii Lifeguard
Surf Instructors SURFING
(HLSI; Map p120; ☑ 808-324-0442; www.surflessonshawaii.com; 75-5909 Ali'i Dr; group/private lessons from $75/110; ⊙ 8am-8pm) Skilled, professional HLSI instructors have a minimum of 15 years surfing experience and are all certified lifeguards. Join a group surfing or SUP lesson, or book a private one-on-one session (which is the only way that kids aged three to 10 years are taught at this school). Offers lessons in Japanese. Call in advance to book.

Snorkeling

For easy-access snorkeling, Kahalu'u Beach Park (p98), 5 miles south in Keauhou, is your closest and best option. To snorkel further afield, take a cruise from Honokohau Harbor or Keauhou Pier. Opt to depart in the morning, when conditions are calmer and clearer. Tour prices typically include snorkel gear, beverages and snacks; book ahead online for discounts.

Zodiac rafts are zippy and thrilling, capable of exploring sea caves, lava tubes and blowholes, but expect a bumpy ride and no shade or toilets. Catamarans are much larger, smoother and comfier but can't get as close into coves. Alternatively, many dive boats let snorkelers ride along at a cheaper rate.

Wild Hawaii Ocean Adventures SNORKELING
(WHOA.; Map p120; ☑ 808-854-4401; www.wildhawaii.com; Honokohau Marina; tours $100-160) We'd give this outfitter a thumbs up just for its Hawaii-appropriate acronym, but it's actually a great tour runner too. WHOA operates a US Navy Special forces assault boat, a maneuverable little number that the owners of this outfit aren't afraid to push to the limit. No participants under 4ft tall, and no pregnant passengers. Operates out of Honokohau Marina.

Snorkel Bob's SNORKELING
(☑ 808-329-0770; www.snorkelbob.com; 75-5831 Kahakai Rd; mask, fins, net bag & defogger from $9/week; ⊙ 8am-5pm; 🐾) Snorkeling is a great

way of getting underwater, but substandard gear will leave you with cloudy vision and a nose full of water. Enter Snorkel Bob's: enthusiastic, friendly staff, who rent snorkel masks (including corrective lenses for nearsighted folks), fins, reef walkers, wetsuits and flotation aids. They're pretty lenient about returning gear after hours, and prices are fantastic.

Swimming

With rocky shores and rough waters, Kailua-Kona isn't ideal for swimming – for that head to North Kona Coast beaches. Still, Kahalu'u Beach Park (p98), 5 miles south, is a good bet when conditions are calm, as are parts of the Old Kona Airport State Recreation Area (p82), especially with kids in tow. Another nearby spot that's good for families is Wawaloli (OTEC) Beach (p125).

☞ Tours

Kayak Fishing Hawai'i　　　　　FISHING
(☎808-936-4400; www.kayakfishinghawaii.com; guided tour $300) Ever read *The Old Man and the Sea?* How would you like to live out that tale...er, minus the really tragic Hemingway bits about life's inevitable defeats? Instead, imagine landing a 25lb ahi (yellowfin tuna) or *ono* (wahoo) fish from a kayak, fighting the fish basically on its own turf (or surf). Based at Kawaihae Harbor, but travels islandwide.

Kailua Bay Charter Company　　　CRUISE
(☎808-324-1749; www.konaglassbottomboat.com; Kailua-Kona Pier; 50min tour adult/child under 12yr $50/25; ⊙11am & 12:30pm; ⊕) Gain a new perspective on Kailua-Kona's coastline, its underwater reef and sea life from a 36ft glass-bottomed boat with a cheery crew and onboard naturalist. Easy boarding is available for passengers with mobility issues. Times vary; check the website or call ahead.

Hawaiian Walkways　　　　　WALKING
(☎808-322-2255; www.hawaiianwalkways.com; $120-190) Leads a number of walking tours, including trips to Volcano National Park (p244), the Pololu Valley (p156) and through the upland Kona Cloud Forest Sanctuary (p120). Guides are knowledgeable about botany and geology. All tours for children from seven to 11 years are $99. Wear sturdy shoes. They will pick you up from your hotel.

Aloha Ocean Adventures　　　BOATING
(www.alohaoceanexcursions.com; 74-380 Kealakehe Pkwy, Honokohau Marina; whale-watching/manta snorkel from $70/90) Captain Kris

Henry takes passengers out on his zodiac craft to engage in some of the most exciting aquatic adventures on the Big Island, including whale-watching trips, manta ray snorkeling expeditions and excursions out to Kealakekua Bay. Solid customer service and competitive pricing make this a standout tour operator.

Kona Brewing Company　　　　TOURS
(☎808-334-2739; http://konabrewingco.com; 74-5612 Pawai Pl; ⊙30min tours 10:30am & 3pm) ✔ FREE Since 1994, this eco-conscious company has anchored Hawai'i's microbrewery scene. The once-small, family-run operation is now one of the nation's fastest-growing microbreweries – from Maine to California, you can sip 'liquid aloha,' which circulates throughout 4000 kegs in Hawaii alone. Complimentary tours include tasting samples; note that kids under 15 are not allowed to tag along.

★☆ Festivals & Events

Kailua-Kona maintains a busy events calendar. Elements of these parties and festivals are aimed at visitors to the Big Island, but in the main these are community affairs that celebrate the greater Big Island *ohana* (family).

★Kokua Kailua　　　　　CULTURAL
(http://historickailuavillage.com/kokua-kailua; ⊙1-6pm 3rd Sun of month; ⊕) ✔ If you want to get a taste for the feisty civic spirit of Kailua-Kona, this is a can't miss. Local food vendors, artists and craftspeople set up booths along Ali'i Dr, which closes to vehicular traffic. Free Hawaiian music and hula dancing at Hulihe'e Palace start around 4pm, and despite official hours, festivities tend to last until the sunset.

★Kona Coffee Cultural Festival　　FOOD
(www.konacoffeefest.com; ⊙Nov; ⊕) For 10 days in early November during the harvest season, the community celebrates Kona coffee pioneers and their renowned beans. Dozens of events include a cupping competition, art shows, live music and hula performances, farm tours, coffee tastings, a recipe cook-off and a coffee cherry-picking contest. In many ways, this is a party that celebrates the entire Kona region.

Don's Mai Tai Festival　　　FOOD & DRINK
(☎800-222-5642; www.donsmaitaifest.com; ⊙Aug) The tropical drink with little umbrellas in is one of the great gifts the Hawaiian islands

have given the world, and this genre of libation is celebrated in all of its multicolored, high-proof glory at this festival, which goes off in August at the Royal Kona Resort.

Queen Lili'uokalani Canoe Race SPORTS
(www.kaiopua.org; ⊙ late Aug or early Sep) Over Labor Day weekend the world's largest long-distance outrigger canoe race paddles from Kailua Bay south to Honaunau. The event currently takes up a full Thursday to Monday long weekend, and includes many other smaller races.

Kona Brewers Festival BEER
(www.konabrewersfestival.com; $75; ⊙ Mar) On the second Saturday in March, Kona Brewing Company throws its annual beer bash, with proceeds benefiting local charities. Sample dozens of craft beers and island chefs' gourmet grinds. Buy tickets in advance online.

**Hawaiian International
Billfish Tournament** FISHING
(☑ 808-836-1723; www.hibtfishing.com; ⊙ late summer) Hawaii's most prestigious sportfishing contest encompasses five days of fishing followed by weigh-ins and festivities at Kailua Pier. Traditionally, the tournament has occurred in late summer; dates have ranged from late July to early September. Check the website for details.

✖ Eating

You don't have to spend a lot to eat *'ono kine grinds* (good food), but you'll usually have to venture further afield than Ali'i Dr, where many of the waterfront restaurants are disappointing and overpriced. On the flip side, there's a great concentration of good food in this relatively middle-sized town.

★**Umekes** HAWAII REGIONAL $
(☑ 808-329-3050; www.umekespoke808.com; 75-143 Hualalai Rd; mains $5-14; ⊙ 10am-7pm Mon-Sat; ☑ ⓦ) Umekes takes island-style food to the next level. Local ingredients such as ahi tuna, spicy crab salad and salted Waimea beef are served plate-lunch style with excellent, innovative sides such as seasoned seaweed and cucumber kim chi (along with heaping scoops of rice). It's some of the best-value grinds on the island. There's another location at 74-5563 Kaiwi St.

★**Da Poke Shack** SEAFOOD $
(☑ 808-329-7653; http://dapokeshack.com; 76-6246 Ali'i Dr, Castle Kona Bali Kai; mains & meals $5-12; ⊙ 10am-6pm; ⓦ) *Poke* is a local specialty that blends ceviche and sushi: raw, marinated cubes of fish mixed with soy sauce, sesame oil, chilies, seaweed and...well, really, the sky's the limit. The point is, *poke* is wonderful, and Da Poke Shack is the spot to get it. You'll be eating at a picnic table or, better, bring it to the beach.

**Fresh Off Da Boat
Polynesian Deli** POLYNESIAN $
(FOB's Polynesian Deli; ☑ 808-327-4444; 74-5543 Kaiwi St; mains $7-12; ⊙ 11am-7pm Tue-Fri, 10am-6pm Sat; ⓟ) This takeout joint, run by a husband-and-wife team, serves authentic Polynesian meals from across the Pacific, with a focus on Samoa and New Zealand. The menu varies – you may see oxtail soup, fresh octopus, taro or breadfruit cooked in coconut milk, or New Zealand lamb. It's all solid, filling and very affordable.

Ultimate Burger BURGERS $
(Map p120; www.ultimateburger.net; 74-5450 Makala Blvd; burger $6-15) ✗ Kailua-Kona is likely your introduction to the Big Island; with this in mind, let Ultimate Burger be your introduction to the wonderful world of Big Island beef. There's a big focus on organic ingredients and local sourcing, and we commend such efforts, but also: these burgers are *delicious*. Wash them down some homemade lemonade.

Ba-Le Kona VIETNAMESE $
(☑ 808-327-1212; 74-5588 Palani Rd, Kona Coast Shopping Center; mains $5-12; ⊙ 10am-9pm Mon-Sat, to 4pm Sun; ☑) Don't let the fluorescent-lit dining room and polystyrene plates fool you: Ba-Le serves the sort of Vietnamese that makes you want to pack it all up and move to Hanoi. Flavors are simple, refreshing and bright, from the green-papaya salad to traditional *pho* (noodle soup), and rice plates of spicy lemongrass chicken, tofu, beef or roast pork.

TJ'S BBQ By The Beach BARBECUE $
(Map p120; ☑ 425-308-1815; www.tjsbbqbythebeach.com; 75-6129 Ali'i Dr; mains $8-15; ⊙ 10:30am-5pm Tue-Sat) Located in Ali'i Gardens Marketplace, TJ's does enormous, tasty slabs of ribs and other meaty favorites, smoked and slathered in sauce (lots of sauce; if you're a dry barbecue fan, take note), and served plate-lunch style, with scoops of rice and mac salad. One full meal here and you may be good for food for the day.

Broke Da Mouth Grindz
HAWAIIAN $

(☑ 808-327-1113; www.brokedamouthgrindzkailua
kona.com; 74-5565 Luhia St; mains $6-13;
⊙ 6:30am-9:30pm Mon-Sat, 9am-5pm Sun) A favorite with the plate lunch crowd, Broke Da Mouth lives up to its name via heaping portions of sirloin, *lau lau* (taro-wrapped and steamed meat), teriyaki and Korean *kalbi*, presented with rice and love.

Evolution Bakery & Cafe
BAKERY $

(☑ 808-331-1122; www.evolutionbakerycafe.com;
75-5813 Ali'i Dr; mains $5-10; ⊙ 7-11:30am; 🛜🍴)
🚩 Kailua-Kona has always had room for a spot that's hip enough for a MacBook, and crunchy enough for dreadlocks. Enter Evolution. There's wi-fi, smoothies, vegan bagels, pancakes and sandwiches, Kona coffee and some seriously good mac nut (served to the Mac nuts, get it? Never mind) banana bread. Much of the menu is vegan friendly and gluten free.

KTA Super Store
SUPERMARKET $

(☑ 808-329-1677; www.ktasuperstores.com; 74-5594 Palani Rd, Kona Coast Shopping Center;
⊙ 5am-11pm; 🅿) The Big Island's best grocery chain, featuring many Hawaii-made products.

Scandinavian Shave Ice
DESSERTS $

(☑ 808-326-2522; www.scandinavianshaveice.com;
75-5699 Ali'i Dr; snacks & drinks $3-8; ⊙ 11am-9pm; 🍴) Shave ice is piled up here in huge, psychedelic-colored mounds that are as big as your head. Dither over a rainbow variety of flavored syrups, then borrow a board game to while away an hour.

Basik Acai
CAFE $

(www.basikacai.com; 75-5831 Kahakai Rd; snacks & drinks $6-13; ⊙ 8am-4pm; 🛜🍴) 🚩 Healthy, wholesome acai bowls bursting with tropical fruity goodness, granola, nuts, shredded coconut and even cacao nibs, along with fresh juice smoothies, are made to order at this tiny upstairs kitchen.

Island Naturals Market & Deli
SUPERMARKET $

(www.islandnaturals.com; 74-5487 Kaiwi St;
⊙ 7:30am-8pm Mon-Sat, 9am-7pm Sun; 🍴) 🚩
This health-conscious grocery store has a deli making sandwiches, wraps and salads to go, plus a hot-and-cold takeout bar.

Island Lava Java
CAFE $$

(☑ 808-327-2161; www.islandlavajava.com; 75-5799 Ali'i Dr, Ali'i Sunset Plaza; breakfast & lunch mains $11-30; ⊙ 6:30am-9pm; 🛜🍴🅿)
🚩 A convivial gathering spot for Sunday brunch or a sunny breakfast (served until 11:30am) with ocean-view dining on the sidewalk patio. This upscale diner is a little too fancy to be a greasy spoon; maybe it's a greasy complete cutlery set. Anyways, there are huge portions, Big Island–raised meats and fish, farm-fresh produce and 100% Kona coffee.

Foster's Kitchen
AMERICAN $$

(☑ 808-326-1600; 75-5805 Ali'i Dr; mains $14-32; ⊙ 11am-11pm; 🍴) 🚩 In the midst of the booziest, cheesiest stretch of Ali'i Dr, Foster's comes out with farm to table New American dishes – roast chicken, fresh salads, spring lamb etc – served alongside craft cocktails and a laid-back if semi-sophisticated vibe. It's a little incongruous, and a nice break from flash-fried pub grub.

Original Thai
THAI $$

(☑ 808-329-3459; 75-5629 Kuakini Hwy; mains $8-20; ⊙ 11am-3pm & 5-9pm) Run by a friendly Thai family, this place does a mean line of Thai classics (as the name implies), including the standard rainbow of curries. There's a particularly strong depth of dishes from the Isan region – the *larb* (a kind of spicy and savory salad) is quite excellent.

Kamana
INDIAN $$

(☑ 808-326-7888; http://kamanakitchen.com; 75-5776 Ali'i Dr; mains $13-22; ⊙ 11am-3pm & 5-9:30pm; 🍴) Kamana is about your only option if you're craving Indian food in Kailua-Kona. Fortunately it's a fine restaurant, with a deep menu that caters to carnivores (chicken vindaloo) and vegetarians (mushroom pakoras) in equal measure.

Lemongrass Bistro
ASIAN $$

(☑ 808-331-2708; www.lemongrassbistrokona.com;
75-5742 Kuakini Hwy; mains $13-25; ⊙ 11am-3pm & 5-9pm Mon-Fri, from noon Sat & Sun; 🍴) The food at Lemongrass is clean and elegant but also hearty enough to stick to your ribs, just like the best comfort food. Try the meaty oxtail or crispy duck shellacked in a garlic soy glaze.

Big Island Grill
HAWAIIAN $$

(☑ 808-326-1153; 75-5702 Kuakini Hwy; mains $10-20; ⊙ 7am-9pm Mon-Sat, 7am-noon Sun;
🅿🍴) The grill serves fresh and flavorful Hawaiian soul food such as plate lunches and *loco moco* (rice, fried egg and hamburger patty topped with thick gravy). Choose from fried chicken katsu (deep-fried fillets), fried mahimahi, shrimp tempura and more.

All meals come with two scoops of rice, potato-mac salad and rich gravy.

Kona Brewing Company AMERICAN $$

(☑ 808-334-2739; http://konabrewingco.com; 75-5629 Kuakini Hwy; mains $13-25; ⊙ 11am-10pm; ◀) 🥢 Expect a madhouse crowd at this sprawling, eco-sustainable brewpub, with tiki torch-lit outdoor seating and laid-back waitstaff. Pizza toppings verge on gourmet, but crusts can be soggy; BBQ sandwiches and fish tacos are better bets. Enter the parking lot off Kaiwi St.

★ Sushi Shiono JAPANESE $$$

(☑ 808-326-1696; www.sushishiono.com; 75-5799 Ali'i Dr, Ali'i Sunset Plaza; à la carte dishes $4-18, lunch plates $10-19, dinner mains $20-40; ⊙ 11:30am-2pm Mon-Sat, 5:30-9pm Mon-Sat, 5-9pm Sun) Inside a mini mall, wickedly fresh sushi and sashimi are complemented by a sake list that's as long as Honshu. The joint is owned by a Japanese expat, who employs an all-star, all-Japanese cast of sushi chefs behind the bar. Dinner reservations recommended.

Daylight Mind FUSION $$$

(☑ 808-339-7824; http://daylightmind.com; 75-5770 Ali'i Dr; brunch $10-18, dinner $15-38; ⊙ 8am-9pm) A pretty perch over the water and an airy dining space is complemented by fare that runs the gamut from Hawaii Regional (short ribs braised in local coffee) to Pacific fusion (Hamakua mushroom polenta). It's all delicious, but the morning brunch stands out as a particularly excellent start to a Kona day.

Hayama JAPANESE $$$

(☑ 808-331-8888; 75-5660 Kopiko St; mains $14-35; ⊙ 11am-2pm & 5-9pm Tue-Sat) Hayama imparts that feeling of authenticity you get when the kitchen and service staff don't speak much English, and most of the clientele speaks fluent Japanese. This *izakaya* (Japanese pub serving tapas-style food), tucked into a nondescript strip mall, serves heaping platters of mouthwatering sushi, strong *sake* and delicious *tempura*.

🍷 Drinking & Nightlife

Kailua-Kona's bar scene is pretty touristy, but there are a handful of places for a cocktail or a beer. Always a good fallback, Kona Brewing Company usually has live Hawaiian music from 5pm to 8pm on Sundays.

Sam's Hideaway BAR

(☑ 808-326-7267; 75-5725 Ali'i Dr; ⊙ 9am-2am) Sam's is a dark, cozy (OK, maybe 'dank') little nook of a bar. You'll rarely find tourists but there are always locals, especially on karaoke nights. Trust us: you haven't done Kailua-Kona until you've seen a 7ft Samoan guy tear up as he belts out 'The Snows of Mauna Kea.'

My Bar LGBT

(☑ 808-331-8789; www.mybarkona.com; 74-5606 Luhia St) While My Bar is one of the few dedicated gay bars on the island, it's also just a fun bar – it's neither locals' dive or a crazy club, but occupies a sweet spot between those two extremes. Expect casual vibes during the week, and wilder DJ and themed nights on weekends.

Mask-Querade Bar LGBT

(Mask Bar; ☑ 808-329-8558; 75-5660 Kopiko St; ⊙ 10am-2am) Hidden away in a strip mall is 'the Mask,' one of Kailua-Kona's dedicated gay bars. In a town where drinking options run from tourist traps to sports bars, it's nice to find a place that feels a little playfully kitschy. On some nights it can get pretty sexy; on others it's a cozy neighborhood joint.

Dolphin Spit Saloon BAR

(☑ 808-326-7748; 75-5626 Kuakini Hwy, Unit F; ⊙ 10:30am-2am) In a city full of transplants and tourists, the Dolphin Spit (yum!) is where the locals are: drinking 'til they're merry, rubbing elbows, giving each other crap, watching sports and generally pickling themselves in the Pacific sun.

Kona Coffee & Tea Company CAFE

(☑ 808-365-5340; www.konacoffeeandtea.com; 74-5588 Palani Rd; ⊙ 6am-6pm; 🛜🐕) 🥢 Life is too short for bad coffee: head here for award-winning 100% Kona coffee grown on sustainable farms. Freshly roasted beans and toothsome macnut pies are a match made in heaven and this place makes a point of being dog friendly – woofing and wi-fi, together at last.

Humpy's Big Island Alehouse BAR

(☑ 808-324-2337; http://humpys.com/kona; 75-5815 Ali'i Dr, Coconut Grove Marketplace; ⊙ 8am-2am) With its enviable location on the strip overlooking Kailua Bay, Alaskan Humpy's would probably survive in touristy Kailua-Kona even without having dozens of craft beers on tap. Perch on the upstairs balcony, with its sea breezes and views, while live bands rock out. Regular happy hours, pub quizzes, open mics and an eclectic musical line-up rounds out the Humpy's experience.

Humpy's opens at 7am on Sundays if an NFL game is going and has multiple screens, so you can catch most games.

Don's Mai Tai Bar   BAR

(☑ 808-930-3286; www.royalkona.com; 75-5852 Ali'i Dr, Royal Kona Resort; ⊙10am-10pm) For pure kitsch, nothing beats the lounge-lizard fantasy of Don's, located inside the Royal Kona Resort. Soak up the killer ocean views of the crashing surf, then get sauced on one of several varieties of tropical drinks with plastic accoutrements. Real tiki fans roll in for Don's Mai Tai Festival (p91) in mid-August.

Huggo's on the Rocks   BAR

(☑ 808-329-1493; http://huggosontherocks.com; 75-5828 Kahakai Rd; ⊙11am-10pm Sun-Thu, to 11pm Fri & Sat) Huggo's is as adjacent to the water as you can get in Kailua-Kona (ordinances now prevent other bars from getting this close to the waves). You'll be drinking under thatch with live music, sunsets and occasionally a spray of surf dusting your hair. In the mornings this place reverts to **Java on the Rock** (☑ 808-324-2411; www.javaontherock.com; ⊙6-11am; 🔊), serving coffee and espresso.

Kanaka Kava   CAFE

(https://kanakakava.com; 75-5803 Ali'i Dr, Coconut Grove Marketplace; ⊙10am-11pm) 🍃 This tiny, locals' grass-shack hangout is the place to try Hawaiian-style kava (the mildly sedative juice of the *'awa* plant) or organic *noni* (Indian mulberry) juice, another herbal elixir.

☆ Entertainment

Kailua-Kona's hokey, cruise ship–friendly luau include a ceremony, a buffet dinner with Hawaiian specialties, an open bar and a Polynesian dinner show featuring a cast of flamboyant dancers and fire twirlers. Forego if any rain is forecast – an indoor luau ain't worth it. There's also a little live music going down on the weekends at area bars.

Island Breeze Lu'au   LUAU

(☑ 866-482-9775; www.islandbreezeluau.com; 75-5660 Palani Rd, Courtyard Marriott King Kamehameha's Kona Beach Hotel; adult/child 5-12yr $97/50; ⊙5pm Tue, Thu & Sun; 🐾) Family-friendly luau benefiting from a scenic oceanfront setting.

> **ⓘ PARKING LOT PROBLEMS**
>
> The parking lot behind Sunset Plaza (where Oceans is located) is convenient if you've got a designated driver and want to park near Ali'i Dr's most popular boozing strip. Be careful walking back to your car later in the evening. There's usually a high level of alcohol/testosterone around and fights aren't uncommon. If you're in a group you should be fine; just keep your wits about you.

Voyagers of the Pacific   LUAU

(☑ 808-329-3111, 888-359-7674; www.konaluau.com; 75-5852 Ali'i Dr, Royal Kona Resort; adult/child 6-11yr $91/45; ⊙6pm Mon, Tue, Wed & Fri; 🐾) Hula lessons, complimentary mai tais, roast pig, waterfront views and graceful dancers are all on the menu.

Gertrude's Jazz Bar   LIVE MUSIC

(☑ 808-327-5299; www.gertrudesjazzbar.com; 75-5699 Ali'i Dr; ⊙5-10:30pm Mon-Sat, 2-10:30pm Sun) There are a lot of cheesy bars on Ali'i, but Gertrude's classes the joint up a little with live music (usually from around 6pm to 9pm), cocktails and frequent dance nights.

Regal Makalapua Stadium 10   CINEMA

(☑ 844-462-7342; Makalapua Shopping Center, 74-5469 Kamaka'eha Ave; adult/child $12/8) Catch first-run Hollywood movies on 10 screens.

🛍 Shopping

Although the situation is improving, and local goods are becoming more commonplace, Ali'i Dr is also swamped with run-of-the-mill, dubious-quality Hawaiiana and souvenir shops. Beware of 'Made in China' fakes.

★ Kona Bay Books   BOOKS

(☑ 808-326-7790; http://konabaybooks.com; 74-5487 Kaiwi St; ⊙10am-6pm) The Big Island's largest selection of used books, CDs and DVDs, including Hawaiiana titles, is piled floor to ceiling in this warehouse-sized bookstore.

Ali'i Gardens Marketplace   SHOPPING CENTER

(Map p120; ☑ 808-937-8844; 75-6129 Ali'i Dr; ⊙10am-5pm; 🐾) This open-air shopping center is an exceedingly pleasant spot to while away an hour or so while perusing arts, crafts and produce. There are plenty of stalls and kiosks to get lost among, and kids can run around. Note that the above hours

TRAVEL WITH CHILDREN

The following spots are all great for kids in Kailua-Kona:

Kahalu'u Beach Park (p98)

Ocean Rider Seahorse Farm (p125)

Scandinavian Shave Ice (p93)

Fair Wind (p100) snorkel cruise to Kealakekua Bay

Hawaii Lifeguard Surf Instructors (p90)

Three Ring Ranch Exotic Animal Sanctuary (p87)

are for the marketplace as a whole; different shops within the space maintain their own hours.

Big Island Jewelers JEWELRY
(☎888-477-8571, 808-329-8571; http://bigisland jewelers.com; 75-5695A Ali'i Dr; ⊙9am-5:30pm Mon-Sat) Family owned for nearly four decades, with master jeweler Flint Carpenter at the helm, this storefront sells high-quality Hawaiiana bracelets, pendants, earrings and rings, including pieces made with Tahitian pearls. Custom orders welcome.

Conscious Riddims Records MUSIC
(☎808-322-2628; 75-5719 Ali'i Dr, Kona Marketplace; ⊙10am-7pm Mon-Fri, 10am-5pm Sun) Drop by for reggae and Jawaiian (Hawaii-style reggae) music and dope clothing.

Wyland Kona Oceanfront Gallery ART
(☎808-334-0037; http://wylandbigisland.com; 75-5770 Ali'i Dr; ⊙9:30am-9pm) Robert Wyland is known for his maritime-themed, neon-palette artwork – the pride of many a waterfront hotel or condo. His originals, and the works of many Big Island locals, are for sale in this huge space, which regularly hosts art events and special gallery nights.

Honolua Surf Co CLOTHING
(☎808-329-1001; www.honoluasurf.com; 75-5744 Ali'i Dr, Kona Inn Shopping Village; ⊙9am-9pm) This island-grown surfwear shop is split right down the middle between styles for *kane* (men) and *wahine* (women). Board shorts, bikinis, hoodies, T-shirts and beach cover-ups will last you as long as an endless summer.

Kona Farmers Market GIFTS & SOUVENIRS
(☎808-961-5818; www.konafarmersmarket.com; Hualalai Rd, cnr Ali'i Dr; ⊙7am-4pm Wed-Sun; 🖐) Like Kailua-Kona itself, this busy little market hovers between catering to tourists and locals, and in the process, veers between tacky and touching. Sure, there's a lot of phony shell jewelry and pseudo-Hawaiian knickknacks, but you can also find fresh produce, flower leis, and a high level of enjoyable market chatter and gossip.

ℹ Information

MEDIA

Popular radio stations:

KAGB 99.1 FM (www.kaparadio.com) West Hawai'i home of Hawaiian and island music.

KKUA 90.7 FM (www.hawaiipublicradio.org) Hawaii Public Radio; classical music, talk and news.

KLUA 93.9 FM Native FM plays island tunes and reggae beats.

Newspapers:

Hawaii Tribune-Herald (www.hawaiitribune-herald.com) The Big Island's main daily newspaper.

West Hawaii Today (www.westhawaiitoday.com) Kona Coast's daily newspaper covers Kohala to Ka'u.

MONEY

The Bank of Hawaii and First Hawaiian Bank have 24-hour ATMs and island-wide branches.

Bank of Hawaii (☎808-326-3900; www.boh.com; 74-5457 Makala Blvd; ⊙8:30am-4pm Mon-Thu, 8:30am-6pm Fri, 9am-1pm Sat) Local branch office for Bank of Hawaii.

First Hawaiian Bank (☎808-329-2461; www.fhb.com; Lanihau Center, 74-5593 Palani Rd; ⊙8:30am-4pm Mon-Thu, 8:30am-6pm Fri, 9am-1pm Sat) Local branch of Bank of Hawaii.

RESOURCES

Big Island Visitors Bureau (www.gohawaii.com/big-island) Travel planning info and comprehensive listings for festivals and special events.

CVS (☎808-329-1632; www.cvs.com; 75-5595 Palani Rd; ⊙store 7am-10pm daily, pharmacy 7am-8pm Mon-Fri, 8am-7pm Sat, 8am-6pm Sun) Centrally located drugstore and pharmacy.

Kona Hawaii Fishing Report (http://aloha-kona.com) Info on fishing charters in the area.

KonaWeb (www.konaweb.com) Homegrown website for locals and visitors, with an island-wide calendar of events.

Manta Pacific Research Foundation (www.mantapacific.org) Information on the area's cycling trails.

ⓘ Getting There & Away

AIR

Kona International Airport (KOA; Map p120; ☑ 808-327-9520; http://hawaii.gov/koa; 73-200 Kupipi St) Mostly interisland and some US mainland and Canada flights arrive at Hawai'i's main airport, 7 miles northwest of Kailua-Kona.

BUS

Hele-On (www.heleonbus.or) public buses run between Kailua-Kona and Captain Cook in South Kona (one to 1¾ hours) up to 10 times daily except Sunday (when service goes down to one north and southbound bus per day); one or two also stop at the airport. Buses connect Kailua-Kona with Hilo (three hours) via Waimea (1¼ to 1¾ hours) three times daily except Sunday; two go via South Kohala's resorts.

Buses on the Pahala–South Kohala route (four hours) make stops in Kailua-Kona, South Kona, Ka'u and sometimes at Kona's airport and in Keauhou.

All schedules and fares are subject to change; check the website. A $1 surcharge applies for luggage, backpacks or bicycles; no surfboards or boogie boards allowed on board. Children under six years old ride free.

Keauhou Trolley (www.sheratonkona.com; one-way $2; ⊘ 9am-9:15pm), also called the 'Honu Express,' is a tourist trolley that makes six daily round-trips between Keauhou and Kailua-Kona. Stops include White (Magic) Sands Beach, Kona Brewing Company, Kailua Pier and various shopping centers and resort hotels. Check schedules and fares online.

The breezy **Kona Trolley** (www.konaweb.com/forums/shuttle.shtml; ⊘ 9am-9:15pm) service makes six trips a day with stops running from central Kailua-Kona to the Keauhou resort area.

CAR

The drive from Kailua-Kona to Hilo is 75 miles and takes at least 1¾ hours via Saddle Rd, 95 miles (two hours) via Waimea and 125 miles (three hours) via Ka'u and Volcano.

To avoid snarly commuter traffic on Hwy 11 leading into and away from Kailua-Kona, try the Mamalahoa Hwy Bypass Rd. It connects Ali'i Dr in Keauhou with Haleki'i St in Kealakekua, between Miles 111 and 112 on Hwy 11.

ⓘ Getting Around

BICYCLE

Home of the Ironman Triathlon World Championship, Kailua-Kona is a bike-friendly town. At the time of research, a **bike share** ($3.50 per half

hour) program was just getting off the ground. Kiosks are located at Hale Halawai Park, Huggo's On the Rock's and Courtyard King Kamehameha's Kona Beach Hotel. The kiosks accept credit cards.

Bike Works (☑ 808-326-2453; www.bikeworkskona.com; 74-5583 Luhia St, Hale Hana Center; bicycle rental per day $40-60; ⊘ 9am-6pm Mon-Sat, 10am-4pm Sun) is a full-service bike shop renting high-quality mountain and road-touring bikes; rates include helmet, lock, pump and patch kit. Multiday and weekly discounts available. Second location in Waikoloa. You can also try **Kona Beach and Sports** (☑ 808-329-2294; www.konabeachandsports.com; 75-5744 Ali'i Dr, Kona Inn Shopping Village; bicycle rental per day $25-30; ⊘ 9:30am-8pm).

Consider checking out the website for **Peoples Advocacy for Trails Hawaii** (☑ 808-326-7284; https://pathhawaii.org), which has an excellent database of local cycling routes (they're also one of the main backers for the bike share program).

BUS

Both the public Hele-On Bus and privately operated Keauhou and Kona Trolley make stops within Kailua-Kona.

CAR

Ali'i Dr in downtown Kailua-Kona is almost always congested. Free public parking is available in a lot between Likana Lane and Kuakini Hwy. Many shopping centers along Ali'i Dr have free parking lots for customers.

MOPED & MOTORCYCLE

Doesn't it look fun zipping down Ali'i Dr on a moped? And what a breeze to park!

Scooter Brothers (☑ 808-327-1080; www.scooterbrothers.com; 75-5829 Kahakai Rd; per 8/24/48hr from $40/50/90; ⊘ 9am-5pm) Get around town like a local, on a moped or electric scooter. The official riding area is from Hapuna Beach up north to Honaunau down south.

TAXI

A car is almost a necessity on Hawai'i, but for those who are not renting one upon arrival at the airport, taxis are available curbside (book late-night pickups in advance). Taxi fares average $25 to Kailua-Kona or $35 to Keauhou, plus tip.

Speedi Shuttle (p305) is economical if you're in a group. Book in advance, and beware, they've been known to run on island time.

Call ahead for pickups from local taxi companies:

Aloha Taxi (☑ 808-329-7779; www.alohataxihi.com)

Dakine Taxi (☑ 808-329-4446; www.dakinetaxi.com)

Laura's Taxi (☑ 808-326-5466; www.laurastaxi.com)

AROUND KAILUA-KONA

Keauhou Resort Area

With its wide streets and manicured landscaping, Keauhou feels like a US mainland suburb: easy, pleasant and bland. Like most suburbs, there's no town center (unless you count the shopping mall that is Keauhou Shopping Center). Rather, it's a collection of destinations: Keauhou Harbor for boat trips, beaches for snorkeling and surfing, condos and resort hotels for sleeping, and farmers markets for local flavor.

◉ Sights

End of the World   NATURAL FEATURE
(Kuamo'o Bay; Map p106; Ali'i Dr) Rarely do geographic titles so convincingly live up to their names, but then comes Keauhou's End of the World. A Mordor-esque lava plain of jagged *'a'a* rock crinkles to the deep blue coast, and then drops steeply into the ocean. To get here, drive all the way to the end of Ali'i Dr and look for a trailhead to the water. It's a short, rocky hike to the cliffs. *Do not attempt to swim here* – serious injuries are commonplace.

Sometimes waves crash like thunderheads on the rocks, sometimes the ocean is calm as a pond and, often, local teenagers jump off the cliffs into the water; we'll give them a pass because locals know the tides here (although even they get hurt at this spot).

The End of the World marked the end of an era. When Kamehameha the Great's son Liholiho (Kamehameha II) was crowned king, the new monarch took major steps to abolish the rigid *kapu,* the taboo system that regulated daily life. So Liholiho took the then-drastic step of eating at a table with women. His cousin Chief Kekauokalani was incensed (or perhaps he coveted the crown, or maybe a bit of both) and challenged Liholiho to battle at the End of the World. In the resulting Battle of Kuamo'o some 300 were killed, including Kekauokalani and his wife. The dead were interned in cairns on the lava field, Liholiho's rule was firmly established, and the *kapu* system was broken.

Kahalu'u Beach Park   BEACH
(78-6710 Ali'i Dr; 🚻) Whether young or old, triathlete or couch potato, everyone appreciates the island's most easy-to-access (and admittedly busy) snorkeling spot. Protected by an ancient breakwater (which, according

to legend, was built by the *menehune,* or 'little people'), the bay is pleasantly calm and shallow. You'll spot tropical fish and *honu* (green sea turtles) without even trying. The lifeguard-staffed park has outdoor showers, restrooms, drinking water, snorkel and locker rentals and picnic tables. Water can sometimes get cloudy later in the day.

Kahalu'u can be too popular for its own good, with snorkelers literally bumping into one another. The salt-and-pepper beach (made of lava and coral sand) is often a mass of humanity, which you may find sociable or nauseating, depending. Come early; the parking lot often fills by 10am. Treading lightly is also important: follow coral-reef etiquette. By law you must stay at least 50yd from all sea turtles in the water (20ft on land).

When the surf's up (and it can rage here), expert surfers challenge the offshore waves and avoid strong rip currents on the bay's north side near the church. When conditions are mellow, beginners can learn to surf or stand up paddle surf.

Kahalu'u Bay
Education Center   NATURE CENTER
(KBEC; ☎808-887-6411; http://kohalacenter.org/kbec; 78-6710 Ali'i Dr; ⊙9:30am-4pm; 🅿🚻) 🎫 **FREE** Located by Kahalu'u Bay beach, Kahalu'u Bay Education Center (KBEC) is a family-friendly educational center that provides teaching and instruction on both snorkeling and 'reef etiquette' – the proper way to interact with the ocean. Also rents out snorkeling gear (a full set of fiks, snorkel and mask will run you $13.50); all proceeds go to educational programs.

Original Hawaiian Chocolate Factory   FARM
(Map p106; ☎888-447-2626, 808-322-2626; www.ohcf.us; 78-6772 Makenawai St; tour adult/child under 12yr $15/free; ⊙9am Wed, 9am & 11am Fri, by reservation; 🚻) A must for chocolate fans, these one-hour farm tours detail how the *only* Hawaiian chocolate is grown, harvested, processed and packaged, followed by chocolate sampling and sales. Hours vary; book tours by phone or email at least a week ahead. The factory is inland from Hwy 11 and King Kamehameha III Rd.

Keauhou Kahalu'u Heritage Center   GALLERY
(www.keauhouresort.com; 78-6831 Ali'i Dr, Keauhou Shopping Center; ⊙10am-5pm; 🅿) 🎫 **FREE** To learn more about the restoration of Keauhou's heiau, visit this unstaffed cultural center, where small exhibits and videos also describe *holua,* the ancient Hawaiian sport

of lava-rock sledding, at nearby He'eia Bay. The center is on the KTA Super Store side of the mall, hidden behind the post office near the public restrooms.

St Peter by the Sea CHURCH
(📞 808-326-7771; http://catholichawaii.org; 78-6684 Ali'i Dr) Ever popular for weddings, the much-photographed 'Little Blue Church' practically sits in Kahulu'u Bay. Made of clapboard and a corrugated-tin roof in the 1880s, the church was moved here from White (Magic) Sands Beach in 1912. The church is on the *makai* (seaward) side of Ali'i Dr, north of Mile 5.

Incidentally, an ancient Hawaiian temple, Ku'emanu Heiau, once stood here. Hawaiian *ali'i* surfed at the northern end of Kahalu'u Bay, praying at the temple before hitting the waves.

There are no set hours to get inside of the church, but most people visit to take a photo from the outside in any case.

Keauhou Bay HARBOR
(Kaleiopapa St) Many tour cruises launch from the small pier at this protected bay. While not worth going out of your way for, the small beach, picnic tables and sand volleyball courts bring out locals. Facilities include restrooms and outdoor showers.

Against the hillside, a plaque marks the site where Kamehameha III was born in 1814. The prince is said to have been stillborn and brought back to life by a visiting

Keauhou

kahuna (priest, healer) who dunked him in a healing freshwater spring here.

To get here, turn *makai* off Ali'i Dr onto Kaleiopapa St.

🏃 Activities

Many tours that explore the west side of the island are operated out of Keauhou.

Ocean Safaris   KAYAKING
(☎ 808-326-4699; www.oceansafariskayaks.com; 78-7128 Kaleiopapa Rd; tours per person $79) This outfit conducts kayak tours of local sea caves and lava tubes where you'll search for dolphins, sea turtles and manta rays; a bit of (safe) cliff jumping is an option at the end.

🧭 Tours

Sea Quest   CRUISE
(☎ 808-329-7238; www.seaquesthawaii.com; 78-7106 Kamehameha III Rd; 2-snorkel cruise adult/child $112/92; ⊗ 7am-9pm; 🚗) Well run Sea Quest has rigid-hull inflatable rafts that take passengers (only a total of 14 per trip) on two- and three-stop snorkel adventures that cover much of the South Kona Coast. This popular outfitter is known for hosting repeat guests to the Big Island. Japanese language tours are also available.

Fair Wind   SNORKELING
(☎ 800-677-9461, 808-322-2788; www.fair-wind.com; 78-7130 Kaleiopapa St; snorkel cruise adult/child 4-12yr from $79/49; 🚗) 🐚 The *Fair Wind II*, a two-story catamaran with two 15ft-long waterslides, sails to Kealakekua Bay every morning. Daytime cruises on the luxury catamaran *Hula Kai* explore less-trafficked waters ($149), while nighttime manta-ray snorkel cruises are hugely popular ($119; minimum seven years old), so book ahead.

Sea Paradise   CRUISE
(☎ 808-322-2500; www.seaparadise.com; 78-6831 Ali'i Dr; snorkel cruise adult/child 5-12yr from $77/47, manta rays adult/child from $112/100) Highly recommended outfitter offering morning snorkel cruises to Kealakekua Bay and excellent nighttime manta-ray trips (free rebooking if you don't spot any the first time out) on a smaller 46ft-long catamaran with a friendly, professional crew.

🍃 Courses

Kona Surf Adventures   SURFING
(Map p120; ☎ 808-334-0033; www.konasurf adventures.com; 75-5995 Kuakini Hwy, Ali'i Gardens Marketplace; surfing lesson $99-150) This surf school is run by California-born 'Kona Mike,' who comes with endorsements from novice students and veteran wave riders alike.

🍴 Eating

Don't be put off by the strip mall setting – there's some great eating here. Drop by Keauhou's **farmers market** (8am to noon Saturdays) for tasty, cheap grinds.

Peaberry & Galette   CAFE $
(☎ 808-322-6020; www.peaberryandgalette.com; 78-6831 Ali'i Dr, Keauhou Shopping Center; mains $7-14; ⊗ 7am-5pm Mon-Sat, 8am-5pm Sun; 🅿) Brewing 100% Kona estate-grown coffee and Illy espresso, this cafe with Euro-bistro style also dishes up sweet and savory French crepes, plus satisfying salads, sandwiches, quiches and *liliko'i* (passion fruit)-lemon bars for dessert.

KTA Super Store   SUPERMARKET $
(www.ktasuperstores.com; 78-6831 Ali'i Dr, Keauhou Shopping Center; ⊗ 6am-10pm; 🅿❄) Locally owned supermarket chain stocking groceries, beach snacks and drinks, with a full-service deli and bakery.

Bianelli's   ITALIAN $$
(☎ 808-322-0377; http://bianellis.com; 78-6831 Ali'i Dr, Keauhou Shopping Center; pizza $14-25; ⊗ 4:30-9pm Mon-Sat; 🍴🚗) There's not a ton of pizza places in Keauhou, which is a shame, as it's been scientifically proven that pizza is the most important food group in the universe (not really, but still). And, honestly, Bianelli's is quite good; the Bufala, layered with garlic sauce and white mozzarella, is pretty perfect after a day of snorkeling.

Kenichi Pacific   JAPANESE $$$
(☎ 808-322-6400; www.kenichihawaii.com; 78-6831 Ali'i Dr, Keauhou Shopping Center; dishes $4-18, mains $25-42; ⊗ 4:30-9:30pm; 🅿) Ignore the mall setting. Just savor the beautifully presented Pacific Rim fusion cuisine including tender miso black cod, Hawaiian *ono* topped with a cloud of *ponzu* (Japanese citrus sauce) and macadamia-nut-encrusted lamb. Sushi and sashimi cuts are fresh and generous. Happy hour (4:30pm to 6:30pm daily) brings half-price sushi rolls and drinks (hello, sake!) to the bar.

Sam Choy's Kai Lanai   HAWAII REGIONAL $$$
(☎ 808-333-3434; www.samchoyskailanai.com; 78-6831 Ali'i Dr, Keauhou Shopping Center; mains lunch $10-15, dinner $21-39; ⊗ 10am-9pm Mon-Thu, from 8am Sat & Sun; 🅿🍴🚗) Sam Choy is one of

the pioneers of Hawaii Regional Cuisine, an island-grown version of Pacific Rim fusion. At this casual eatery with dynamite sunset panoramas, the dinner menu is stuffed with fusion gastronomy such as lamb chops broiled with soy, ginger and local bird-peppers, although execution falls short of the chef's sterling reputation.

🍷 Drinking & Nightlife

There are a few sports bar–type spots within the main shopping center.

Tropics Tap House   SPORTS BAR
(📞808-498-4507; www.tropicstaphousekona.com; 78-6831 Ali'i Dr; ⊙11am-midnight) This is a pretty basic sports bar, an extension of a Honolulu-based franchise. It hits all the usual targets of the genre: there's a good beer line-up, passable pub grub and games playing on the TV watched by mainlanders looking for a brew and a taste of home.

☆ Entertainment

Keauhou Shopping Center   DANCE
(📞808-322-3000; www.keauhouvillageshops.com; 78-6831 Ali'i Dr; ♿) This shopping mall has hula shows from 6pm to 7pm most Friday nights. It also usually runs free Hawaiian craft workshops from 10am to noon every Thursday. Check the website for more cultural activities and special events.

Haleo Luau   LUAU
(📞866-482-9775; www.haleoluau.com; 78-128 Ehukai St, Sheraton Keauhou Bay Resort; adult/child 6-12yr $95/45; ⊙4:30pm Mon; ♿) The Sheraton's touristy luau weaves together Hawaiian themes and tales of ancient kings and battles, along with fiery dances from across Polynesia. The buffet is about as generic as you'd expect, but there's an open bar.

Regal Keauhou Stadium 7   CINEMA
(📞844-462-7342; 78-6831 Ali'i Dr, Keauhou Shopping Center) Hollywood flicks fill big multiplex screens. Showings before 6pm are discounted.

🛍 Shopping

For many locals, 'Keauhou' is synonymous with Keauhou Shopping Center, which has lots of businesses ranging from the locally owned to big chains. Past that, there are also some noteworthy farmers markets in the area.

★**Ho'oulu Community Farmers Market**   MARKET
(📞808-930-4900; www.hooulufarmersmkt.com; 78-128 Ehukai St, Sheraton Keauhou Bay Resort; ⊙9am-2pm Wed) 🍃 Unlike the touristy Kailua-Kona farmers market selling knick-knacks from who-knows-where, this weekly event focuses on small-scale farm and fishing bounty, including genuine Kona coffee and flower lei. Live music, island artists and takeout food vendors make this a must-do lunchtime stop.

Kona Stories   BOOKS
(📞808-324-0350; www.konastories.com; 78-6831 Ali'i Dr, Keauhou Shopping Center; ⊙10am-6pm Mon-Fri, 10am-5pm Sat, 11am-5pm Sun) Independent bookstore with a strong Hawaiiana section, which hosts community events for kids and adults. It's near KTA Super Store.

Keauhou Farmers Market   MARKET
(www.keauhoufarmersmarket.com; 78-6831 Ali'i Dr, Keauhou Shopping Center; ⊙8am-noon Sat; ♿) 🍃 At this parking-lot farmers market with live Hawaiian music and a neighborly spirit, everything is Big Island–grown including seasonal fruits and veggies, organic coffee, homemade preserves and fresh flowers.

ℹ Information

Bank of Hawaii (www.boh.com; 78-6831 Ali'i Dr, Keauhou Shopping Center, Suite 131; ⊙9am-6pm Mon-Fri, 9am-2pm Sat & Sun) ATM available inside KTA Super Store.

CVS (📞808-322-6627; www.cvs.com; 78-6831 Ali'i Dr, Keauhou Shopping Center; ⊙store 7am-10pm, pharmacy 8am-7pm Mon-Fri, 9am-7pm Sat, 9am-6pm Sun) Convenient drugstore and pharmacy.

Keauhou Urgent Care Center (📞808-322-2544; www.konaurgentcare.com; 78-6831 Ali'i Dr, Suite 418, Keauhou Shopping Center; ⊙9am-7pm) Walk-in clinic for nonemergency medical matters.

ℹ Getting There & Away

Nicknamed the 'Honu Express,' **Keauhou Trolley** (www.sheratonkona.com; one-way $2; ⊙9am-9:15pm) makes five daily round trips between Keauhou and Kailua-Kona, stopping at White (Magic) Sands Beach, Kailua Pier, various shopping centers, resort hotels and elsewhere. Check current schedules and fares online.

Hele-On (www.heleonbus.or) buses pass through Keauhou Shopping Center around ten times a day, with times clustered around commuting hours (ie 8am to 10am and noon to 7:45pm). There are no services on Sundays.

Otherwise, Keauhou, located about 6 miles south of Kailua-Kona, is easily accessible if driving down Ali'i or along the Belt Rd.

Holualoa

📞 808 / POP 8540

The further up the mountain you get from Kailua-Kona, the artsier, more residential and more rural (not to mention cooler and damper) it gets, until all of these qualities mush into one misty bohemian village: Holualoa. Perched at 1400ft on the lush slopes of Mt Hualalai, this town – village, really – has come a long way from its days as a tiny, one-donkey coffee crossroads. Today Holualoa's ramshackle buildings hold a lovely collection of artist-owned galleries, which lends this spot a distinct bohemian vibe.

Most businesses close on Sunday and Monday. Note that the census designated area called 'Holualoa' extends to the sea and includes much of Ali'i Dr. Generally, when locals speak of Holualoa they are referring to the artsy, upcountry village described here.

◉ Sights

Donkey Mill Art Center　　　ARTS CENTER
(Map p106; 📞808-322-3362; www.donkeymill artcenter.org; 78-6670 Mamalahoa Hwy; ◉10am-4pm Tue-Sat Aug-May, 9am-3pm Mon-Fri Jun & Jul; P ♿) 🅵🆁🅴🅴 The Holualoa Foundation for Arts & Culture created this community art center in 2002. There are free exhibits, a plethora of locally made art, plus lectures and workshops – taught by recognized national and international artists – all open to visitors. If you're wondering where the name comes from, the center's building, built in 1953, was once a coffee mill with a donkey painted on its roof. It puts on lots of family-friendly arts education programs. Located 3 miles south of the village center.

Japanese Cemetery　　　CEMETERY
(Map p120; 76-6018 Mamalahoa Hwy) The upland coffee country of the Kona coast has historically been settled and worked by Japanese immigrants and their descendants, and this cemetery, which clings to the mountain slopes and is full of coral and lava rock headstones inscribed with kanji, speaks to that heritage. Be respectful, and remember the cemetery is actively visited by locals.

🏃 Activities

Hula Daddy Kona Coffee　　　FARM
(Map p120; 📞808-327-9744; www.huladaddy. com; 74-4944 Mamalahoa Hwy; ◉10am-4pm Mon-Sat) 🅵🆁🅴🅴 With jaw-dropping ocean views from a breezy lanai, this epicurean tasting room and eco-conscious farm is the place to learn about cupping. Ask about unusual coffee-production techniques used to create its signature Kona Oli and Kona Sweet beans. It's less than 5 miles north of Holualoa.

Malama I'ka Ola Holistic Health Center　　　HEALTH & FITNESS
(Map p120; 📞808-324-6644; www.malamatherapy. com; 76-5914 Mamalahoa Hwy) Inside a 19th-century doctor's office, this alternative-minded oasis offers yoga and Pilates classes, as well as massage, acupuncture, Chinese herbal medicine and organic skin treatments.

👉 Tours

Holualoa Kona Coffee Company　　　FARM
(📞800-334-0348, 808-322-9937; www.konalea. com; 77-6261 Mamalahoa Hwy, Holualoa; ◉8am-4pm Mon-Fri) 🅵🆁🅴🅴 Kona Le'a Plantation does not use pesticides or herbicides on its small organic-certified farm, less than 2 miles south of Holualoa. As you drive up, watch out for the free-ranging geese, who do double duty as lawn mowers and fertilizers.

Kona Blue Sky Coffee　　　FARM
(📞877-322-1700; www.konablueskycoffee.com; 76-973 Hualalai Rd, Kailua-Kona; ◉visitor center & gift shop 9am-4pm Mon-Sat, tours 10am-3pm on the hour, except noon) 🅵🆁🅴🅴 A convenient choice if your time is limited, this tiny coffee estate in Holualoa village offers a free walking tour that passes traditional open-air drying racks and includes an educational video.

Kona Gold Rum Company　　　BAKERY
(Map p106; 📞808-769-4322; www.konagoldrum. com; 78-1377 Bishop Rd; ◉9am-5pm Mon-Fri, to 2pm Sat, closed Sun) 🅿 Things that go well with Kona coffee include: sitting on a lanai, watching the ocean, and rum cake. See how that last product is made and order some in the tasting room of this local institution. On-site is Buddha's Cup, a local coffee purveyor that harvests some exceptionally fine local beans, which you can taste along with the aforementioned cake.

✿ Festivals & Events

First Friday ART
(Art After Dark; www.holualoahawaii.com; ⊙ 5:30-8:30pm 1st Fri of the month; ⚑) ☞ On the first Friday of the month, the little village of Holualoa becomes a veritable mountain-side art gallery...which, to be fair, is an apt description of Holualoa at any time of year. But during the 'Art After Dark' walk, said galleries throw their doors open, visitors mill about, and there's a general sense of bohemian conviviality.

Music & Light Festival ART
(www.holualoahawaii.com; ⊙ mid-Dec) A small-town Christmas celebration with live music and a tree-lighting ceremony.

Coffee & Art Stroll FOOD
(www.konacoffeefest.com) During early November's Kona Coffee Cultural Festival (p91), Holualoa hosts an incredibly popular, day-long block party.

✕ Eating

Beyond Holuakoa Gardens, **Doris Place**, at 77-6108 Mamalahoa Hwy, is a well loved local grocery store if you need to stock up on supplies.

★Holuakoa Gardens & Café HEALTH FOOD $$
(Map p120; ☎ 808-322-5072; www.holuakoa cafe.com; 76-5900 Mamalahoa Hwy; mains brunch $12-25, dinner $17-35; ⊙ cafe 6:30am-6pm Mon-Fri, 8am-6pm Sat, 8am-2:30pm Sun, restaurant 10am-2:30pm Mon-Fri, 9am-2:30pm Sat & Sun, 5:30-8:30pm Mon-Sat; ☑) ☞ The storefront cafe serves 100% Kona coffee, baked goods and sandwiches. Out back, an organic, slow-food restaurant dishes up a sophisticated yet casual bistro-style menu that makes the most of fresh, Big Island–grown produce. Book ahead for dinner.

As this is one of Hawai'i's most dedicated supporters of local farmers, it's no surprise there's a seasonal farmers market here.

🔒 Shopping

Holualoa is a tiny village, but don't underestimate the quality of its artists. Along the Mamalahoa Hwy (Hwy 180) you'll find internationally known, highly commissioned artists creating art beyond the stereotypical tropical motifs. Most galleries and shops are closed on Sunday and Monday.

Holualoa Ukulele Gallery MUSIC
(Map p120; ☎ 808-324-4100; www.konaweb.com/ukegallery; 76-5942 Mamalahoa Hwy; ⊙ 11am-4:30pm Tue-Sat, other times by appointment) Inside a historic post office, owner Sam Rosen displays beautifully handcrafted ukuleles made by himself and other island luthiers. He's happy to show you his workshop and, if you've got 10 days, he'll even teach you how to build your own uke.

Studio 7 Fine Arts ARTS & CRAFTS
(Map p120; ☎ 808-324-1335; www.studio7hawaii.com; 76-5920 Mamalahoa Hwy; ⊙ 11am-5pm Tue-Sat) A serene, museum-like gallery featuring prominent artist-owner Hiroki Morinoue's watercolor, oil, woodblock and sculpture pieces, and the pottery of his accomplished wife, Setsuko. Pieces draw on Japanese influences and history, but are also excellent executions of contemporary art.

Ipu Hale Gallery ARTS & CRAFTS
(Map p120; ☎ 808-322-9069; www.holualoahawaii.com/member_sites/ipu_hale.html; 76-5893 Mamalahoa Hwy; ⊙ 10am-4pm Tue-Sat) ☞ Magnificent *ipu* (gourds) are decoratively carved with Hawaiian imagery and dyed using an ancient method unique to Ni'ihau island, knowledge of which had been lost for over a century until a scholar rediscovered it in 1980.

Holualoa Farmers Market MARKET
(Map p120; 76-5901 Mamalahoa Hwy; ⊙ 9am-noon Sat Apr-Oct) ☞ Local produce and an eclectic cast of neighbors set the scene at this market.

Dovetail Gallery & Design ARTS & CRAFTS
(Map p120; ☎ 808-322-4046; www.dovetailgallery.net; 76-5942 Mamalahoa Hwy; ⊙ gallery 11am-4pm Tue-Sat, woodworking shop 8am-4:30pm Mon-Fri) Showcases elegant contemporary work by Big Island sculptors, painters, photographers and furniture designers.

Kimura Lauhala Shop ARTS & CRAFTS
(☎ 808-324-0053; www.holualoahawaii.com/mem ber_sites/kimura.html; Hwy 180, cnr Hualalai Rd; ⊙ 9am-5pm Mon-Fri, 9am-4pm Sat) ☞ Four generations of Kimuras have sold *lauhala* (hala tree) products in this shop, making it as much a landmark as a business. There's a beautiful selection of handcrafted artisan goods on display. Don't fall prey to cheap imports sold elsewhere – the *lauhala* hats, placemats, baskets and tote bags here are the real deal.

ⓘ Getting There & Away

Holualoa village straggles along Hwy 180 (Mamalahoa Hwy), north of the Hualalai Rd intersection. Parking in the free village lot or along the highway's shoulder is easy most of the time, except during special events. There are no public transportation options out here.

SOUTH KONA COAST

South Kona, more than any other district of Hawai'i, embodies the many strands that make up the geo-cultural tapestry of the Big Island. There is both the dry lava desert of the Kohala Coast and the wet, misty jungles of Puna and Hilo; fishing villages inhabited by country-living locals next to hippie art galleries established by counterculture exiles from the US mainland, next to condos plunked down by millionaire land developers.

In addition, the dozen or so miles south from Kailua-Kona to Kealakekua Bay are among Hawai'i's most action-packed, historically speaking. It's here that ancient Hawaiian *ali'i* secretly buried the bones of their ancestors, *kapu* breakers braved shark-infested waters to reach the *pu'uhonua* (place of refuge), and British explorer Captain Cook and his crew fatally first stepped ashore in Hawaii.

ⓘ Getting There & Away

The Belt Rd that rings the island becomes Hwy 11 in South Kona, and it's a twisty, sometimes treacherous route – while there aren't many hairpin turns, folks who are used to flatland driving will need to acclimate themselves to driving in the mountains.

In some places the highway is quite narrow; while cycling is relatively common, make sure to wear reflective gear and sport good lighting on your rig. Note that mile markers decrease as you head further south; this may seem weird given that mile markers decrease going *north* in North Kona, but you're technically on Hwy 11, as opposed to Hwy 19, down here.

The Hele-On Bus (www.heleonbus.org) passes through the area sporadically, mainly in the mornings and early evening, taking commuters to and from resorts; it can also drop travelers off along the way.

Honalo

📞 808 / POP 2423

At a bend in the road where Hwys 11 and 180 intersect, little time-warped Honalo is your first sign that more than miles separate you from touristy Kailua-Kona. The heavy presence of Japanese culture within the Kona coffee belt is palpable in the form of temples and restaurants.

⊙ Sights

Daifukuji Soto Mission TEMPLE
(Map p106; 📞 808-322-3524; www.daifukuji.org; 79-7241 Mamalahoa Hwy; ⊙ 8am-4pm Mon-Sat; 🅿) The first building you see in Honalo resembles a cross between a low-slung red barn, a white-roofed villa and a Japanese shrine. Well, one out of three ain't bad: this is the Buddhist Daifukuji ('Temple of Great Happiness') Soto Mission. Slip off your shoes and admire the two ornate, lovingly tended altars. Everyone is welcome to join Zen meditation sessions, tai chi lessons and *taiko* (Japanese drum) practices, which are held across the week; call or check the website for details.

Higashihara Park PARK
(Map p106; ⊙ 9:45am-6:30pm Mon-Thu, 7:45am-4:30pm Fri; 🅿 👪) If you have young kids, head north a mile or so from Honalo and enjoy shady Higashihara Park. Its unique Hawaii-themed wooden play structure is both attractive and endlessly climbable. It is on the *makai* side, between Miles 114 and 115.

🧭 Tours

Aloha Kayak Co KAYAKING
(Map p106; 📞 808-322-2868; www.alohakayak.com; 79-7248 Mamalahoa Hwy; kayak per day single/double/triple $35/60/85, tours $54-130; ⊙ 7:30am-5pm) This Hawaiian-owned outfit knows local waters, offers half-day (noon to 5pm) kayak rentals and stand up paddle surfing (SUP) gear rental. Kayak-snorkel tours go to Kealakekua Bay and other spots along the coast, seeking out sea caves and manta rays at night.

✕ Eating

If you like Japanese diners, you're in luck! There's also a convenience store by Teshima's.

Teshima's Restaurant JAPANESE $$
(Map p106; 📞 808-322-9140; www.teshimarestaurant.com; 79-7251 Mamalahoa Hwy; dinner mains $13-23; ⊙ 6:30am-1:45pm & 5-9pm; 👪) For a real window into local life, grab a table at this family-run restaurant, which has been dishing up Japanese comfort food since the 1950s. The vintage atmosphere and the

country-style Japanese home cooking come together into a lovely whole; the sashimi is always super fresh and the tempura lightly crisp and golden.

ⓘ Getting There & Away

Honalo is located just south of Keauhou. The Hwy 11 and 180 merge forms a tricky pattern, especially when it's raining (not uncommon here in the coffee belt). Traffic also gets backed up here in the mornings and early evening during rush hour.

Kainaliu

📞 808 / POP 1600

Packed with antiques shops, art galleries and eclectic boutiques, Kainaliu is a lunch-and-linger kind of place – handy if you get caught in the infamous 'Kainaliu crawl' traffic jam along the two-lane Mamalahoa Hwy. This is the first bonafide town you'll hit in upcountry South Kona, and while it's barely 20 minutes from Kailua-Kona, the change in atmosphere is palpable – the vibe here is a lot more bohemian, eco-conscious and generally funky.

✕ Eating

As in the rest of the region, the eating options are conveniently located just off Hwy 11.

★ Annie's Island
Fresh Burgers BURGERS $

(Map p106; 📞 808-324-6000; www.anniesisland freshburgers; 79-7460 Mamalahoa Hwy, Mango Court; burgers $14-20; ⊙ 11am-8pm; 🅿️ 🖉 🔄) 🖉 Sometimes you just need a burger. The sort of burger that makes you sigh and smile and say 'Damn' and feel uncomfortably full afterwards. Enter Annie's, which uses local veggies and grass-fed Big Island beef to make some of Hawai'i's best burgers. Vegetarian? No worries – dig into a portobello mushroom stuffed with parmesan cheese.

Gypsea Gelato GELATO $

(Map p106; 📞 808-322-3233; www.gypseagelato. com; 79-7460 Mamalahoa Hwy; gelato from $3.50; ⊙ noon-8:30pm; 🅿️ 🕸) We first came here after Ironman, where we saw a wiry Italian, without an ounce of fat on his body, walk by, then walk in, saying to his partner, 'It's always a good time for gelato.' And if an Ironman can indulge here and not feel guilty, we're following suit! Flavors run from island-inspired to decadent chocolate.

Rebel Kitchen SANDWICHES $$

(Map p106; 📞 808-322-0616; www.rebelkitchen. com; 79-7399 Mamalahoa Hwy; mains $10.50-18; ⊙ 11am-8pm; 🖉) There's a sense of playful anarchy here, from the young counter staff to the punk and reggae coming out of the kitchen. You know what else comes out of the kitchen? Amazing sandwiches. We'll fight you for the blackened *ono* with cajun mayo, although you could pacify us with the jerk chicken sandwich served on a rosemary roll.

☆ Entertainment

Aloha Theatre THEATER

(Map p106; 📞 808-322-9924; www.apachawaii. org; 79-7384 Mamalahoa Hwy; tickets $10-25; 🖑) Meet one of the liveliest little community theater troupes in the islands: the Aloha Performing Arts Company, with quality plays, indie films and live music on its program. Budget tip: buy tickets in advance to save money. Pro tip: on the opening night of locally produced shows, the cast cooks the audience dinner.

🛍 Shopping

A glut of cute antique shops and galleries lines the 'main street' (ie the bit of Hwy 11 that passes through town).

Kiernan Music MUSIC

(Map p106; 📞 808-323-4939; www.kiernanmusic. com; 79-7401 Mamalahoa Hwy; ⊙ 10am-6pm Tue-Fri, 10am-5pm Sat) Friendly owner Brian Kiernan has a talent for restoring vintage ukuleles and guitars, and he's a wonderful resource whether you're a curious beginner or a serious musician looking to buy a custom-made uke or archtop guitar.

Lavender Moon Gallery ARTS & CRAFTS

(Map p106; 📞 808-324-7708; www.lavendermoon gallery.com; 79-7404 Mamalahoa Hwy; ⊙ 11am-6pm Tue-Fri, 11am-5pm Sat) High-quality original paintings, prints, jewelry, pottery and handmade bags by Big Island artists fill the colorful storefront windows.

Donkey Balls SWEETS

(Map p106; 📞 808-322-1475; www.alohahawaiian store.com; 79-7411 Mamalahoa Hwy; ⊙ 8am-6pm Mon-Sat, from 9am Sun) When it comes to sweets, we love Donkey Balls – and we promise it's not just for the saucy name, but for the excellent quality and diverse varieties of these beefy chocolates. Sure, the pure version is amazing, but check out the Jitter

South Kona Coast

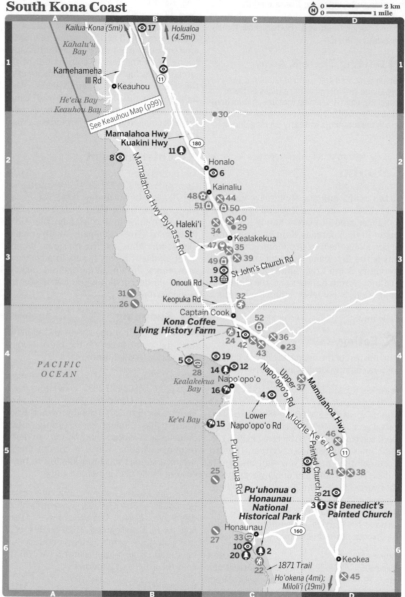

Balls, coated in 100% Kona coffee, or the Blue Balls, which come in a layer of blue-colored white chocolate.

...OK, maybe we're a little enamored of the saucy names. The local factory store also contains a pretty excellent cafe if you need some espresso to go with your punny chocolates.

Blue Ginger Gallery ART
(Map p106; ☑ 808-322-3898; www.blueginger gallery.com; 79-7391 Mamalahoa Hwy; ◎10am-

South Kona Coast

5pm Mon-Sat) This idiosyncratic little gallery is supremely eclectic and friendly. There's a definite blue-turquoise aura about, as well as plenty of paintings, prints and crafts produced by local artists and artisans. A great spot for original island souvenirs.

Kimura H Store ARTS & CRAFTS
(Map p106; 79-7408 Mamalahoa Hwy; ⊙9am-5pm Mon-Sat) This long-standing family shop rolls out yards of colorfully patterned Hawaiian and Japanese fabrics.

❶ Getting Threre & Away

Although you'll hit Honalo first, Kainaliu feels like the gateway to the South Kona upcountry. The town spreads along Miles 112–114, and is about a 20-minute drive south of Kailua-Kona.

Kealakekua
🌙 808 / POP 2020

Hawaiian heiau and the secret burial caves of *ali'i* sat high upon these cliffs centuries ago, and this was once a sacred place – the name means 'pathway of the gods.' Today, Kealakekua is a workaday town – the commercial center of South Kona – spread along the busy Mamalahoa Hwy.

◉ Sights

Greenwell Farms FARM
(Map p106; 🌙808-323-2295; www.greenwellfarms.com; 81-6581 Mamalahoa Hwy; ⊙tours 8am-4:30pm; 🅿) FREE This 150-acre family farm, established in 1850, is run by fourth-generation Greenwells and is one of Kona's

oldest and best-known coffee plantations. It currently roasts coffee cherries from more than 200 local growers. Take a free tour and sample coffee and fruit at a shady picnic table. You can also purchase Kona Red (www. konared.com), a juice made from coffee cherry pulp. The farm is between Miles 110 and 111.

HN Greenwell Store Museum   MUSEUM
(Map p106; ☑ 808-323-3222; www.konahistorical. org; 81-6551 Mamalahoa Hwy; adult/child 5-12yr $5/2; ⊙ 10am-2pm Mon & Thu, museum only Tue; ℙ) ⌀ Housed in one of Kona's oldest buildings, this museum is a taste of 19th-century Hawai'i. Built in 1875 and meticulously restored, it has educational docents in period dress who bring Kona's multicultural and agricultural history to life as they wield dry goods and talk story. You'll usually smell sweet bread baking in the traditional Portuguese bread oven after 11am on Thursdays. The museum, sans docents, is open on Tuesdays.

The museum is between Miles 111 and 112 on Hwy 11.

👉 Tours

Kona Boys   OUTDOORS
(Map p106; ☑ 808-328-1234; www.konaboys. com; 79-7539 Mamalahoa Hwy; single/double kayak per day $54/74, tours $139-189; ⊙ 7:30am-5pm) This laid-back pro water-sports outfitter is South Kona's largest, and a fixture of the local tourism scene. Kayaking, snorkeling and outrigger-canoe sailing trips visit Kealakekua Bay, and you can learn surfing and SUP from these brahs. Snorkel gear, SUP, surfboard and kayak rentals available. Call ahead for tour and gear-rental reservations.

🍴 Eating

Your restaurant options line Hwy 11, and include some fine locally sourced spots.

Cafe Florian   CAFE $
(Map p106; ☑ 808-238-0861; www.caffeflorian kona.com; 81-6637 Mamalahoa Hwy; mains $5.50-12; ⊙ 6:30am-4pm Mon-Fri, 7am-2pm Sat, closed Sun; ℙ❄☕) This clean, cozy cafe has a back porch for sitting, watching geckos and sipping strong Kona coffee while dining on salads, sandwiches, bagels, scrambles and other breakfast and lunch mainstays. Has one of the more extensive vegetarian menus in this corner of the island.

Dave's Hawaiian Ice Cream   ICE CREAM $
(Map p106; ☑ 808-345-8042; www.daveshawaiian icecream.com; 81-6592 Mamalahoa Hwy; snacks $3-6; ⊙ 11:30am-9pm, to 5pm Sat & Sun; 🚗) Made on O'ahu, Dave's creamy concoctions are bursting with island flavors: *poha* (cape gooseberry), guava, *liliko'i*, coconut, *ube* (purple yam), chocolate mac nut, Kona coffee and more. Get your scoop served inside a cup of rainbow shave ice.

Ke'ei Café   BISTRO $$
(Map p106; ☑ 808-322-9992; www.keeicafe.net; 79-7511 Mamalahoa Hwy; mains $17-31; ⊙ 5-9pm Tue-Sat; 🚗) If you're craving some fine dining while in South Kona, it's hard to do better than Ke'ei Cafe, which has carved a name for itself as an excellent outpost of haute Hawaiian cuisine. Cracking peanut miso salad sets the stage for powerful mains like roasted chicken served with red curry sauce – or, if you're in the mood, a more Western peppercorn gravy.

Reservations recommended; request a lanai table.

🍸 Drinking & Nightlife

Korner Pocket Bar & Grill   BAR
(Map p106; ☑ 808-322-2994; 81-970 Haleki'i St; ⊙ 11am-1am) This is about it when it comes to bar options in South Kona. It's a pretty local joint, with live music on weekends and packed pool tables any day of the week. On slow nights, it may close earlier. A popular spot to catch sports on big-screen TVs.

🛍 Shopping

As in much of the region, there are good antique shops scattered along the highway.

Discovery Antiques   ANTIQUES
(Map p106; ☑ 808-323-2239; 81-6593 Mamalahoa Hwy; ⊙ 10am-5pm Mon-Sat, 11am-4pm Sun) Tin toys and aloha shirts, bric-a-brac and vintage Hawaiiana – who knows what you'll find at this secondhand antiques and curiosities shop. Bonus: it sells delicious scoops of Tropical Dreams ice cream, made in Hilo.

ⓘ Information

First Hawaiian Bank (☑ 808-322-3484; www. fhb.com; 81-6626 Mamalahoa Hwy; ⊙ 8:30am-4pm Mon-Thu, to 6pm Fri)

Kona Community Hospital (☑ 808-322-9311; www.kch.hhsc.org; 79-1019 Haukapila St; ⊙ 24hr) West Hawai'i's most advanced (level-III) trauma center, about 10 miles south of Kailua-Kona.

ⓘ Getting There & Away

Kealakekua is on Mamalahoa/Hwy 11 and starts just south of Kainaliu, at Mile 111. If you need to get between Keauhou and Kealakekua, consider skipping the Belt Rd and using the Mamalahoa Hwy Bypass Rd that connects the two communities. This cut-through allows savvy drivers to avoid the worst of commuter traffic in and out of Kailua-Kona.

The road connects Haleki'i St in Kealakekua – turn *makai* off Hwy 11 between Miles 111 and 112 – to Kamehameha III Rd in Keauhou, and Ali'i Dr and Hwy 11 (Mamalahoa) beyond.

Captain Cook

📞 808 / POP 3429

As Hwy 11/Mamalahoa Hwy winds southward, the greenery thickens and the ocean views become more compelling and it can be hard to tell where towns start and stop. Captain Cook is signaled by the historic Manago Hotel, which began in 1917 as a restaurant catering to salesmen on the then-lengthy journey between Hilo and Kona. The stout building remains a regional touchstone for travelers and residents alike.

Captain Cook is also where you access Kealakekua Bay, plus a great selection of B&Bs and down-home cooking. Sinewy Napo'opo'o Rd, which eventually becomes Middle Ke'ei Rd, webs between the mountain and the ocean and is a pretty place to drive without an agenda. The many 'No Spray' signs are put up by organic farms (or even just homeowners) that are warding against state pesticide spraying.

◎ Sights

Middle Ke'ei Road and **Painted Church Road**, which both run toward the sea from Hwy 11, are two of the prettiest roads on the island, and are well worth a drive. Many souls choose to cycle down here, but beware – the road is narrow with no shoulder. It's also a huff getting back to the main highway.

★ Kona Coffee Living History Farm   HISTORIC SITE
(Map p106; 📞 808-323-3222; www.konahistorical. org; 82-6199 Mamalahoa Hwy; 1hr tour adult/child 5-12yr $15/5; ⏰ 10am-2pm Mon-Fri; P) Many coffee-farm tours are perfunctory 15-minute affairs. This tour, run by the Kona Historical Society, an affiliate of the Smithsonian Institute, is different and deep. More than just an exploration of how coffee is grown and harvested, it's an evocative look at rural Japanese immigrant life in South Kona throughout several decades of the 20th century. Restored to Hawai'i's pre-statehood era, this 5.5-acre working coffee farm once belonged to the Uchida family, who lived here until 1994.

Several of the docents grew up on area coffee farms, so they speak from experience as they show you around the orchards, processing mill, drying roofs and main house. On easy walking tours, you'll learn how to pick coffee cherries and prepare a traditional *bentō* (Japanese boxed lunch).

The farm is between Miles 110 and 111.

Big Island Bees   FARM
(Map p106; 📞 808-328-7318; www.bigislandbees. com; 82-1140 Meli Rd; ⏰ 10am-4pm Mon-Fri, to 2pm Sat; P) At this roadside gift shop and tiny historical museum, genial staff will let you in on all the secrets of beekeeping, then give you a peek inside a living apiary and teach you how their award-winning, single-varietal and certified organic honey is made. Taste a free sample of ohia lehua blossom honey spiced with cinnamon or the macnut blossom honey.

🏃 Activities

Captain Cook Monument Trail   HIKING
(Map p106; off Napo'opo'o Rd) 🥾 Your only landbound access to the Cook Monument is this trail, which offers nice lookouts on the way down and leads right to the snorkeling cove. The descending path is an easy (if buggy) hour, but after snorkeling, the uphill return seems twice as steep (in reality it's a 1300ft elevation gain in 1.8 miles); allow two hours to return.

To get to the trailhead, turn *makai* off the Mamalahoa Hwy onto Napo'opo'o Rd; within the first 10th of a mile, park along the narrow road shoulder, wherever it's safe and legally signposted to do so. To find the trailhead, count five telephone poles from the start of the road – it's *makai* across from three tall palm trees.

The route is fairly easy to follow; when in doubt, stay to the left. For the uphill return, you should stay alert for the trail's right-hand turn back up onto the lava ledge, or you'll end up on a 4WD road heading north along the coast – for miles.

Mamalahoa Hot Tubs & Massage   SPA
(Map p106; 📞 808-323-2288; www.mamalahoa-hottubs.com; 81-1016 St John's Church Rd; hot tub per hr 2 people $35-50; ⏰ noon-9pm Wed-Sat)

THE CAPTAIN COOK STORY

On January 17, 1779, Captain Cook sailed into Kealakekua Bay, kicking off one of the most controversial months in Hawaii's history.

Cook's visit coincided with the annual makahiki festival, a four-month period when all warfare and heavy work was suspended to pay homage to Lono – the god of agriculture and peace. Makahiki was marked by an islandwide procession to collect the chief's annual tribute, which set off celebrations, sexual freedom and games.

Cook's welcome in Kealakekua Bay was spectacular: more than 1000 canoes surrounded his ships and 9000 people hailed him from shore. Once landed, Cook was treated with supreme deference – feted as any ruling chief would be, with huge celebrations and overwhelming offerings. The Hawaiians also bartered for goods – particularly for metals, which they'd never seen before. Though Cook tried to keep his sailors from fraternizing with Hawaiian women, he failed utterly and ultimately gave up: sailors frequently bartered nails in exchange for sex.

On February 4, restocked and ready to go, Cook departed Kealakekua Bay. But only a short way north he encountered a huge storm, and the *Resolution* broke a foremast. Unable to continue, Cook returned to the safety of Kealakekua Bay on February 11.

This time, no canoes rowed out in greeting. Chief Kalaniopu'u instead seemed to indicate Cook had worn out his welcome. For one, captain and crew had already depleted the Hawaiians' supplies of food, plus the makahiki season had ended; the party was over.

As Hawaiian generosity decreased, petty thefts increased, and insults and suspicion replaced politeness on both sides. After a rowboat was stolen, Cook ordered a blockade of Kealakekua Bay and took chief Kalaniopu'u hostage until the boat was returned.

Cook convinced Kalaniopu'u to come to the *Resolution* to resolve their disputes. But as they walked to shore, Kalaniopu'u learned that sailors had killed a lower chief attempting to exit the bay in his canoe. At this, Kalaniopu'u apparently sat and refused to continue, and a large angry crowd gathered.

Thinking to frighten the Hawaiians, Cook fired his pistol, killing one of the chief's bodyguards. Incensed, the Hawaiians attacked. In the deadly melee, Captain Cook was stabbed with a dagger and clubbed to death.

Cook's death stunned both sides and ended the battle. In the days afterward, the Hawaiians took Cook's body and dismembered it in the custom reserved for high chiefs. The Englishmen demanded Cook's body back, and in a spasm of gruesome violence torched homes and slaughtered Hawaiians – women and children included.

Eventually the Hawaiians returned some bits and pieces – a partial skull, hands and feet – which the English buried at sea, per naval tradition. The Hawaiians kept the bones that held the most mana, such as his femurs.

Soak away your blisters or blues in a lush garden mini-oasis. The two teak tubs, sheltered by thatched roofs that allow for stargazing, are open-sided yet private. Many types of massage, from Swedish to traditional Hawaiian *lomilomi* and hot stone, are available. Reservations are required; ask about discount packages.

Tours

Adventures in Paradise   KAYAKING
(Map p106; ☎808-447-0080; www.bigisland kayak.com; 82-6020 Mamalahoa Hwy; kayak-snorkel tour $100; ☺ office 7am-3pm) At this professional water-sports outfitter, guides look after beginners and lead excellent kayak-snorkeling trips to Kealakekua Bay. Also offers boat tours and can arrange gear rentals.

Eating

Manago Restaurant   JAPANESE $
(Map p106; ☎808-323-2642; www.manago hotel.com; 82-6155 Mamalahoa Hwy; mains breakfast $4-6, lunch & dinner $6-14; ☺7-9am, 11am-2pm & 5-7:30pm Tue-Sun; P♿) The Bingo parlor dining room of the Manago is an iconic Big Island experience. It feels like an early-20th-century diner, but one made for South Kona's ethnic blend: a mix of Japanese, Chinese, Portuguese, Filipino, a few mainlanders and Native Hawaiians. Thus, the Manago's meals are hearty,

American-size portions, yet come with bowls of rice and diced Japanese vegetables.

Coffee Shack CAFE $
(Map p106; ☑ 808-328-9555; www.coffeeshack. com; 83-5799 Mamalahoa Hwy; meals $11-15; ☺ 7:30am-3pm; ℗) Perched precariously next to the highway, the Shack is famous for insane views of Kealakekua Bay from its open-air deck. We can say, with no hyperbole, you may never have a cup of coffee with a better vista. The food – sandwiches, salads and the like – is pretty kick-butt too, especially homemade desserts such as *liliko‘i* cheesecake.

Look for the historic building on the *makai* side of Hwy 11, between Miles 108 and 109.

Patz Pies PIZZA $
(Map p106; ☑ 808-323-8100; www.patzpies.com; 82-6127 Mamalahoa Hwy; slice/whole pizza from $3/17; ☺ 10am-8pm, to 9pm Fri & Sat; ℗) Thin crust and zesty sauce makes us happy travelers. Claims to authentic NYC pizza are only slightly exaggerated at this native NYer's kitchen, just south of the Manago Hotel.

ChoiceMart SUPERMARKET $
(Map p106; ☑ 808-323-3994; www.choicemart. net; 82-6066 Mamalahoa Hwy; ☺ 5am-10pm; ℗) South Kona's largest grocery store lets you stock up on beach picnic supplies. Also has a very good beer, wine and liquor selection.

🛍 Shopping

South Kona Green Market MARKET
(Map p106; 82-6160 Mamalahoa Hwy; ☺ 9am-2pm Sun; 🖈) 🖉 The Green Market is, in many ways, a gossip center, town hall and temporary village green for the eclectic community of South Kona. That said, it's also a place to buy fresh fruit, organic island-grown produce, artisanal foodstuffs and funky crafts. Live music is usually served up with the locally sourced goodness.

ℹ Getting There & Away

'Central' Captain Cook is about 13 miles south of Kailua-Kona on Hwy 11/Mamalahoa Hwy. Hele-On buses (www.heleonbus.or) can drop you off along the way to Kailua-Kona.

Kealakekua Bay

Kealakekua Bay is one of Hawai‘i's seminal sites, a location that manages to blend incredible natural beauty with supreme his-

torical importance. Besides being one of the major religious sites of Native Hawaiians, the bay marks the spot where Captain Cook and, by extension, the outside world first set foot in the archipelago, irrevocably altering the fate of the islands and their residents.

A wide, calm bay is shouldered by a low lava point to the north, tall reddish *pali* (cliffs) in the center and miles of green mountain slopes to the south. The bay is both a state park and a marine-life conservation area, and is famous for its rich variety of sea life, including spinner dolphins. This entire area is considered sacred, and deserves your respect.

👁 Sights

Kealakekua Bay State Historical Park PARK
(Map p106; www.hawaiistateparks.org; 82-6099 Pu‘uhonua Beach Rd; ☺ sunrise-sunset; ℗) 🖉 Beautiful, historical Kealakekua Bay is the big draw on the south coast. Local organizations and businesses are working hard to keep it that way, as more people communing with the wildlife increases pressure on this marine-life conservation district famous for its rich variety of sea life, including spinner dolphins. To this end, new kayak regulations have been issued.

To reach the park, take Napo‘opo‘o Rd, off Mamalahoa Hwy, for 4.5 miles. At the bottom of the road you'll turn right for Hiki‘au Heiau, a broad stone platform temple dedicated to war god Ku that was Kealakekua's religious center, or left for the wharf. There are bathrooms and showers near the heiau.

Ke‘ei Beach BEACH
(Map p106; off Pu‘uhonua Rd) Just south of Kealakekua Bay, Ke‘ei Beach is an attractive cove that's mostly too rough and rocky for swimming, except for a *very* narrow sandy stretch at its northern end. When conditions are right, local surfers ride the long reef break. Bayside, there's a small canoe and kayak launch and a few fishing shacks but no public facilities. Be respectful of local residents – you're essentially walking in their front yards.

To get here, take the ragged 4WD road leading *makai* off Pu‘uhonua Rd, about 0.3 miles south of Manini Beach Rd (if you hit Ke‘ei Transfer Station, you've gone too far). Paved Pu‘uhonua Rd continues another few miles south to Place of Refuge.

Pali Kapu o Keoua
HISTORIC SITE

(Map p106) Above Kealakekua Bay, the 'sacred cliffs of Keoua' were named for a chief and rival of Kamehameha I. Several high, inaccessible caves in these cliffs served as burial places for Hawaiian royalty, and it's speculated that some of Captain Cook's bones ended up here as well. In case you're wondering: there really is no way up to these caves, and they're sacred and off limits in any case.

Manini Beach
BEACH

(Map p106) On its southern side, Kealakekua Bay is rocky and exposed to regular northwest swells, so swimming and snorkeling conditions are poor. That said, Manini Beach makes a scenic, shady picnic spot. If you do want to take a dip, despite the scattered, sharp coral and 'a'a (rough, jagged lava) along the shoreline, the best ocean access is to your right upon arriving at the beach.

From Napo'opo'o Rd, turn left onto Pu'uhonua Rd, then right onto Manini Rd. There's limited roadside parking.

Captain Cook Monument
HISTORIC SITE

(Map p106) This tall white obelisk is visible a mile away at Ka'awaloa Cove. It marks the spot where Captain Cook was killed in an armed confrontation with Hawaiians in 1779. In 1877, as an act of diplomacy, the Kingdom of Hawai'i deeded the land that the monument stands on to Britain (so yes: this is technically British soil – makes sense, as it's pretty damp). Behind lie some scattered stones and foundation marks, the ruins of the ancient village of Ka'awaloa.

Hiki'au Heiau
TEMPLE

(Map p106; P) Veer right at the base of Napo'opo'o Rd to reach this large platform temple. In front of the heiau, a stone beach makes a moody perch from which to observe the stunning scenery, but the surf is too rough to swim in. Climbing on the ruins is kapu.

🏃 Activities

Kayaking

Controversy over overcrowding and environmental impact on the bay has resulted in new legal regulations for kayakers. Special recreational permits for transiting the bay, but not for landing at Ka'awaloa Cove or launching from Napo'opo'o Wharf, are currently available to individual kayakers in advance from the Division of State Parks.

Otherwise, your only other option (for now) is a guided kayaking tour by a state-permitted outfitter; check www.hawaii stateparks.org for a current list. Most tours launch from Napo'opo'o Wharf, paddling 30 to 45 minutes across the bay to Ka'awaloa Cove. Prevailing winds are from the northwest, so returning is usually faster and easier.

Diving

There are many good dive sites clustered around Kealakekua Bay, including Ka'awaloa Cove, with its exceptionally diverse coral and fish. Other sites further north include Hammerhead (Map p106), a deep dive with pelagic action; Coral Dome (Map p106), a big, teeming cave with a giant skylight; and Driftwood (Map p106), featuring lava tubes and white-tip reef sharks.

In the aptly named Long Lava Tube (Map p106), an intermediate site just north of Kealakekua Bay, lava 'skylights' shoot light through the ceiling of the 70ft-long tube, and you may see crustaceans, morays and maybe even Spanish dancers. Outside are countless lava formations sheltering conger eels, triton's trumpet shells and squirrelfish.

Snorkeling

At Kealakekua Bay's northern end, protected Ka'awaloa Cove ranks among Hawai'i's premier snorkeling spots. Protected from ocean swells, its aquamarine waters are especially clear. Tropical fish and coral are brilliantly abundant, and those with iron stomachs can swim 100ft from shore to hang over the blue abyss of an underwater cliff.

If you're lucky, honu and spinner dolphins might join you, but remember not to approach these wild animals. By law, you must remain at least 50yd away from turtles and 100yd from dolphins, whales and seals in the water. All Hawaiian sea turtles are endangered, so give them a break and never touch or try to ride them.

At the time of research, and for the foreseeable future, you could only visit Ka'awaloa Cove on a snorkel cruise leaving from Kailua-Kona or Keauhou, on a guided kayaking tour by a South Kona outfitter or by hiking the Captain Cook Monument Trail.

Ka'awaloa Cove
SNORKELING

(Map p106) Snorkeling at wildly popular Ka'awaloa Cove in Kealakekua Bay is stellar. The coral gardens, tropical fish and an underwater cliff just 50yd from shore are electrifying. If you're visiting in winter, consider wearing a rashguard. Enormous coral cliffs and drop-offs are inhabited by wandering clouds of brightly colored fish, which congregate in the bay in a wash of neon hues. If you don't want to paddle or hike into the cove, you can catch a **snorkeling cruise**.

The popularity of this spot for wild dolphin encounters has alarm bells ringing in environmental and animal rights circles, since human contact can disturb the habitat, and the eating, sleeping or mating habits of wildlife. Note that if you don't want to go to Kealakekua Bay, some tour outfits visit less-trafficked (if less spectacular) coves nearby.

⊙ Getting There & Away

There is no public transportation to Kealakekua Bay; if you're not hiking down to the Captain Cook Monument or arriving by boat with a permit, you need a car or a bicycle. Napo'opo'o Rd, off Hwy 11, winds 4.5 miles down to the bay, leaving behind the lush foliage of the rainier uplands for the perpetually sunny coast (never assume that rain on the highway means rain in the bay). The road ends at the parking lot for Napo'opo'o Beach and Wharf.

Honaunau

🖉 808 / POP 2600

Little more than some scattered, friendly businesses hidden amid thick coffee and macadamia nut groves, Honaunau is fun to explore without a guidebook. The nearby 'Place of Refuge' remains the star attraction, but meander down Painted Church Rd, stopping at fruit stands and coffee shacks with sea views, for another type of retreat.

⊙ Sights

★**St Benedict's Painted Church**   CHURCH
(Map p106; 🖉808-328-2227; www.thepaintedchurch.org; 84-5140 Painted Church Rd; ⊙9am-6pm, services 7am Tue, Thu & Fri, 4pm Sat, 7:15am Sun; P) A pulpit with a view, gravestones cradled by tropical blooms and a little chapel with floor-to-ceiling 'outsider art' make this church a picturesque side trip. A self-taught artist and Catholic priest, John Velghe, came to Hawai'i from Belgium in 1899 and he modeled the vaulted nave on a Gothic cathedral in Burgos, Spain. His trompe l'oeil art work merges European structure with Polynesian scenery, such as Jesus casting out the

devil in front of what looks like the Pololu Valley.

Although admission is free, we suggest leaving a little donation to help upkeep this fascinating, living piece of culture.

Society for Kona's Education & Art   ARTS CENTER
(SKEA; Map p106; 🖉808-328-9392; www.skea.org; 84-5191 Mamalahoa Hwy; P) ✎ SKEA is a hotbed of activity, with pilates, Polynesian dance, tai chi and Japanese ink painting classes, art shows and poetry readings; check the online calendar or give them a call. Around back at the **Kona Potter's Guild**, you can watch potters at work and buy their handmade creations.

It's between Miles 105 and 106.

Paleaku Gardens Peace Sanctuary   GARDENS
(Map p106; 🖉808-328-8084; www.paleaku.com; 83-5401 Painted Church Rd; adult/child 6-12yr $10/3; ⊙9am-4pm Tue-Sat; P) ✎ Near the church on Painted Church Rd, these tranquil 7-acre gardens contain shrines to the world's major religions and a staggeringly impressive 'Galaxy Garden,' in which famous space painter Jon Lomberg has created a scale model of the Milky Way – in plants. You'll also find yoga and tai chi classes and plenty of general interfaith good vibes.

✖ Eating

A few very tasty roadside options are just what the vacation calls for after a hard day of having a great time.

★**Super J's**   HAWAIIAN $
(Ka'aloa's Super J's; Map p106; 🖉808-328-9566; 83-5409 Mamalahoa Hwy; plates $8-12; ⊙10am-6:30pm Mon-Sat; P⊞) The full title of this place is 'Ka'aloa's Super J's Hawaiian Food,' but everyone calls it Super J's. They also call it freakin' delicious. The *laulau* (pork, chicken or fish wrapped inside taro or *ti* leaves) is steamed until it's so tender it melts under your fork, the *lomilomi* salmon is perfectly salty – you'll even want second helpings of *poi* (mashed taro).

Best of all is the setting: you're basically eating in a welcoming Hawaiian family's kitchen. It's on the *makai* side of Hwy 11, between Miles 106 and 107.

Da Poke Shack   SEAFOOD $
(Map p106; 🖉808-328-8862; www.dapokeshack.com; 83-5308 Mamalahoa Hwy; mains $5-12; ⊙11am-6pm Sun-Thu, to 7pm Fri & Sat; P) This

DMITRI KOTCHETOV/SHUTTERSTOCK ©

1. Mokuʻaikaua Church (p82)
The oldest Christian church in the Hawaiian Islands.

2. Diving off the Kona Coast (p88)
Clear, calm water makes for a perfect view of lava
formations and coral reefs.

3. Sunset at Kailua Bay (p83)
Once a major commercial harbour, the bay is now a
tranquil swimming and canoeing spot.

4. *Honu* (green sea turtle; p295)
If you encounter this endangered species swimming or
sun bathing, be sure to keep your distance.

sister location to Kailua-Kona's excellent outpost (p92), Da Poke Shack serves up the same screamingly fresh, marinated or dressed in multiple iterations, be it with *shōyu* (soy sauce) or dynamite style (avocado aioli), the spicy Pele's Kiss. All dishes officially come with scoops of rice and unofficial praise from on high.

South Kona Fruit Stand   MARKET $

(Map p106; 808-328-8547; www.southkona fruitstand.com; 84-4770 Mamalahoa Hwy; items $3-10; ⊙9am-6pm Mon-Sat, 10am-4pm Sun;) Baskets overflow with everything from tart apple bananas to filling breadfruit, creamy *abiu* (sapote) and purple jaboticaba berries. Slurp a smoothie on the outdoor patio with gorgeous coastal views. Look for the pineapple flags on the *mauka* (inland) side of Hwy 11, between Miles 103 and 104.

Big Jake's Island B-B-Q   BARBECUE $

(Map p106; 808-328-1227; 83-5308 Mamalahoa Hwy; mains $7-12; ⊙11am-3pm;) Barbecued ribs, pork and chicken are slowly cooked in the barrel smoker parked by Mile 106. Chow down at picnic tables out back, or for DIY surf-and-turf pick up some *poke* from the next-door Da Poke Shack.

Keoki's Roadside Cafe   SEAFOOD $$

(Map p106; 808-328-2259; 83-5293 Mamalahoa Hwy; mains $11-22; ⊙10am-6:30pm;) This roadside business dishes out fish and chips made with locally caught seafood species such as *ono* and mahimahi. It's decent enough, and pretty filling after a swim or a hike; not our top fish and chips on the island, but the garden seating area is sweet. There's island art for sale, too!

❶ Getting There & Away

The Intra-Kona line of the Hele-On Bus (www. heleonbus.org) passes Honaunau about three to four times daily and is timed for commuters (ie northbound buses depart toward Kailua-Kona from around 5am to 9:30am, and southbound buses bring workers home from around 4am to 6:30pm). If you're driving, Honaunau is about 7 miles south of Captain Cook.

Pu'uhonua o Honaunau National Historical Park

Standing at the end of a long semi-desert of thorny scrub and lava plains, the national park fronting Honaunau Bay provides one of the state's most evocative experiences of ancient Hawai'i, and easy access to some of the best snorkeling anywhere. In short, Pu'uhonua o Honaunau combines a seminal historical experience with some of the best wildlife-spotting on the island, and to access all this, you just need to be able to fit a snorkel in your mouth. The park's tongue-twister name simply means 'place of refuge at Honaunau.'

Early morning or late afternoon is an optimal time to visit to avoid the midday heat and crowds. On the weekend closest to July 1, show up for the park's annual **cultural festival**, an extravaganza of traditional food, hula dancing, Hawaiian crafts and cultural demonstrations.

History

In ancient Hawai'i the *kapu* system regulated every waking moment. A *maka'aina* (commoner) could not look at *ali'i* or walk in their footsteps. Women couldn't cook for men, nor eat with them. Fishing, hunting and gathering timber were restricted to certain seasons. And on and on.

Violators of *kapu* were hunted down and killed. After all, according to the Hawaiian belief system, breaking *kapu* infuriated the gods. And gods wrought volcanic eruptions, tidal waves, famine and earthquakes, which could be devastating to the entire community.

There was one loophole, however. Commoners who broke *kapu* could stave off death if they reached the sacred ground of a *pu'uhonua*. A *pu'uhonua* also gave sanctuary to defeated warriors and wartime noncombatants (men who were too old, too young or unable to fight).

To reach the *pu'uhonua* was no small feat. Since royals and their warriors lived on the grounds surrounding the refuge, *kapu* breakers had to swim through violent, open ocean, braving currents and sharks, to safety. Once inside the sanctuary, priests performed ceremonies of absolution to placate the gods. *Kapu* breakers could then return home to start afresh.

The *pu'uhonua* at Honaunau was used for several centuries until 1819, when Hawai'i's old religious ways were abandoned after King Kamehameha II and regent Queen Ka'ahumanu ate together in public, overthrowing the ancient *kapu* system forever.

◉ Sights

After wandering the self-guided trail, you might try some wildlife watching: humpback whales can be seen offshore in winter, and turtles, dolphins and even hoary bats can be seen year-round (after sunset is best for the bats).

★ Pu'uhonua o Honaunau
National Historical Park   PARK

(Map p106; ☎808-328-2326; www.nps.gov/puho; off Hwy 160, Honaunau; 7-day entry per car $5; ⏱park 7am-sunset, visitor center 8:30am-4:30pm; P ♿) ✐ This awesome park is an ancient place of refuge – or *pu'uhonua,* a sanctuary where *kapu*-breakers could have their lives spared. A half-mile walking tour encompasses major sites – the visitor center provides a brochure map with cultural information. You enter the park in the village-like royal grounds, where Kona *ali'i* and their warriors lived; the spiritual atmosphere is greatly enhanced by gently breaking waves and wind-rustled palms. Throughout the grounds are wooden *ki'i* standing up to 15ft high.

Picnic Area   NATIONAL PARK

(Map p106; Pu'uhonua o Honaunau National Historical Park; ♿) ✐ Just south of the park's central village area, an oceanfront palm-tree grove holds one of South Kona's choicest picnic areas. Parking, picnic tables and BBQs face a wide slab of *pahoehoe* (smooth-flowing lava), which is littered with wave-tumbled lava-rock boulders and pockmarked with busy tide pools where you may encounter sea turtles. Swimming is possible but can be dicey; judge the surf and entry for yourself. Note that it's *kapu* to snorkel here.

Hale o Keawe Heiau   TEMPLE

(Map p106; Pu'uhonua o Honaunau National Historical Park) 'The temple on the point of the cove,' located a few hundred yards past the main park entrance, was built around 1650 and contains the bones of 23 chiefs. It was believed that the mana of the chiefs remained in their bones and bestowed sanctity on those who entered the grounds. A fishpond, lava tree molds, a hand-carved koa canoe and a few thatched huts and shelters are scattered through here.

Great Wall   RUINS

(Map p106; Pu'uhonua o Honaunau National Historical Park) Leading up to Hale o Keawe Heiau is the Great Wall, separating the royal grounds from the *pu'uhonua.* Built around 1550, this stone wall is over 1000ft long and 10ft high. Inside the wall are two older heiau platforms and legendary standing stones.

Keone'ele Cove   LANDMARK

(Map p106; Pu'uhonua o Honaunau National Historical Park) Once this was the royal canoe landing; now it's a tongue of sand that hooks into the waters (wave to those snorkelers at Two-Step just across the way) and a favorite resting spot for sea turtles.

⟨ Activities

★ Two-Step   SNORKELING

(Map p106; Honaunau Beach Rd) Immediately north of the national historical park, concealed within a (usually) placid bay, are a series of ridiculously vibrant coral gardens where the reef and marine life seem locked in a permanent race to outstrip each other with the gaudiest color palette. From above the water, your only indication of the action is the presence of boats and crowds gathering at the titular two steps.

There's no beach here – snorkelers use a stepped lava ledge beside the boat ramp to access about 10ft of water, which quickly drops to about 25ft.

Once you're in the water you'll feel like a supporting cast player in Disney's *The Little Mermaid.* Visibility is usually excellent, especially with the noon sun overhead; good-size reef fish and a fine variety of coral are close to shore. The predatory 'crown of thorns' starfish can be seen feasting on live coral polyps. Cool, freshwater springs seep out of the ground, creating blurry patches in the water. Divers can investigate a ledge a little way out that drops off about 100ft.

The best time to go is during rising tide, when there are more fish. High winter surf means rough waters. The morning is also always better for undersea wildlife watching.

A privately operated parking lot costs $3. You can also park in the national park lot ($5, but you can go in and out for 10 days) or try to squeeze in along the road's shoulder.

1871 Trail   HIKING

(Map p106; Pu'uhonua o Honaunau National Historical Park) ✐ Back in – you guessed it! – 1871, a section of derelict coastal trail that extended south all the way to Ho'okena was cleared and opened to the public, re-establishing what had once been a main artery for coastal villages in the region. Today, said trail crosses wild stretches of South Kona countryside; see our self-guided tour (p80) for more details.

❶ Getting There & Away

To get here, turn *makai* on to City of Refuge Rd (about 17 miles south of Kailua-Kona). Follow the signs along the curvy road for about 2 miles to Pu'uhonua o Honaunau. There are no public transportation links here.

Ho'okena & Around

Most tourists zip right by the turnoff for Ho'okena. But meander just a couple of miles downhill to this fishing community and you'll be surprised by a gorgeous bayfront beach that locals love and, more importantly, are willing to share.

Ho'okena was once a bustling Hawaiian village. Novelist Robert Louis Stevenson wrote about his 1889 visit here in *Travels in Hawaii*. In the 1890s, Chinese immigrants moved in, a tavern and a hotel opened, and the town got rougher and rowdier. In those days, Big Island cattle were shipped from the Ho'okena landing, but when the circle-island road was built, Honolulu-bound steamers stopped coming and most people moved away.

◉ Sights

★ **Ho'okena Beach Park**   BEACH
(www.hookena.org; off Ho'okena Beach Rd; 👪)
This modest, charcoal-colored beach is backed by a steep green hillside. When calm, the bay's waters are good for swimming, kayaking and snorkeling (although the bottom drops off quickly). Coral abounds, as do strong currents further out. When the winter surf is up, local kids hit the waves with bodyboards. You might spot dolphins and humpback whales offshore between December and April. Facilities include restrooms, outdoor showers, drinking water, campsites, a picnic pavilion and a concession stand.

Camping is right on the sand at the base of the cliffs. Ongoing security issues have been addressed by implementing a guard patrol and through the activism of the Friends of Ho'okena Beach Park; you can obtain required camping permits and rent camping gear from them online or in person. Camping permits can also be obtained in advance from the county.

Pebble Beach   BEACH
(off Kaohe Rd) Not quite pebbles, the smoky stones of this nonsandy beach at the bottom of the Kona Paradise subdivision range from gumdrop- to palm-size. It's a popular kayak put-in and offers a good dose of peace and quiet. Lounge for a bit, paddle a while or just watch the sun go down, although note that those rocks do get hot. If you enter the water, watch out for waves – the currents here are powerful and treacherous.

The beach is a mile down very steep, winding Kaohe Rd, accessed between Miles 96 and 97 on Hwy 11. Signs say 'private road' and 'keep out,' although the subdivision is ungated. Always ask permission from locals before entering.

❶ Information

Friends of Ho'okena Beach Park (📞 808-328-8430; http://hookena.org) Community organization that manages maintenance and cleaning efforts at Ho'okena Beach Park.

❶ Getting There & Away

Three Hele-On buses pass by very early in the morning (around 5am) and in the late afternoon (around 4pm). But you really need your own wheels to properly explore the area, which is 10 miles south of Captain Cook; look for the turnoff between Miles 101 and 102.

Miloli'i

📞 808 / POP 8110
Miloli'i is a fishing village fighting to maintain its traditional ways while an upscale subdivision rises from the lava landscape around it. Miloli'i means 'fine twist,' and historically the village was known for skilled sennit twisters, who used coconut-husk fibers to make fine cord and highly valued fishnets. Villagers here still live close to the sea, and many continue to make a living from it.

Privacy is paramount in these parts, but curious tourists are treated well – as long as they act like courteous guests. Just bear in mind the citizens of Miloli'i have made a conscious decision to reject tourism development in their backyards.

◉ Sights

★ **Honomalino Beach**   BEACH
The top sight in Miloli'i is about a mile's walk south of the town itself. Honomalino Bay is simply gorgeous; with sand the color of all Big Island beaches crushed into one – green,

gold, tawny and black – this beach also has gentle swimming and reef snorkeling. Look for the marked public path beginning just beyond Miloli'i's public basketball courts by the yellow church and up the rocks.

When in doubt, keep to the right fork along the trail. Respect all private property and *kapu* (no trespassing) signs.

Miloli'i Beach Park   BEACH
(off Milolii Rd; ☺ sunrise-sunset; P ☃) / This county beach park is pocked with tide pools. On weekends in particular, locals are pretty protective of this park, and facilities are limited to restrooms and picnic tables. Camping along the rocky shore is allowed with an advance county permit.

ℹ Getting There & Away

The turnoff to Miloli'i is just south of Mile 89 on Hwy 11; the village is 5 miles down a steep, winding, single-lane road that cuts across a 1926 lava flow. There is no public transportation down to the village.

NORTH KONA COAST

If you thought the Big Island was all jungle mountains and white sand beaches, the severe North Kona Coast and its beige deserts and black-and-rust lava fields will come as a shock. Yet always, at the edge of your eyesight, is the bright blue Pacific, while bits of green are sprinkled like jade flecks amid the dry. Turn off the Queen Ka'ahumanu Hwy and make your way across the eerie lava fields to snorkel with sea turtles, bask on almost deserted black-sand beaches and catch an iconic Kona sunset. On clear days, gaze *mauka* at panoramas of Mauna Kea and Mauna Loa volcanoes, both often snow-dusted in winter, and in the foreground between the two, Mt Hualalai.

North Kona technically runs 33 miles along Queen Ka'ahumanu Hwy (Hwy 19) from Kailua-Kona up the Kona Coast to Kawaihae. Honokohau Harbor is an easy 2-mile drive from downtown Kailua.

ℹ Getting There & Away

The Hele-On Bus (www.heleonbus.org) runs at least one daily line out to the resorts at Kohala that pass through North Kona. Otherwise, North Kona is an easy drive north of Kailua-Kona; just be aware of heavy traffic conditions around the airport during rush hour (7am to 9am and 3:30pm to 6pm). You can also cycle out here

(bring water); this is one of the few areas of the Belt Rd with a wide shoulder. Note that mile markers *decrease* as you head north.

Honokohau Harbor

Almost all of Kona's catch comes in at this harbor, about 2 miles north of downtown Kailua-Kona, including granders (fish weighing over 1000lb). Most fishing charters, dive boats and snorkeling and whale-watching cruises booked out of Kailua-Kona depart from here.

◉ Sights

The harbor provides public access to Honokohau Beach inside Kaloko-Honokohau National Historical Park. Park at the end of the lot and you should see signs pointing toward the beach; it's about a 10-minute walk.

★**Honokohau Beach**   BEACH
(Map p120; ☺ daylight hours; ⊞) / At this beautiful hook-shaped beach with a mix of black lava, white coral and wave-tossed shells, the water is usually too cloudy for snorkeling, but just standing on shore you'll see *honu*. You may spot more *honu* munching on *limu* (seaweed) around the ancient 'Ai'opio fishtrap, bordered by a Hawaiian heiau at the beach's southern end. Inland are anchialine ponds – pools of brackish water that make unique habitats for marine and plant life.

To get here, turn right into the first parking lot at Honokohau Harbor (look for the small public coastal access sign). Near the end of the road is the signposted trailhead; a five-minute walk on a well-beaten path leads to the beach. You could also take the more scenic, if longer, route by hiking to the beach along the 0.75-mile Ala Hele Iki Trail from the visitor center.

Kaloko-Honokohau National Historical Park   PARK
(Map p120; ☎ office 808-329-6881, visitor center 808-326-9057; www.nps.gov/kaho; off Hwy 19; ☺ visitor center 8:30am-4pm, park 24hr; P)
/ FREE Just north of Honokohau Harbor, on the ocean side of Hwy 19, this 1160-acre national park may be the Kona Coast's most underappreciated ancient Hawaiian site. Hidden among lava fields lies evidence of the innovations that allowed Hawaiians to thrive in this hostile landscape: fish traps, lava planters used to grow taro and other staples, plus the *ahupua'a* (land division)

North Kona Coast

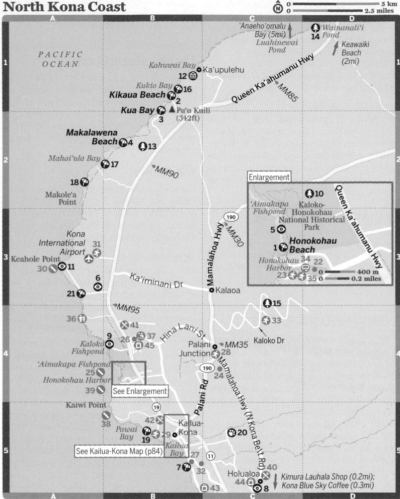

between Kaloko and Honokohau that gives the park its name. There are also heiau, burial caves and petroglyphs.

Despite the seemingly endless expanse of lava rock and unbearable midday heat, this is a good place to explore. Go in the early morning, late afternoon or when skies are overcast. *Kokua* (please) remember not to climb on, move, alter or deface any rock structures. Take special care not to disturb the endangered *honu*, who haul out here to rest, feed and bask in the sun – it's illegal to approach them closer than 20ft away on land, or 50yd in the water.

The park's main entrance is off Hwy 19 between Miles 96 and 97, where there's a parking lot and a small but informative ranger-staffed visitor center.

Kona Cloud Forest
Sanctuary   FOREST
(Map p120; ☎808-325-6440; www.konacloud forest.com; [P]) ✎ Above 3000ft on the slopes of Mt Hualalai, the Kaloko Mauka subdivision is the home of this spectacular 70-acre sanctuary. It's not just any forest – a cloud forest is a moist woodland where mist and fog are constants. The sanctuary is a lush ha-

North Kona Coast

ven for native plants and birds, and thanks to a consistent carpet of gray-green fog, it always feels as mysterious as it is beautiful.

Visits are by guided tour only; contact KapohoKine Adventures (p208) or Hawaiian Walkways (p91) to organize one.

The forest also contains demonstration gardens of non-native species, including more than 100 varieties of bamboo, which local experts study for their viability for use. Sustainable-agriculture types and horticulturists won't want to miss a visit to this well-kept Kona secret most locals don't even know about.

Kaloko Fishpond   HISTORIC SITE
(Map p120; www.nps.gov/kaho) ✦ At the northern end of Kaloko-Honokohau National Historical Park, this fishpond is especially fascinating because its massive rock retaining wall is being completely rebuilt in the traditional way – dry stacking, with no mortar or shaping of the rocks – so it can once again be fished in the traditional way. Some speculate that the bones of Kamehameha the Great were secretly buried in a cave nearby.

From the park's visitor center, drive north on Hwy 19 until you reach a separate gated entrance at Ala Kaloko Rd. Alternatively, it's about a 1-mile hike north from the visitor center along the coastal Ala Kahakai National Historic Trail (p127), a restored ancient Hawaiian footpath.

'Aimakapa Fishpond
HISTORIC SITE

(Map p120; www.nps.gov/kaho) *✦* In the southern section of Kaloko-Honokohau National Historical Park, 'Aimakapa is the largest fishpond on the Kona Coast. It's home to *ae'o* (Hawaiian black-necked stilt) and *'alae kea* (Hawaiian coot), both of which are endangered native waterbirds. Nearby look for the ancient remains of a *holua* (lava-sledding course).

🏃 Activities

Scads of fishing charters leave from Honokohau Harbor. If you're just after the money shot, you can watch the boats as they pull up and weigh their haul at around 11:30am and 3:30pm. Entering the harbor area, take the first right, park near the gas station and walk toward the dock behind Bite Me Fish Market Bar & Grill.

Plenty Pupule
KAYAKING

(Map p120; ☎808-880-1400; www.plentypupule. com; 73-4976 Kamanu St, Kaloko Industrial Park; kayak rental per day s/d $25/38, tours $80-250; ⏱10am-5:30pm Mon-Fri, 10am-5pm Sat) One of the island's top outfitters for adventure kayaking, these folks can recommend the best put-ins and snorkel spots, customize tours, teach you to kayak surf or take you kayak sailing, the latter particularly memorable during winter whale-watching season.

Charter Desk
FISHING

(Map p120; ☎888-566-2487, 808-326-1800; www.charterdesk.com; Honokohau Marina; ⏱6am-6pm) Reputable agency that can match you with over 60 boats.

Diving

From Honokohau Harbor south to Kailua Bay is a marine-life conservation district, accessible only by boat. This stretch of coast is littered with dive sites, including **Turtle Pinnacle** (Map p120), a premier turtle-spotting site straight out from the harbor. Northbound toward the airport is **Garden Eel Cove** (Map p120), aka 'Manta Heaven.'

Another good diving spot is off **Kaiwi Point** (Map p120), south of Honokohau Harbor, where sea turtles, large fish and huge eagle rays swim around some respectable drop-offs. Nearby is **Suck 'Em Up** (Map p120), a couple of lava tubes you can swim into, letting the swell pull you through.

🎓 Courses

FBI Surf School
SURFING

(Map p120; ☎808-557-7089; www.fbisurf school.com; 74-4966 Mamalahoa Hwy; group/semi-private/private per person $99/125/165) While the name implies you'll be hitting the waves with Mulder and Scully while wearing a trenchcoat, FBI actually stands for 'From Big Island.' This friendly outfit is run by Ossian (Ocean), a big surf dude who's a beloved local instructor. While FBI's office is in Holualoa, lessons are at Ali'i Dr or Kaloko-Honokohau National Historical Park. Call in advance to book.

👉 Tours

Dan McSweeney's Whale Watch
WHALE-WATCHING

(Map p120; ☎888-942-5376; www.ilovewhales. com; 2½-hr cruise adult/child 2yr $110/99; ♿) *✦* Captain Dan McSweeney is a nice, patient guy who genuinely loves the sea and marine biology – just the sort of tour leader you'd want. His winter excursions focus on humpback whale sightings, marine conservation and education, but several other species of whales and dolphins can be seen in Kona waters year-round. Hydrophones allow passengers to listen in on whale songs.

Hawaii Forest & Trail
TOURS

(Map p120; ☎808-331-8505; www.hawaii-forest. com; 73-5593 A Olowalu St; tours from $169) *✦* This multi-award-winning outfitter caters to active travelers who want to delve into the Big Island's greenest depths. From the always popular Mauna Kea summit and stargazing van tours, to hikes that run by volcanic lava, to guided bird-watching hikes in Hakalau Forest National Wildlife Refuge, you won't regret an adventure with these expert naturalists and eco-sustainability stewards.

Mountain Thunder Coffee Plantation
FARM

(Map p120; ☎tours 808-325-2136; www.mountain thunder.com; 73-1944 Hao St; 20min tour free, 3hr VIP tour adult/child under 6yr from $135/free; ⏱tours hourly 10am-4pm, VIP tours 10am Mon-Fri) *✦* This award-winning farm lies upland in lush Kaloko Mauka, a 20-minute drive from downtown Kailua-Kona or Holualoa village. VIP tours (call to reserve at least one day in advance) give you a more in-depth look at Kona coffee, and let you roast half a pound of beans to take home. It

OFF THE BEATEN TRACK

KIHOLO BAY

With its pristine turquoise waters and shoreline fringed with coconut trees, **Kiholo Bay** (Map p120; www.hawaiistateparks.org; off Hwy 19; ⊙7am-7pm Apr-Aug, to 6pm Sep-Mar; P⛺) ⚡ is yet another off-the-beaten-track Big Island beauty. It's more of a series of beaches than one contiguous stretch of sand, and it's relatively unvisited.

The main beach (near the parking lot) is pebbly and swimming is fine when seas are calm. Follow a trail south (left if facing the water) over the lava to find secluded pockets of fine black sand and, further south, a coconut grove surrounding **Luahinewai**, a pretty spring-fed pool.

Walking north at low tide reveals tide pools that are popular feeding and napping grounds for sea turtles and offer plenty of snorkeling possibilities. Inland near the end of the gravel path is a lava tube/Queen's Bath filled with clear freshwater; adventurous swimmers can check it out. Rumor has it other tubes in the area are some of the longest in the island. Lots of folks stop here to wash off salt water, but please note there is an actual ecosystem within the pond, and coming in while wearing suncreen can harm this environment. Just past the Queen's Bath is a sandy patch with a keiki pool perfect for the little ones.

Keep going north. You'll pass a gargantuan private estate with a yellow mansion and tennis courts, and then a huge Balinese house. This estate was built in Indonesia, then taken apart and reassembled here. Keep a respectful distance from this private residence, then continue to the north end of Kiholo.

You'll see more black sand fronted by smooth *pahoehoe* (lava) rocks. Follow a circular bay, crossing a bridge over a fishpond, and you'll come to **Wainanali'i Pond**, also known as the Blue Lagoon (Brooke Shields was absent when we visited). Green sea turtles love this spot; on our last visit we saw no less than 10 sunbathing on the sand. You may see them swimming around if you want to snorkel, although the presence of freshwater stream outflow clouds underwater visibility. Remember to stay at least 50yd from all sea turtles in the water and 20ft on land. The beach here is pebbly black sand – not great for sunbathing or walking, but pretty unbeatable for natural beauty.

To get to Kiholo, turn seaward on the unmarked, graded gravel road between Miles 82 and 83. Follow the road for a mile, taking the left-hand fork, and park in the parking lot. An alternate way in, which we prefer for the scenery, is hiking from a trailhead located by a small, rocky parking lot just north of Mile 81. Hike along the trail at the bottom of the lot for 20 to 30 minutes (bring water), and say hi to the goats. You'll pop out just north of the Balinese house. Kiholo is a popular camping spot for locals, and you can join them with a permit from Hawaii state parks; just be aware that there's no potable water. Watch out for kiawe thorns!

also offers small tours of an organic coffee farm and mill ($65).

Ocean Eco Tours   SNORKELING
(Map p120; ☎808-324-7873, 808-331-2121; www.oceanecotours.com; 74-425 Kealakehe Pkwy; snorkel/dive boat trip from $99/150, group/private surfing lesson $95/150) Combine sport and history with surfing lessons conducted within the boundaries of Kaloko-Honokohau National Historical Park. This outfit also guides snorkeling and scuba trips along the coast, including night dives with manta rays. Stop by the small shop at the harbor to rent surfboards, boogie boards and snorkel or scuba gear.

Kamanu Charters   CRUISE
(Map p120; ☎808-329-2021; www.kamanu.com; manta ray snorkel $95) Offers a great slate of watery activities, including manta ray snorkeling on both a catamaran and a zodiac, sunset cruises, and humpback whale-watching in the winter. Check out trips to Pawai Bay, a snorkeling wonderland that is off the tourist track. Kamanu specializes in catering to first-time snorkelers and nonswimmers.

Captain Zodiac   SNORKELING
(Map p120; ☎808-329-3199; www.captainzodiac.com; 74-425 Kealakehe Pkwy; snorkel cruise adult/child 4-12yr from $89/59) In business with a

jaunty pirate theme since 1974, Captain Zodiac makes daily trips down the coast to sites like Kealakekua Bay in 24ft-long rigid-hull inflatable rafts that each carry up to 16 passengers.

✗ Eating

Pine Tree Cafe
HAWAIIAN $

(Map p120; ☑ 808-327-1234; 73-4038 Hulikoa Dr; mains $9-13; ☉ 6am-8pm Mon-Sat, from 6:30am Sun; P ✷ ⬆) If some freak climatic event ever brought winter hibernation to the Big Island, you could survive the lean season by storing the calories away after a single plate lunch at this institution. The food here – short ribs, garlic fried chicken, *loco moco* etc – is both delicious and served in simply awe-inspiring portions.

🍷 Drinking & Nightlife

Kona Mountain Coffee
CAFE

(Map p120; ☑ 808-329-5005; www.konamountain coffee.com; 73-4038 Hukiloa Dr; ☉ 7am-6pm Mon-Fri, 8am-5pm Sat & Sun) Just over 2 miles north of the harbor turnoff along Hwy 19, this farm-grown coffee roaster's retail shop and coffee bar also stocks baked goodies and snacks. It's a quick stop on the way to the airport, or a nice way to pack in some caffeinated rocket fuel as you drive along the Belt Rd.

🛍 Shopping

Kailua Candy Company
FOOD

(Map p120; ☑ 808-329-2522, 800-622-2462; https://kailuacandy.com; 73-5612 Kauhola St, Kaloko Industrial Park; ☉ 9am-5pm Mon-Sat) A detour to this chocolate factory shop is mandatory for every sweet tooth. Savor free samples of Mauna Kea 'snowballs' (white chocolate with shredded coconut), Kona coffee swirls, Hawaiian 'turtles' and tropically flavored truffles. To get here, turn *mauka* onto Hina Lani St off Hwy 19, then right on Kamanu St.

ℹ Getting There & Away

To reach the harbor, turn *makai* on Kealakehe Pkwy, just north of Mile 98 on Hwy 19.

Keahole Point

Funny place, Keahole Point. Just offshore, the seafloor drops abruptly, providing a continuous supply of both cold water from 2000ft depths and warm surface water. These are ideal conditions for ocean thermal-energy conversion (OTEC), deep sea water extraction and aquaculture. All of this is happening here, plus there's a beach and one of the island's best surf breaks.

Also nearby is Kona International Airport, so likely as not, you'll end up passing here at some point, unless you've decided to just move to the Big Island, in which case: congratulations! Do you have a spare room?

◉ Sights

Kanaloa Octopus Farm
AQUARIUM

(Map p120; ☑ 818-514-5997; www.kanaloaoctopus. com; off Makako Bay Dr; tours $20; ☉ tours 10am & 2pm; P) ✐ If you're hoping to see hayseeds in overalls teaching cephalopods how to drive tractors (we entertained the fantasy), the world's only octopus farm may miss the mark, but if you're interested in both sustainable aquaculture and the general biology (and dare we say, psychology) of one of the world's most fascinating creatures, this spot is pretty awesome.

Kampachi Farms
FARM

(Map p120; www.kampachifarm.com; HOST Park; P) ✐ The aquaculture gurus responsible for yellowfin tuna seen on haute island restaurant menus. Tours can be organized through Hawaii Ocean Science & Technology Park.

Hawaii Ocean Science & Technology Park
NOTABLE BUILDING

(HOST Park; Map p120; ☑ 808-327-9585; www. nelha.hawaii.gov; 73-4660 Queen Ka'ahumanu Hwy; lecture & tour adult/child under 9yr $10/free, conservation & aquaculture tour adult/child under 9yr $32/free; P) ✐ That funny-looking building with the gigantic solar panels is the Natural Energy Laboratory of Hawaii Authority (NELHA). This 'zero-net energy facility' was voted one of the USA's 10 greenest buildings in 2007. Learn about OTEC and research into alternative and renewable-energy technologies at NELHA's public presentations (on Monday). Come on Wednesday and Friday for tours of sustainable aquaculture facilities like Kampachi Farms and Big Island Abalone, or Tuesday and Thursday for tours of Ke Kai Ola and Kanaloa Octopus Farm. Reservations required.

The turnoff is just over a mile south of Kona International Airport, between Miles 94 and 95.

Wawaloli (OTEC) Beach
BEACH
(Map p120; Makako Bay Dr; ☉ sunrise-sunset; P 🚻) At the *makai* end of the access road to the Natural Energy Laboratory of Hawaii Authority, this quiet locals' beach is perfectly positioned for sunsets – never mind the jets flying overhead. At high tide, the protected tide pools along the lava-rock coastline overflow; at other times, the same pools (especially the more southerly one) are a perfect spot for teaching kids to swim. Bring a picnic and the family. Facilities include restrooms and outdoor showers.

Ocean Rider Seahorse Farm
FARM
(Map p120; ☎ 808-329-6840; www.seahorse. com; 73-4388 Ilikai Pl; tours adult/child 4-9yr $42/32; ☉ 9:30am-3:30pm Mon-Fri; P 🚻) 🅿 Ocean Rider sustainably raises seahorses for research and aquariums, thus avoiding the perils of catching these creatures in the wild. Biologist-led tours will give you as good a grounding in the seahorse as you'll ever get – reserve in advance.

🏃 Activities

Pine Trees
SURFING
(Map p120) Pine Trees is one of west Hawai'i's best surfing breaks. The break stretches along a beach that is rocky enough to make swimming difficult. The final bay gets the most consistent yet forgiving waves. An incoming midtide is favorable, but as the swell picks up in winter these breaks often close out.

Get friendly with local regulars if you want in on the action – this hot spot draws crowds, especially on weekends. Where the access road to NELHA veers to the right, look left for a rutted dirt road leading about 2 miles further south. You'll need a high-clearance 4WD to make it, or you can walk, but it's hot. The access road gates are locked between 8pm and 6am.

Ke Kai Ola
WILDLIFE
(Marine Mammal Center; Map p120; ☎ 808-987-0765; www.marinemammalcenter.org) *Ke Kai Ola* means 'the healing sea' – an appropriate name for this wildlife hospital which cares for the endangered Hawaiian monk seal. Tours can be arranged through the Hawaii Ocean Science & Technology Park.

👉 Tours

Big Island Abalone
AQUARIUM
(Map p120; ☎ 808-334-0034; www.bigisland abalone.com; 73-357 Makako Bay Dr; adult/child $12/free) 🅿 Abalone – otherwise known as

sea snails – have delicious flesh and gorgeous shells, and as such, this outfit is trying to figure out a sustainable way of raising and harvesting them. Take a tour of this facility (offered in English and Japanese) to see responsible aquaculture in action.

❶ Getting There & Away

Keahole is about 7 miles north of Kailua-Kona and (depending where you're staying) 20 to 25 miles south of the Kohala resorts; most people pass right by it on their way to the airport or Kona town. Note that traffic tends to jam at the airport intersection during rush hour (7am to 9am and 3:30pm to 6pm). Hele-On buses only stop by once around 8:30am.

Ka'upulehu

Once a thriving fishing village among many dotting this length of coast, Ka'upulehu was wiped out by the 1946 tsunami and abandoned until the Kona Village Resort opened here in 1965. The resort closed in 2011 after more tsunami damage caused by the massive earthquake in Japan, and is currently slated to reopen in 2019. The luxurious Four Seasons Resort Hualalai remains open and, by law, these and other resorts must provide public coastal access, meaning you can enjoy some fine beaches without the resort price tag.

◉ Sights

Ka'upulehu Cultural Center
GALLERY
(Map p120; ☎ 808-325-8000; www.fourseasons. com/hualalai; 72-100 Ka'upulehu Dr, Four Seasons Resort Hualalai; ☉ 8:30am-4pm Mon-Fri; P) 🆓 Inside the Four Season's Hawaiian cultural center is a small, museum-quality exhibit organized around a collection of 11 original paintings by Herb Kawainui Kane. Each painting is accompanied by a hands-on exhibit about traditional Hawaiian culture: shake an *'uli'uli* (feathered hula rattle), test the heft of a *kapa* (bark-cloth) beater or examine stone adze heads. On-site Hawaiian cultural practitioners actively link the present with the past by teaching classes (usually reserved for resort guests only) and giving impromptu Hawaiian arts-and-crafts demonstrations.

At the Four Seasons security guardhouse, tell them you're visiting the cultural center. Drive all the way downhill to the resort's self-parking lot, from where it's a short walk to the center.

KAILUA-KONA & THE KONA COAST KA'UPULEHU

Beaches

★ Kua Bay
BEACH

(Manini'owali Beach; Map p120; www.hawaii
stateparks.org; ⊘8am-7pm; P⚹) ◐ This
crescent-shaped white-sand beach is
fronted by sparkling turquoise waters that offer first-rate swimming and
bodyboarding, and good snorkeling on the
north side of the bay (by the large rock outcroppings) when waters are calm. A paved
road leads right up to it, and thus the beach,
also known as Manini'owali, draws major
crowds, especially on weekends. Arrive late
and cars will be parked half a mile up the
road. The parking area has bathrooms and
showers.

To get here, take the paved road between
Miles 88 and 89 (north of the main Kekaha
Kai entrance). Hikers will enjoy the scenic
coastal trail from here to Kukio Beach.

★ Makalawena Beach
BEACH

(Map p120) If what you're after is an almost
deserted, postcard-perfect scoop of soft,
white-sand beach cupping brilliant blue-
green waters (got your attention?), head
to 'Maks.' Although popular, this string of
idyllic coves absorbs crowds so well you'll
still feel like you've found paradise. The
northernmost cove is sandier and gentler,
while the southernmost cove is (illegally) a
naked sunbathing spot. Swimming is splen-
did, but beware of rough surf and rocks in
the water. Bodyboarding and snorkeling are
more possibilities.

Practice aloha during your visit by pack-
ing out all trash and respecting the privacy
of others. For locals, this is an unofficial
camping and fishing getaway, and the growing popularity of these beaches among out-
siders is contentious for some. Always give
endangered sea turtles a wide berth – it's
illegal to approach them closer than 20ft on
land or 50yd in the water.

Getting to Makalawena requires extra
effort. Take the unpaved Kekaha Kai (Kona
Coast) State Park access road (4WD recommended, although many locals drive it in a
standard passenger car), off Hwy 19 between
Miles 90 and 91. Less than 1.5 miles later, at
the road junction before the parking lot for
Mahai'ula Beach, turn right. Park on the
road shoulder near the cables restricting
vehicle access to a service road, then walk
north for 30 minutes across the lava flow
and sand dunes to the beach, either following the service road or a much rougher footpath over crunchy 'a'a lava.

Kekaha Kai State Park
PARK

(Kona Coast State Park; Map p120; www.hawaii
stateparks.org; ⊘8am-7pm; P) ◐ The gorgeous beaches of Kekaha Kai are all the
more memorable for being tucked on the
far side of a vast desert of unforgiving black
lava. This 1600-acre park has four beaches,
only one of which has paved access. The others are best approached with a 4WD or on
foot; if you hike, bring good shoes, food and
water. It can be brutally hot, and once you
reach the sand you'll want to stay till the last
drop of sunlight.

★ Kikaua Beach
BEACH

(Map p120; off MM 87, Hwy 19; P⚹) Though
obviously artificial (a thin layer of sand laid
over concrete is hard on the feet), Kikaua
Beach is also effortlessly beautiful. Palm
trees do the whole sway in the breeze thing,
the sand is white, and the completely protected cove that makes up the main swimming area is perfect for teaching *keiki* to
swim and snorkel. As a bonus, sea turtles
frequently congregate nearby. Facilities
include restrooms, outdoor showers and
drinking water.

Public beach access is through a private
country club and residential development.
It's limited to 28 cars per day, so it never
feels that crowded. To get here, turn *makai*
onto Kuki'o Nui Rd near Mile 87 on Hwy
19. Drive to the security guardhouse and request a parking pass and directions to the
beach.

Mahai'ula Beach
BEACH

(Map p120; P) Kekaha Kai (Kona Coast)
State Park's largest beach has salt-and-
pepper sand, rocky tide pools, shaded picnic tables and pit toilets. Swimming usually
isn't good, but during big winter swells,
there's plenty of surfing. Walk a few minutes
north along the coast to find a second, less
rocky beach with soft tawny sands (nicknamed Magoon's), perfect for sunbathing
and swimming. Access to Mahai'ula is via a
chunky lava road between Miles 90 and 91
on Hwy 19.

Although a 4WD is recommended, many
locals drive the unpaved beach access road
in a standard passenger car. If you want to
attempt this, drive *very* carefully. Alternatively, you could traverse the 1.5 miles on
foot from Hwy 19. Park at an improvised lot
just inland from the highway and start walking or thumb it – drivers may take pity on
your sun-beaten head and give you a lift. The

end of this road is the junction for Makalawena and Makole'a Beaches.

Makole'a Beach   BEACH

(Map p120) Amazingly, this secluded black-sand beach belongs to Kekaha Kai (Kona Coast) State Park. Although there's no shade and it's too rocky for swimming, its natural beauty rewards those who make the effort to visit (which is usually some local fishing-folk). To reach this small, dark treasure on foot, head south along Mahai'ula Beach and either follow the road or the coastline while making toward a lone tree.

With a 4WD, turn left at the road junction by Mahai'ula Beach, drive south for about 1000yd until you reach a path marked by white coral, then get out and hoof it as the lava becomes too rough.

Kukio Beach   BEACH

(Map p120; ▣) The scalloped, palm-fringed coves of Kukio Bay are officially part of the Four Seasons Resort Hualalai. Here the sand is soft, the swimming is good (even for kids) and there's a paved trail leading north along the rocky coastline to another beach. Facilities include restrooms, outdoor showers and drinking water.

To drive here, turn onto Ka'upulehu Rd (unsigned) between Miles 86 and 87 on Hwy 19. Drive straight ahead to the Four Seasons security guardhouse and request a beach parking pass. The 50-car beach parking lot almost never fills up.

Keawaiki Beach   BEACH

Keawaiki is as isolated as Big Island beaches get, mainly because the quickest way here is via a 15 to 20 minute walk over an 'a'a lava trail that looks like it was plucked from Dante Alighieri's darkest dreams. Your reward for getting here: a rocky, black-sand beach overlooked by a lone palm tree, and the blue ocean – which can be quite rough, so be careful if you swim. The path begins at a parking pull-off near Mile 79.

🏃 Activities

Ala Kahakai National
Historic Trail   HIKING

(Map p136; www.nps.gov/alka) 🖉 Diehard sun worshippers access South Kohala's signature beaches via a 6-mile stretch of the 175-mile Ala Kahakai National Historic Trail. You'll

also pass pristine shoreline and natural anchialine ponds (pools which provided the ancients with drinking water).

From the north, start at the southern end of Spencer Beach Park, where you'll pass thick kiawe groves until you reach Mau'u-mae Beach and eventually the Mauna Kea Resort Area, including the renowned golf course. After you navigate the Hapuna Beach, the trail continues down to Beach 69. The whole hike, especially the last leg, is scorching. Of course, you can turn back at any point, and can start at any point along the way.

🍴 Eating

Beach Tree   CALIFORNIAN $$$

(Map p120; ☑ 808-325-8000; www.fourseasons.com/hualalai; 72-100 Ka'upulehu Dr, Four Seasons Resort Hualalai; mains lunch $14-24, dinner $16-39; ☉ 11:30am-8:30pm; ▣) Do you know what's better than enjoying *pupu* or one of the island's best burgers on the breezy, beachside porch of the Beach Tree on a perfect Hawaiian day? Not much. Thin-crust brick-oven pizzas come with toothsome toppings and sit alongside a variety of surf-and-turf delights, including a fierce paella. Also, you can eat barefoot. Bonus!

'ULU Ocean Grill
+ Sushi Lounge   HAWAII REGIONAL $$$

(Map p120; ☑ 808-325-8000; www.uluoceangrill.com; 72-100 Ka'upulehu Dr, Four Seasons Resort Hualalai; mains $24-52, tasting menu from $65; ☉ restaurant 6:30-11am & 5:30-9pm, sushi lounge 5:30-10pm; ℗) 🖉 *'Ulu* means 'breadfruit,' and this sustainably minded restaurant is all about locally sourced produce, seafood and meat – some 75% of its dishes are made with Hawai'i-grown ingredients. The menu mixes tastes from *makai* to *mauka*: curried Kona mussels, kiawe-smoked potatoes and wild boar glazed with *liliko'i*. That said, the food doesn't always live up to the hype – or the sky-high prices.

ℹ️ Getting There & Away

Ka'upulehu is located about 15 miles north of downtown Kaliua-Kona via Hwy 19. Look for signs to the Four Seasons Resort Hualalai and turn toward the ocean. You'll have to clear security to enter the resort; feel free to let the guards at the gate know you're just visiting.

Kohala & Waimea

🔊 808

Best Places to Eat

➡ Kohala Burger & Taco (p148)

➡ Merriman's (p161)

➡ Sushi Rock (p151)

➡ Anuenue (p148)

➡ Bamboo (p151)

Best Activities with Kids

➡ Horseback riding in Waimea (p159) or North Kohala (p155)

➡ Splashing around at Spencer Beach Park (p147)

➡ Ziplining in and around the Kohala canopy (p149)

➡ Exploring the Puako Tide Pools (p145)

Why Go?

The Kohala coast is a land of long deserts bending to bleached white-sand beaches, before giving way to the fuzzy grass hills of cattle country and the thick jungles of the north coast. Out here the wind howls a gale, the sun shines like a broiler, and a land of wild extremes waits to be discovered.

South Kohala is the archetypal sun-and-sea resort mecca. From Waikoloa to Kawaihae, Hawaiian history is preserved in ancient trails, heiau (temples), fishponds and petroglyphs – although all you'll see from the highway is stark lava desert and the edges of resort golf courses.

In counterpoint to the south's desert climate and man-made attractions, North Kohala is lushly otherworldly, with magnificent pastureland, quaint plantation towns and Pololu Valley's cascading cliffs. It proudly remains rural with nary a high-rise in sight. Waimea, a ranch town in between, is a central stop for cross-island travelers.

When to Go

Jun Celebrate the life of King Kamehameha with a North Kohala-style parade from Hawi to Kapa'au.

Feb In Waimea, the Cherry Blossom Heritage Festival is a must-see cultural event.

Sep The Taste of the Hawaiian Range brings out the best of local produce and livestock.

Kohala & Waimea Highlights

1 Hawi (p149) Pottering around this quirky little town.

2 Kohala Mountain Road (p155) Driving over one of the state's most beautiful roads.

3 Mo'okini Heiau (p153) Making the trek to this ancient Hawaiian temple.

4 Hapuna Beach (p144) This classically gorgeous beach does wonders for the Instagram feed.

5 Mahukona (p153) A gorgeous snorkeling spot that's off the beaten track.

6 Mau'umae Beach (p146) Another picture-perfect Kohala beach? Why not.

7 Pu'ukohola Heiau (p148) Wandering around

the base of this enormous Hawaiian temple.

8 Pololu Valley (p156) Sheer cliffs plunge into this Edenic green sanctuary.

9 Beach 69 (p144) Guess what? We're not done with Kohala's gorgeous beaches.

10 Flumin' Kohala (p151) Exploring a historic irrigation canal.

HIKING & CYCLING AROUND KOHALA & WAIMEA

CYCLING TOUR: HAWI TO POLOLU VALLEY LOOKOUT

START HAWI
END POLOLU VALLEY LOOKOUT
LENGTH 8 MILES, 3 HOURS

The trip from Hawi to the Pololu Valley takes you through verdant forests, over hills and into narrow gullies, and in the process through the settled communities of modern North Kohala all the way to a seminal ancient Hawaiian site, now a carved pocket of utterly Edenic nature.

Start in Hawi town, and fuel yourself up at one of this little village's excellent restaurants – you can grab a sushi lunch at **Sushi Rock** (p151), or a heart vegetarian meal at **Sweet Potato Kitchen** (p151). Or ride a mile and a half east to the **Takata Store** (p151), a grocery store that stocks plenty of organic goodies. But don't leave Hawi without checking out one of its plethora of local galleries and artisan shops – head to **Elements** (p152) for jewelry or **Kohala Mountain Gallery** (p152) for local art.

It's about 2.5 miles from Hawi to Kapa'au – you'll cycle past the **statue of Kamehameha** (p154), who grew up on this windy coast and once carried the **Kamehameha Rock** (p153; further along the road) as a sign of his great strength.

As you leave Kapa'au, the road narrows and the shoulders thin out, to the point of vanishing as you get closer to Pololu (you'll even have to cross a one-lane bridge at one point). Be aware of wind conditions; they can make cycling dangerous.

The roads rise and fall rapidly; the **Pololu Valley Lookout**, scalloped out of the Kohala Mountains like a green scar is your eventual reward. Enjoy the view, and consider a hike into the valley.

DESIGN PICS INC/ALAMY ©

Pololu Valley Trail

A journey across this region takes you through diverse landscapes and culture both ancient and modern. Whether you're strolling or pedaling, you'll finish with better-than-postcard views.

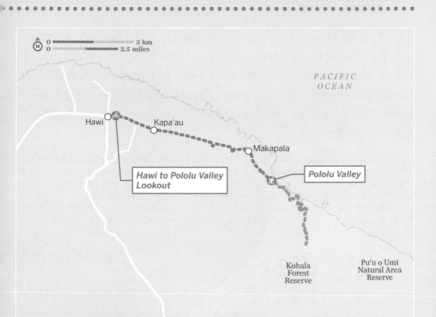

WALKING TOUR: POLOLU VALLEY

START POLOLU VALLEY LOOKOUT
END HONOKANE NUI LOOKOUT
LENGTH 3 MILES; 2–4 HOURS

There's a dramatic finality to the Pololu Valley. The word Pololu means 'long spear,' and that's a fitting appellation – the valley looks as if it were carved out of the jungle and mountains by a vengeful deity.

Follow the tourists and signs from the lookout to find the beginning of the trail. Note that even if you don't want to walk this path to its conclusion, you should really attempt at least the very start of this trail. The view into the valley from the Hwy 270 lookout is *much* improved after a couple of switchbacks.

The valley floor is located about a third of a mile below the beginning of the trailhead. The trees are lush on the way down, but they turn into alien jungle beings down here. You'll need to cross the (shallow) Pololu River where it flows into the sea.

Marvel at the beautiful beach but don't venture into the water – the currents around here are particularly dangerous. From here you'll walk on flat, verdant ground east into the valley; this short jaunt is about 0.4 miles long. Keep your eyes peeled for a faint, upward climbing trail that wends for just over a mile to the Honokane Nui Valley lookout. The view is as lovely as you might expect.

MAHUKONA TO KAPA'A WALKING TRAIL

Mahukona and Kapa'a Beach Parks are linked by a beautiful, little-known, 2-mile oceanside walking trail. From Kapa'a Beach Park, start by the old railway bed on the left, visible on the way in. From Mahukona Beach Park, go past the two-story brown metal building and park at the turnout on the right. Scoot left around the metal pipe gate to find the trail sign. Bring water and a hat and stay on the trail.

ROAD TRIP:
KOHALA MOUNTAIN ROAD

The Kohala Mountain Road is gorgeous, although some may scoff at the designation 'mountain.' Fair enough – maybe these are 'high hills.' Either way, most of this drive is at 2000– 3000ft of elevation. You're welcome to go from Waimea to Hawi, but we prefer the north–south version, as it saves the best views for last.

The road is well paved, two lanes wide and in very good condition. There isn't a ton of switchbacks, so even amateur mountain drivers shouldn't feel too nervous. The main hazards are speeders, who always seem to ride your tail in a giant pickup truck just as you're reaching a pretty area you want to slow down in, and the occasional wandering cow. Note that there aren't many pull-offs.

You can do this drive at any time of day. Early evening sunsets are beautiful, but

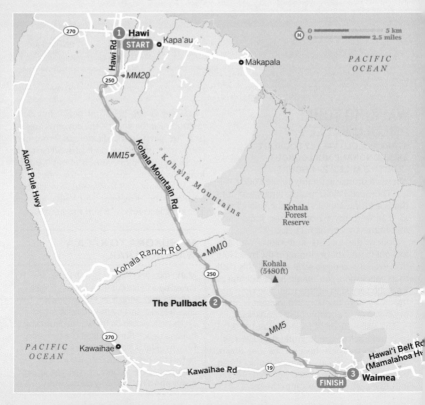

Start Hawi

End Waimea

Length 22 miles, 1 hour

ALVIS UPITIS/GETTY IMAGES ©

Kohala Mountains (p155)

it doesn't make sense to drive at night, as the scenery will be blacked out. Note that thick fog is sometimes an issue, so check the weather before you drive.

① Hawi

Start in Hawi. Grab some coffee and breakfast at the colorful **Kohala Coffee Mill** (p151) – it's never too early for their Tropical Dreams ice cream. Once you're sated turn onto Hawi Rd/Hwy 250 – other names for the Kohala Mountain Road. You'll immediately reach the space where the **Hawi Farmers Market** (p149) is held. If you're driving on a Saturday or Tuesday, this is your chance to pick up some provisions, listen to some live music or just enjoy the atmosphere.

The Drive > The Kohala Mountain Road initially climbs through dense forests, which start clearing into open pastureland after about 4 miles. From here on out you'll be driving through a mix of grassy upland pasture country and ironwood tunnels.

② The Pullback

As you proceed along, you'll pass the gates to various ranch properties and catch glimpses of the peaks of Hualalai, Mauna Kea and Mauna Loa. As the road starts sloping down toward Waimea, you'll come across an **official scenic pull-off point**. Park, take a picture, and make everyone jealous on social media.

The Drive > From here, it's a short hop on to Waimea.

③ Waimea

Once you reach Waimea, make a beeline for **Hawaiian Style Cafe** (p160). Whether your have a yearning for *loco moco* (rice, fried egg and hamburger patty topped with gravy or other condiments), pancakes or burgers, their portions will satisfy your calorie count for the next few months. Then browse local and international art at the **Isaacs Art Center** (p157) – you may find a painting of the perfect scenery you just traversed.

ⓘ Getting There & Away

Kohala lies north of Kailua-Kona; the big resorts are about 30 or so miles up the road, while Hawi and North Kohala are 55 miles away. Hwy 19 banks east just past Mauna Kea resort, where it goes on to Waimea. Hwy 270 splits from the belt road here and climbs north to North Kohala and Hawi, and eventually terminates at the Pololu Valley. The **Hele-On Bus** (☑ 808-961-8744; www. heleonbus.org; adult one-way $2, 10-ride ticket $15, monthly pass $60) runs past the resorts, while another Hele-On line connects to Hilo, but in general it's easiest to get around via your own car.

Hwy 250, one of the prettiest roads on the island, connects Hawi to Waimea.

SOUTH KOHALA

The Queen Ka'ahumanu Hwy (Hwy 19) cuts through stark fields of lava, but as you head toward the ocean, rolling emerald golf course slopes edge onto condo complexes and electric teal pools. This is the Gold Coast of the Big Island, and whatever your feelings are on resorts, this is where you'll find some of the area's best beaches.

Oddly enough, South Kohala also contains numerous ancient Hawaiian sights. This coast was more populated at the time of their creation than it is now, and the region is packed with village sites, heiau, fishponds, petroglyphs and historic trails – areas that are often preserved for visitors.

The waters off the coast in South Kohala are pristine and teeming with marine life – and they're relatively uncrowded. The reef drops off more gradually here than along the Kona Coast, so you might see sharks, dolphins, turtles and manta rays.

ⓘ Getting There & Away

The resorts and sights of South Kohala are located north of Kailua-Kona off of Hwy 19 – depending on which resort you're going to, they're located about 25 to 35 miles away from town.

The Pahala–South Kohala Hele-On bus line (www.heleonbus.org) plies this route three times a day Monday to Saturday, and once a day on Sundays.

Traffic jams around KOA airport during rush hours can eat up your travel time.

Waikoloa Resort Area

Among South Kohala's resort areas, the Waikoloa Beach Resort area is the most affordable and bustling. Its mega hotels and golf courses aren't as prestigious as those further up the coast, but it does offer two shopping malls and the lion's share of events. As at Mauna Lani further up the road, the management at Waikoloa has effectively and admirably integrated historic Hawaiian sites into the layout of the resort itself – whole series of fishponds, petroglyph preserves and ancient trails run adjacent to condo blocks and outdoor malls. Beyond this fascinating cultural heritage, the Waikoloa area includes one of the finest beaches on the Kohala coast.

Note that the Waikoloa Beach Resort is not Waikoloa Village, a residential community located further inland.

⊙ Sights

'Anaeho'omalu Beach Park　　　　　BEACH
(A Bay; Waikoloa Beach Dr; ⊙6am-8pm; 🚶) Don't worry about that tongue twister of an official name; everyone on the island calls this beach 'A Bay.' 'A plus' is another way of putting it: this beach boasts easy access, salt-and-pepper sand and calm waters that are well suited to windsurfing. Classically beautiful, it's backed by hundreds of palm trees and makes for fantastic sunset viewing. Drinking water, showers and restrooms are available. To get here, turn left off Waikoloa Beach Dr opposite the Kings' Shops.

The Waikoloa Beach Marriott fronts the beach's north end, but ancient fishponds add a buffer zone between the two. In that area, there's decent snorkeling directly in front of the sluice gate, where you'll find coral formations, a variety of fish and possibly sea turtles. Remember that, by law, you must remain at least 50yd away from turtles in the water.

Archaeologists have found evidence of human habitation dating back more than 1000 years. A short footpath with interpretive plaques starts near the showers.

Waikoloa Anchialine
Pond Preservation Area　　　　　LANDMARK
(WAPPA) 🏊 Here's your daily dose of science in a travel guidebook: anchialine ponds are coastal ponds that have no surface connection to the ocean, but that nonetheless rise and fall with the tides. A series of such ponds can be found within Waikoloa, where they are maintained and studied by the University of Hawaii. Have a peek at (but don't step in) the clear water to see mollusks, fish and other sea life.

The pond trail takes about five minutes to walk.

Ku'uali'i and
Kahapapa Fishponds ARCHAEOLOGICAL SITE

An entire ancient aquaculture system once formed an important backbone of Native Hawaiian foodways, and physical evidence of this system is located smack dab behind Anaeho'omalu Beach (side note: Anaeho'omalu means 'restricted mullet,' a reference to food stocked in the fishponds, and really, the best name for a beach ever). The two fishponds were well stocked with seasonal marine foodstuffs; stories say runners would deliver fresh fish to royalty by sprinting down the nearby Ala Kahakai trail.

Ala Kahakai NATIONAL PARK

(www.nps.gov/alka) A portion of Ala Kahakai (p127) – the King's Trail – winds through Waikoloa, offering a somewhat incongruous dose of ancient Hawaiian history and heritage within Waikoloa's pruned landscape and resort amenities. The trail is accessible via several points located along 'Anaeho'omalu Bay beach; note that sharp lava rocks start cropping up as the trail edges near the golf course. Any ruins you may spot along this area fall within protected federal lands.

Waikoloa
Petroglyph Preserve HISTORIC SITE

(Waikoloa Beach Dr) FREE This collection of petroglyphs carved in lava rock is so easy-access that it merits a stop, although the Puako Petroglyph Preserve (p140) further north is more spectacular and doesn't abut a shopping mall. Many petroglyphs date back to the 16th century; some are graphic (humans, birds, canoes) and others cryptic (dots, lines). Western influences appear in the form of horses and English initials. To get here, park at the Kings' Shops and walk for five minutes on the signposted path.

Free one-hour guided tours of the petroglyphs are offered most Thursdays and Fridays, starting at the mall.

🏃 Activities

You can book outdoor activities through companies that are either based here or have satellite offices within the resort area.

Hilton Waikoloa Village Pools SWIMMING

(☑808-886-1234; www.hiltonwaikoloavillage.com; 425 Waikoloa Beach Dr; nonguest pool pass up to 4 people $90; ☉ sunrise-sunset; ⋒) The chances are that the elaborate pools at this over-the-top resort will thrill your kids. They've got three enormous pools with waterfalls and water slides, plus an artificial beach and saltwater lagoon. All stuff that can be found in the wild, of course, but if your group numbers four, the fee *might* be worth a splash.

Waikoloa Beach & Kings' Courses GOLF

(☑808-886-7888; www.waikoloabeachgolf.com; 69-275 Waikoloa Beach Dr, Waikoloa Beach Marriott; greens fees $145) The Waikoloa Beach Marriott boasts two top golf courses: the coastal Beach course is known for its par-five 12th hole; the Kings' course is the more challenging and offers Scottish-style links. Tee off later in the day and pay less (11:30am/1pm/2pm $120/119/95). Carts are mandatory.

DON'T MISS

DON'T MISS: HAWAIIAN SACRED SITES

Ancient Hawaiians built a variety of heiau (temples) for different gods and different purposes: healing the sick, sharing the harvest, changing the weather, offering human sacrifice and succeeding in warfare.

While some were modest thatched structures, others were enormous stone edifices, which today exist in eroded ruins that only hint at their original grandeur. After Kamehameha II (Liholiho) abolished the *kapu* (taboo) system in 1819, many were destroyed or abandoned. But on the Big Island, two of the largest and best-preserved heiau remain: **Pu'ukohola Heiau** (p148) and **Mo'okini Luakini Heiau** (p153).

Luakini heiau, for human sacrifice, were always dedicated to Ku, the war god. Only Ku deserved the greatest gift, a human life, and only the highest chiefs could order it. An enemy slain in battle was an acceptable sacrifice. But the victim had to be a healthy man, never a woman, a child or an aged or deformed man.

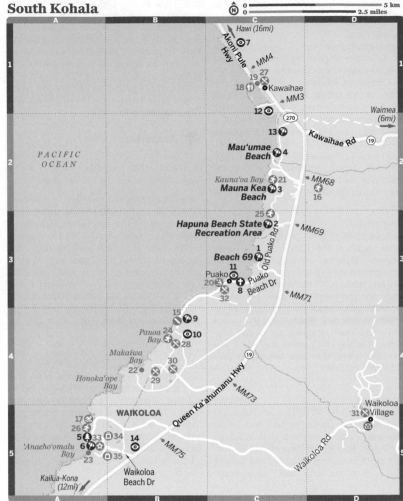

Tours

Ocean Sports OUTDOORS
(☎ 808-886-6666; www.hawaiioceansports.com;
69-275 Waikoloa Beach Dr; snorkeling adult/child
$147/73.50; ⊙ 7am-9:30pm) Ocean Sports
monopolizes the ocean-activity market in
South Kohala. Fortunately the company
is well run, if slightly steep in its pricing.
Cruises include whale-watching ($119)
and glass-bottom boat tours ($27) aboard
a 49-passenger catamaran. Departures are
from 'Anaeho'omalu Bay and Kawaihae
Harbor.

At 'Anaeho'omalu Beach Park and the
Hilton Waikoloa Village, this outfit also
rents beach equipment.

Festivals & Events

**A Taste of the
Hawaiian Range** FOOD & DRINK
(www.tasteofthehawaiianrange.com; Hilton Waikoloa Village; admission advance/door $40/60)
Celebrated Big Island chefs work magic with
local range-fed meats and local produce in
late September or early October. As of late,
there's been an effort the make the event

South Kohala

KOHALA & WAIMEA WAIKOLOA RESORT AREA

zero-waste, and themes of food sustainability have been explored.

Moku O Keawe   CULTURAL
(www.mokif.com; Waikoloa Resort Area; admission per night $15-25; 🔊) This early November hula competition includes *kahiko* (ancient), *'auana* (modern) and *kupuna* (elder) categories. This is a decent alternative to the sell-out, similarly themed Merrie Monarch Festival in Hilo around Easter.

✕ Eating

Sushi Shiono   SUSHI $
(📞 808-886-3588; www.sushishiono.com; Queens' MarketPlace; sushi $5-18; ⊙ 7am-9:30pm; 🅿) An excellent little sushi bar that prepares rolls

and *nigiri (*oblong-shaped sushi) by request, as well as packs to go.

Island Gourmet Markets   MARKET $

(Queens' MarketPlace; ☑808-886-3577; www.island gourmethawaii.com; ☺7am-11pm; Ⓟ🐾) Spectacularly maintained and stocked, this is a one-stop shop for takeout food, freshly made sushi, basic and specialty groceries, magazines, gifts and more. It's a great option for healthy eats, and there's a small patio for diners. Inside the market, an excellent little sushi bar called Sushi Shiono (p137) prepares rolls and *nigiri* (oblong-shaped sushi) by request.

Lava Lava Beach Club   FUSION $$

(☑808-769-5282; http://lavalavabeachclub.com/bigisland; 69-1081 Ku'uali'i Pl; mains $15-37; ☺11am-9pm; Ⓟ🐾) This cheerful spot is a favorite with tourists and locals, who snack on excellent coconut shrimp with ginger-guava sauce, ginger-crusted ahi with ponzu and slow-roasted chicken. Be sure to order the fries, which come with Parmesan and *furikake* (Japanese seasoning). Cocktails and live music make the food go down smoothly. Reservations are a good idea.

Sansei Seafood Restaurant
& Sushi Bar   JAPANESE $$$

(☑808-886-6286; www.sanseihawaii.com; Queens' MarketPlace; mains $25-52, rolls $5-23; ☺5:30-10pm Sun-Thu, to midnight Fri & Sat; Ⓟ) Local celebrity chef DK Kodama is known for innovative, fusion Japanese cuisine, such as his signature flash-fried ahi roll, and an extensive wine list. This branch of Kodama's empire has the sort of inconsistent performance we've come to expect at resorts, so fair warning – still, when the kitchen is on, it's great.

Roy's Waikoloa
Bar & Grill   HAWAII REGIONAL $$$

(☑808-886-4321; www.roysrestaurant.com; Kings' Shops; mains $31-50; ☺5:30-9:30pm) Always ridiculously bustling and noisy, Roy's will either delight or disappoint. We suggest that you focus on the food and not the buzzy atmosphere. The main courses, such as rack of lamb in a *liliko'i* (passion fruit) cabernet sauce or blackened ahi with pickled ginger, are less than cutting-edge today, but they're still pretty tasty.

Waikoloa Kings' Shops
Farmers Market   MARKET

(www.kingsshops.com; Kings' Shops; ☺8:30am-2pm Wed; Ⓟ) Features 100% locally grown and produced edibles (no crafts), including produce, honey, baked goods, coffee, tea and orchids.

☆ Entertainment

Check Waikoloa Nights (www.waikoloa beachresort.com) for special nightlife events, from rock concerts to hula shows. Free early-evening concerts featuring slack key guitar, ukulele and hula can be had at the Kings' Shops and Queens' MarketPlace shopping malls.

Legends of the Pacific   LUAU

(☑808-886-2929; www.hiltonwaikoloavillage.com; Hilton Waikoloa Village; adult/child $125/68; ☺5:30pm Tue, Fri & Sun; 🛋) Features various South Pacific dances and includes a dinner buffet and one cocktail. This luau is particularly family-friendly, and opens with an interactive artisan market aimed at kids.

Waikoloa Beach
Marriott Sunset Luau   LUAU

(☑808-886-8111; www.waikoloabeachmarriott.com; 69-275 Waikoloa Beach Dr; adult/child 6-12yr $102/48; ☺5pm Mon & Wed; 🛋) This oceanfront luau features a Hawaiian-style dinner buffet, open bar and various Polynesian perfomances, including the Samoan fire dance.

🔒 Shopping

Queens' MarketPlace   MALL

(☑808-886-8822; www.queensmarketplace.net; 201 Waikoloa Beach Dr; ☺9:30am-9:30pm, individual store hours vary) Landscaped shopping arcade in the heart of the resort. A luxury cinema is slated to open here soon.

Kings' Shops   MALL

(☑808-886-8811; www.kingsshops.com; 250 Waikoloa Beach Dr; ☺9:30am-9:30pm, individual store hours vary; 🐾) A large outdoor complex of upscale shops.

Waikoloa Village

🍴 Eating

KTA Waikoloa Village   SUPERMARKET $

(☑808-883-1088; www.ktasuperstores.com; 68-3916 Paniolo Ave, Waikoloa Highlands Shopping Center; ☺6am-9pm; Ⓟ) Located *mauka* (inland) of the highway in Waikoloa Village, this branch of the excellent KTA Super Stores is a full-service grocery store with deli, bakery and ATM.

★ **Pueo's Osteria** ITALIAN $$

(☑808-339-7566; http://pueososteria.com; 68-1845 Waikoloa Rd, Waikoloa Highlands Shopping Center; pizzas $18-22, mains $18-36; ⊙5-9pm daily, bar to 1am Mon-Thu, to 2am Fri & Sat, to 10pm Sun; P) Run by a former top resort chef, this hidden gem will satisfy your cravings for gourmet-rustic Italian fare: pizzas, pastas and classics, including a yummy gorgonzola gnocchi. Everything is homemade, and the attention to detail is obvious. The Sunday brunch menu, from lemon-ricotta pancakes to a cherrywood bacon BLT, surpasses the standard buffet line. Reservations are recommended.

Located in the Waikoloa Highlands Shopping Center, inland of the highway.

🍷 Drinking & Nightlife

Banjy's Paradise Bar & Grill SPORTS BAR

(☑808-883-3853; 68-1790 Melia St; ⊙11am-11pm) This bar and grill does a pretty busy stock in trade with locals and resort guests who are seeking something a little more laid-back. It's a sports bar with not many frills other than a nice lanai, decent fish tacos and cold beer, and at the end of the day, that's about all we need.

🛍 Shopping

Waikoloa Highlands Shopping Center MALL

(68-1845 Waikoloa Rd) The local shopping center for the folks who work in the shopping centers at the resorts (or, y'know, just work at the resorts).

ℹ Information

Post Office (☑808-885-6239; 68-1875 Pua Melia St; ⊙9am-4:30pm Mon-Fri, 10am-noon Sat, closed Sun) This is the main post office for the South Kohala region.

ℹ Gettting There & Away

To get to the resort area, turn *makai* (seaward) just south of Mile 76 on Hwy 19. Hele-On buses (www.heleonbus.org) come through daily at 6:20 and 7:50am, and 11am and 3:05pm from Monday to Saturday.

Mauna Lani Resort Area

Constructed in 1983 by a Japanese company, the Mauna Lani Resort Area resembles its neighbors in the sense that it is a manicured bit of high-amenity green studded with high-end hotels, condos and golf courses located in the midst of a searing lava desert. But it deserves special attention for its significant historic sites and for the Mauna Lani Bay Hotel & Bungalows' open attitude toward nonguests who come to explore its fishponds and trails.

It's fair to say large mega-resorts don't have the best reputation when it comes to preserving heritage sites, but Mauna Lani proves that this kind of sensitivity doesn't just have to be an afterthought or an obligation – it can actually become an integral draw of a resort itself.

The northern end of the Mauna Lani golf course abuts the southern fringe of Puako.

◉ Sights

While Holoholokai (p140) is lovely, our merciless judgement is that the truly world-class beaches of the Kohala coast are located within other resorts. That's a shame, as the Mauna Lani area gets so many other elements of a great resort right.

Kalahuipua'a Historic Trail HISTORIC SITE

(68-1400 Mauna Lani Dr, Mauna Lani Bay Hotel & Bungalows; P) 🎫 FREE The first segment of this easy trail meanders through a 16th-century Hawaiian settlement, passing **lava tubes** once used as cave shelters and a few other archaeological and geological sites marked by interpretive plaques. The trail then skirts ancient fishponds lined with coconut palms and continues to the beach, where there's a thatched shelter with an outrigger canoe and a **historic cottage**. Continue southwest past the cottage to loop around the fishponds and back to the start (about 1.5 miles round-trip).

Located on Mauna Lani Bay Hotel & Bungalows grounds, the trail starts at a marked parking lot opposite the hotel convenience store.

Kalahuipua'a Fishponds HISTORIC SITE

(www.maunalani.com) 🎫 FREE These ancient fishponds are among the island's few remaining working fishponds and, as in ancient times, they're stocked with *awa* (Hawaiian milk fish). Water circulates from the ocean through traditional *makaha* (sluice gates), which allow small fish to enter but keep mature, fattened catch from escaping. The area is shaded by groves of spindly trees, forming a serene, even romantic panorama. To access the fishponds directly (without taking the Kalahuipua'a Historic

Trail) exit the hotel lobby and go south toward the beach.

Puako Petroglyph Preserve   HISTORIC SITE

FREE With more than 3000 petroglyphs, this preserve is among the largest collections of ancient lava carvings in Hawaii. The simple pictures might not make sense to you, but viewed together, they are fascinating and worth a visit.

The ¾-mile walk from Holoholokai Beach Park to the preserve adds to the experience: take the well-marked trail at the parking lot. The walk is easy but rocky; wear sturdy footwear and expect blazing sun.

Beaches

The best beaches for swimming or snorkeling are small and located around the two large hotels.

The beach fronting the Mauna Lani Bay Hotel & Bungalows is protected and relatively calm, but the water is shallow. Just 10 minutes' south of the hotel by foot, in **Makaiwa Bay**, there's a small, calm lagoon fronting the Mauna Lani Beach Club condo. To get here, park at the hotel and walk south along the path past the fishponds.

One mile south of the hotel, there's a small salt-and-pepper beach at **Honoka'ope Bay**. When seas are calm, swimming and snorkeling are fine but not fantastic. The resort development fronting the beach reserves 20 daily parking spaces for nonresidents. To get here, drive toward the golf courses, turn left at Honoka'ope Place and check in at the entry gate.

Located at the Fairmont Orchid, **Pauoa Bay** is an excellent, little-known snorkeling spot, but you have to pay to park here. You can also park for free at the Puako Petroglyph Preserve and walk here (a little over half a mile).

Holoholokai Beach Park   BEACH

(Holoholokai Beach Park Rd; ⊙6:30am-6:30pm) Forget about sand and enjoy picnicking and strolling at this pleasantly uncrowded beach, blanketed by chunks of coral and lava. Facilities include restrooms, showers, drinking water, picnic tables and grills. The swimming isn't that great; if you need a dip, head to one of the area's other beaches.

To get here, take Mauna Lani Dr and veer right at the circle; turn right on the marked road immediately before the Fairmont Orchid. The trail to the Puako petroglyphs starts here.

☆ Activities

A full slate of activities, adventures and relaxation programs await guests of (and visitors to) the Mauna Lani area. Also, there's golf, of course. Star Gaze Hawaii makes regular visits here.

Star Gaze Hawaii   STARGAZING

(☑808-323-3481, 808-987-9582; www.stargaze hawaii.com; 62-100 Kauna'oa Dr; adult/child $40/20; ⊙8-9pm) Take advantage of Kohala's consistently clear night skies with these 'star tours,' conducted by professional astronomers. The pros come to the resorts to lead beachside stargazing lessons, usually from around 8pm to 9pm, but they can also be hired out for private sessions (one/two hours $550/800). Check the website to see when your Kohala resort is scheduled for a stargazing session.

Francis I'i Brown North & South Golf Courses   GOLF

(☑808-885-6655; www.maunalani.com/golf; 68-1400 Mauna Lani Dr, Mauna Lani Bay Hotel & Bungalows; greens fees guest/nonguest $170/225) Mauna Lani boasts two world-class golf courses. The South course is more scenic, with its signature 15th hole featuring a tee shot over crashing surf. The North course is more challenging and interesting, with a par-three 17th hole within an amphitheater of black lava. The prices we list are for morning tee times; play later in the day and rates drop.

Spa Without Walls   SPA

(☑808-887-7538; www.fairmont.com/orchid-hawaii/spa; 1 North Kaniku Dr, Fairmont Orchid; massages & facials from $159; ⊙7am-7pm) Treatments can be done in open-air *hale* (houses), hidden amid orchids, coconut palms, streams and lily ponds; that tinkling waterfall really accentuates your reflexology treatment. The spa services tend to feature botanicals, from Kona coffee to matcha green tea. The facility is upscale, if not quite luxurious.

Yoga at the Shops at Mauna Lani   YOGA

(☑808-638-2928; www.shopsatmaunalani.com/yoga/; 68-1330 Mauna Lani Dr, Suite 306; per class $15; ⊙8:30am Tue, Thu & Fri, 6pm Tue, 10am Sun) Several weekly yoga classes are held at the Shops at Mauna Lani, focusing on Vinyasa courses and stretching. Practitioners of all skill levels, from novice beginners to advanced students, are welcome. Call ahead to determine specific course offerings and times, which may change with the season.

Mauna Lani Spa
SPA

(☑ 808-881-7922; www.maunalani.com; 68-1365 Pauoa Rd, Mauna Lani Bay Hotel & Bungalows; massages & facials from $165; ⊗ treatments 10am-4pm) A vast indoor/outdoor space landscaped with exotic tropical flora and a beautiful outdoors lava-rock sauna. There's an enormous range of treatments, from lymphatic draining to shiatsu massage and Brazilian waxes, but with that said, those treatments are pricey, perhaps overpriced. Insist on something Hawaiian (eg *lomilomi* massage or hot stones) for the memory.

☞ Tours

Mauna Lani Sea Adventures
OUTDOORS

(☑ 808-885-7883; http://maunalaniseaadventures. com; 68-1292 S Kaniku Dr, Mauna Lani Bay Hotel & Bungalows; snorkeling tour adult/child 3-12yr $99/45, whale-watching cruise $85/45; ⛵) For snorkeling, whale-watching and diving, this outfit offers almost daily tours at decent prices. While Kailua-Kona is the Big Island's hub for snorkeling and scuba diving, the waters off Mauna Lani are excellent and much less crowded. Also has a beach center that offers outrigger lessons ($150 for 90 minutes), surf lessons ($99) and SUP rental (30 minutes/one hour $30/50).

✖ Eating

For fine dining, the restaurants in Mauna Lani are among the west side's finest and priciest, although more mid-range opportunities have been presenting themselves as of late.

Under the Bodhi Tree
VEGETARIAN $

(☑ 808-895-2053; www.underthebodhi.net; 68-1330 Mauna Lani Dr, Ste 116; mains $9-16; ⊗ 7am-7pm; P ✿ ☑) Vegetarians flock to this organic-friendly spot, where the dishes show a commitment to local produce and Pacific Rim influences. Kalbi-style tofu is served up with kimchi and brown rice, or you can opt for coconut green curry noodles with Hamakua mushrooms. Breakfast goodies, multigrain sandwiches and a juice menu round out the offerings, which can all be made vegan.

Foodland Farms
SUPERMARKET $

(☑ 808-887-6101; 68-1330 Mauna Lani Dr, Shops at Mauna Lani; ⊗ 6am-11pm; P) Full-service gourmet supermarket with an impressive deli selection.

Monstera
JAPANESE $$

(☑ 808-887-2711; www.monsterasushi.com; 68-1330 Mauna Lani Dr; plates $16-30, sushi rolls $13-20; ⊗ 5:30-10pm) Chef Norio Yamamoto left his namesake restaurant at the Fairmont Orchid to launch his own *izakaya* (Japanese pub). It's a looser, cooler place, where the menu ranges from classic *nigiri* sushi and tuna *tataki* (tuna seared and seasoned with ginger) to sizzling plates of kimchi stir-fried pork loin and teriyaki chicken. You'll want to make reservations.

★ Brown's Beach House
HAWAII REGIONAL $$$

(☑ 808-887-7368; 1 North Kaniku Dr, Fairmont Orchid; mains $41-69; ⊗ 5:30-8:30pm Thu-Mon, 5:30-9pm Tue-Wed; P) The prices might be intimidating, but Brown's remains a standout for those willing to pay. Expect gracious service and the finest local ingredients: the surf and turf features locally raised beef and Kona lobsters, wild boar ribs are served with local fern shoots and Puna chicken comes dressed with semolina and black garlic. There's an extensive vegan menu as well.

Napua
FUSION $$$

(www.napuarestaurant.com; 68-1292 Mauna Lani Point Dr; lunch mains $15-18, dinner mains $38-42; ⊗ 11am-4pm & 5-9pm; P ✿) Fine dining and Pacific influences come together at this breezy gem, which overlooks a fine sweep of the Mauna Lani oceanfront. Give the rib-eye steak a whirl, try the slow cooked guava barbecue pork rubs, or indulge in the always excellent catch of the day. The salads are a particular winner, combining the fruits (literally) of local agricultural bounty. Reservations recommended.

CanoeHouse
HAWAII REGIONAL $$$

(☑ 808-881-7911; 68-1400 Mauna Lani Dr, Mauna Lani Bay Hotel & Bungalows; mains $32-48; ⊗ 6-9pm; P ✿) The Mauna Lani's flagship restaurant showcases local ingredients creatively but simply. Island ingredients are crafted with care; the risotto with Hamakua mushrooms is a creamy treat. For those looking for something extra special, a decadent option is the 'Captain's Table' (two to eight diners; $125 per person, with wine pairings $175), a five-course meal specially designed in collaboration with the chef. Both the setting and service are lovely.

ANDRE NANTEL/SHUTTERSTOCK ©

1. Petroglyphs (p135)
Hawaiian history is preserved in these ancient lava carvings.

2. Pololu Valley (p156)
A lush, emerald slice of jungle paradise.

3. Pu'ukohola Heiau National Historic Site (p148)
The rock foundations of a massive heiau dedicated to war god Kuka'ilimoku.

4. Ranch horses in Waimea (p156)
With its rich pastureland, Waimea is *paniolo* (cowboy) country.

🍸 Drinking & Nightlife

For evening drinks (and a more affordable dinner), try an oceanfront bar.

Luana Lounge　　　　　　　　BAR
(📞808-885-2000; 1 North Kaniku Dr, Fairmont Orchid; ⊘5pm-midnight) A nice spot to unwind at sunset, with specialty drinks and *pupus* (small plates). There's a big list of homemade cocktails on tap, although they don't come cheap ($11 to $16). Live music sometimes goes from 6pm to 9pm.

☆ Entertainment

The resort keeps a couple of blue-chip acts on tap to keep the guests entertained, but you don't need to be staying here to enjoy the shows.

Kona Cozy Comedy & Tiki Club　　COMEDY
(📞808-430-1957; http://konakozy.com; Shops at Mauna Lani; tickets from $60; ⊘shows 8pm daily, gallery 10am-7pm) Half comedian, half magician, and all character, 'Kozy' Kozak and his raucous hybrid comedy-magic show are a Big Island original. Kozak's rapid-fire routine is matched in oddity by a truly surreal gallery setting, where the concept of pseudo-Polynesian kitsch – otherwise known as 'tiki' – is elevated to near worship. This show is for those 18 and older only.

Hawaii Loa Luau　　　　　　　LUAU
(📞808- 892-2082, 866-482-9775; www.gatheringofthekings.com; Fairmont Orchid; adult/child 6-12yr $115/80; ⊘5:30pm Sat; 👶) This luau spins a thread of storytelling to highlight slightly modernized versions of Polynesian and Hawaiian dance and music. It's notable for its above-average Polynesian dinner buffet and open bar, and a narrative that focuses on the Polynesians' oceanic exploration and eventual settlement of the Hawaiian islands.

🛍 Shopping

After you enter the resort, you'll soon pass by the Shops at Mauna Lani, an outdoor mall that is a bit of a nerve center for the resort. Plentiful parking and piped in music contribute to the sense that you've discovered a slice of mainland suburbia in the midst of the Kohala lava desert.

Shops at Mauna Lani　　　　　MALL
(📞808-885-9501; www.shopsatmaunalani.com; 68-1330 Mauna Lani Dr; ⊘10am-9pm, individual store hours vary; 👶) This outdoor mall contains many of the stores, businesses and restaurants that form the backbone of mainland-style amenities and entertainment options in the Mauna Lani resort.

ⓘ Getting There & Away

The Mauna Lani area is located about 29 miles north of Kailua-Kona via Hwy 19. The Pahala–Kohala Hele-On Bus (www.heleonbus.org) passes by at 2:50pm and 6:40am daily, and at 11:20am and 7:35am Monday to Saturday.

Puako

📞808 / POP 772

Standing in contrast to the mega-resorts to the south, Puako is essentially a mile-long row of homes. The single road through 'town' is marked with numerous 'shoreline access' points that are popular with locals and the semi-locals who make up the part-time population of Puako. There is some very fine diving and snorkeling along the Puako coastline, some of which is accessible independently, and some of which you may find easier to access on a tour.

◉ Sights

★Hapuna Beach State Recreation Area　　　　　　　BEACH
(⊘gate 7am-8pm; 🅿👶) Hapuna Beach is a postcard snapshot of what a beach can be – it's world famous for a magnificent half-mile sweep of white powder sand and fabulously clear waters. In summer, waves are calm and allow good swimming, snorkeling and diving. When the surf's up in winter, bodyboarding is awesome, thanks to reliable swells from the northwest. In general, Hapuna waters are too choppy for tots or nonswimmers. Waves over 3ft should be left for experts; drownings are not uncommon here.

The restrooms and picnic area at this state recreation area can be crowded and, at worst, grungy. Lifeguards are on duty. For nonresidents, parking costs $5 per vehicle.

To get here, take Hapuna Beach Rd just south of Mile 69. Arrive early to snag a parking space and a good spot. Bring industrial-strength sunscreen because there's virtually no shade.

★ Beach 69　　　　　　　　BEACH
(Waialea Beach; Old Puako Rd; ⊘7am-7:30pm; 🅿👶) This lovely crescent of white sand is a local favorite but remains somewhat off the tourist radar. Both family-friendly and

gay-friendly, its calm, protected waters are ideal for a bout of casual snorkeling. Around the boundary of the beach, copses of shady trees provide welcome relief from the sun. The north end of the beach is the best area for snorkeling; be aware that this area is popular with nudists as well. Restrooms and showers are available; there are no lifeguards.

From Puako Beach Dr, take the first right turn onto Old Puako Rd. Find telephone pole No 71 (originally numbered No 69) to the left and park. Follow the 'road' to its end, and then tramp along the footpath that runs parallel to a wooden fence.

Puako Tide Pools LANDMARK
(Puako Beach Dr) Puako is known for giant tide pools, some deep enough to shelter live coral and other marine life. There's no sandy beach, but a narrow strip of pulverized coral and lava covers the shore. It's ideal for beach walks and you might even see *honu* (sea turtles) sunning on the rocks. To get to the pools, park along the road near the 'beach access' paths. If you swim out past the pools, note the waters here can be temperamental.

Hokuloa United Church CHURCH
(☑ 808-883-8295; 69-1600 Puako Beach Dr; P) Heading toward Puako 'town' you'll pass the Hokuloa United Church on your right. This may be the cutest little white seaside church on the Big Island. Originally built in 1860, the structure fell apart and was then restored in 1990. Call ahead for service times.

🏃 Activities

Puako is considered one of the best diving spots in the Big Island. The signs for 'shoreline access' are all potential entry points, but in many of these spots the water is too shallow and rough for proper entry. For diving tours, book with Kawaihae-based Kohala Divers (p148).

End of the Road DIVING
(N 19°57'30.9", W 155°51'28.8") The End of the Road is widely considered one of the best dive sites on the Big Island – there's easy entry for divers, clear water and excellent coral viewing, including canyons with 20–40ft vertical coral walls. Snorkeling here is pretty great as well. Be on the lookout for wave conditions – if folks are surfing, don't go diving.

To get here, drive about three miles down Puako Beach Dr and pull over before the road ends. Walk toward the water and look for a natural pool formed by lava rocks – this constitutes an easy access point. Once you're underwater, be on the lookout for small lava caves – turtles love to sleep in these. Check with Kohala Divers (p148) to see if they're running trips out here if you're looking for a tour.

Lat 20 KAYAKING
(☑ 808-785-4466; www.lat20hawaii.com; Off Puako Beach Dr) Lat 20 is an ocean equipment rental company above all else, and they're great folks to go to if you need kayaks, bicycles (day/week $30/120) and stand up paddle boards ($75). They've got a solid local reputation, and are willing to go over ocean safety (and enjoyment) tips with you, whatever your level of experience in the water.

👉 Tours

Kohala Kayak Club KAYAKING
(☑ 808-882-4678; www.kohalakayak.org; 3hr tour or 2hr SUP lesson $70; ⊙ departing around 9am; 👪) Paddle and snorkel in Puako's pristine, less-traveled waters with knowledgeable, customer service–oriented guides. All levels are welcome, and stand up paddle surfing lessons are offered. There is no office for the 'club,' but boats tend to put out from Puako.

🍴 Eating

Puako General Store STORE $
(☑ 808-882-7500; www.thepuakostore.com; 69-1649 Puako Beach Dr; prepared meals $8-13; ⊙ 8am-7pm; ✳ 👪) There may not be an official city hall in Puako, but this general store more or less fulfills that purpose. It's basically a shop selling all kinds of sundries, but there are groceries, yummy, Hawaiian-inspired prepared meals prepared by the chefs at Kawaihae's excellent Blue Dragon (p149), and lots of chatter about the town and its populace.

Three Frogs AMERICAN $
(Hapnua Beach State Recreation Area; mains $9-12; ⊙ 10am-4pm; P) A pair of friendly brothers run this Hapuna Beach (p144) concession stand, which sells enormous fish tacos, burgers and other variations of food that all go down a treat after a good swim. Located adjacent to the path leading down to the sand.

ℹ Getting There & Away

To get here, turn *makai* (seaward) down Puako Beach Dr between Miles 70 and 71. You can ask Hele-On (www.heleonbus.org) bus drivers to drop you at the head of the road, but you'll still need to walk down here, which is a hike with bags. Puako is about 32 miles north of Kailua-Kona.

Mauna Kea Resort Area

The Mauna Kea Resort may not have the historic heritage and sheer quantity of dining amenities possessed by resorts to the south, but it does have proximity to two of the Big Island's great beaches – one of which, despite being located within a resort, still feels decently off the tourism trail.

Development began here when the late Laurance Rockefeller obtained a 99-year lease on the land around Kauna'oa Bay. 'Every great beach deserves a great hotel,' Rockefeller apparently said. Not everyone would agree, but he sure got his way here.

⊙ Sights

★Mauna Kea Beach   BEACH
(ℙ) Crescent-shaped Kauna'oa Bay (nicknamed 'Mauna Kea Beach' after Rockefeller built his landmark hotel on it) is blanketed in powdery white sand, while the clear waters are calm and shallow (generally less than 10ft). Snorkeling is best at the north end along the rocky ledge. This wonderfully uncrowded beach is open to the public through 40 parking spaces set aside daily for nonguests. Arrive by 9am and stop at the entry gate for a parking pass and directions.

★Mau'umae Beach   BEACH
(ℙ) White sand, teal water, shady trees and protected waters – and it's even more private than Kauna'oa Bay. What's not to love about Mau'umae? (pronounced Mao-oo-my) Locals are proprietary about this gem, and for good reason. There's great snorkeling on either end of the bay. Only 10 parking spots are given out, so arrive by 9am on weekdays, and possibly earlier on weekends. You can also walk here from Spencer Beach Park to the north; it's about a quarter-mile hike.

To get here, go toward Mauna Kea Beach Hotel, turn right on Kamahoi and cross two wooden bridges. Look for telephone pole number 22 on the left and park next to the other cars. Walk down the trail to the Ala Kahakai sign and turn left toward the beach.

🏃 Activities

Beyond the beach, you'll find the usual golf-friendly country club resort spaces. For other outdoor adventures, many outfitters

in Kailua-Kona (p86) can arrange excursions for you departing from the resort.

Hapuna Golf Course   GOLF
(☑808-880-3000; www.princeresortshawaii.com; Hapuna Beach Prince Hotel; greens fees $160) Set amid lava fields, with Maui glittering in the distance, this course has a 700ft elevation gain and was designed by Arnold Palmer and Ed Seay. It's known for its signature set of par-five holes and tricky elevated greens.

Mauna Kea Golf Course   GOLF
(☑808-882-5400; www.princeresortshawaii.com; Mauna Kea Beach Hotel; greens fees $275) A 72-par championship course that consistently ranks among the top courses in the USA. Designed by Robert Trent Jones Sr, it was remodeled in 2008 by his son, Rees Jones.

★☆ Festivals & Events

Big Island
Chocolate Festival   FOOD & DRINK
(www.bigislandchocolatefestival.com; tickets from $75; ☉late Apr) Chocolate in all of its delicious iterations is celebrated and served up at this annual culinary party, which goes off at the Hapuna Beach Prince Hotel (☑888-977-4623; www.princeresortshawaii.com; 62-100 Kauna'oa Dr).

✗ Eating

For dining options beyond hotel fare, head to Waimea, Kawaihae or the Waikoloa Resort Area. The Mauna Kea (☑808-882-7222, 877-880-6524; www.maunakeabeachhotel.com; 62-100 Mauna Kea Beach Dr) holds a seaside clambake buffet featuring all the critters of the sea from 6pm to 8pm on Saturday evenings (adult/child $120/60).

Copper Bar   HAWAIIAN $$
(☑808-882-5707; mains $18-26; ☉11am-9:30pm; ℙ❄) Hawi-born Rio Miceli cranks out eclectic, island-themed dishes at this spot, such as cold soba noodles with lobster, kalua pork flatbreads and kung pao ahi. We're not always fans of spiffed-up traditional Hawaiian fare, but this kitchen is doing the genre justice, and prices are reasonable.

Hau Tree   HAWAIIAN $$
(☑808-882-5707; lunch mains $13-22, dinner mains $18-29; ☉7am-3:30pm daily, 5:30-8:30pm Sun-Wed; ℙ) Casual dining and outdoor dress codes, all overlooking the deep blue Pacific. The solid if not super-original menu includes grilled mahi with miso

butter, pork barbecue with guava sauce and a kick-butt brunch that gets the week started right.

Coast Grille AMERICAN $$$

(☑ 808-880-1111; Hapuna Beach Prince Hotel; mains $23-38; ⏱ 6-9pm, bar to 10pm; 🅿) If you're going to dine on fresh Hawaiian seafood and steak, it's best to do so in the open air with the wind in your hair, right? That's the philosophy at this restaurant, at least. Try the seafood trio, with three varities of locally caught fish – *ono,* mahimahi and ahi, or down some ahi *poke* nachos.

☆ Entertainment

Mauna Kea Hawaiian Luau LUAU

(☑ 808-882-5707; www.princeresortshawaii.com; 62-100 Mauna Kea Beach Dr; adult/child 5-12yr $106/53; ⏱ 5:30pm Tue & Fri) This outdoor luau features standard entertainment (thrilling fire dance, group hula) and a gorgeous beach setting. The buffet is generous and above average.

ℹ Getting There & Away

Located 33 miles north of Kailua-Kona via Hwy 19, the Mauna Kea area is the northernmost resort in South Kohala. Almost immediately after you pass, you'll come to the Hwy 19–Hwy 270 split, which leads off east to Waimea and north and west to Hawi and Pololu. The Pahala–Kohala Hele-On Bus (www.heleonbus.org) heads south from here at 2:30pm daily, and at 7:15am from Monday to Saturday.

Kawaihae & Around

Kawaihae is more functional than recreational, a working port 'town' (if such can be said for a settlement that's a couple of blocks long) where fuel tanks and cargo containers give off an industrial sense of identity. For all its compact utilitarianism, there is noteworthy dining, a family beach, decent surf and a historic heiau (temple) toward the south. Scrappy little Kawaihae marks the end of South Kohala resort country and the beginning of North Kohala, which is possessed of an altogether more funky vibe. Sitting as it does on a border, Kawaihae has a hybrid nature; you'll find outfitters catering to the big resorts, and local farmers loading for a community market all on the same block.

For an insider's view of Kawaihae, check out the Pacific Worlds Kawaihae website (www.pacificworlds.com/kawaihae).

◉ Sights

Spencer Beach Park BEACH

(☑ 808-323-4322; www.hawaiicounty.gov; ⏱ lifeguard 7am-4pm; 🅿 🚻) Shallow, sandy and gentle, this beach lacks the dramatic sweep of Mauna Kea or Hapuna, but it's ideal for kids and popular with local families. Come to swim rather than to snorkel; the waters are slightly silty due to being close to Kawaihae Harbor (to the north). Located off the Akoni Pule Hwy just north of the 2-mile

---

ATOMIC ARCHITECTURE: KAWAIHAE HARBOR

Back in the bad old days of the Cold War, when nuclear annihilation seemed like it was only one bad morning in the White House or Kremlin away, the US government funded a program called Project Plowshare. The idea: use controlled nuclear explosives for peaceful construction, and in the process normalize the idea of the 'friendly atom' at a time when the word 'atomic' was synonymous with 'apocalypse.'

The program was terminated in 1977 after outcry over fallout disposal and water contamination, but not before it quite literally altered the American landscape – including a dry northwestern corner of the Big Island known as Kawaihae.

In the summer of 1969, the US Army Corps of Engineers' Nuclear Cratering Group (NCG) came to Kawaihae. The year before, the US Congress had approved the construction of a small boat harbor in the town. The NCG was on hand to dredge the harbor – and prove a well-supervised nuclear explosion could be bent toward peacetime purposes.

While no nuclear material was employed by the NCG, they did get the go ahead to prime 120 tons of aluminized ammonium nitrate, which apparently creates an explosion that's close enough to an atomic boom. The chemicals did the trick – the harbor was dredged out, and there was no damage to local heiau, which had even been braced to protect against the shockwave of the explosions. For a program that has attracted its fair share of controversy and criticism, Project Plowshare did, at the end of the day, help bring a small boat harbor to Kawaihae.

marker, the park has a lifeguard, picnic tables, barbecue grills, restrooms, showers, drinking water and campsites (permit required).

Pu'ukohola Heiau National Historic Site
HISTORIC SITE

(808-882-7218; www.nps.gov/puhe; 62-3601 Kawaihae Rd; 8am-4:45pm; P) FREE By 1790 Kamehameha the Great had conquered Maui, Lana'i and Moloka'i. But power over his home island of Hawai'i was a challenge. When told by a prophet that he would rule all of the Hawaiian Islands if he built a heiau dedicated to his war god Kuka'ilimoku atop Pu'ukohola (Whale Hill) in Kawaihae, Kamehameha built this massive structure. Today only the basic rock foundation remains, but it's still a massive 224ft by 100ft, with 16–20ft walls.

Hamakua Macadamia Nut Company
FACTORY

(888-643-6688, 808-882-1690; www.hawnnut. com; 61-3251 Maluokalani St; 9am-5:30pm; P) FREE It's a tourist stop, but a darned good one, featuring a spanking-clean factory, gift shop and generous free samples. This eco-conscious company generates 75% of its energy needs from solar power and 10% from ground mac-nut shells. The Hamakua-grown nuts are excellent in quality and reasonably priced. To get here, turn *mauka* (inland) just north of Mile 4.

Activities

Kawaihae Harbor
SURFING

This surfing break is beloved by locals and often totally passed up by visitors. The waves are created by northwest swells that hit the coast and the harbor breakwater, producing running righthanders. The presence of the breakwater provides a nice shelter if you start getting tired.

Tours

★ Kohala Divers
OUTDOORS

(808-882-7774; www.kohaladivers.com; 61-3665 Akoni Pule Hwy, Kawaihae Shopping Center; 1-/2-tank dive from $109/149; 8am-6pm) This long-running outfit leads excellent diving trips throughout Kohala waters, plus snorkeling and seasonal whale-watching. One memorable trip visits a *honu* (sea turtle) 'cleaning' station where the turtles allow fish to pick parasites off their bodies.

Eating

★ Kohala Burger & Taco
BURGERS, MEXICAN $

(808-880-1923; www.kohalaburgerandtaco.com; Akoni Pule Hwy, Kawaihae Shopping Center; mains $9-16; 11am-7:30pm Mon-Sat, to 4pm Sun; P) When only a real burger will do, come here for local grass-fed quarter-pounders with specialty toppings that are, in short, absolutely gorgeous. If you're not into beef, have a go at the fish tacos, quesadillas and dreamy shakes and malts.

★ Anuenue
DESSERTS $

(808-882-1109; Akoni Pule Hwy, Kawaihae Shopping Center; cones from $4; P) Since 1998, Tim Termeer has delighted all comers with snowy shave ice and premium ice cream, which is perfect on a hot day, or following, say, a gut-busting burger from Kohala Burger & Taco. Among his dozens of flavors are ginger lemongrass, citrus mint and lavender lemonade. He also offers hot dogs, veg burgers and chili bowls.

Original Big Island Shave Ice Co, Inc.
DESSERTS $

(www.obisic.com; 61-3616 Kawaihae Rd; shave ice $3.75; 11am-5:30pm Mon-Sat; P) Kawaihae's only food truck, parked in the lot of the Blue Dragon Restaurant, is also a supremely good shave ice stand. The flavors are good and the ice texture is smooth, but we say the standout is the ice cream and the *halo-halo*, with *ube* (sweet potato) ice cream, azuki beans, taro, coconut and jelly. It's oddly delicious.

Dragon Wagon
HAWAIIAN $

(808-882-7500; 61-3616 Kawaihae Rd; mains $6-9; 11am-4pm Wed-Sun; P) The folks at the Blue Dragon host a food truck in their own parking lot during the day, so if you aren't swinging by here for an evening dinner, you can still enjoy local sliders, *musubi* and creative spins on the hot dog (wasabi mayo and kimchi pickle – *nice*) served out of said restaurant's mobile satellite.

Hale I'a Da Fish House
SEAFOOD $

(808-882-1052; 61-3659 Akoni Pule Hwy; poke $8-13; 9am-5pm Mon-Fri, to 3pm Sat) Also known as just 'Da Fish House,' this spot mainly sells fresh fish, but you can also score some fresh, delicious *poke* here for a picnic meal.

Cafe Pesto
BISTRO $$

(808-882-1071; www.cafepesto.com; Akoni Pule Hwy, Kawaihae Shopping Center; lunch $11-14, pizza $10-20, dinner mains $17-33; 11am-9pm

Sun-Thu, 11am-10pm Fri & Sat; P) This well-loved favorite serves eclectic, innovative cuisine you might call Mediterranean with an Asian twang or Italian with an Island twist. Choose from curries and Greek salads, seafood risotto and smoked salmon alfredo, piping-hot calzones and thin-crust gourmet pizzas.

Blue Dragon Restaurant   HAWAII REGIONAL $$$
(☑808-882-7771; www.bluedragonhawaii.com; 61-3616 Kawaihae Rd; mains $18-38; ⊙5-10pm Wed-Thu & Sun, 5-11pm Fri & Sat; P ♿) The cuisine at this retro-chic roofless restaurant is hard to pin down. The haute regional menu runs from stir-fries to curries to rib-eye steaks, but generally it's all good. This is a convivial, family-oriented place for dinner; later, the potent specialty cocktails might tempt you to the dance floor.

ℹ Getting There & Away

Kawaihae is 35 miles north of Kailua-Kona, 12 miles west of Waimea and 19 miles south of Hawi. It is just north of the split between Hwy 19 and Hwy 270. The North Kohala–Waimea Hele-On Bus (www.heleonbus.org) passes by at 10:20am (to Waimea) and 12:30pm (to Hawi).

NORTH KOHALA

Where the winds scream out of the Pacific, bending the tall grass into stiff yellow prairies that drop to a frothy ocean held adjacent to a black lava rock coastline – there, friend, you've reached North Kohala, and North Kohala is a world unto itself. This is the birthplace of Kamehameha, 'The Lonely One,' a fitting nickname given the austerity of this landscape, which in some ways is utterly removed from the clichéd lush garden image you may have of the Hawaiian Islands. This applies to the west side of North Kohala, anyway; drive east and the rains lash out with the winds, greening the hills until one reaches the fertile jungle cleft of the Pololu Valley. The distinctive nature of the landscape and the population here give North Kohala an undeniable sense of place, and locals have an enormous well of pride in this windswept corner of the Big Island.

ℹ Getting There & Away

About 33 miles north of Kailua-Kona, Hwy 19 – the belt road – veers east. Hwy 270 goes north, hugging the coast, and this is the road you take

into the heart of North Kohala; you can also connect via Hwy 250 from Waimea.

Public transportation options are limited to a Hele-On Bus (www.heleonbus.org) that comes through daily in the mornings and early afternoon.

Hawi & Around

📍 808 / POP 1081

Hawi (hah-vee) is a little slice of picturesque North Kohala that's been massaged by mainlanders (and their money) into a bohemian enclave of cafes, locavore dining, galleries and artisan gifts: all in about two blocks, which is as big as this town gets. Rarely will you see a 'snowbird' community settle into such a permanent nest; transplants and locals have built something special in Hawi, and it's quite simply one of the nicest places to stop and smell the organic coffee.

This was once a major plantation town for the Kohala Sugar Company, and many local residents are descendants of sugar workers. For all the town has evolved from rustic boondocks to tourist destination, there is still a very Kohala-esque sense of feisty isolation – an independent streak that's easy to love.

Note that Kohala Mountain Rd (Hwy 250) is called Hawi Rd close to town.

◉ Sights

Hawi Farmers Market   MARKET
(www.hawifarmersmarket.com; Hwy 250; ⊙8am-2pm Sat, noon-5pm Tue; ♿) ✿ All of the funky, organic, crunchy goodness of North Kohala is sold by all of its funky, organic, crunchy characters at this weekly farmers market, held under the shade of the huge banyan tree off Hwy 250. Pick up honey, mushrooms or sweet potatoes, listen to live, local music and generally revel in the region's idiosyncrasies.

🏃 Activities

Many of the outdoor activities that North Kohala is famous for can be accessed via tour companies based out of (or nearby) Hawi.

Kohala Zipline   ADVENTURE SPORTS
(☑800-464-1993, 808-331-3620; www.kohalazipline.com; 55-515 Hawi Road; adult/child from $169/129) ✿ Nine ziplines crisscross the Kohala canopy, specifically designed to blend into the trees and account for their growth. On this awesome tour, you're not just a

North Kohala

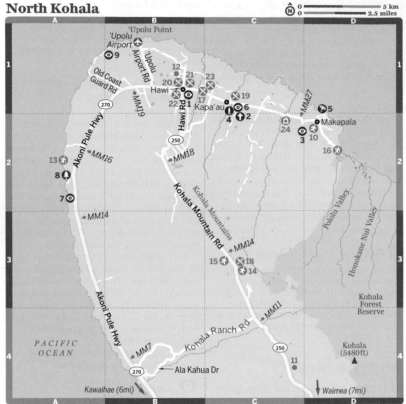

North Kohala

customer sitting back on a zipline – you're directing the flow of the journey across the forest canopy itself. Also offers a 'zip 'n' dip' into a Pololu waterfall (adult/child $249/209).

🖝 Tours

★ Flumin' Kohala
KAYAKING

(☑844-933-4294, 808-933-4294; http://flumin kohala.com; 55-517 Hawi Rd; adult/child $135/75; ⊙7:30am-5pm) 🥢 After an off-road excursion deep into the North Kohala bush, you embark on a leisurely 3-mile kayaking trip through a series of historic plantation irrigation ditches or flumes, including 10 tunnels. Guides are well versed in island history, and the entire experience comes off as a unique cultural journey, as opposed to a fast-paced action adventure. Highly recommended.

Lokahi Garden Sanctuary
FOOD

(☑808-889-0001; http://lokahigardensanctuary. com; 55-448 Hoea Rd; adult with/without lunch $65/45, child 3-12yr with/without lunch $40/25; ⊙tours 11am-12:30pm Mon-Fri) 🥢 This working farm focuses on growing sustainable crops and includes extensive plots of herbal and medicinal plants. A tour takes in the aforementioned flora, plus fauna (sheep, chickens, dogs etc), and visitors can throw in a true farm-to-table lunch with the experience.

Palili 'O Kohala
FOOD

(☑808-960-3727; www.kahuapaamua.org; tour $50; ⊙9am-12:30pm Fri) 🥢 Taro is the historic staple of the Hawaiian people, and the reason for this sustainable farm's existence. Come here to learn about the agricultural heritage (and future) of North Kohala, all while seeing taro fields, wetland plots and naturally raised pigs.

🍴 Eating

The food scene here is fantastic, thanks to a collision of the two demographics that make up North Kohala – quirky transplants and proud locals. Both groups have been espousing the seasonal, locavore approach to food since before that mindset gained pop-culture cachet. There is a wide range of price points, but very little white-tablecloth atmosphere – laid-back elegance is as fancy as it gets.

Sweet Potato Kitchen
VEGETARIAN $

(☑808-345-7300; http://sweetpotatokitchen. com; 55-3406 Akoni Pule Hwy; dishes $4-14; ⊙9am-3:30pm Tue-Sat, 10am-2pm Sun; 🖝) 🥢

This cozy kitchen serves heaping plates of vegetarian and vegan fare, from congee (rice porridge) cooked with black rice, garlic and local greens to a 'BeetSteak' patty burger that's as hearty as any Waimea steer. Dairy-free coconut ice cream, banana bread and some sinful mushroom gravy round out the offerings.

Kohala Coffee Mill
CAFE $

(☑808-889-5577; 55-3412 Akoni Pule Hwy; drinks $2-4, sandwiches $6-10; ⊙6am-6pm Mon-Fri, 7am-6pm Sat & Sun) 🥢 A comfy place to hang out and treat yourself to muffins, fresh-brewed Kona coffee and heavenly Tropical Dreams ice cream. For breakfast, the souffléd eggs with cheese, onion, tomato, pesto and/or bacon is a winner. Frequently hosts live music on Sunday mornings.

Mi Ranchito
MEXICAN $

(808-756-4636; 55-3419 Akoni Pule Hwy; mains $7-15; ⊙11am-8pm, to 9pm Fri) Hawi folks and West Coast transplants (to be fair, there's a lot of overlap between those categories) love this little Mexican place, which is basically a window counter and a few tables. We say it's filling, if just fine – the usual menu of tacos, enchiladas and burritos served with scoops of rice and beans. Cash only.

Takata Store
SUPERMARKET $

(☑808-889-5413; Akoni Pule Hwy; ⊙8am-7pm Mon-Sat, to 1pm Sun; ℗) For groceries, try this well-stocked, family-run market between Hawi and Kapa'au.

★ Bamboo
HAWAII REGIONAL $$$

(☑808-889-5555; www.bamboorestaurant.info; 55-3415 Akoni Pule Hwy, Kohala Trade Center; lunch $12-17, dinner $25-38; ⊙11:30am-2:30pm & 6-8pm Tue-Sat, lunch only Sun; 🖝) Always-packed Bamboo offers interesting takes on old standbys, such as mahimahi on focaccia with shredded papaya. It shares space with a gallery and gift shop, making you feel like you're eating in a general store – which you are. The inviting interior – suspended Balinese umbrellas, twinkling Christmas lights and warm wood walls – is cheerful and pure Hawi.

★ Sushi Rock
SUSHI $$$

(☑808-889-5900; www.sushirockrestaurant.net; 55-3435 Akoni Pule Hwy; sushi rolls $5-20, mains $18-36; ⊙noon-3pm & 5:30-8pm) 🥢 This ever-popular sushi bar is famous all over the island for its fusion tropical rolls, which might include papaya, mac nuts, Fuji apple or goat cheese. Some work better than others, but we always leave satisfied. The menu also includes vegetarian/vegan rolls, creative salads and sandwiches, plus a wild selection of cocktails.

Trio   FUSION $$$
(📱 808-889-5900; www.sushirockrestaurant. net; 55-3435 Akoni Pule Hwy; 3-course menu $29; ⊗ noon-3pm & 5:30-8pm) Trio specializes in three-course, creative Hawaiian fusion cuisine. The menu has a lot of variation; on one night you might mix Indonesian chicken with Waimea beef sliders finished with some vegetarian *poke*. For a town as small as Hawi, this is a heady gastronomic adventure. It's attached to and operated by Sushi Rock.

🍸 Drinking & Nightlife

As fun as Hawi is, there's no real nightlife – Sushi Rock may stay open a little late if folks are knocking back drinks, and there's often live music at Bamboo, but on the flip side, we've been here around 8pm and the town has felt as dead as a mausoleum.

🛍 Shopping

Hawi Gallery   MUSIC
(📱 206-452-3697; www.hawigallery.com; 55-3406 Akoni Pule Hwy; ⊗ 11am-4pm) The ukulele as a work of art? Definitely, as this fascinating collection proves. In addition to classics, check out the Cuban model made from a cigar box and the curvaceous Polk-a-lay-lee, a rare 1960s promotional item from a Chicago furniture store. Also sells vintage Hawaiian shorts and great line of Hawaiiana.

L Zeidman Gallery   ARTS & CRAFTS
(📱 808-889-1400; http://zeidmangallery.wix.com/ aloha; 55-3419 Akoni Pule Hwy; ⊗ 10am-5pm) The exquisitely crafted, museum-quality wood bowls made by the owner are mesmerizing en masse. Take one home for between $150 and $2500.

MakiSun   GIFTS & SOUVENIRS
(www.makisun.com; 55-3410 Akoni Pule Hwy; ⊗ 10am-6pm Mon-Sat) This adorable little 'lifestyle' boutique specializes in the sort of boho-chic goods and gifts you'd fully expect out of the heart of Hawi. Soy candles, surf art cards, Big Island themed pendants, crafted beach towels and tote bags, sea salt soap, sunscreen and that staple of 21st-century Hawaiian formal dress – the trucker hat – are all for sale.

Note that MakiSun is officially open 'most' Saturdays.

As Hawi Turns   CLOTHING
(📱 808-889-5023; 55-3412 Akoni Pule Hwy; ⊗ 9:30am-6pm) Forgive us this day that groan-worthy name and focus instead on a range of breezy, bohemian clothes, locally designed jewelry and crafts, handmade ukuleles and a general slate of gifts that are more interesting than an 'I Heart the Big Island' T-shirt. The shop's goods aren't all that's nice here; it's housed in the 1932 Toyama Building.

Kohala Mountain Gallery   ART
(55-3435 Hawi Rd; ⊗ 10:30am-5:30pm, closed Sun) Local artists show off their stuff in this classy gallery – the work embraces a wide range of prices, but this is original artwork, and the prices tend to skew correspondingly high. Note that the hours here can be fungible based on upcoming exhibitions and special events.

Elements   JEWELRY
(📱 808-889-0760; www.elementsjewelryandcrafts. com; 55-3413 Akoni Pule Hwy; ⊗ 10am-6pm Tue-Sat, to 5pm Sun & Mon) This jewelry and gift shop carries an eclectic collection of locally made finery.

❶ Information

North Kohala Community Center (📱 808-889-5523; www.northkohala.org; 55-3393 Akoni Pule Hwy; ⊗ 9am-4pm Mon-Fri, 10am-2pm Sat, 11am-1pm Sun) Contains the Kohala Welcome Center and a veritable army of volunteers who are more than willing to give you tips on how to explore North Kohala.

❶ Getting There & Away

Hawi is about 22 miles from Waimea via Hwy 250 (Kohala Mountain Rd, also known as Hawi Rd closer to town) and 18 miles from Kawaihae via Hwy 270. The town itself spreads along a few blocks on either side of Hwy 270, so you can't really miss it.

Akoni Pule Highway

The land along the Akoni Pule Hwy (Hwy 270) remains largely undeveloped, affording spectacular views of the Pacific (and Maui in the distance). This is a beautiful drive where the contrasts of North Kohala are on full display; in the southern portion of Hwy 270, you're surrounded by red rocks, thorn bushes and dusty prairie. As you round the top of the North Kohala peninsula, you leave the dry, rain-less portion of Kohala behind and enter the wet zone. The land becomes noticeably greener – the change is so abrupt it feels as if you'd stepped into a new level in a video game.

The winds here are something fierce, and many trees look as if they've been erected sideways. That's funny – what isn't is the way the wind can sometimes even shift your car. Be particularly aware of these conditions if you choose to cycle out here.

◎ Sights

★ Mo'okini Heiau TEMPLE

(☉ sunrise-sunset) ⊘ It's off the beaten path, but this heiau, near 'Upolu Point at Hawai'i's northernmost tip, is among the oldest (c AD 480) and most historically significant Hawaiian sites. Measuring about 250ft by 125ft, with walls 6ft high, the massive stone ruins sit brooding on a wind-rustled grassy plain. The sheer isolation of this spot adds to its stark appeal. The hike out here is a sight in and of itself – a lonely, sometimes eerie trek along gorgeous isolated coastline.

★ Mahukona Beach Park PARK

(off Hwy 270, between Mile 14 & 15; ☉ sunrise-sunset; ℗) ⊘ This abandoned harbor offers no sandy beach, so what's the appeal? *Excellent* snorkeling and diving. Head into the blue and you'll see coral-encrusted underwater mooring chains that lead to the wreckage of an old ship in the center of the harbor; said ship is home to multicolored fish and creeping eels. The left side of the park leads into a county park, where a shabby cluster of picnic tables and restrooms overlooks a scenic, if formidable, beach.

Lapakahi State Historical Park HISTORIC SITE

(☎ 808-587-0300; www.hawaiistateparks.org; off Hwy 270, Mile 14; ☉ 8am-4pm, closed state holidays; ℗) ⊘ This park was a remote fishing village 600 years ago. An unshaded, 1-mile loop trail traverses the 262-acre grounds, passing the remains of stone walls, house sites, canoe sheds and fishing shrines. Visitors can try their hand at Hawaiian games, with game pieces and instructions laid out for *'o'o ihe* (spear throwing), *konane* (checkers) and *'ulu maika* (stone bowling). Nothing is elaborately presented, so visitors need an imagination to appreciate the modest remains. Located just south of Mile 14.

Site of Kamehameha's Birth LANDMARK

⊘ A series of low stone walls overlaid on windy grassy fields is all that is left of the birthplace of the most famous monarch in Hawaiian history. Located adjacent to Mookini Heiau.

🏃 Activities

See p131 for information on the Mahukona to Kapa'a Walking Trail.

ℹ Getting There & Away

The Akoni Pule Highway – Hwy 270 – splits from Hwy 19 just south of Kawaihae and heads around the coast to Hawi. While Hele-On buses (www.heleonbus.org) traverse this route twice a day (around 9am and noon), it's nicest to drive or cycle at your own pace.

'Upolu Airport (☎ 808-327-9520; http://hawaii.gov/upp) Airport serving small-craft flights, located near the north point of the island.

Kapa'au

☎ 808 / POP 1734

Kapa'au isn't quite as bohemian and consciously crunchy as Hawi, and thus feels more authentically rustic and/or undeveloped and quiet, depending on your point of view. Either way, this is another former sugar town refashioned into an attractive tourist destination. You'll feel a lot of North Kohala regional pride, just as you did in Hawi, and in a similar vein to that town, there's an attractive degree of assimilation between transplants and locals.

Kapa'au has an ever-expanding range of good eateries and serves as a meeting point for several outdoor adventure tours. It's more spread out than Hawi, but basically follows the same plan: Hwy 270 cuts through the heart of town, which radiates off either side of the road.

◎ Sights

Kamehameha Rock LANDMARK

According to legend, Kamehameha carried this rock uphill from the beach to demonstrate his prodigious strength. Much later, when a road crew attempted to move it elsewhere, the rock stubbornly fell off the wagon – a sign that it wanted to stay put. Not wanting to upset Kamehameha's *mana* (spiritual essence), the workers left it alone. Don't blink or you'll miss it, on the inland roadside about 2 miles east of Kapaʻau, on a curve just past a small bridge.

Keokea Beach Park
BEACH

(📋808-961-8311; www.hawaiicounty.gov; 52-128 Keokea Park Road, off Akoni Pule Hwy; ⊙6am-11pm; 🅿) 🏄 While it has no beach to speak of, this county park, about 3.5 miles from Kapaʻau, has the best picnic spot around: an elevated pavilion with smashing views of a rocky bay and the motley crew of local surfers brave enough to test its dangerous shore breaks and strong currents. Besides picnic tables, there are barbecue grills, showers, drinking water and portable toilets. The marked turnoff is about 1.5 miles before the Pololu Valley Lookout.

Kamehameha the Great Statue
MONUMENT

(Akoni Pule Hwy) The statue on the front lawn of the North Kohala Civic Center has a famous twin in Honolulu, standing across from Iolani Palace. The Kapaʻau one was the original, constructed in 1880 in Florence, Italy, by American sculptor Thomas Gould. When the ship delivering it sank off the Falkland Islands, a duplicate statue was cast from the original mold and erected in downtown Honolulu in 1883. Later the sunken statue was recovered and sent here, to Kamehameha's childhood home.

🏃 Activities

⭐Hawaii Paso Finos
HORSEBACK RIDING

(📋808-884-5625; rides $85-130) Paso Finos are incredibly smooth-riding horses. Experience their bounceless gait and engaging demeanor with this outfit; they're obsessive about the care and treatment of their horses, and you'll engage your equine charge on a deep level that's unique on the Big Island. Learn horse handling, riding, therapeutic communication and even yoga on horseback. A special activity, even for experienced equestrians.

🎊 Festivals & Events

North Kohala Kamehameha
Day Celebration
CULTURAL

(www.kamehamehadaycelebration.org) On June 11 join islanders in honoring Kamehameha the Great in his birthplace. The spectacular parade of floral-bedecked horseback riders and floats culminates in an all-day gathering with music, crafts, hula and food.

🍴 Eating

King's View Cafe
HAWAIIAN $

(📋808-889-0099; www.kingsviewcafe.com; 54-3897 Akoni Pule Hwy; mains $10-15, pizza $15-26; ⊙7am-8:30pm; 🅿) The King's View has quickly become a community fixture in North Kohala, offering hot subs, creative pizzas (rosemary garlic anyone?), omelets, burgers and plate meals at competitive prices, especially when compared to the regional competition. Has a nice range of salads as well, although they almost all come with some kind of meat on top.

Gill's Lanai
CAFE $

(📋808-315-1542; 54-3866 Akoni Pule Hwy; mains $7-14; ⊙11am-5pm; 🚲🖶) With its umbrella-shaded patio and tiny kitchen, this avocado-colored roadside cafe offers a beach vibe and unfairly good food, given Kapaʻau's small size. Favorites include fish tacos, fish and chips, savory sandwiches, bowls of ahi *poke* (cubed, marinated raw fish) and veg quesadillas. Fair warning: the seating area is small and this little place gets packed for lunch.

CSC Cafe
HAWAIIAN $

(📋808-889-0208; 54-3615 Akoni Pule Hwy; mains $6-13; ⊙6am-9pm; 🅿🖶) There's a lot of focus on organic, healthy, gluten-free, name-your-food-trend dining in the Hawi and Kapaʻau area. Not at CSC – this place is all about straight-up, big Hawaiian portions served local style – plate lunches with teriyaki or Korean chicken, big breakfast plates with three-egg omelets and, of course, *loco moco*. Popular with local families.

🔒 Shopping

Rankin Gallery & Studio
ART

(📋808-889-6849; www.patricklouisrankin.net; 53-4380 Akoni Pule Hwy; ⊙11am-5pm Tue-Sat & noon-4pm Sun-Mon) Located midway between Pololu Valley and Kapaʻau, this gallery is noted for its landscapes of Hawaii and the American West (and for the conviviality of Patrick Rankin, a local character happy to show you around his studio).

ℹ Getting There & Away

Kapaʻau is 2.5 miles past Hawi heading east on Hwy 270. A Hele-On Bus (www.heleonbus.org) rolls through in the mornings and the early afternoons.

THE KOHALA INSTITUTE

A pioneering blend of indigenous cultural activity, historical preservation and environmental education is taking root in North Kohala. 'Iole, a 2400-acre tract of land extending from the Pacific Ocean into the Kohala Mountains, is now owned and managed by the **Kohala Institute** ('Iole; ☑ 808-889-5151; www.kohalainstitute.org; 53-580 'Iole Rd; ⊘ 8am-4pm Mon-Fri; ℗) ✿ **FREE**.

The Institute offers a large range of educational activities on this huge parcel of traditional land, many of which are aimed at families. Kids and parents are taught about sustainable cultivation and Native Hawaiian folkways on traditional farms. Check the website for more information on its ever-changing program schedule.

The area also encompasses the 54-acre **Bond Historic District**, which contains three historic properties all built by missionary Elias Bond (1813–62), a seminal figure in numerous aspects of Kohala life, from education to roads to the sugar industry. The **Bond Homestead** (1889) was the original base for Elias' work. The **Kohala Girls School** is an atmospheric throwback to the merger of New England missionary sensibilities with Hawaii. So too is the **Kalahikiola Church** (☑ 808-889-6703; www.kalahikiola congregationalchurch.com; 53-496 'Iole Rd; ⊘ services 9:30am; ℗). Connected by walking paths that are open to visitors, all properties are currently being restored, and are managed by the Kohala Institute.

Kohala Mountain Road

Arguably the Big Island's best scenic drive, Kohala Mountain Rd (Hwy 250) affords stupendous views of the Kohala–Kona coastline and three majestic volcanic mountains: Mauna Kea, Mauna Loa and Hualalai. Start from Waimea, climb past an overlook, and then follow the spine of the peninsula through green pastures until you finally descend to the sea at Hawi. The name changes to Hawi Rd close to that town.

🏃 Activities

Paniolo Riding
Adventures   HORSEBACK RIDING
(☑ 808-889-5354; www.panioloadventures.com; Kohala Mountain Rd, Mile 13.2; rides $69-175) Paniolo Adventures offers five different horseback rides ranging from one to four hours, enough for anyone to find their comfort level, whether it's walking or cantering. Of particular note is the Sunset Ride, allowing you to finally – ahem – ride off into the sunset. Horses are selected for the rider's experience and all necessary equipment is provided.

Na'alapa Stables   HORSEBACK RIDING
(☑ Kahua Ranch 808-889-0022, in Waipi'o 808-775-0419; www.naalapastables.com; Kahua Ranch Rd; rides $73-94) Na'alapa Stables organizes rides both into the Waipi'o Valley, and across the rolling hills and pastures of the

8500-acre Kahua Ranch, which affords exceptionally fine views of the coast from its 3200ft elevation. Either way, this is mostly a nose-to-tail ride, set at the level of the most inexperienced rider. Na'alapa's guides are personable and knowledgeable. No kids aged under 8 years.

☞ Tours

Kohala Mountain
Educational Farm   FARM
(☑ 808-937-7432; www.kohalamountainpumpkin patch.com; Kohala Mountain Road, Mile 12.5; ⊘ 7am-5pm Mon-Fri; ♿) ✿ Farm tours and a busy list of events keep the calendar full at this educational outfit, which aims to teach visitors and youngsters about the importance of agriculture on the Big Island. Both tours and events reflect the passing of the seasons; in fall, for example, hayrides are offered to a pumpkin patch.

🍴 Eating

Kahua Ranch   BARBECUE $$$
(☑ 808-882-7954; www.exploretheranch.com; Kahua Ranch Rd; per person without/with transportation $115/139, child 6-11yr half price, child under 5yr free; ⊘ 6-9pm Wed summer, 5:30-8:30pm Wed winter; ♿) Looking for a down-home country barbecue? Well they've got a doozy at the Kahua Ranch. One of the ranch owners, who missed his calling in stand-up comedy, gets things rolling with jokes on ranching life. Busloads of lei-wearing tourists then line

up for a hearty buffet of meat and beer in a nearby Quonset hut.

❶ Getting There & Away

The Mountain Road extends for about 22 miles between Hawi and Waimea. You can access it via an easy turnoff from both towns.

Pololu Valley

Followed to its absolute terminus, Hwy 270 takes you from the sparse habitation and gale-driven semi-desert north of Kawaihae to an utterly fecund emerald vision: the Pololu (Long Spear) Valley, a toothy hump of jungle ribboned by a black sand beach that together form an utterly unforgettable vista.

The area was once abundant with wetland taro, when Pololu Stream carried water from the deep, wet interior to the valley floor. When the Kohala Ditch was built in 1906, it diverted the water for sugar production. Unlike its sister valley, Waipi'o, Pololu Valley has not been inhabited since the 1940s. So, instead of territorial residents, you are met by a forest reserve.

If you're going to hike into the valley, be prepared for a series of tense switchbacks and steep drop-offs, but with that said, walking into the Pololu isn't as intensely difficult as trekking the Waipi'o.

🏃 Activities

For information on hiking the Pololu Valley, see p131.

☞ Tours

Hawaii Forest & Trail HIKING

(📞 808-331-8505; www.hawaii-forest.com; adult/child under 12yr $179/129) The Kohala Waterfalls Adventure includes a leisurely 1.5-mile loop trail to waterfalls (swimming included), as well as stops in Hawi and by ancient Hawaiian ruins. Transportation from the Waikoloa Resort Area or Kailua-Kona is included. Other adventures in the area include a shorter waterfalls-only trek (adult/child $89/79).

❶ Getting There & Away

The Pololu Valley is about 8 miles east of Hawi on Hwy 270. This is the end of the road, quite literally. If you're coming from Kailua-Kona, the valley is about 55 miles away and takes about 1½ hours to get to in decent traffic.

WAIMEA (KAMUELA)

📞 808 / POP 9212

The misty rolling pastureland surrounding Waimea is perhaps Hawai'i's most unexpected face. This is *paniolo* (cowboy) country, and nearly all of it, including Waimea itself, is controlled by Parker Ranch, the fifth-largest cow-calf ranch in the USA.

But don't leap to any conclusions: this is no company town. For its size, Waimea contains extraordinary depths, and one of the joys of visiting is to plumb them. From the highway all you see are bland strip malls, but closer inspection finds an vibrant arts scene, a long list of dining options,

---

DON'T MISS

RANCH LIFE

Windswept pastureland. Grazing cattle. Cloud-dappled skies. North Kohala makes city slickers yearn to be a *paniolo* (cowboy), at least for a day. These working ranches give you that chance. (Also see Hawaii Paso Finos (p154) in Kapa'au.)

For horseback riding, **Paniolo Riding Adventures** (p155) offers a variety of rides (short, long, picnic and sunset) across 11,000-acre Ponoholo Ranch and accommodates all levels. Horses are matched to a rider's level. This is the best choice for experienced riders. Boots, hats, chaps and jackets are provided.

Na'alapa Stables (p155) offers rides across the pastures of 8500-acre Kahua Ranch, with nice views of the coast from its 3200ft elevation. Group rides are adjusted to the level of the least-experienced rider, so most rides are nose-to-tail.

If a down-home country barbecue is more your style, join the Richards family of **Kahua Ranch** (p155) for a hearty buffet dinner (including beer) followed by country music, line dancing, a campfire and Piggly Wiggly, the performing pig. The sprawling pastureland is perfect for sunset watching and stargazing by telescope.

outstanding shopping, farmers markets and a rich cowboy heritage. Then there are all the fascinating transplants – organic farmers, astronomers, artists, teachers – an enlightened, well-traveled bunch. Old West courtesy and small town pace prevail, making it easy to strike up a conversation.

◉ Sights

Until the late 2000s, Waimea's main attractions were the Parker Ranch museum and 19th-century historic homes. They're now closed permanently, but there are other worthy stops.

Isaacs Art Center
GALLERY

(☑ 808-885-5884; http://isaacsartcenter.hpa.edu; 61-1268 Kawaihae Rd; ⊘ 10am-5pm Tue-Sat; P) FREE Set in a meticulously relocated 1915 schoolhouse, this series of bright, charming galleries displays a diverse collection of local and international fine art. The permanent collection features mostly renowned late masters, while the pieces for sale are by living artists. Works include paintings, pottery, furniture, jewelry and Hawaiian arts. As you enter, take note of Herb Kawainui Kane's classic *The Arrival of Captain Cook at Kealakekua Bay in January 1779*. The gallery is affiliated with the prestigious Hawaii Preparatory Academy.

Paniolo Heritage Center
MUSEUM

(☑ 808-854-1541; www.paniolopreservation.org; 67-139 Pukalani Rd; ⊘ 9am-2pm Tue, Thu & Fri, to 4pm Wed, noon-7pm Sat; P) FREE The Paniolo Preservation Society is developing this museum at Pukalani Stables, where Parker Ranch once bred horses. It's a work-in-progress, currently housing a photo exhibit and a saddle-making operation. The real reward is the personal touch: staffers are happy to talk story about *paniolo* (cowboy) history and the legacy of ranching in this corner of Hawaii.

Want ranching history and farmers market goods? Both the Waimea MidWeek Market (p160) and Kamuela Farmers Market (☑ 808-960-1493; www.kamuelafarmersmarket.com; ⊘ 7am-noon Sat; P) are held at the stables.

Waimea Nature Park
PARK

(Ulu La'au; ☑ 808-443-4482; www.waimeaoutdoorcircle.org; suggested donation $3; ⊘ 7am-5:30pm; ⊕) 🖋 Not to be confused with adjacent Waimea Park, this is a 10-acre green space in the center of town with picnic tables and

---

OF CATTLE & COWBOYS

Big Island ranching goes back to 1793, when British Captain George Vancouver gifted King Kamehameha with a herd of long-horned cattle. Protected by the king's *kapu* (taboo), the herd proliferated and by 1815 was a menace.

Massachusetts mariner John Palmer Parker, who arrived here in 1809 at age 19, was deft with a rifle and was hired to control the cattle problem. After successfully cutting the herd down to size, he received not only top-quality cows but also the hand of one of Kamehameha's granddaughters and a prime piece of land. Parker Ranch (p158) was founded in 1847.

---

free wi-fi. It's also a native plant restoration project. An excellent booklet on said plants and efforts to re-establish them in the region is available on site ($3, or free if you return it). The park is surprisingly easy to miss: follow the road by the side of the large Canada France building.

Church Row
CHURCH

(Church Rd) Home to Christians, Buddhists and Mormons, Church Row is a living history of religious life on the island. There are several noteworthy, if humble, structures along this curved street, including the much-photographed, all-Hawaiian Ke Ola Mau Loa Church. Look for the green steeple.

Ke Ola Mau Loa Church
CHURCH

(Green Church; Church Rd) A much-photographed, historic Hawaiian church with an eye-catching green steeple. There are no set times when the church is open, although Sunday mornings are obviously a safe bet.

Imiola Congregational Church
CHURCH

(www.imiolachurch.com; 65-1084 Mamalahoa Hwy; ⊘ service 9:30am; P) Waimea's first Christian church originated as a grass hut in 1830 and was built entirely of koa in 1857. Here lies the grave of missionary Lorenzo Lyons, who arrived in 1832 and spent 54 years in Waimea. He wrote many hymns in Hawaiian, including the classic 'Hawai'i Aloha.' You will need to turn onto Church Rd to find the building.

Waimea (Kamuela)

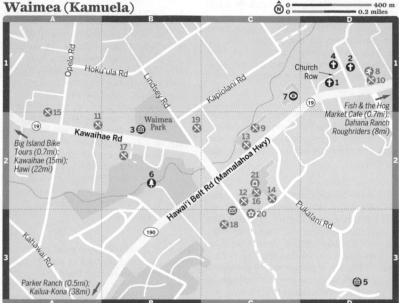

Parker Ranch

RANCH

(☎ 808-885-7311; www.parkerranch.com; 66-1304 Mamalahoa Hwy; P) Once the nation's largest privately owned ranch, peaking at 250,000 acres. Throughout the years, the ranch has had to sell off parcels, including 24,000 acres to the US military in 2006. For all that, today it's the fifth-largest cow-calf ranch in the USA, with at least 12,000 mother cows on 130,000 acres, and producing 12 million pounds of beef annually.

WM Keck Observatory Office

OBSERVATORY

(☎ 808-885-7887; www.keckobservatory.org; 65-1120 Mamalahoa Hwy; ⊙10am-2pm Mon-Fri; P) 🖉 FREE The lobby of this working office is open to the public. See models of the twin 10m (33ft) Keck telescopes, fascinating photos and a telescope trained on Mauna Kea. Informative volunteers prep you for a trip to the Mauna Kea summit.

🏃 Activities

⭐ Mountain Road Cycles CYCLING
(☎ 808-885-7943; www.mountainroadcycles.com;
64-1066 Mamalahoa Hwy; bikes per day from $30;
⊙ 9:30am-5:30pm Mon-Fri, 10am-3pm Sat) In
addition to renting bicycles, this full-service
bike shop arranges mountain biking and
road tours starting at $50. It prefers small
groups and serious riders, and gives fantastic advice on riding in the Big Island.

👉 Tours

Big Island Bike Tours CYCLING
(☎ 800-331-0159; http://bigislandbiketours.com;
65-1480 Kawaihae Rd; tours from $159) Runs a
bunch of bicycle ride tours on the Big Island,
including rides to the Hamakua Coast and
Waipiʻo Valley (both $159); if you feel like
exploring further afield, these guys can even
arrange tours as far afield as Kaʻu ($239).
They can also drop you off at a high point
overlooking Waimea ($35) so you can enjoy
a downhill ride into town.

Dahana Ranch Roughriders HORSEBACK RIDING
(☎ 808-885-0057; www.dahanaranch.com; 90min
ride adult/child $80/70; ⊙ 9am, 11am, 1pm & 3pm;
🚸) Ride American quarter horses bred, raised
and trained by third- and fourth-generation
paniolo (cowboys). On offer are open-range
rides for kids as young as three years, as well
as advanced rides ($115) and a cattle drive
($150) for those who can canter. The ranch,
owned and operated by a Native Hawaiian
family, is 7.5 miles east of Waimea, off Mamalahoa Hwy. Reservations required.

✨ Festivals & Events

Waimea Ukulele & Slack Key Guitar Institute Concert MUSIC
(☎ 808-885-6868; www.kahilutheatre.org; tickets from $20) This annual concert in mid-November is a dream opportunity to see
Hawaii's musical greats. Past headliners include Ledward Kaʻapana and Cyril Pahinui.

Waimea Paniolo Parade and Hoʻolauleʻa PARADE
(www.waimeatown.org; ⊙ mid-Sep) This mid-September parade of authentic paniolo
(cowboys), island princesses and beautiful
steeds begins at historic Church Row Park
and makes its way through town, followed
by a lively fair in Waimea Park. Run in
conjunction with statewide Hawaii Island
Festivals.

Waimea Cherry Blossom Heritage Festival CULTURAL
(waimeacherryblossom@gmail.com; Parker Ranch
Center & Church Row Park) Dark pink blossoms
are greeted with taiko drumming, mochi
(sticky rice cake) pounding and other Japanese cultural events on the first Saturday
in February.

Christmas Twilight Parade CHRISTMAS
(http://waimeatown.org; ⊙ early Dec) In early
December, the town gets into the Kalikimaka (Christmas) spirit with a block party.

Round-Up Rodeo RODEO
(☎ 808-885-7311; www.parkerranch.com; 67-1435
Mamalahoa Hwy, Parker Ranch Rodeo Arena; $8)
This whip-cracking event is held on the
first Monday in September after Labor Day
weekend.

🍴 Eating

The eating scene here is fantastic. You can
stock up on groceries at KTA Super Store
(☎ 808-885-8866; www.ktasuperstores.com; 65-
1158 Mamalahoa Hwy, Waimea Center; takeout $8-
11; ⊙ 6am-11pm; 🅿), a large supermarket with
a pharmacy, and at Healthways II (Kona
Natural Foods; ☎ 808-885-6775; www.konanatural
foods.net; 67-1185 Mamalahoa Hwy, Parker Ranch
Center; ⊙ 9am-7pm Mon-Sat, to 5pm Sun; 🅿), a
natural food store; both have delis.

Be sure to visit the Waimea Homestead
Farmers Market (☎ 808-333-2165; www.
waimeafarmersmarket.com; 67-1229 Mamalahoa
Hwy; ⊙ 7am-noon Sat; 🅿) 🍽 and MidWeek
Market (p160).

It kind of goes without saying, but this is
cowboy country, and as such, the beef here
is pretty great.

⭐ Aka Sushi Bar SUSHI $
(☎ 808-887-2320; www.bigakasushi.com; 65-
1158 Mamalahoa Hwy, Waimea Shopping Center;
sushi $5-14, bowls $12-18; ⊙ 10:30am-2:30pm
& 5-8:30pm Tue-Fri, 5-8:30pm Sat, closed Sun &
Mon; 🅿) Ignore the strip-mall setting: this
is a gem for reasonably priced or takeout
sushi, and a beloved local institution. Nigiri
(oblong-shaped sushi) and rolls have a high
fish-to-rice ratio, and everything is fresh. Be
sure to try the succulent hamachi kama
(grilled yellowtail collar).

⭐ Village Burger BURGERS $
(☎ 808-885-7319; www.villageburgerwaimea.com;
67-1185 Mamalahoa Hwy, Parker Ranch Center;
burgers $8-14; ⊙ 10:30am-8pm Mon-Sat, 10:30am-
6pm Sun) Burger connoisseurs, prepare to be

OFF THE BEATEN TRACK

WAIMEA BACK ROADS

For a peaceful, scented back road meander, turn right off Hwy 19 onto the **Old Mamalahoa Hwy**, just west of the 52-mile marker. (Coming from Hilo, turn left at the 43-mile marker opposite Tex Drive-In and then take the next immediate right.) This 10-mile detour winds through hill country, with small roadside ranches, old wooden fences and grazing horses. Take it slow, snap some pictures and get a taste of what Waimea used to be like. This makes a picturesque **cycling** route, but take care on the narrow, winding road, especially once you enter the forested curves of Ahualoa.

Diehards may want to explore the old miner's **quarry cave**, along the roadside 4 miles from the turnoff coming from Waimea. The entrance is at the bend in the road hemmed in by root-encrusted escarpments. Beyond the dying ferns of the most easterly cave, there's litter, beer bottles and a labyrinth of tunnels dug by early miners. Another set of caves just west looks like two eye sockets and requires an uphill scramble to enter.

Another back road drive is a long, hard 44 miles southeast along **Mana Rd**, wending around Mauna Kea. The landscapes are even more spectacular here, with expansive mountain vistas and green as far as the eye can see, but after 1.7 miles you are violating your rental car contract *in flagrante* when the road turns to dirt. You'll need a good 4WD to go the whole way, but you'll definitely be on the road less traveled. This is a great **mountain biking** excursion. Mana Rd is at the Mamalahoa Hwy 55-mile marker.

impressed. Big Island beef, veal and lamb burgers are juicy and tender, while vegetarian options (Waipi'o Valley taro or Hamakua mushroom) are equally scrumptious. All major ingredients pass muster with locavores, and freshly cut fries and aptly named 'Epic Shakes' top it off. Seating is very limited, but there's ample space in the adjacent food court.

★**Hawaiian Style Cafe**   DINER $
(☏808-885-4295; http://hawaiianstylecafe.com; 64-1290 Kawaihae Rd, Hayashi Bldg; dishes $7.50-13; ☺7am-1:30pm Mon-Sat, 7am-noon Sun) Think you can eat a lot? If the portions at this local favorite greasy spoon don't satisfy you, we nod our heads in awe (and maybe a little in disgust). Expect enormous portions of *loco moco* (rice, fried egg and hamburger patty topped with gravy or other condiments), pancakes, fried rice, burgers and more. Health nuts and dieters need not apply.

Waimea Town Farmers Market   MARKET $
(http://waimeatownmarket.com; 65-1224 Lindsey Rd; ☺7:30am-noon Sat) ✔ With a circle of vendors around a grassy field, this farmers market has a friendly, cohesive vibe. Find artisan edibles, including handcrafted pasta and sausages, bread freshly baked in a mobile oven, goat diary products, local sea salt and fresh juices. Located in front of Parker School.

Waimea MidWeek Market   MARKET $
(☏808-747-4300; 67-139 Pukalani Rd; ☺9am-3pm Wed; ℙ) ✔ This midweek market offers goodies including local organic produce, honey, handmade soaps, hot plate lunches and live *paniolo* music. Before browsing, visit the Paniolo Heritage Center (p157), also at the stables.

Lilikoi Cafe   CAFE $
(☏808-887-1400; 67-1185 Mamalahoa Hwy, Parker Ranch Center; meals $7-15; ☺7:30am-4pm Mon-Sat; ☑) ✔ This cheery cafe serves healthy, innovative food such as a breakfast burrito with eggs, tofu and sweet red pepper, and hearty vegetable lasagne. Drink the fresh carrot, apple, beet and ginger 'House Cocktail' ($5.50) and conquer the world. Hidden in the back of the shopping center.

Waimea Coffee & Co   CAFE $
(☏808-885-8915; www.waimeacoffeecompany. com; 65-1279 Kawaihae Rd, Parker Sq; sandwiches $3-12; ☺6:30am-3pm Mon-Fri, 7am-noon Sat, 8am-noon Sun; ☏) If you can snag a patio table, this is a lively hangout for espresso drinks and light fare. As one might expect, the excellent coffee is locally sourced.

Big Island Brewhaus & Taqueria   MEXICAN $
(☏808-887-1717; www.bigislandbrewhaus.com; 64-1066 Mamalahoa Hwy; mains $7.50-16; ☺11am-8:30pm Mon-Sat, noon-8pm Sun; ℙ) ✔ This

quality brewpub nails the intersection of booze and belly-busting meals. Owner Thomas Kerns has created more than a dozen memorable beers, including White Mountain Porter, rich with coffee and coconut, and Golden Sabbath Belgian Ale, which has a tremendous aroma. The setting is casual verging on sloppy. Much of the food is locally sourced.

Fish and the Hog Market Cafe   BARBECUE **$$**
(☑ 808-885-6268; 64-957 Mamalahoa Hwy; sandwiches $10-13, barbecue $15-26; ⊙ 11am-8pm; ℗) Barbecue isn't the first food genre folks tend to associate with Hawaii, but this is an island that loves smoked meat. This sit-down restaurant serves ribs, pulled pork, beef brisket and other kiawe-smoked meats with their signature barbecue sauces. Fish dishes, from gumbo to tacos, are also fabulously well done. Save room for the famous banana cream pie.

Pau   PIZZA **$$**
(☑ 808-885-6325; www.paupizza.com; 65-1227 Opelo Rd, Opelo Plaza; pizzas $17-28; ⊙ 11am-8pm) This casual eatery serves reliably creative, tasty and healthful salads, sandwiches, pastas and more than a dozen crisp, thin-crust pizzas.

★**Merriman's**   HAWAII REGIONAL **$$$**
(☑ 808-885-6822; www.merrimanshawaii.com; 65-1227 Opelo Rd, Opelo Plaza; lunch $13-18, dinner $28-58; ⊙ 11:30am-1:30pm Mon-Fri, 5:30-8pm daily; ℗) 🥢 Chef-owner Peter Merriman's Waimea namesake has long wowed diners with its creative use of organic, island-grown ingredients. Today there are four sister restaurants anchored by this, the original flagship. It's still the best fine-dining spot in town. The mahimahi marinated in *ponzu* (Japanese citrus sauce), wok-charred ahi and crispy molten chocolate 'purse' are classics. Lunch offers good value.

☆ Entertainment

★**Kahilu Theatre**   THEATER
(☑ 808-885-6868; www.kahilutheatre.org; 67-1185 Mamalahoa Hwy, Parker Ranch Center; ⊙ box office 9am-1pm Mon-Fri, show times vary) A hot spot for

music and dance, this theater has its finger on the pulse of the Big Island, and offers a variety of top performances – for example from Hawaii icons the Brothers Cazimero, the latest Van Cliburn winner and the annual Waimea Ukulele & Slack Key Guitar Institute Concert. Check the website for upcoming shows.

🔒 Shopping

Wishard Gallery   ART
(☑ 808-887-2278; www.wishardgallery.com; 67-1185 Mamalahoa Hwy, Parker Ranch Center; ⊙ 10am-6pm Mon-Sat, 11am-4pm Sun) Apart from Harry Wishard's own work – imaginative landscapes that pop up in houses and restaurants around the island – this gallery represents over two dozen other artists. Of note are Ethan Tweedie's stunning panoramas of Mauna Kea transferred to aluminum.

Gallery of Great Things   ARTS & CRAFTS
(☑ 808-885-7706; www.galleryofgreatthingshawaii.com; 65-1279 Kawaihae Rd, Parker Sq; ⊙ 9am-5:30pm Mon-Sat, 10am-4pm Sun) This unpretentious gallery is crammed with antiques, high-quality art and collectibles from Hawaii, Polynesia and Asia. Among the Hawaiian crafts for sale is *kapa:* bark cloth painstakingly handmade by traditional methods. There's something for every budget.

ℹ Information

North Hawaii Community Hospital (☑ 808-885-4444; www.nhch.com; 67-1125 Mamalahoa Hwy; ⊙ 24hr) Emergency services available 24 hours.

Post Office (☑ 808-885-6239; 67-1197 Mamalahoa Hwy; ⊙ 9am-4:30pm Mon-Fri, 9am-noon Sat) Address all Waimea mail to Kamuela.

ℹ Getting There & Away

Kailua-Kona is 37 miles away along Hwy 190; Hilo is 51 miles away on Hwy 19. You can also take Hwy 19 to Kailua-Kona if you want to check out the Kohala coast.

On Monday to Saturday the Hele-On Bus (www.heleonbus.org) goes from Waimea (Parker Ranch Center) to both Kailua-Kona and Hilo.

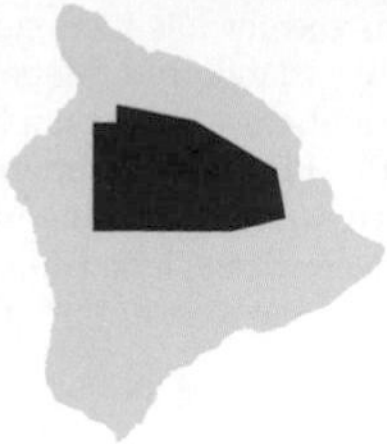

Mauna Kea & Saddle Road

♪ 808

Mauna Kea Webcams

➡ Keck Cosmic Cams (www.
keckobservatory.org/video)

➡ Gemini Cloud Cams
(www.gemini.edu/sciops/
telescopes-and-sites/
weather/mauna-kea/cloud-
cam)

➡ CFH Telescope Timelapse
Webcam (www.cfht.hawaii.
edu/webcam)

➡ MKVIS Live Allsky Cam
(www.ifa.hawaii.edu/info/
vis/photo-gallery/live-
webcam.html)

➡ NASA Infrared Telescope
Facility Cameras (http://
irtfweb.ifa.hawaii.
edu/~irtfcameras)

➡ Subaru Telescope
Webcams (www.naoj.org/
Weather)

Why Go?

You won't find much on the grassy lava-strewn plains between the massive shoulders of Mauna Loa and Mauna Kea, except for overwhelming scenery and an acute sense of your own insignificance.

Hastily built by the army to move troops across the island, the original Saddle Road's tight turns, blind hills and poor surface made it terrifying and downright dangerous, which motivated most rental companies to prohibit driving it. Now officially named Daniel K Inouye Hwy, a major reconstruction is almost complete that has removed Saddle Road's claws and teeth – but it's still an impressive beast with astounding views across the lonely heart of Hawai'i Island (when those views aren't obscured by fog – one remaining, real danger).

Just before Mile 42, the old road splits north toward Waimea, while the new section begins a zippy 9-mile, 3000ft descent toward Hwy 190.

When to Go

Nov–Mar Winter definitely visits the high country, making road and trail conditions less appealing and more dangerous; though it can snow any month of the year.

Aug & Dec Watching a meteor shower from the slopes of Mauna Kea is worthy of planning your trip around. Check StarDate (http://stardate.org/nightsky/meteors) for information. The Perseids (August) and Geminids (December) usually give reliable shows.

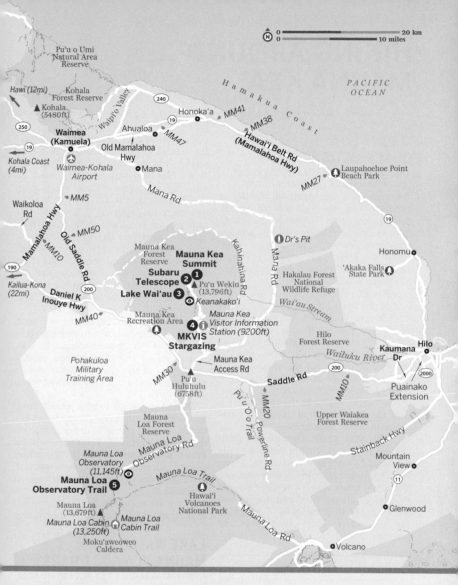

Mauna Kea & Saddle Road Highlights

1 **Mauna Kea Summit** (p170) Standing among the giants of astronomy, contemplating your own relationship with the heavens.

2 **Subaru Telescope** (p170) Inspecting the inner workings of a gargantuan precision instrument.

3 **Lake Wai'au** (p170) Paying respects to the Hawaiian gods of the earth and sky at the Hawaiian Islands' *piku* (navel).

4 **MKVIS Stargazing** (p172) Taking an optical journey through the cosmos from the top of the world.

5 **Mauna Loa Observatory Trail** (p164) Staring into the gaping maw of the world's largest above-water volcano.

HIKING AROUND MAUNA KEA

MAUNA LOA OBSERVATORY TRAIL

START/END MAUNA LOA OBSERVATORY
LENGTH 6.4 MILES ONE-WAY; ALL DAY

The easiest way to stand on the top of Mauna Loa is via this trail, but easiest doesn't mean 'easy' The 2500ft climb starts from Mauna Loa Observatory. It's a steep, exhausting adventure, but also an exceptional one. Prepare for snow at any time, and take a flashlight; it'll take longer than you think.

Start early; you want to be off the mountain or descending if afternoon clouds roll in. The trail is marked by *ahu* (cairns), which disappear in the fog. If fog does roll in, stop hiking; find shelter in one of several small tubes and hollows along the route until you can see again, even if this means waiting till morning – it's dangerously easy to get lost up here.

It is nearly 4 miles to the trail junction with the **Mauna Loa Trail** (p238; an alternative multiday backpacking route to the summit). Allow three hours for this gradual ascent of nearly 2000ft. Proceed slowly but steadily, keeping breaks short. If you feel the onset of altitude sickness, descend. About two hours along, you enter Hawai'i Volcanoes National Park, and the old lava flows appear in a rainbow of sapphire, turquoise, silver, ocher, orange, gold and magenta.

PU'U HULUHULU TRAIL

This easy 0.6-mile **trail** (junction Saddle Rd & Mauna Kea Rd) up the cinder cone **Pu'u Huluhulu** (Shaggy Hill; 6758ft) makes a piquant appetizer, and an acclimatization opportunity, before going up Mauna Kea. Inside a *kipuka* (volcanic oasis), the 20-minute hike climbs through protected native forest to the hilltop, from where there are panoramic views of Mauna Kea, Mauna Loa and Hualalai on clear days. Leave gates closed.

Once at the trail junction, the majesty of the summit's Moku'aweoweo Caldera overwhelms you (or maybe it's the exhaustion). Day hikers have two choices: proceed another 2.6 miles (about three hours) along the Summit Trail to the peak at 13,677ft, or explore the caldera by following the 2.1-mile Mauna Loa Cabin Trail. The second option is extremely interesting, leading to even grander caldera views and a vertiginous peek into the awesome depths of **Lua Poholo** (Falling Pit) – a pit crater that collapsed inward when lava left the summit. To do both would be an exhausting feat; choose wisely.

Descending takes half as long as ascending; depending on how far you go, prepare for a seven- to 10-hour round-trip hike. Bring copious amounts of water, food, a flashlight and rain gear, and wear boots, a winter coat and a cap – it's cold and windy year-round.

Day hikers do not need a permit, but if you would like to overnight at Mauna Loa Cabin, obtain a permit ($10 per group) the day before at Hawai'i Volcanoes National Park's **Backcountry Office** (p252), where rangers can inform you about current trail conditions and water-catchment levels at the cabin.

There are no visitor facilities or toilets at the trailhead or Mauna Loa Observatory.

LAKE WAI'AU & MAUNA KEA ADZ QUARRY

START/END MAUNA KEA ACCESS RD MILE 6 PARKING
LENGTH 3.6 MILES RETURN; 2 HOURS

This trail takes in two of the most important cultural sites on Mauna Kea.

Start by heading back down the road from the parking lot a few hundred feet, and look for a faint trail heading west toward a sign in the middle of the valley. Above and to the left is **Pu'u Wai'au** whose flanks are lighter colored and lined with channels of erosion, making it distinctly different from other nearby cinder cones. Steam, hot water

Snow-kissed winds whip over fields of alpine needlegrass and gray scree slopes. Tropical Hawai'i? Not quite – but the trails and moonscapes around Mauna Kea are just as magical and unique.

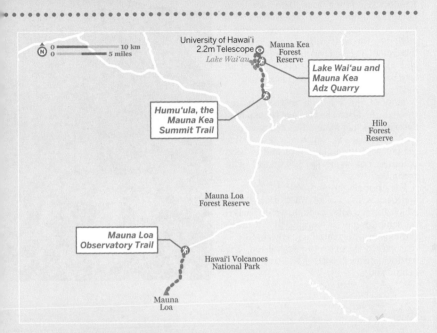

N
0 — 10 km
0 — 5 miles

University of Hawai'i
2.2m Telescope
Lake Wai'au

Mauna Kea
Forest
Reserve

Lake Wai'au and
Mauna Kea
Adz Quarry

*Humu'ula, the
Mauna Kea
Summit Trail*

Hilo
Forest
Reserve

Mauna Loa
Forest Reserve

**Mauna Loa
Observatory Trail**

Hawai'i Volcanoes
National Park

Mauna
Loa

and sulfur percolating up through the cone changed the composition of the rock, breaking it down into a finer, clay-like grain.

The trail heads uphill until it intersects with the **Mauna Kea Summit Trail**. Continue straight over the saddle directly west and you'll see tiny **Lake Wai'au** (p170) in the valley below. Although the area receives an average of only 8in of rain each year, it's enough to keep the sacred lake filled.

Return to the trail intersection, only this time head downhill (south) on the Summit Trail while looking for the light-gray areas of **glacial till**, the result of lava being pulverized by the moving glaciers that once covered the mountaintop. Also watch for darker, almost black outcroppings. When lava erupts under ice, the rapid cooling can form dense, fine-grained blocks of basalt, which ancient Hawaiians prized for making adz heads.

Exactly 1 mile below the intersection you'll find an astonishing pile of black chips below a tiny cave. This virtual mountain is the result of hundreds of years of adz-making: craftsmen chipping sharp edges into chunks of hard rock **quarried** (p171) nearby.

This is a highly revered place; leave all rocks where you found them.

HUMU'ULA, THE MAUNA KEA SUMMIT TRAIL

START MAUNA KEA VISITOR INFORMATION STATION
END UH 2.2M TELESCOPE
LENGTH 6 MILES ONE-WAY; 5 HOURS

Start the Humu'ula trail very early – by 6am if possible. It typically takes five hours to reach the summit, half as long coming down, and you'll want some time to explore in between. Register at the Visitor Information Station (p173) where you can also get advice from the staff. Be prepared for serious weather – snow and 100mph winds are possible.

From the Visitor Information Station walk 1000ft up the road toward the

Onizuka Center for International Astronomy.
Where the pavement ends, go left on the
dirt road, following several 'Humu'ula
Trail' signs to the trail proper.

Reflective T-posts and cairns mark the
route as the trail traverses up above the
10,000ft vegetation zone. After about an
hour the summit road comes back into
view on your right. As you weave around
cinder cones and traipse over crumbled
'a'a (rough, jagged lava) and slippery scree,
you pass various spur trails – which all
lead back to the access road in case you are
having second thoughts.

Most of the way you will be passing
through the **Mauna Kea Ice Age Natural Area
Reserve**. Much of Mauna Kea was once covered with glaciers, which are responsible
for much of the unique lava and erosion
patterns not typically associated with
volcanoes.

For example, around Mile 1.7, the trail
approaches the top of **Waikahalulu Gulch**,
which formed after enough water backed
up behind a glacial moraine that it broke
through in a torrential, cataclysmic flood
that carved deeply into the hillside. The
hardest, steepest part of the trail is now
behind you.

Mauna Kea

Lake Wai'au

At Mile 3.1, begin looking for outcroppings of dark gray or black basalt. The value of this material was not lost on the ancient Hawaiians who established a **major mining operation** (p171) to make adz heads. The trail passes just to the west of an impressive pile of flakes accumulated over likely hundreds of years as craftsmen sat at the mouth of the caves chipping away the days.

At the trail intersection at Mile 4, take a 10-minute detour to the west that takes you over the saddle and down to **Lake Wai'au** (p170), the sacred *piku* of the Hawaiian Islands. Likely this place remained flooded for some time during the glacial melt before draining to form **Pu'u Pohakuloa Gulch**.

Return to the four-way junction and head north (uphill) for the final push to the Mauna Kea Summit Rd at a parking area. Suddenly **Millimeter Valley** comes into view, nicknamed for its submillimeter and mil-

limeter observatories. The trail officially ends at the access road's Mile 7, but the true summit still snickers at you another 1.5 miles away.

For Native Hawaiians, the summit is a region, a realm, not a point on a map. But if you really need to place a boot toe on **Pu'u Wekiu** (p172), Mauna Kea's true summit, soldier on till you reach the **UH 2.2m Telescope** (p172), where the short spur trail to the summit begins. However, keep in mind that this is a sacred mountain, which some believe has already suffered enough disrespect from the development here.

The return route is via the same way you came up, only this time the sprawling vistas will be in your face; but so will the breeze. As an alternative, return along the shoulder of the access road rather than retracing the trail. Though the road is 2 miles longer, it's smoother walking and easier to follow as sunlight fades.

ROAD TRIP: MAUNA KEA ACCESS ROAD

Winding from unique volcanic formations to the brilliant domes of the Astronomy Precinct, this road trip will leave you feeling a world away from tropical island clichés.

❶ Pu'u Huluhulu

This epic drive to the lofty 13,776ft summit of Hawai'i starts at an already respectable 6578ft, so it's worth taking a moment here to climb **Pu'u Huluhulu**, the forested *kipuka* (oasis) across the highway, just to get your lungs used to the thinner air. Altitude can affect anyone, and impair driving.

Mauna Kea Access Rd, aka Mauna Kea Summit Rd, aka John A Burns Way (named after Hawaii's second governor) starts easy enough, darting off through the grasslands past the sign warning of (invisible) cows toward the historic **Humu'ula Sheep Station** (p172).

The Drive > Continuing up Mauna Kea, you'll wind between a few cinder cones until Mile 6 and an off-road track that marks the entrance of a true off-the-beaten-path 4WD adventure: Kahinahina Road. The 37-mile route circles the mountain back to Saddle Road, and yes, it voids everything about your rental-car contract.

❷ Mauna Kea Visitor Information Station

Stop at the **visitor center** (p173) to acclimatize, check road conditions, and see if there are any budget travelers looking for a ride up. Don't forget to reset your odometer; the mile markings start over here and we'll go by those.

Pass **Onizuka Center for International Astronomy** on your right where visiting researchers and observatory staff reside. The center is named for Hawaiian-born Ellison Onizuka. He was the first Asian-American astronaut to reach space, but tragically died in the Challenger explosion.

The Drive > 4WD is highly recommended for the road beyond. Although the gravel is usually smooth, 2WD vehicles (even 2WD SUVs) ruin the road surface by spinning out on the way up, and 2WD simply does not have a low enough gear to descend safely. The road begins the big climb almost immediately beyond the center. Use caution, and park only in designated areas.

❸ Apollo Valley

At Mile 4.4 you pass a gravel turnout, and just to the east is a gray gravelly wash nicknamed **Apollo Valley** (p172). Astronauts and engineers alike have trained for moon- and Mars-bound missions here over the decades. The unique surface is glacial till which formed when giant rivers of ice pulverized the lava rock beneath them. Glaciers as thick as 560ft covered Mauna Kea as recently as 13,000 years ago, creating some unique geological features not usually associated with Hawai'i volcanoes. If you want a closer look, there's a parking lot at Mile 5.1.

The Drive > Keep along the access road until you reach Mile 5.6.

❹ Very Long Base Array

At Mile 5.6, a side road takes you east to the westernmost antenna in the **Very Long Base Array** (p172). To the west you may be able to see outcroppings of black rock – from here it's hard to appreciate the scale of the **Mauna Kea Adz Quarry** (p171), the source of the island's hardest rock. The tight-grained, dense basalt formed when lava from eruptions under glaciers cooled almost instantly against the ice.

The Drive > Back on the Mauna Kea Access Rd, it's not even a mile to your next stop.

5 Lake Wai'au

At Mile 6.5 is the trailhead to both the quarry and Lake Wai'au, a short but powerful trip into Mauna Kea's sacred realms. If you look west up the trail, you'll notice the lighter almost yellowish-orange hue of the cinders on Pu'u Wai'au. Geologists believe that hot water and sulfur gas steaming through the cinders caused them to break down into a fine, almost clay-like silt, which is why the cone has more visible evidence of water erosion.

The Drive > Continue along the access road to Mile 7.4. As you curve around the flank of Pu'u Haukea, the gleaming white domes of the Astronomy Precinct begin popping into view. There's $600 million worth of science happening up here – an awesome sight.

6 Telescopes & Twins

The access road splits at Mile 7.4, and either way will take you around the partially paved summit loop to each of the observatories. We prefer to take the right, which zigzags up the final 1.2 miles to the parking area beside the **UH 2.2m Telescope** (p172) where you'll have commanding views of the summit caldera and beyond.

Welcome to the top of the Pacific. How you choose to proceed is up to you. Definitely stop by the **Keck Twins**, a pair of the largest astronomical telescopes in the world, to get a glimpse of what's happening on the inside of these massive monoliths.

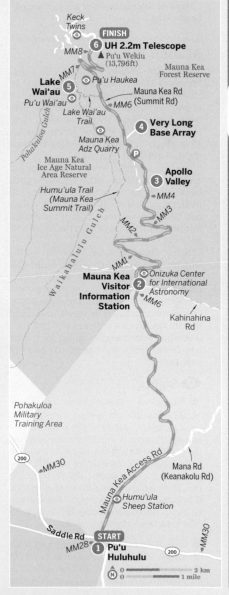

ℹ Getting There & Away

As you drive east toward Hilo along Hwy 200, the road splits at Mile 6. Hwy 200 turns northeast as Kaumana Dr into downtown, while Hwy 2000 continues through suburbia toward Hwy 11. It's an easy junction to miss.

At the other end, a new re-route at Mile 41.6 sends traffic down toward Hilo while the Old Saddle Road continues right to Waimea.

There are no gas stations, or any services, on Saddle Road.

Mauna Kea

Mauna Kea (White Mountain) is called Mauna O Wakea (Mountain of Wakea) by Hawaiian cultural practitioners. While all of the Big Island is considered the first-born child of Wakea (Sky Father) and Papahanaumoku (Earth Mother), Mauna Kea has always been the sacred *piko* (navel) connecting the land to the heavens.

For the scientific world, it all began in 1968 when the University of Hawai'i (UH) began observing the universe from atop the mountain. The summit is so high, dry, dark and pollution-free that it allows investigation of the furthest reaches of the observable universe.

Many Hawaiians are opposed to the summit 'golf balls' – the white observatories now dotting the skyline. While not antiscience, they believe unchecked growth threatens the mountain's *wahi pana* (sacred places), including heiau (temples) and burial sites. Litter, vandalism and pollution (including toxic mercury spills) have been a problem. Visit with respect, and pack out your trash.

◉ Sights

★ Mauna Kea's Summit Area   LANDMARK

At 13,796ft in the air, you are above 40% of the atmosphere and 90% of its water vapor – apparently perfect conditions for growing the giant mushroom-like observatories that have popped up around the summit. Glistening in the sun against the desolate terrain like a human colony on an alien planet, this is the greatest collection of telescopes on earth. You can practically feel the knowledge being sucked out of the sky.

★ Lake Wai'au   ARCHAEOLOGICAL SITE

On an island with a conspicuous dearth of surface water, tiny Lake Wai'au's existence on a porous lava mountain is something of an enigma. Hawaiian legends say it's bottomless, connecting the realm of the heavens and the earth. As the *piku* of the island chain, its waters are the most sacred. Some still place their newborn's umbilical cord in the lake to ensure a strong connection to the gods. To say this place feels significant would be an understatement.

Geologists disagree about what's trapping the water and, frankly, both theories kind of blow our mind: glacial silt, or permafrost...in the tropics. Glaciers covered the peak as recently as 13,000 years ago and eruptions under the ice may have formed fine ash. Permafrost (underground ice that never melts) has been found on the nearby summit cone **Pu'u Wekiu**, though there is no evidence of it here, yet. A third theory – that percolating sulfur gas altered the cinder composition and created clay – is probably most likely correct. Regardless of what's keeping the water here, however, it most certainly comes from rain and snow, as confirmed when the lake almost dried up in 2015 after a long drought.

Park at the paved area on the east side of the Mauna Kea Access Rd just past Mile 6. The 0.7-mile trail to Lake Wai'au is on the west side of the road just a short way back down the hill.

★ Subaru Telescope   OBSERVATORY

(📞 808-934-7788; www.subarutelescope.org; ⏱ tours English/Japanese 11:30am/10:30am & 1:30pm Tue-Thu) **FREE** When it came online in 1999, Japan's 8.2m (29.6ft) Subaru Telescope was the most expensive observatory ever constructed. The 22-ton mirror is one of the largest optical mirrors in existence. The telescope recently helped create a 3D map of 3000 galaxies that shows Einstein's theory of relativity still holds true. Observatory tours (which, sadly, don't include looking through the telescope) are given in Japanese or English but not both; they fill up fast so register online early.

WM Keck Observatory   OBSERVATORY

(📞 808-935-6268; www.keckobservatory.org; ⏱ visitors gallery 10am-4pm Mon-Fri) **FREE** Mirrors larger than 8m (26.2ft) are so heavy that gravity distorts them as they move. Keck's breakthrough design overcame that limitation in 1993 by using a series of 36 hexagonal mirror segments mounted and independently adjusted that function as a single piece of glass 10m (32.8ft) in diameter. The results were so good, they built

Mauna Kea Summit Area

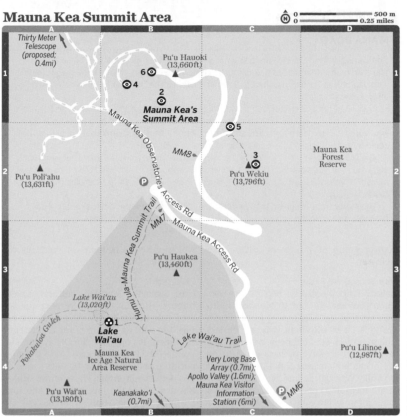

Mauna Kea Summit Area

Keck II next door in 1996. Visitors are welcome into the gallery, which has brief displays, public restrooms and views inside the Keck I dome.

Mauna Kea Adz Quarry HISTORIC SITE
(Keanakako'i) Quarries scattered over 7.5 sq miles produced tons of exceptionally dense and fine-grained basalt (dubbed Hawai'iite) used to make a tool similar to

an ax called an adz. The scale of the operation is difficult to appreciate until you're standing next to one of the enormous piles of leftover chippings. The site is on the **Mauna Kea Trail** (Humu'ula Trail; p165), 1 mile and 650ft below its intersection with the Lake Wai'au trail. It's a registered National Historic Landmark and considered a sacred place.

Thirty Meter Telescope
(planned) OBSERVATORY
(TMT; www.tmt.org) Walk behind the Keck Twins and look northwest and you'll see... nothing. Down there is the ideal location for the TMT, which supersizes Keck's many-small-mirrors design to create the world's most advanced and powerful optical telescope. Once complete, the 492 individually mounted mirrors will peer into the deepest mysteries of the universe. We say once, not if, because the TMT will be built, just maybe not atop Mauna Kea if

OFF THE BEATEN TRACK

MANA ROAD

Contouring around Mauna Kea to Waimea just above the tree line, the 50-mile 4WD Mana Rd (sometimes called Keanakolu Rd) has more scenery than it knows what to do with. It also has a monument to the Scottish botanist the Douglas fir tree was named after: David Douglas.

In 1833, at the age of 35, Douglas was hiking alone through the area when he fell into a pit dug to trap wild bulls. Unfortunately, the pit was still occupied by a previous victim who gored him to death. Or so the story goes. Another telling claims that the fall was not accidental, but caused by a local escaped convict with an ax.

The first section from Saddle Road is fairly decent gravel, but the going gets increasingly rough as you approach the Dr's Pit (as the monument is known) 17.6 miles in. A few miles further is **Keanakolu Ranger & Bunkhouse Cabins** (http://camping.ehawaii.gov; cabins $50-90).

The road can be rough on the Waimea side (check current conditions) but is always passable on a mountain bike – our preferred method of locomotion here.

a vocal group of protesters (p173) have their way.

Very Long Base Array OBSERVATORY
(National Radio Observatory; http://science.nrao.edu/facilities/vlba) One of 10 identical radio receivers that span 5351 miles from Mauna Kea to St Croix, US Virgin Islands. The $85 million project went online in 1993 and has tackled some massive projects equal to its size, including creating a full 3D model of the Milky Way Galaxy, and getting more accurate measurements of the mass of black holes. All units are controlled remotely by a base station in Socorro, New Mexico. At Access Rd Mile 5.

Apollo Valley HISTORIC SITE
(Moon Valley) Just past Mile 4 on the east side of the summit road, a washed-out valley full of grayish glacial till and rocks is a dead ringer for the surface of the moon. So much so that the Apollo astronauts trained here for their missions. It has continued to test the mettle of moon and Mars rovers over the years, and some of their knobby tire tracks are still faintly visible. Park only in designated areas.

Humu'ula Sheep Station HISTORIC SITE
For 100 years these pastures were filled with sheep, and that historical legacy is marked by nearby rock walls stacked by Japanese laborers and the Humu'ula Sheep Station at the corner of Saddle and Mauna Kea Access Rds. By 1963, the station was no longer used for sheep, but did support cattle operations –

which proved to be more commercially viable – until 2002.

Pu'u Wekiu MOUNTAIN
(True Summit) Hawaiian cultural practitioners ask that visitors respect the sacred true summit of Mauna Kea and not hike the trail to the top of the cinder cone (13,796ft). It's opposite the **UH 2.2m Telescope** (UH2.2, UH88) where there is ample parking, and which – at 13,776ft – already has perfectly stunning views of the sunset. Besides, given the biting winds, the high altitude sapping your strength, and the extreme cold, it all just sounds like a miserable time.

🏃 Activities

For information on the Mauna Kea Summit Trail, see p165.

⭐ **MKVIS Stargazing Program** STARGAZING
(www.ifa.hawaii.edu/info/vis; ⊘ 6-10pm; 🚼) **FREE**
The Mauna Kea Visitor Information Station offers a terrific nightly stargazing program. Numerous telescopes are set up outside the station, each trained on a different celestial object. On an average night you might move from the Ring Nebula to the Andromeda Galaxy to a galactic cluster to Jupiter's moons. It is a unique and profoundly memorable experience.

MKVIS Volunteer Program VOLUNTEERING
(www.ifa.hawaii.edu/info/vis/volunteer-program.html) Long-term volunteers staff the visitor center and bookstore and assist with public stargazing programs.

☞ Tours

Hawaii Forest & Trail TOURS
(📞 808-331-8505; www.hawaii-forest.com; tour per person $209; ☺ tours nightly, weather permitting) 🥾 Top-notch tour of sunset and stargazing, with knowledgeable guides who take you to the summit, then return down for a tour of the heavens with an 11in Celestron telescope. Pick-ups are from near Kailua-Kona, Waikoloa and the Hwys 190/200 junction. Includes parkas, gloves and picnic dinner at a private location. Participants must be at least 16 years old. Book early.

Mauna Kea Summit Adventures TOURS
(📞 808-322-2366; www.maunakea.com; tours per person $212) The granddaddy of Mauna Kea tours has been taking folks to the summit for over 30 years. A hot dinner outside MKVIS, cold-weather parkas to borrow and stargazing through an 11in Celestron telescope are included. Pick-ups from Kailua-Kona, Waikoloa and Hwys 190/200 junction. Children must be at least 13 years old.

Arnott's Lodge Summit Tours TOURS
(📞 808-339-0921; www.arnottslodge.com; tours per person $180; ☺ tours nightly Wed-Mon) Summit and stargazing tours depart from Hilo regardless of weather conditions. Guides point out constellations with a laser-pointer, but they do not bring a telescope, or food. Guests of Arnott's Lodge get discounted rates.

❶ Information

Mauna Kea Visitor Information Station
(MKVIS; 📞 808-961-2180; www.ifa.hawaii.edu/info/vis; ☺ 9am-10pm) Modestly sized MKVIS packs a punch with astronomy and space-exploration videos and posters galore, and information about the mountain's history, ecology and geology. Budding scientists of all ages revel in the gift shop, while knowledgeable staff help you pass the time acclimatizing to the 9200ft altitude. Check the website for upcoming special events, such as lectures about science and Hawaiian culture, typically held on Saturday nights.

Excellent free stargazing programs happen from 6pm until 10pm nightly, weather permitting.

❶ Getting There & Away

Coming from Waimea or Kona take Saddle Road (Hwy 200) or the the new Daniel K Inouye reroute. From Hilo, drive *mauka* (inland) on Kau-

---

TMT: CONTROVERSY AT THE SUMMIT

The sacred summit of Mauna Kea provides humans with a link to the heavens. For astronomers, it's an ideal location above the clouds that provides a clearer window to the origins of the universe. For Hawaiians, it is the *piku* connecting the earth with the sky – and some of them believe the observatories are a desecration.

These sentiments reached a head in 2014 when peaceful protesters halted the groundbreaking ceremony for the $1.4 billion **Thirty Meter Telescope** (p171) (TMT). This act surprised developers who had conducted dozens of community meetings during the long permitting process, and chose a site a mile away from known burials, free from endangered plants and below the summit where it would be less visible. In addition, TMT committed to donating $1 million a year to science education in Hawaii.

For those opposed, however, none of that matters. The mountain is sacred, and management plans don't consider the Hawaiian people, but rather continue a pattern of colonial disregard that has long disenfranchised them. Along with their demand to scrap the TMT, the protesters want the gratis lease of the summit area held by University of Hawai'i to be turned over to a community-based authority representing all interests.

In 2015, protest blockades, petitions and lawsuits sent the TMT case to the Hawaiian Supreme Court, which sent it back to the permitting stage.

Meanwhile, the governor made an agreement to decommission 25% of existing telescopes at the summit before the TMT is operational, and promised that this would be the last new site developed. Final hearings into the TMT's fate were being held at time of research.

Regardless of the outcome, those backing the TMT said they will begin construction in 2018 – if not in its scientifically ideal location atop Mauna Loa, then at a backup site in the Canary Islands.

TO BUY A SUMMIT TOUR OR NOT, THAT IS THE QUESTION

Tours have many positives: transportation from other parts of the island to the visitor station, 4WD to the summit, warm clothing, a box dinner, excellent guides with deep knowledge of astronomy, and the ease of it all. The negatives to consider include the considerable cost (around $200 per individual), a fixed and limited schedule, and the herd factor.

Itinerary-wise, a typical sunset tour starts in the early afternoon, stops for dinner, arrives at the summit just before sunset, stays about 40 minutes (this is not long enough to allow for hiking), descends to the visitor station area for private stargazing with a single telescope, and gets you home after 9pm. There is no tour of summit telescopes.

Now assess the DIY alternative. If you have the proper vehicle (or know someone who does) you can do some hiking on your own, poke into the Keck observatory, and experience a sacred mountain at your own pace. Finally, you can come back down to the visitor station for a smorgasbord of stargazing amid multiple telescopes. You'll have to pack your dinner and bring warm clothing, but the total cost is zero, apart from the car, which you might have rented anyway.

mana Dr (Hwy 200) or Puainako Extension (Hwy 2000), both of which become Saddle Road. Start with a full tank of gas – there are no service stations out here.

The Visitor Information Station (MKVIS) and the summit beyond are on Mauna Kea Access Rd, near Mile 28 on Saddle Road. MKVIS is 6 miles uphill from Saddle Road; the summit is another 8 miles beyond that. Call ☑ 808-935-6268 for current road conditions.

❶ Getting Around

Driving to the summit is best done in a low-gear 4WD vehicle – there have been many accidents that underscore this point. Over half of the summit road is loose gravel, sometimes at a 15% grade. Not only can the wrong vehicle be deadly to you, but spinning tires create washboard bumps that put everybody at risk.

Check with your rental-car company if your contract even allows driving past the visitor center; if in doubt, there is always the option of taking a guided summit tour.

Drive in low gear and be particularly careful on the way down not to ride your vehicle's brakes: they can overheat and fail. Driving around sunrise or sunset can create hazardous, blinding conditions. Fog and ice are terrifying.

Plan to drive up to the summit during the daytime as headlights interfere with astronomical observations. All vehicles are required to descend 30 minutes after sunset.

Saddle Road

If you're driving Saddle Road from Hilo, you'll pass a few interesting, mid-elevation hiking trails through *kipuka* (oases) and

lava flows before reaching Mauna Loa Observatory Rd to the south and Mauna Kea Access Rd to the north 0.3 miles later. Beyond this, much of the rolling grassland punctuated with cinder cones is occupied by the US Army's **Pohakuloa Training Area**, a 133,000-acre complex complete with (what looks from above to be) fake villages, networks of trenches and a bombed-out airstrip.

◉ Sights

Mauna Kea Recreation Area　PARK
(☑ 808-961-8311; http://hawaiicounty.ehawaii.gov/camping; Saddle Rd Mile 34; cabins/bunkhouse $150/480; ⊙ 6am-7pm; ⊞) Desperately needed renovations have made the only public facilities along Saddle Road an altogether pleasant stop. Clean restrooms and a playground with plenty of ropes to climb mean it's an excellent spot to stretch your legs and let antsy children exhaust themselves. Cabins were still under construction at time of research, but hopefully the improvements include thicker walls to block the sound of the neighbors: a military training center that occasionally performs large-scale maneuvers.

Mauna Loa Observatory　OBSERVATORY
(MLO; www.esrl.noaa.gov/gmd/obop/mlo/) The weather measurements made here are so sensitive that when the observatory was built in 1956 scientists asked the national park to ban stoves at the summit cabin, fearing those emissions 6 miles away would throw off their readings. The park didn't,

but the observatory managed to adjust. It has continuously recorded carbon dioxide (CO_2) and other human-produced greenhouse gas levels ever since, defining much of our understanding of global climate change. Tours of the facility are by appointment only.

Activities

For information on the Mauna Loa Observatory Trail and the Pu'u Huluhulu Trail, see p164.

Mauna Loa

Observatory Road   SCENIC DRIVE

If the hulking mass of Mauna Loa proves too tantalizing to resist (but not tantalizing enough for the three- to five-day south-side backpacking trip (p238), drive its north flank on this one-lane, 17.5-mile paved road that punches through piles of *'a'a* (rough, jagged type of lava) and crosses rivers of *pahoehoe* (smooth-flowing lava) as it climbs to Mauna Loa Observatory (11,145ft). It's a fun, if exhausting, drive in a car, and an abso-

lute blast on a motorcycle (or bicycle). Just watch for oncoming vehicles; they're infrequent but consistent.

Entertainment

Mauna Kea Polo Club   SPORTS

(☑ 808-960-5098; www.maunakeapoloclub.com; Waiki'i Ranch; adult/child under 12yr $5/free; ⊙ 11am-3:30pm Sun Oct-Dec) And now for something completely different: polo! An ancient game involving a ball, mallets and ponies played on an impressive, large field. The games are sponsored by Mauna Kea Polo Club and held 6.4 miles up Old Saddle Rd from Waimea on exclusive Waiki'i Ranch. More Big Island than Long Island, they are very low key, with BBQ eats and T-shirts for sale. Tailgating encouraged.

It's the perfect excuse for a beautiful drive and picnic, and you might even learn something about polo. Turn west off Old Saddle Rd half-way between the Daniel K Inouye and Mamalahoa Highways; the gate house attendant will let you in.

MAUNA KEA & SADDLE ROAD SADDLE ROAD

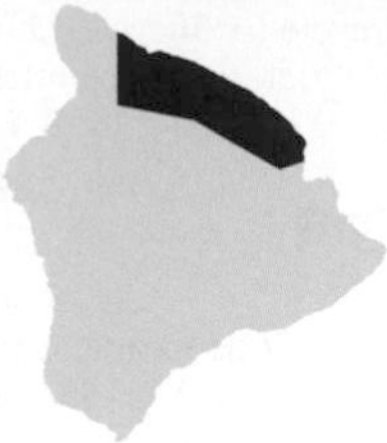

Hamakua Coast

☎ 808

Best Places to Eat

➡ Gramma's Kitchen (p185)

➡ Papa'aloa Country Store & Cafe (p192)

➡ Honoka'a Farmers Market (p185)

➡ Waipi'o Cookhouse (p190)

➡ Cafe il Mondo (p188)

➡ Sea DandeLion Cafe & Awa Bar (p185)

Best Farm Tours

➡ Hamakua Mushrooms (p191)

➡ Mauna Kea Tea (p184)

➡ Onomea Tea Company (p194)

➡ Hawaiian Vanilla Company (p185)

➡ Long Ears Coffee (p184)

Why Go?

Stretching from Waipi'o Valley to Hilo, the Hamakua Coast combines rugged beauty and bursting fertility. Here you'll find rocky shores and pounding surf, tropical rainforests and thunderous waterfalls. The color green takes on new meaning, especially in Waipi'o Valley, which you can explore on horseback or on a steep, exhilarating hike.

On the slopes of Mauna Kea, farmers grow vanilla, tea, mushrooms and other boutique crops, modernizing and diversifying island agriculture. Visit these small-scale farms for a close-up look at island life (and to sample its delicious bounty). Sugarcane once ruled the Hamakua Coast, with acres of plantations and massive trains chugging along the coast and across towering bridges spanning the tremendous gulches. Stop at old-time museums and delve into the rich history here. Pause to imagine the 'old plantation days.' Go slow, explore the back roads and step back in time.

When to Go

May–Sep Less chance of rain, especially if hiking in Waipi'o Valley (although the windward Hamakua Coast can see showers year-round).

Dec–Feb Accommodations will be pricier and booked well in advance during the winter high season.

Mar–Apr The Laupahoehoe Music Festival offers genuine Hawaiian music and community spirit.

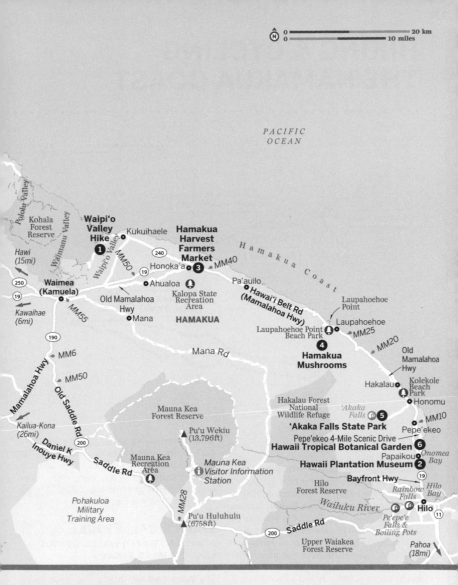

PACIFIC OCEAN

Hamakua Coast Highlights

1 **Waipi'o Valley Hike** (p178) Struggling down the steep road to Waipi'o's black-sand beach.

2 **Hawaii Plantation Museum** (p194) Viewing fascinating artifacts from the days when sugar was king.

3 **Hamakua Harvest Farmers Market** (p185) Shopping for locally grown items in neighborly Honoka'a.

4 **Hamakua Mushrooms** (p191) Touring the efficient indoor farm that produces Hawai'i's famous Ali'i Oyster mushrooms.

5 **'Akaka Falls State Park** (p193) Taking an easy stroll through soaring rainforest to the touristy yet impressive 420ft falls.

6 **Hawaii Tropical Botanical Garden** (p194) Strolling nicely landscaped gardens with eye-popping foliage.

HIKING & CYCLING THE HAMAKUA COAST

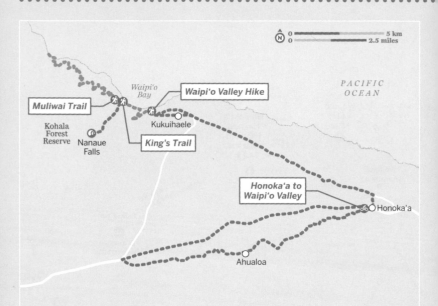

WAIPI'O VALLEY

If you are hiking on your own, it is strongly advised that you stick to established trails and avoid trespassing on private property if you enter the valley. You can explore Waipi'o Beach and take the **King's Trail** to Nanaue Falls, but go no further, unless you pay for a tour (and even those are limited in range). Hiking along Waipi'o Stream to Hi'ilawe is no longer recommended as you must either traverse private land or walk in the stream itself, which is difficult and somewhat hazardous. For the average person the beach and the King's Trail are enough. Avid outdoors people can trek over the ridge toward Waimanu on the **Muliwai Trail**.

Less-experienced hikers should consider exploring Waipi'o backcountry with a **tour** (p189). Not only are they safer, but they also allow venturing into otherwise inaccessible areas.

It is always important to leave no trace when hiking, and this is particularly critical in pristine, sacred places such as Waipi'o Valley. Inexcusably, some people stick their garbage into crevices in the lava-rock walls surrounding the campsites. This attracts roaches and other pests. Some even abandon unneeded gear in the valley. Always carry out what you carry in.

WAIPI'O VALLEY HIKE

START/END WAIPI'O VALLEY LOOKOUT
LENGTH 3 MILES, 2 HOURS

Start at the trailhead to the left of the **Waipi'o Valley Lookout** (p189). The road looks innocent, but the steep grade averages 25%. Wear snug-fitting shoes that you don't mind getting muddy to avoid jamming your toes, and watch out for 4WDs sharing the road.

Going down, you can observe the valley floor growing closer. The beach is not yet visible due to thick foliage. After three-quarters of a mile, you'll reach a dirt-road turnoff toward the right, leading to Waipi'o Beach. The paved road goes toward the residences and taro farms.

The jungle spreads across the mountains, and the mountains plunge into the ocean, along the Hamakaua Coast. Along the way, you'll find some superlative treks and cycling routes.

Follow the dirt road, which can be muddy and riddled with huge puddles, for about half a mile. Under a jungly canopy, it's shady and much cooler here. Finally you'll reach **Waipi'o Beach**. Look for spinner dolphins and whales offshore. There are bathrooms near the beginning of the beach, which has rip currents and a treacherous undertow. Experienced local surfers catch waves here, but visitors should just enjoy being spectators.

If it's been rainy, you might catch a glimpse of **Kaluahine Falls**, which cascade down the cliffs below the lookout. Go east along the coastal boulders for just under half a mile. Don't go if the tide is high and covering the boulders.

If you walk westward across the beach, cross the stream, but only if shallow; if in doubt, observe the locals and ask them for advice. The trail forks shortly thereafter, with the **Muliwai Trail** zig-zagging up the cliffs on the other side of the valley, on its way to distant Waimanu, and, at the base of the far cliffs, the **King's Trail** heading inland, along a fence.

When ready, turn around and brace yourself for a heart-pumping climb uphill!

KING'S TRAIL

START/END WAIPI'O BEACH
LENGTH 1.7 MILES ONE-WAY, 90 MINUTES

If hiking to Waipi'o Beach is too civilized for you, take it up a notch with this trail. From the beach, cross the stream (only if safe) to the far western end. This trail goes inland for about 45 minutes to **Nanaue Falls**, a stepped series of three pools that are a popular swimming hole for residents. Be respectful of locals and farmers: stick to the trail and don't litter.

The trail parallels the valley walls and passes through a natural botanic garden. You'll encounter coffee plants, *liliko'i* (passion fruit), massive monkeypods, papaya, elephant ear, avocado and lots more, making you realize what a cornucopia the valley is. You'll also come across small groups of friendly wild horses, the descendants of domesticated animals left behind after the tsunami.

About 30 minutes in, the trail will end in a 'T'; go right and continue along a fence farther into the valley. Ten minutes later, you'll reach a gate, which you can go through because the trail is public. Several minutes later you'll see the falls. This is the end of the public trail, so take a dip and head back.

MULIWAI TRAIL

START WAIPI'O VALLEY
END WAIMANU VALLEY
LENGTH 8.5 MILES, 6½ TO 8 HOURS
ONE-WAY

For expert trekkers only, this trail traverses steep, slippery and potentially treacherous ground. It crosses 13 gulches – brutal to ascend and descend but lovely, with little waterfalls and icy pools for swimming. Plan on camping in Waimanu Valley for at least two nights. For safety reasons, do not attempt this hike during or after rains. For detailed hiking information, contact Na Ala Hele (www.hawaiitrails.org/trails) in Hilo.

You can park your car at the signposted 24-hour parking area. The Muliwai Trail begins at the base of the cliffs on the far side of the valley; you can see it zig-zagging up the cliff face as you approach. A shaded path at the end of the beach takes you to a dual trailhead: head right and up for Muliwai (straight ahead leads to the King's Trail). The ancient Hawaiian footpath now rises over 1200ft in a mile of hard laboring back and forth up the cliff face; it's nicknamed 'Z-Trail' for the killer switchbacks. The hike is exposed and hot, so cover this stretch early.

MULIWAI TRAIL SAFETY

➡ Streams in the valley are subject to flash floods during heavy rains. Don't cross waters above knee level.

➡ Don't drink unboiled or untreated water; leptospirosis is present.

➡ Beware of wasps and centipedes.

➡ Bring a signal device for emergencies, as sightseeing helicopters regularly pass.

Eventually the trail moves into ironwood and Norfolk pine forest, and tops a little knoll before gently descending and becoming muddy and mosquito-ridden. The trail crosses a gulch and ascends past a sign for **Emergency Helipad No 1**. For the next few hours the trail finds a steady rhythm of gulch crossings and forest ascents. A waterfall at the third gulch is a source of fresh water; treat it before drinking. For a landmark, look for Emergency Helipad No 2 at about the halfway point from Waipi'o Beach. Beyond that, there's an open-sided **emergency shelter** with pit toilets and Emergency Helipad No 3.

Rest at Helipad No 3 before making the final difficult descent. Leaving the shelter, hop across three more gulches and pass Emergency Helipad No 4, from where it's less than a mile to Waimanu Valley. This final section of switchbacks starts out innocently enough, with some artificial and natural stone steps, but over a descent of 1200ft the trail is poorly maintained and hazardous. A glimpse of Wai'ilikahi Falls (accessible by a 45-minute stroll) on the far side of the valley might inspire hikers to press onward, but beware: the trail is narrow and washed out in parts, with sheer drop-offs into the ocean and no handholds apart from mossy rocks and spiny plants. If the descent is questionable, head back to the trail shelter for the night.

Waimanu Valley is...well, this is as good as God's green Earth gets, a deep valley framed by cliffs, waterfalls and a boulder-strewn beach. There was once a sizable settlement here, and the valley contains many ruins, including house and heiau terraces, stone enclosures and old *lo'i*. In the early 19th century an estimated 200 people lived here, but the valley was abandoned by its remaining three families after the 1946 tsunami.

From the bottom of the switchbacks, **Waimanu Beach** is 10 minutes past the camping regulations signboard. To ford the stream to reach the campsites on its western side, avoid the rope strung across the water, which is deep there. Instead cross closer to the ocean entry where it is shallower. Camping requires a state permit from the **Division of Forestry & Wildlife** (📞808-974-4221; http://camping.ehawaii.gov/camping; 19 E Kawili St, Hilo; ⊙8am-4:30pm Mon-Fri) for a maximum of six nights.

Facilities include fire pits and composting outhouses. There's a spring 10 minutes behind campsite No 9, with a PVC pipe carrying water from a waterfall; all water must be treated.

On the return trip, be careful to take the correct trail. Walking inland from Waimanu Beach, don't veer left on a false trail-of-use

Wild horses on the banks of the Waipi'o Valley River

Waimanu Beach

that attempts to climb a rocky stream bed. Instead keep heading straight inland past the camping regulations sign to the trail to the switchbacks. It takes about two hours to get to the trail shelter, and another two to reach the waterfall gulch. Exiting the ironwood forest soon after, the trail descends back to the floor of Waipi'o Valley.

CYCLING TOUR: HONOKA'A TO WAIPI'O VALLEY

START/FINISH TEX DRIVE-IN
LENGTH 40 MILES, HALF-DAY

From **Tex Drive-In** (p185), cross Hwy 19 onto the **Old Mamalahoa Hwy**. The old cane-haul road will meander through the misty woods and pastures of Ahualoa. Keep going east for about 10 miles until you meet Hwy 19 again. Cycle back to Tex Drive-In on the highway.

Now take a break for coffee and hot *malasadas* (Portuguese doughnuts). Then take Pakalana St downhill toward Honoka'a town to the north. In less than a mile, you'll reach Mamane St, Honoka'a's main street, which becomes Hwy 240, also called the Honoka'a-Waipi'o Rd, once it crosses Plumeria Rd (where the post office is located).

Go east on **Hwy 240**, which has decent shoulders and is less busy than Hwy 19. You'll pass open fields as well as clusters of houses. At the 8-mile marker, there's a turnoff onto Kukuihaele Rd; stay on Hwy 240 since you'll take Kukuihaele Rd on the way back.

At the end of the road, stop at the **Waipi'o Valley Lookout** (p189). Gaze at the emerald valley and black-sand beach. If you have the legs (and an extra hour and a half) for it, lock your bike near the ranger's station and hike down. The ranger won't take responsibility for your bike, but it's unlikely to be stolen there.

Once done admiring Waipi'o Valley, head back by veering left onto Kukuihaele Rd. Narrow and winding at first, the road crosses a one-lane bridge and then a little neighborhood. Stop at **Waipi'o Valley Artworks** (p190) to browse the souvenirs.

Return to Hwy 240 and cycle back to **Honoka'a**. Check out Mamane St's half-mile of shops, restaurants and old-fashioned theater. The wooden buildings from the early 1900s fit its small-town vibe.

Prepare for an uphill push back to Tex Drive-In, where you can stock up on a few more *malasadas* for the road.

ROAD TRIP: HAMAKUA HIGHLIGHTS

Since most visitors stay in West Hawai'i, this route goes from north to south and then circles back northward. Start early to take advantage of easterly morning light.

❶ Mile 20

Drive south along Hwy 19 until you see the 20-mile marker. Keep your eyes peeled for the Waikaumalo Park sign. Turn *mauka* (inland) onto the off-the-tourist-track Old Mamalahoa Hwy, which is loaded with DIY exploration opportunities. Soon after the turnoff, a grassy slope (with picnic area) leads to a pretty stream.

The Drive > Driving on, the old highway becomes a one-lane road, dipping among a series of stream gulches overhung with thick foliage. A little less than halfway along, watch out for Honohina Cemetery, a historic Japanese graveyard full of flowers.

❷ World Botanical Gardens

The southern end of the road is anchored by the **World Botanical Gardens** (p193) near the 16-mile marker. The fee is a bit steep for the modest gardens, but it is the only viewing access to the beautiful, three-tiered **Umauma Falls**.

The Drive > Back on Hwy 19, head south toward Hilo. In Honomu, turn right just before the 13-mile marker and go 4 miles.

❸ 'Akaka Falls State Park

The easy paved path at **'Akaka Falls** (p193) is best navigated counterclockwise. The route takes you to the opening act, the 100ft **Kahuna Falls**, and then to the 442ft highlight that give this state park it's name.

❹ Honomu village

If you're feeling parched, drive to Honomu village, where you can find locally grown coffee at **Hilo Sharks Coffee** (p194) and a hypnotizing selection of homemade preserves at **Mr Ed's Bakery** (p194).

The Drive > Next, continue along the highway until Papaikou, where you'll pass a school. Then, turn right on Papaikou Rd.

❺ Hawaii Plantation Museum

Hawaii Plantation Museum (p194) is marked by a colorful external mural. Talk story with the founder, a passionate historian, and his welcoming staff to delve into the rich island history.

❻ Alae Cemetery

Pass the 5-mile marker, and slightly after the Honoli'i Bridge, turn right into Alae Cemetery. The cemetery centers on a magnificent 160ft monkeypod tree, standing watch over the gravestones of plantation immigrants and their descendants.

The Drive > Back on Hwy 19, head back northward and veer left between the 7- and 8-mile markers after the Pepe'ekeo 4-Mile Scenic Drive sign.

❼ Pepe'ekeo 4-Mile Scenic Drive

As you turn on **Pepe'ekeo 4-Mile Scenic Drive**, you'll immediately travel back in time (and instinctively slow down on the narrow road, enveloped in lush foliage). Multiple one-lane stone bridges, covered with mossy patina, require careful driving; when in doubt, let the other driver pass first.

In places the sun is almost blocked out by *liliko'i* (passion fruit), guava, mango and soaring African tulip trees. Little waterfalls and streams appear here and there. When you reach a clearing, the ocean and the former Onomea Arch will be visible. Find a spot to pull out and park. The fallen arch now resembles a U-shaped outcropping.

Start Waikaumalo Park Turnoff

End Pepe'ekeo 4-Mile Scenic Drive, northern end

Length 30 miles, full day

The Drive > For a quick, pretty hike down to Onomea Bay, take the Na Ala Hele trailhead on the makai (seaward) side of the road, just north of the botanical garden. After a 10-minute hike down a slippery jungle path, you'll come to a finger of lava jutting into the sea. Enjoy the view, then continue along the scenic drive.

❽ Hawaii Tropical Botanical Gardens

Soon you'll reach **Hawaii Tropical Botanical Garden** (p194), a pleasantly landscaped collection of 2000 species of tropical plants. Walk at your leisure amid streams and waterfalls. Buy your ticket at the yellow building on the *mauka* (inland) side of the road.

The Drive > Back on the road, continue north and you'll reach grassy fields. Keep your eyes peeled for your next stop, a yellow house on the left.

❾ Fuel Stop!

What's Shakin' (p195) is your ticket for the best smoothie on the island (and, some claim, in the world). For heartier fare, head slightly further north to **Low Store** (p195). Once you've refueled, follow the road until it connects back to Hwy 19.

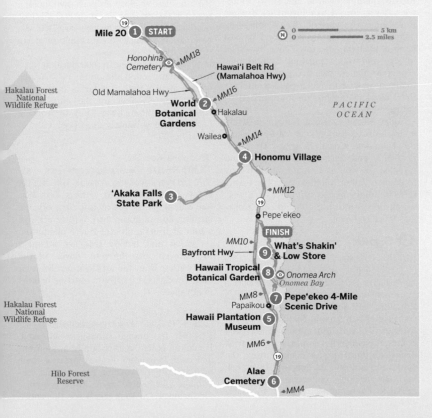

ℹ️ Getting There & Away

A car is essential to navigate the Hamakua Coast along Hwy 19. Honoka'a, the biggest town along the Hamakua Coast, is approximately 50 miles from Kailua-Kona and 40 miles from Hilo. Expect the drive to take 75 minutes from Kona and an hour from Hilo.

The **Hele-On Bus** (📞808-961-8744; www.heleonbus.org; adult one-way $2, 10-ride ticket $15, monthly pass $60) route between Kona and Hilo stops at various towns along the coast, including Honoka'a, Pa'auilo, Laupahoehoe, Hakalau, Honomu and Papaikou. Buses run between Kona and Hilo three times daily. Service between Hilo and Honoka'a is more frequent. Check the website for schedules.

Honoka'a

📞 808 / POP 2258

Honoka'a's slow-paced main street belies the town's former importance as the third-largest town in the Hawaiian Islands, after Honolulu and Hilo. Once a major hub for the dominant cattle and sugar industries, it was forced to reinvent itself when those industries crashed. By the time Honoka'a Sugar Company processed its last harvest in 1993, the town had dwindled in size and was struggling to find new economic niches. Eventually, new farmers found success with niche edibles, such as the Hamakua mushrooms now prized by gourmet chefs.

Today Honoka'a town remains a lively, if tiny, hub, as the only actual town along the Hamakua Coast. It serves the rural residents and farmers of Pa'auilo and Ahualoa, as well as tourists on their way to Waipi'o Valley, 10 miles west. The town's retro buildings have a jaunty western vibe, which bursts into full glory during Honoka'a Western Week.

◉ Sights

NHERC Heritage Center MUSEUM
(📞808-775-8890; www.hilo.hawaii.edu/academics/nherc/HeritageCenter.php; 45-539 Plumeria St; ⊙8am-4pm Mon-Fri, 9am-1pm Sat) FREE Honoka'a will make a lot more sense if you visit this museum. Sponsored by the Northern Hawai'i Education and Research Center, the collection comprises numerous historical photographs documenting the plantation era and its demise. It's a peek into the region's collective grandmother's attic. Each picture speaks a thousand words.

From the main intersection downtown, follow Plumeria St uphill, then turn right on Lehua St.

Katsu Goto Memorial MEMORIAL
(Mamane St) Katsu Goto was a Japanese canefield worker who eventually opened a general store in Honoka'a. Goto was hanged by local sugar bosses and accomplices in 1889 for his attempts to improve labor conditions on Hamakua plantations. Considered one of the first union activists, he has been featured in books, such as *Hamakua Hero: A True Plantation Story,* a graphic novel by PY Iwasaki.

The memorial is only a large plaque with a brief summary of Goto's life, located across the street from Honoka'a High School on Mamane St.

👉 Tours

Although nearby Waipi'o Valley is better known for activities, the back roads in Pa'auilo and Ahualoa make for terrific cycling. If hesitant to explore on your own, book a tour. **Big Island Bike Tours** (📞800-331-0159; www.bigislandbiketours.com; tours from $160; 🚴), based in Waimea, offers a couple of group rides in the Honoka'a area.

If you're interested in food, local agriculture or nature and the outdoors, visit one of the small, family-run farms in pastoral Pa'auilo or Ahualoa, on the *mauka* (inland) side of the highway. They are working farms so you absolutely must book visits in advance.

★ Mauna Kea Tea FARM
(📞808-775-1171; www.maunakeatea.com; 46-3870 Old Mamalahoa Hwy, Ahualoa; 1½hr tour per 2/3/4+ people $30/25/20; ⊙tours 10am Mon, Wed & Thu) 🍃 If you're into tea, organic farming and philosophical inquiry, arrange a tour at this family-run 2-acre plantation. Its green and oolong teas are intended to represent the inherent 'flavor' of the land rather than the artificial fertilizers of mass-produced teas. Tours must be booked in advance.

Long Ears Coffee FARM
(📞808-775-0385; www.longearscoffee.com; tour $35) 🍃 Try unique three-year-old 'aged' Hamakua coffee at this family farm. Wendell and Irmanetta Branco process their own and other Hamakua farms' beans, creating a sustainable agricultural economy for farmers. On tour you'll see the entire

process: growing trees, harvesting cherries, pulping, drying, husking and roasting. Directions to the farm are given upon booking a tour.

Hawaiian Vanilla Company FOOD
(☑ 808-776-1771; www.hawaiianvanilla.com; 43-2007 Paauilo Mauka Rd, Pa'auilo; tour $25, afternoon tea $34, lunch per adult/child $39/19; ☺ tour 1pm Mon-Fri, afternoon tea 3pm Sat, lunch 12:30pm Mon-Fri; ⊞) ✎ The first commercial vanilla operation in the US, this family-run farm is an agritourism success story. The foodie tours (lunch or afternoon tea) are pricey crowd-pleasers, but the farm tour is too superficial to warrant the price.

✖ Eating

Honoka'a has enough restaurants to satisfy most cravings, plus a medium-sized supermarket. Most are located on Mamane St and all are informal and family-friendly. Many are closed on Sunday, which fortuitously is shopping day for the Hamakua Harvest Farmers Market (p185).

★Hamakua Harvest Farmers Market MARKET
(www.hamakuaharvest.org; cnr Hwys 19 & 240; ☺ 9am-2pm Sun) ✎ Featuring over 35 vendors, live music and talks, this market is worth checking out. Everything is locally grown or made, including produce, honey, goat cheese, coconut-milk gelato, smoked fish and much more. To get here, turn *makai* (seaward) off Hwy 19 at the eastern end of Mamane St.

Honoka'a Farmers Market MARKET
(Mamane St; ☺ 7:30am-noon Sat) ✎ A small gathering, with fresh produce, directly from the farmers, baked goods and other edibles. Not the biggest or the best, but possibly the oldest farmers markets on the island. Located in front of Honoka'a Trading Company (p188).

★Gramma's Kitchen AMERICAN $
(☑ 808-775-9943; www.facebook.com/grammas kitchenhonokaa; 45-3625 Mamane St; mains $12-20; ☺ 8am-3pm daily, plus 5-8pm Fri & Sat) The restaurant's storefront sign states 'Very homestyle cooking.' And it's true. Gramma's is your ticket for local dishes, such as hearty Portuguese bean soup, teriyaki cheeseburgers (with pineapple and bacon) and a perfectly seared and crusted ahi roll. Expect a casual diner setting, cheerful staff and small-town aloha.

OFF THE BEATEN TRACK

AHUALOA PASTORAL DETOUR

For a peaceful meander, turn off Hwy 19 onto the Old Mamalahoa Hwy, just west of the 52-mile marker. (Coming from Hilo, turn left at the 43-mile marker opposite Tex Drive-In and then take the next immediate right.) This 10-mile detour winds through hill country, with small roadside ranches, old wooden fences and grazing horses. Take it slowly and get a taste of old-time ranching. It's even more picturesque by bike.

★Tex Drive-In BAKERY $
(☑ 808-775-0598; www.texdriveinhawaii.com; 45-690 Pakalana St; malasadas $1.20, mains $5-10; ☺ 6am-8pm) A *malasada* is just a doughnut, but Tex is famous for serving them hot and fresh. They come plain or filled; either way, folks drive across the island to devour them. Tex also serves decent plate lunches and *loco moco* (rice, fried egg and hamburger patty or other main dish topped with gravy) and seasonal taro burgers. Go elsewhere for health food; come here for local color.

Adjacent to the drive-in, the Tex store (9am to 5pm) sells a variety of locally made gifts, from toiletries to T-shirts.

Hamakua Living LOCAL $
(☑ 808-775-1033; www.hamakualiving.com; 45-3551 Mamane St; meals $5-7; ☺ 7am-3pm & 4-7pm Mon-Thu, 10am-3pm Fri) Experience a plantation-era general store, with freshly cooked plate lunches and a vast selection of local snacks, such as 'seed' (salty-sweet-sour preserved fruit), creamy strawberry ice cake (frozen treat) and chewy dried cuttlefish. The store is immaculately organized. Breakfast is served until 10am, followed by lunch until 3pm.

Sea DandeLion Cafe & Awa Bar VEGETARIAN $
(☑ 808-765-0292; www.facebook.com/seadande lion; 45-3590 Mamane St; meals $8-12; ☺ 11:30am-6:45pm Mon & Thu, 11:30am-2:30pm Tue, 4:15-9pm Fri; ☑) ✎ In a cozy space with a New Age-y vibe, a husband-and-wife team serves creative healthy vegetarian fare. Sample a couple of sliders, savory with a 'superfoods' veg patty and kraut, or sweet with banana, avocado and mac-nut butter. On Friday

GEORGE BURBA/SHUTTERSTOCK ©

1. Waipi'o Valley (p188)
This fertile valley is a natural botanic garden.

2. *Malasada* (Portuguese fried dough)
Tex Drive-In (p185) is famous for these doughy desserts.

3. 'Akaka Falls State Park (p193)
Plunging 400ft, these falls are one of Hawai'i's most iconic sights.

4. Honoka'a People's Theatre (p188)
Honoka'a's retro buildings give it a Wild West feel.

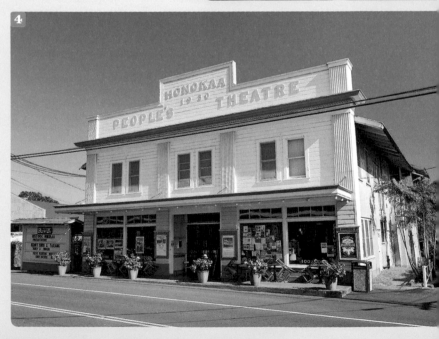

evenings (5pm to 9pm), get a third 'shell' of *'awa* (medicinal drink) free.

Simply Natural CAFE $
(☎ 808-775-0119; 45-3625 Mamane St; dishes $5-12; ⊙ 8:30am-4pm Mon-Sat, 11am-3pm Sun; 🛜 🍴) A cozy go-to spot for wholesome eats, from taro pancakes to an open-faced spicy tuna melt. A kiddie menu, biodegradable takeout containers and a mural showing the whole world coming together to enjoy healthy food add to the appeal.

Cafe il Mondo ITALIAN $$
(☎ 808-775-7711; www.cafeilmondo.com; 45-3580 Mamane St; calzones $14, pizzas $15-20; ⊙ 11am-2pm & 5-8pm Mon-Sat) Honoka'a's fanciest restaurant is this longtime Italian spot, specializing in thin-crust pizzas, pastas and enormous calzones packed to bursting point. With a grand stone-tiled patio, gleaming wood furnishings, sleek bar and live music, the vibe is romantic. But the crowd is refreshingly informal, convivial and diverse.

☆ Entertainment

★ Honoka'a People's Theatre THEATER
(☎ 808-775-0000; http://honokaapeople.com; 45-3574 Mamane St; movie tickets adult/child/senior $6/3/4; ⊙ typical showtimes 5pm & 7pm Tue-Sun) There's something wonderful about watching a movie in a huge, old-fashioned theater – like this one, with a 50ft screen and over 500 seats. Built in 1930, this theater still shows movies and hosts special events. For a bargain movie and a way to immerse yourself with locals, you can't go wrong coming here. Check the website and call to confirm show times.

🛍 Shopping

The Knickknackery ANTIQUES
(raynwatcher@yahoo.com; 45-3611 Mamane St; ⊙ 10am-5pm Tue-Fri, to 4pm Mon) Even if you're not into antiques, this smartly curated shop will charm you. From vintage wood furniture to retro home decor and collectible local art, there's something for all tastes and wallets. The welcoming owner is happy to share his firsthand local knowledge.

Taro Patch GIFTS & SOUVENIRS
(☎ 808-775-7228; www.taropatchgifts.com; 45-3599 Mamane St; ⊙ 9am-5pm) With a little of everything, this is a one-stop shop for browse-worthy souvenirs, from colorful

ceramic dishes and breezy island apparel to Waipi'o Valley mouse pads and organic soaps. The shopkeeper's organic macadamia nuts, roasted in the shell, are addictive.

Honoka'a Trading Company ANTIQUES
(☎ 808-775-0808; 45-3490 Mamane St; ⊙ 10am-4:30pm Thu-Mon) If some of Honoka'a aunties emptied their attics, basements and garages, the results would look like this hangar-size store. Weave through a mesmerizing collection of vintage aloha wear, local antiques, used books (with a decent Hawaiiana selection) and rattan and koa furniture. Then talk story with the owner, quite a character herself (note: she and her daughter keep somewhat flexible hours).

❶ Getting There & Away

From Hwy 19, there are several turnoffs toward Honoka'a town, including Plumeria Rd on the western end and Mamane St on the eastern end. A handy landmark is Tex Drive-In; the road just east of the drive-in leads into town. The drive from Hilo should take around an hour.

You can catch a Hele-On bus (www.heleonbus. org) to Honoka'a from Hilo or Kailua-Kona, but service is infrequent. Check the website for details. In and around town, you'll definitely need a car.

Waipi'o Valley

Waipi'o Valley occupies a special place on an already special island. Reaching the end of Hwy 240, you look out across a spectacular natural amphitheater, as if an enormous scoop was scalloped from the emerald coastline. Waipi'o ('curving water') is one of seven valleys carved into the windward side of the Kohala Mountains; at the other end is the Polulu Valley in North Kohala. The valley goes back 6 miles, its flat floor an emerald patchwork of jungle, huts and taro patches. Hidden (and inaccessible without crossing private property) is Hi'ilawe, a distant ribbon of white cascading 1450ft, making it the longest waterfall in the state. The water flows into a river that ends at Waipi'o's black-sand beach, a rugged beauty surrounded by dramatic running cliffs that disappear around the corner of the island.

History

Known as the Valley of the Kings, Waipi'o was the island's ancient breadbasket and also its political and religious center, home to the highest *ali'i* (ruling chiefs). According to oral histories, several thousand people lived here before Westerners arrived, and the remains of heiau (temples) can still be seen. In 1823 William Ellis, the first missionary to descend into Waipi'o, estimated the population to be around 1300. In the 1880s Chinese immigrants began to settle in the valley's green folds, adding rice to the native taro cultivation.

In 1946 Hawai'i's most devastating tsunami struck the valley, traveling over a mile inland. No one perished despite the massive flooding but, once the waters receded, most people resettled 'topside' in Kukuihaele. The valley floor has been sparsely populated ever since, attracting only a few dozen nature lovers, recluses, pot farmers, hippies and *kama'aina* (people born and raised in Hawaii; literally 'child of the land') seeking to reclaim their history.

Still regarded as a sacred spot, a voluntarily enforced policy of isolationism continues to this day. Taro cultivation and poi production are building blocks of Hawaiian identity, and both valley residents and Native Hawaiians across the island fiercely guard Waipi'o Valley – its residents have a long history of disagreement with the outside world. Said residents point out that their home is sacred in traditional Hawaiian culture, contains an intangible spiritual energy, holds a special place in Hawaii's history, is limited in space, and has a natural beauty that must be protected. Others above the rim say the valley's residents simply wish to separate themselves from the outside world for reasons ranging from misanthropy to marijuana growing.

◉ Sights

★ **Waipi'o Valley Lookout**   VIEWPOINT
Located at the end of Hwy 240, this lookout offers a jaw-dropping view of Waipi'o's emerald amphitheater, black-sand beach and pounding surf. Feast your eyes on one of Hawaii's iconic images.

🏃 Activities

Hiking or riding into the valley is the headline activity in Waipi'o. For more adventure, you can ride horses, ATVs or a mule-drawn wagon in the valley. Note that some tours navigate the valley floor, while others explore the top of the valley – different experiences, but both worthy. If you have any questions, stop at the Information Booth (p191), which is staffed during daylight hours and located near the parking lot. For more information on hiking in Waipi'o, see p178.

Waipi'o beach isn't swimmable for most people due to rip currents and a treacherous undertow. Only expert local surfers dare to challenge the waves. Experienced sea kayakers can arrange custom tours with Plenty Pupule (p122) in Kona.

👉 Tours

Waipi'o on Horseback   HORSEBACK RIDING
(📞 808-775-7291;   www.waipioonhorseback.com; 2½hr tours $90; ⊘ tours 9:30am & 1:30pm Mon-Sat; 🐎) Explore the valley floor on horses matched to you by experience and personality. Even beginners will feel secure.

Waipi'o Ridge Stables   HORSEBACK RIDING
(📞 877-757-1414, 808-775-1007; www.waipioridge stables.com; 2½hr tours $90/175; ⊘ tours 9am & 1:30pm; 🐎) Tour the valley rim to the top of Hi'ilawe Falls (2½ hours) or add more waterfall sightings plus a picnic and swim (five hours). Great guides. Maximum 10 per group.

Na'alapa Stables   HORSEBACK RIDING
(📞 808-775-0419; www.naalapastables.com; 2½hr tours $90; ⊘ tours 9am & 12:30pm Mon-Sat; 🐎) This longtime outfit offers a reliable 2½-hour horseback ride on the valley floor; children aged eight and over are welcome. Maximum 12 per group.

Ride the Rim   DRIVING
(📞 808-775-1450; www.ridetherim.com; 3hr tours adult/child from $160/100; ⊘ tours 8:45am & 12:45pm) If riding horses is too old fashioned for you, you can drive an all-terrain vehicle (ATV) around the upper parts of Waipi'o Valley. Driving along dirt roads and across

---

❶ BEWARE OF NIGHT MARCHERS

Kukuihaele means 'light that comes and goes' in Hawaiian, referring to the *huaka'ipo* ('night marchers') – torch-bearing ghosts of Hawaiian warriors who pass through Kukuihaele to Waipi'o. As the legend goes, if you look at the night marchers or get in their way, you die. Survival is possible if one of your ancestors is a marcher – or if you lie face down on the ground.

Waipi'o Valley

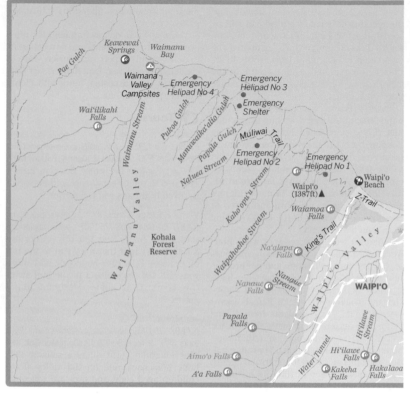

mini streams, you cross otherwise inaccessible private forest land, with an optional stop at a swimming hole (brr, the water is chilly). Those younger than 16 or wary about driving can ride in two-seaters or with the guide. Tours depart from Waipi'o Valley Artworks (p190).

Hawaiian Walkways　　　　　　　　HIKING
(☑808-322-2255; www.hawaiianwalkways.com; 8hr tours adult/child under 11yr $190/100; ☑) All day tours explore Honoka'a, ride 4WD into Waipi'o Valley, hike to a heiau (ancient Hawaiian temple) and to a waterfall viewing spot. Lunch is provided. All guides speak English and Japanese.

Waipi'o Valley Wagon Tours　　　　TOURS
(☑808-775-9518; www.waipiovalleywagontours. com; 1½hr tours adult/child $60/30; ☑tours 10:30am, 12:30pm & 2:30pm Mon-Sat; ☑) A quaint option ideal for tots, this 1½-hour jaunt navigates the valley floor in an old-fashioned mule-drawn wagon.

✖ Eating

Waipi'o Cookhouse　　　　　　　　LOCAL
(☑808-775-1443; 48-5370 Honoka'a-Waipi'o Rd; mains $12-14; ☑7:30am-6pm) ☑ The walk-up counter and patio seating are reminiscent of a drive-in, but this farm-to-table restaurant serves healthy food, locally sourced and all made to order. The smoky *kalua loco moco* gives you two local dishes in one, while the grilled eggplant sandwich features local veggies and creamy Big Island goat cheese. Restrooms are portable toilets.

🔒 Shopping

★ **Waipi'o Valley Artworks**　　ARTS & CRAFTS
(☑808-775-0958, 800-492-4746; www.waipiovalley artworks.com; 48-5416 Kukuihaele Rd; ☑8am-5pm) ☑ This inviting little shop wears many

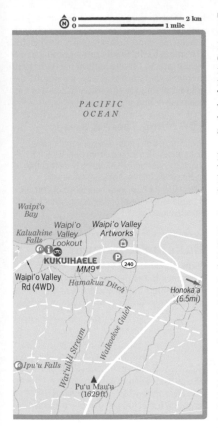

hats. Browse the handmade koa pieces, from rocking chairs to calabash bowls and chess sets. Snack on ice cream or sandwiches. Talk story with the friendly owner. Or park your car overnight, if camping in Waimanu Valley ($15 per day).

ℹ Information

Information Booth (Waipi'o Valley; ⊘ 8am-dusk) Located near the parking lot, this booth is staffed during daylight hours with a knowledgeable official who can answer questions about access to the valley.

ℹ Getting There & Away

From Honoka'a, Hwy 240 runs just under 10 miles to the Waipi'o Valley Lookout. The turnoff onto Kukuihaele Rd is around the 8-mile marker, and it connects again with Hwy 240 near the lookout. There is no bus service here.

Laupahoehoe

Laupahoehoe, meaning 'leaf of *pahoehoe* (smooth-flowing lava),' is aptly named for its landmark point, a flat lava peninsula formed by a late-stage Mauna Kea eruption. This small town had its heyday when sugar was king, but it remains a solid community with a pleasant beach park and a handful of attractions.

On April 1, 1946, tragedy hit the small plantation town when a 30ft-high tsunami wiped out the schoolhouse on the point, killing 20 children and four adults. After the tsunami the whole town moved uphill.

⊙ Sights & Activities

Laupahoehoe Point Beach Park   BEACH
(off Hwy 19) Only real crazy *buggahs* would swim at windy, rugged Laupahoehoe, where the fierce surf sometimes crashes over the rocks and onto the parking lot. But it's strikingly pretty, with a scenic breakwater and fingers of lava rock jutting out of the waves. It's popular with local families for picnics and camping (full facilities available).

Laupahoehoe Train Museum   MUSEUM
(☑ 808-962-6300; www.thetrainmuseum.com; 36-2377 Mamalahoa Hwy; adult/student/senior $6/3/5; ⊘ 10am-5pm Thu-Sun, by appointment Mon-Wed; ℙ) If you love little quirks of history, be sure to pop into this unassuming museum. It's essentially a house (specifically an old station agent's house) of cool stuff, brimming with fascinating artifacts and photographs of the plantation railroad era. Don't miss the video of the long-gone coastal train, which showcases the amazing bridges that once curved along (and across) Hamakua gulches, until demolished by tsunami. Located between Miles 25 and 26.

★**Hamakua Mushrooms**   FARM
(☑ 808-962-0305; www.hamakuamushrooms.com; 36-221 Manowaiopae Homestead Rd; 70min tour per adult/senior/child 3-11yr $20/17.50/10; ⊘ tours 9:30am & 11:30am Tue & Thu) 🍃 A hugely successful boutique crop, Hamakua Mushrooms are favored by top chefs statewide. Its signature specialty mushroom, the Ali'i Oyster, is cultivated in bottles and immediately recognizable by thick meaty stems and smooth, fawn-colored caps. The reasonably priced guided tours are very informative, covering cultivation, production

and the owners' circumstances in starting a mushroom farm. Enjoy a sample taste at the end.

This all-indoor farm and production plant is all-solar powered and uses an ecofriendly eucalyptus growing medium.

🎊 Festivals & Events

Laupahoehoe Music Festival   MUSIC
(📞808-962-2200; www.laupahoehoemusicfestival. org; Laupahoehoe Point Beach Park; $10-15; ⊘Apr) In early April, this 'down home' music festival comes to the Laupahoehoe Point Beach Park to raise scholarship money for local students. Come for local eating, hula and especially Hawaiian music inspired by the memory of festival founder Braddah Smitty.

🍴 Eating

★ Papa'aloa Country
Store & Cafe   MARKET, CAFE
(📞808-339-7614; 35-2032 Old Mamalahoa Hwy; ⊘cafe 7am-6:30pm Mon-Sat, market to 7pm Mon-Sat) 🍴 In the 'middle of nowhere,' this neat little market-cafe serves delicious meals, plus pastries baked in house. Try the fresh fish tacos, hand-tossed pizzas and eclairs. The market sells locally grown produce and locally made products. Run by two local brothers, the store is a new version of the original plantation-era store, which was meticulously restored.

ℹ Getting There & Away

The 25-mile drive from Hilo to Laupahoehoe takes about 40 minutes. From Honoka'a, it's about 20 miles and 30 minutes. Note that Papa'aloa is slightly east of Laupahoehoe.

The Hele-On Bus (www.heleonbus.org) stops in Laupahoehoe several times daily. Check the website for details.

Hakalau & Around

While Hakalau and Wailea were actual villages back in the day, they are now just residential communities of close-knit old-timers and newcomers. Since there are no restau-

---

OFF THE BEATEN TRACK

KALOPA STATE RECREATION AREA

Secluded like a storybook forest, the **Kalopa State Recreation Area** (www.dlnr. hawaii.gov/dsp/parks/hawaii/kalopa-state-recreation-area; off Hwy 19; ⊘dawn-dusk) is offers 100 acres of camping, cabins and various gentle trails. Set amid native trees at 2000ft, it's a quiet spot with few visitors, maybe too deserted for solo travelers. But it's fantastically lush and a great place for group or family camping. For a sightseeing stop, take the easy 0.75-mile **Nature Trail**, which passes through old ohia forest, where some trees measure over 3ft in diameter. The path can be overgrown so watch for the established trail.

The park comprises two overall trail systems (see the large map near the cabins). The Nature Trail starts where the road by the cabins ends. Skip the Dryland Forest Trail, which only goes 100yd, and the Arboretum Trail, which is so overgrown that you might get lost. A small **Polynesian garden** contains a dozen of the original 25 canoe plants, introduced to Hawaii by the original Polynesian voyagers for food, medicine and clothing.

The second, more-interesting **trail system** leads into the adjoining forest reserve with old-growth forest and tremendous tree ferns. It starts along Robusta Lane, on the left between the caretaker's house and the campground, and goes about 600yd to the edge of Kalopa Gulch, through a thick eucalyptus forest. The trail continues along the gulch rim for another mile, while several side trails branch off and loop back into the recreation area via the Perimeter Trail. Signage is confusing so you should sketch the map near the cabins for reference along the way. You can go over 4 miles on these scenic but spottily maintained trails.

For **camping** (per night residents/nonresidents $12/18), you must reserve a permit in advance. **Group cabins** (per night residents/nonresidents $60/80) sleep up to eight people and include bunk beds, plus shared restrooms, hot showers and kitchen.

To get to the park, turn mauka off the Hawai'i Belt Rd near Mile 42, at Kalopa Dr. Follow park signs for 3 miles.

rants or shops, there's no reason to detour here unless you're staying in the area.

Sights

World Botanical Gardens GARDENS
(☑ 808-963-5427; www.worldbotanicalgardens.com; 31-240 Old Mamalahoa Hwy; adult/teen 13-17yr/child 5-12yr $15/7/3; ⊗ 9am-5:30pm; ▥)
Under development since 1995, this garden remains a work in progress. Sprawling grounds include a shrubbery maze, waterfall and arboretum – nothing outstanding. You can up the ante with Segway ($57 to $187 per person) or go ziplining with on-site Zip Isle Zipline Adventures. It is an admirable effort but plays second fiddle to the Hawaii Tropical Botanical Garden closer to Hilo. To get here from Hwy 19, turn *mauka* (inland) near Mile 16, at the posted sign.

Kolekole Beach Park PARK
Beneath a highway bridge, this park sits alongside Kolekole Stream in a verdant tropical valley. The river-mouth break is a local surfing and bodyboarding hot spot, but ocean swimming is dangerous. There are small waterfalls and full facilities. Camping is allowed with a county permit, but the narrow area can get crowded and boisterous with picnicking local families.

Activities

Ziplining in Hamakua's rainforests will almost always guarantee lots of mosquitoes; cover up or wear repellent. Also be prepared for showers.

Umauma Falls
& Zipline Experience ZIPLINE
(☑ 808-930-9477; http://umaumaexperience.com; 31-313 Old Mamalahoa Hwy; per person $190; ⊗ 8am-3pm; ▥) This is the most consistently thrilling of Hamakua's ziplines. On the basic tour you'll ride nine ziplines (including four dual lines), cross a 200ft suspension bridge and see 18 waterfalls. Weight 35lb to 275lb, ages four and up.

Zip Isle Zipline Adventures ZIPLINE
(☑ 808-963-5427, 888-947-4753; www.zipisle.com; per person $165; ⊗ 9:30am-2:30pm; ▥) A good choice for kids and anxious first-timers. There are seven gentle zips, including a dual line, and a 150ft suspension bridge. Located at World Botanical Gardens, which you can enter for free. Weight limit 70lb to 270lb.

❶ Getting There & Away

From Hilo to Hakalau the 15-mile drive takes about 15 minutes. Drive slow when approaching any destinations here; if you blink, you'll miss your turnoff.

The Hele-On Bus (www.heleonbus.org) stops in Hakalau several times daily. Check the website for details.

Honomu

Honomu is a quaint old sugar town that might be forgotten today if not for its proximity to 'Akaka Falls, a popular tourist stop. However, life remains rural and slow paced, as the town comprises only a handful of shops and eateries in historic wooden buildings.

Sights

★ **'Akaka Falls State Park** PARK
(www.hawaiistateparks.org; 'Akaka Falls Rd; car/pedestrian $5/1; ▥) ∅ The island's best 'tourist waterfall' is found at this outstanding, family-friendly park. Walk the paved path counterclockwise, on a loop that traverses lush cliffs above a river. You'll first pass the modest opening act, **Kahuna Falls** (100ft), and then behold the grand **'Akaka Falls**, which plunge 442ft into a deep emerald pool. You'll also enjoy a verdant garden that goes wildly into bloom during specific months (June to July is heliconia season).

For ideal photo conditions, go in the morning since the falls face eastward. To get here turn onto Hwy 220 between Miles 13 and 14, and head 4 miles inland. You can avoid paying the parking fee if you park outside the lot, but you must still pay the walk-in fee.

Activities

Skyline EcoAdventures
Akaka Falls ZIPLINE
(☑ 888-864-6947, 808-878-8400; www.zipline.com; 28-1710 Honomu Rd; per person $170; ⊗ 10am-3pm; ▥) Skyline has the single best zip along the Hamakua Coast and it's a jaw dropper. The seven zips on this course get progressively longer and higher until you whoosh directly over a 250ft waterfall on a 3350ft ride! Weight 80lbs to 260lb, ages 10 years and up.

✖ Eating

The cafes in Honomu are perfect for coffee and refreshments, but you must drive the short distance to Hilo for groceries and evening meals.

★**Mr Ed's Bakery**   BAKERY **$**
(☏808-963-5000; www.mredsbakery.com; Hwy 220; ☉6am-6pm Mon-Sat, 9am-4pm Sun) ✐ Check out the staggering selection of homemade preserves featuring local fruit ($7.50 per jar). *Liliko'i* (passion fruit) is a classic. Low-sugar and sugar-free varieties too. Pastries are hit or miss, but the Portuguese sweet bread is a winner.

★**Woodshop Gallery & Cafe**   CAFE **$**
(☏808-963-6363; www.woodshopgallery.com; Hwy 220; lunch dishes $6-9; ☉11am-5:30pm) ✐ From burgers and lemonade to homemade ice cream and espresso, it's all good Americana served with a side of aloha here. Following lunch, browse or splurge on the extraordinary collection of handcrafted koa pieces, from rocking chairs to classic bowls to jewelry boxes.

Hilo Sharks Coffee   CAFE **$**
(☏808-963-6706; www.hilosharkscoffee.com; 28-1672 Old Mamalahoa Hwy; sandwiches $6-7; ☉8am-6pm Mon-Sat, to 4pm Sun; 🛜✐) ✐ Every village has its hangout spot, and in Honomu, this is it. Locally grown coffee (and chocolate), outdoor seating, tasty sandwiches, refreshing smoothies and rock-bottom prices.

❶ Getting There & Away

Driving the 13.5 miles from Hilo to Honomu takes less than 15 minutes. The turnoff to 'Akaka Falls State Park (p193) is signposted.

The Hele-On Bus (www.heleonbus.org) stops in Honomu several times daily. Check the website for details.

Pepe'ekeo to Papaikou

From east to west, Pepe'ekeo, Onomea and Papaikou are three plantation villages admired for their gorgeous landscapes and views. There are several worthy attractions here (and a post office in Pepe'ekeo), but no actual towns. In fact, those who live from Papaikou to Hakalau consider themselves Hilo residents (and indeed these villages are part of North Hilo).

◉ Sights

★**Hawaii Plantation Museum**   MUSEUM
(☏808-964-5151; www.plantationmuseum.org; 27-246 Old Mamalahoa Hwy, Papaikou; adult/senior/child $8/6/3; ☉10am-3pm Tue-Sat) ✐ This well-done museum highlights Hawai'i's sugar industry, which spanned the period from the mid-1880s to 1996. Museum curator Wayne Subica has single-handedly amassed this collection, which includes plantation tools, memorabilia from mom-and-pop shops, vintage photos and retro signage. Subica is also a prolific author, with 16 books highlighting Hawai'i's past with carefully selected archival photos. His passion for history is contagious.

To get here from Hilo, turn left just past the 6-mile marker on the main highway; from Kona, turn right just past the 8-mile marker. Veer right and park in front of the colorful mural.

★**Hawaii Tropical
Botanical Garden**   GARDENS
(☏808-964-5233; www.hawaiigarden.com; 27-717 Old Mamalahoa Hwy, Papaikou; adult/child $15/5; ☉9am-5pm, last entry 4pm; ♿) ✐ A guaranteed crowd-pleaser, this rainforest garden is beautifully situated by the ocean and superbly managed. A paved trail meanders through 2000 species of tropical plants set amid streams and waterfalls. Give yourself at least an hour for the walk, which ends at Onomea Bay. The garden is located halfway along the Pepe'ekeo 4-Mile Scenic Drive (p182). Park and buy your ticket at the yellow building on the *mauka* (inland) side of the road.

✖ Activities

The main activities in the area are along the Pepe'ekeo 4-Mile Scenic Drive (p182), which includes the opportunity for a short hike down to Onomea Bay.

☞ Tours

Onomea Tea Company   FARM
(☏808-964-3283; www.onomeatea.com; 27-604 Alakahi Pl; 2½hr tour $40) ✐ Established in 2003, this 9-acre tea plantation has produced unique and all-organic green, white, oolong and black teas. Tours cover tea growing, processing and tasting (accompanied by freshly baked scones). The owner-hosts enthusiastically answer your every question

about tea and its cultivation. Reservations required.

🍴 Eating

For more eating options, simply drive to Hilo, less than 10 miles away. There are no supermarkets here, so self-caterers should be sure to stock up on groceries in Hilo as well.

★ What's Shakin'   HEALTH FOOD $

(☑ 808-964-3080; 27-999 Old Mamalahoa Hwy; smoothies $7.25; ⊙ 10am-5pm; 🥗) 🍃 Your fondest memory of the Pepe'ekeo 4-Mile Scenic Drive might be this roadside eatery. On the northern end of the drive, look for the cheerful yellow cottage, which pumps out killer smoothies (all fruit, no filler). Generously stuffed fish wraps and taro burgers come with heaping greens and a sampling of tropical fruit.

Low Store   LOCAL $

(☑ 808-964-1390; www.facebook.com/lowscorner; 28-1099 Old Mamalahoa Hwy; meals $8-10; ⊙ 6am-6pm) Tropical fruit stand. General store. Patio cafe. And oh so picturesque! The Low Store, on the northern end of the Pepe'ekeo 4-Mile Scenic Drive, serves tasty, inexpensive wraps, burgers and their signature 'island nachos' with *kalua* pork, mango salsa, avocado, fresh veggies and cheese. Save room for shave ice or ice cream. Compostable packaging is another plus.

❶ Getting There & Away

Driving from Hilo to these communities takes about 10 minutes. Papaikou, which is closer to Hilo, blends into Pepe'ekeo. Most attractions are along the Pepe'ekeo 4-Mile Scenic Drive (p182).

The Hele-On Bus (www.heleonbus.org) stops in Papaikou several times daily. Check the website for details.

Hilo

POP 45,380 / ☎ 808

Best Places to Eat

➡ Hilo Bay Cafe (p215)

➡ Pineapples (p216)

➡ Paul's Place (p214)

➡ Sweet Cane Cafe (p214)

➡ Moon & Turtle (p216)

Best for Children

➡ Lili'uokalani Park (p200)

➡ Coconut Island footbridge (p201)

➡ Onekahakaha Beach Park (p200)

➡ Pana'ewa Rainforest Zoo & Gardens (p201)

➡ 'Imiloa Astronomy Center of Hawai'i (p201)

Why Go?

Kailua-Kona may host more visitors, but Hilo is the beating heart of Hawai'i Island. Hidden beneath its daily drizzle lies deep soil and soul, from which sprout a genuine community and aloha spirit. Hilo's demographics still mirror its sugar-town roots, with a diverse mix of Native Hawaiians, Japanese, Filipinos, Portuguese, Puerto Ricans, Chinese and Caucasians.

People might seem low-key, but they're a resilient lot. Knocked down by two tsunami, threatened with extinction by Mauna Loa lava flows, deluged with the highest annual rainfall in the USA and always battling for its share of tourist dollars, Hilo knows how to survive and to thrive.

Hilo had a life before tourism, and it remains refreshingly untouristy. Yet it offers many attractions: compelling museums, a walkable downtown, two thriving farmers markets and dozens of indie restaurants. Hilo is an ideal base for exploring Hawai'i Volcanoes National Park, Mauna Kea, Puna and the Hamakua Coast.

When to Go

Mar & Apr Hilo is booked solid during the Merrie Monarch Festival, which starts on Easter Sunday. If planning to attend the festival, order tickets immediately after December 1 (prior year) and book accommodations up to a year ahead.

Jun–Nov Summer tends to be hot and humid, and Hilo's rainiest month is November

Dec–Feb Winter temperatures are balmy and comfortable. During winter high season, accommodations are pricier and often booked solid.

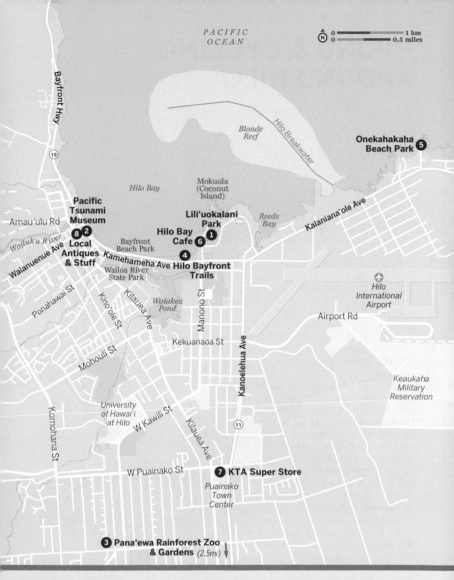

Hilo Highlights

❶ **Lili'uokalani Park** (p200) Strolling through serene Japanese gardens.

❷ **Pacific Tsunami Museum** (p201) Learning about the two historical tsunami that tested Hilo's mettle.

❸ **Pana'ewa Rainforest Zoo & Gardens** (p201) Meeting Bengal tigers and other fascinating creatures amid tropical flora.

❹ **Hilo Bayfront Trails** (p206) Walking or cycling from downtown to Banyan Dr on a family-friendly path.

❺ **Onekahakaha Beach Park** (p200) Splashing with kids and local families in a shallow pool.

❻ **Hilo Bay Cafe** (p215) Dining on Hawaii Regional Cuisine overlooking the bay.

❼ **KTA Super Store** (p211) Stocking up on fresh *poke* (marinated raw fish) sold by the pound at fantastic prices.

❽ **Local Antiques & Stuff** (p218) Browsing eclectic local artifacts and memorabilia.

HIKING & CYCLING AROUND HILO

CYCLING TOUR: HILO TO 'AKAKA FALLS

START DOWNTOWN HILO
END 'AKAKA FALLS
LENGTH 30 MILES, 3 HOURS

Note that this ride includes stretches of narrow shoulder along bridges on Hwy 19. If you're not an experienced cyclist comfortable with highway traffic, stick to in-town rides.

Plan your ride for an early morning departure on a clear day. Start in downtown Hilo, where you can grab on-road supplies such as super-high-SPF sunblock at **Abundant Life Natural Foods** (p211). Go north across the Singing Bridge and you'll ride for about 5 miles along Hwy 19. Be careful crossing the Honoli'i Bridge, since the road shoulder narrows due to the raised bridge structure.

Turn right at the sign for the **Pepe'ekeo 4-Mile Scenic Drive**. This road is narrow and winding, with multiple one-lane bridges, but traffic is lighter. If you're in no rush, succumb to each photo op: jungly foliage, old plantation houses, twinkling waterfalls, weather-worn one-lane bridges. Expect gentle ups and downs and blind turns. When you reach a clearing within sight of the ocean, stop and see the fallen remains of the **Onomea Arch** (which now looks like a U-shaped landmark).

You'll bypass **Hawaii Tropical Botanical Garden** (p194; save it for another day), and wind through more lush rainforest and some scattered houses. To the left, pass the cheerful yellow facade of What's Shakin' and then tidy green-roofed Low Store, both worth roadside eateries for another day. Cross a final one-lane bridge, veer left and you'll return to Hwy 19.

After a couple of miles, turn left onto Hwy 220 to **'Akaka Falls State Park** (p193). Pace yourself for 4 miles of uphill climbing. If you're lucky, Mauna Kea will stand towering before you. If riding in the afternoon, the sun in your face could be brutal.

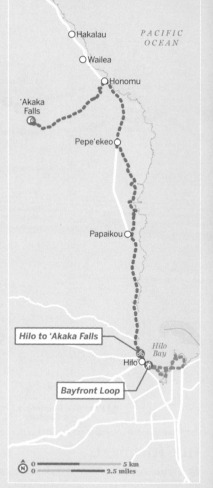

At the state park, either lock your bike to a post or, if cycling with others, take turns visiting the falls. The fee per walk-in visitor is $1. On your way back, stop in Honomu for a celebratory coffee break and browse at the **Woodshop Gallery & Cafe** (p194).

Take your pick: small-town scenic cruising or steep climbs that lead to big rewards?

Lili'uokalani Park (p200)

WALKING TOUR: BAYFRONT LOOP

START/END MO'OHEAU BANDSTAND
LENGTH 4 MILES, 2 HOURS

This scenic walk, which highlights Hilo Bay, can also be done by bicycle. You'll be navigating on a safe paved path, Hilo Bayfront Trails, for most of the way.

Start at the **Mo'oheau Bandstand** (p218), an iconic landmark that serves as a gathering spot for concerts, hula shows, political rallies and more. If you plan to picnic during your walk, cross Kamehameha Ave and cobble together a meal from the farmers market or find your favorite takeout. The path starts slightly east of the bandstand.

At the end of the highway, see **Suisan Fish Market** (p214; another option for delicious *poke* bowls) to your left. Go in that direction toward **Lili'uokalani Park** (p200). With its Japanese-style bridges, vast lawns and magnificent trees, the park is a wonderful place to stroll or picnic. Views of Hilo Bay and the Hamakua Coast, with Mauna Kea in the background, are spectacular.

At the northern end of the park, find the footbridge to **Mokuola** (Coconut Island; p201), a mini island that surely reflects every kid's fantasy. Next head left onto Banyan Dr, iconic for its massive banyan trees.

You'll soon reach **Reeds Bay Beach Park** (p206), a sleepy cove with still waters ideal for learning stand up paddle surfing. Circle back toward Kamehameha Ave, where you'll walk along the golf course. Stop at the tall green **Tsunami Clock** (p206), just opposite Coqui's Hideaway, stopped by Hilo's second catastrophic tsunami at 1:04 on the morning of May 23, 1960.

Continue on Kamehameha Ave, cross to the *mauka* (inland) side of the street and veer left into **Wailoa River State Park** (p205). Cross the pretty rainbow-shaped bridges over ponds of fish and ducks. On the western side of the river, stop at **Wailoa Center** (p205) if an exhihit is running, and at the **Vietnam War** and **Shinmachi Tsunami memorials**.

Join Kamehameha Ave again and continue west past the sports fields until you reach downtown Hilo.

History

Since its first Polynesian settlers farmed and fished along the Wailuku River, Hilo has been a busy port town. In the 20th century it was the trading hub for sugarcane grown in Puna and Hamakua, connecting in both directions with a sprawling railroad, the Hawaii Consolidated Railway.

Back then, townsfolk set up homes and shops along the bay. But after being slammed by disastrous tsunami in 1946 and 1960, no one wanted to live downtown anymore. Today you'll find parks, beaches and open space along Kamehameha Ave.

When the sugar industry folded in the 1980s and '90s, Hilo focused its economy on diversified agriculture, the university, retail and, of course, tourism. While downtown Hilo is still the charming heart of town, the main retail destinations are now the big chain stores south of the airport.

◎ Sights

Most sights are found in downtown Hilo, where historic early-20th-century buildings overlook the coast, which locals call 'bayfront.' Further east sits Hilo's landmark dock, Suisan Fish Market (p214), and the Keaukaha neighborhood, where all of Hilo's beaches are located, except for Honoli'i Beach Park. On weekends, expect jammed parking lots and steady traffic along Kalaniana'ole Ave. Otherwise parking is readily available, whether on the street or in a lot.

★ **Lili'uokalani Park** PARK
(189 Lihiwai St; ⊞) Savor Hilo's simple pleasures with a picnic lunch in scenic Japanese gardens overlooking the shimmering bay. Named for Hawaii's last queen (r 1891–93), the 30-acre county park features soaring trees, sprawling lawns and quaint footbridges over shallow ponds. At sunrise or sunset, join the locals jogging or power walking the perimeter, or simply admire the Mauna Kea view.

Adjacent to the park is Banyan Dr, Hilo's mini 'hotel row,' best known for the giant banyan trees lining the road. Royalty and celebrities planted the trees in the 1930s and, if you look closely, you'll find plaques beneath the trees identifying Babe Ruth, Amelia Earhart and Cecil B DeMille. Also nearby is the paved footbridge to Mokuola (Coconut Island) (p201), a tiny island that will captivate kids of all ages.

★ **Carlsmith Beach Park** BEACH
(Kalaniana'ole Ave; ⊞) Although this beach may look rocky, the swimming area is protected by a reef, making it family-friendly. The anchialine ponds, which flow to the ocean, are ideal for kids. Snorkeling is decent during calm water conditions. Has lifeguards on weekends and holidays, plus restrooms, showers and picnic areas.

★ **Richardson's Ocean Park** BEACH
(Kalaniana'ole Ave; ⊙7am-7pm; ⊞) Near the end of Kalaniana'ole Ave, this little pocket of black sand is a favorite all-round beach. When calm, the protected waters are popular for swimming and snorkeling, with frequent sightings of sea turtles (keep your distance; at least 50yd in the water). High surf, while welcome to local bodyboarders, can be hazardous. Bring water shoes for protection from rocks. There are lifeguards every day, plus restrooms, showers, picnic areas and a parking lot.

★ **Onekahakaha Beach Park** BEACH
(Kalaniana'ole Ave; ⊙7am-9pm; ⊞) Perfect for kids, this spacious beach has a broad, shallow, sandy-bottomed pool, protected by a boulder breakwater. The water is only 1ft to 2ft deep in spots, creating a safe 'baby beach.' An unprotected cove north of the kiddie pool is deeper but can be dangerous due to rough surf and needle-sharp *wana* (sea urchins). Surrounding grassy lawns shaded by trees are ideal for picnicking. There are lifeguards on weekends and holidays, plus restrooms, showers, covered pavilions and picnic areas.

★ **Lyman Museum & Mission House** MUSEUM
(Lyman Museum; Map p202; ☑808-935-5021; www.lymanmuseum.org; 276 Haili St; adult/child $10/3; ⊙10am-4:30pm Mon-Sat; ⊞) Compact yet comprehensive, this small museum encompasses the tremendous variety of Hawaii's natural and cultural history. Downstairs, geologic exhibits include fascinating examples of lava rock, minerals and shells. Upstairs, learn about Native Hawaiians, with exhibits on ancient sports, religion and the *kapu* (taboo) system. The adjacent Mission House, built by the Reverend David Lyman and his wife, Sarah, in 1839, adds a human element to the historical facts. Well-trained docents give half-hour tours of the house at 11am and 2pm.

★ **'Imiloa Astronomy Center of Hawai'i** MUSEUM
(📞 808-969-9700; www.imiloahawaii.org; 600 'Imiloa Pl; adult/child 6-17yr $17.50/9.50; ⏲ 9am-5pm Tue-Sun; ♿) 'Imiloa, which means 'exploring new knowledge,' is a $28 million museum and planetarium complex with a twist: it juxtaposes modern astronomy on Mauna Kea with ancient Polynesian ocean voyaging. It's a great family attraction and the natural complement to a summit tour. One planetarium show is included with admission. On Friday catch special evening programs, including a mind-blowing Led Zeppelin planetarium rock show.

★ **Pana'ewa Rainforest Zoo & Gardens** ZOO
(📞 808-959-9233; www.hilozoo.com; off Hwy 11; ⏲ 9am-4pm, petting zoo 1:30-2:30pm Sat; ♿) FREE Hilo's 12-acre zoo is a terrific family-friendly freebie. Stroll through tropical gardens to see a modest but interesting collection of monkeys, reptiles, sloths, parrots and more. The star attraction? A pair of Bengal tigers: Sriracha (orange female) and Tzatziki (white male). Two play structures and a shaded picnic area are perfect for kids. Generally uncrowded and wheelchair accessible.

To get here, turn *mauka* (inland) off the Volcano Hwy onto W Mamaki St, just past the 4-mile marker.

★ **Pacific Tsunami Museum** MUSEUM
(📞 808-935-0926; www.tsunami.org; 130 Kamehameha Ave; adult/child $8/4; ⏲ 10am-4pm Tue-Sat) You can't understand Hilo without knowing its history as a two-time tsunami survivor (1946 and 1960). This modest museum is chock-full of riveting information, including a section on the Japanese tsunami of 2011, which damaged Kona. Allow enough time to experience the multimedia exhibits, including chilling computer simulations and heart-wrenching first-person accounts.

Mokuola PARK
(Coconut Island; ♿) Tiny Mokuola, commonly called Coconut Island, connects to land near Lili'uokalani Park (p200) by a footbridge. The island is a county park with picnic tables and swimming, and it's popular with local fishing folk. It's worth stopping for a stroll and spectacular views of Hilo Bay and Mauna Kea.

East Hawai'i Cultural Center/HMOCA GALLERY
(📞 808-961-5711; www.ehcc.org; 141 Kalakaua St; suggested donation $5; ⏲ noon-6pm Wed-Fri, 10am-4pm Sat) The best venue for local art is this downtown center, which displays the

HILO SIGHTS

HILO IN...

One Day
Stroll around downtown, the heart of Hilo, with dapper historical buildings, unique shops and a variety of eateries. On Wednesday and Saturday, the **Hilo Farmers Market** (p215) will be teeming. Visit the **Pacific Tsunami Museum** (p201) for a sense of Hilo's true grit. In the afternoon, pack a picnic or pick up a *poke* bowl at **Suisan Fish Market** (p214) and leisurely explore the picturesque Japanese gardens of **Lili'uokalani Park** (p200). End you day with dinner at **Hilo Bay Cafe** (p215), a foodie favorite for gourmet locavore dining.

Three Days
Next morning head to **Richardson's Ocean Park** (p200) for a beach day. Got little kids? Opt for the safe shallow pools at **Onekahakaha Beach** (p200). In the aftenoon, visit **Lyman Museum & Mission House** (p200) for a primer on geology, ancient Hawai'i and plantation life. (Don't miss the two antique shops across the street.) For dinner, head to **Moon & Turtle** (p216) for delicious Hawaii Regional Cuisine or, for a fancier night out, to **Jackie Rey's Ohana Grill** (p216), in a classy historical building downtown.

    On day three, walk along the **Hilo Bayfront Trails** (p206) in the morning and then later visit **'Imiloa Astronomy Center of Hawai'i** (p201), especially if heading to Mauna Kea. Finally, stop at **Big Island Candies** (p211) for scrumptious gifts (or splurge-worthy snacks for the road).

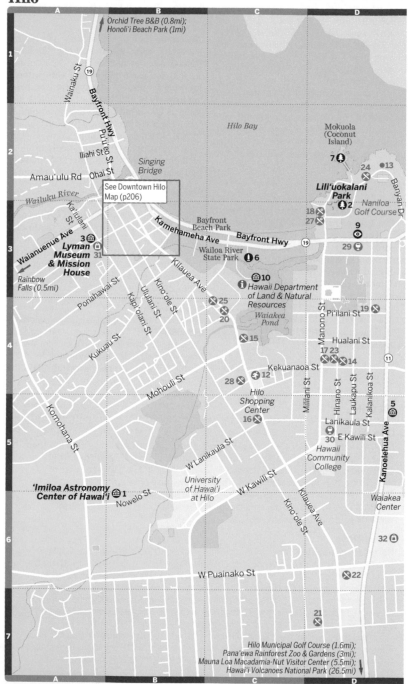

Orchid Tree B&B (0.8mi);
Honoli'i Beach Park (1mi)

Wainaku St

Bayfront Hwy

Pu'u'eo St

Iliahi St

Ohai St

Amau'ulu Rd

Wailuku River

Ka'iulani St

Singing Bridge

See Downtown Hilo Map (p206)

Hilo Bay

Mokuola (Coconut Island)

7

24 13

Lili'uokalani Park

2

18
27

Naniloa Golf Course

9

29

Banyan Dr

Waianuenue Ave

3
31

Lyman Museum & Mission House

Rainbow Falls (0.5mi)

Kamehameha Ave

Bayfront Beach Park

Bayfront Hwy

Wailoa River State Park

6

10

Hawaii Department of Land & Natural Resources

Ponahawai St

Ululani St

Kapi'olani St

Kilauea Ave

Kino'ole St

Waiakea Pond

Manono St

Pi'ilani St 19

Hualani St

17 23
14

Kukuau St

Mohouli St

28

12

Kekuanaoa St

Mililani St

Hinano St

Laukapu St

Kalanikoa St

5

Komohana St

16

Hilo Shopping Center

W Lanikaula St

University of Hawai'i at Hilo

Lanikaula St

30 E Kawili St

Hawaii Community College

Kanoelehua Ave

Waiakea Center

'Imiloa Astronomy Center of Hawai'i

1

Nowelo St

W Kawili St

Kino'ole St

Kilauea Ave

32

W Puainako St

22

21

Hilo Municipal Golf Course (1.6mi);
Pana'ewa Rainforest Zoo & Gardens (3mi);
Mauna Loa Macadamia-Nut Visitor Center (5.5mi);
Hawai'i Volcanoes National Park (26.5mi)

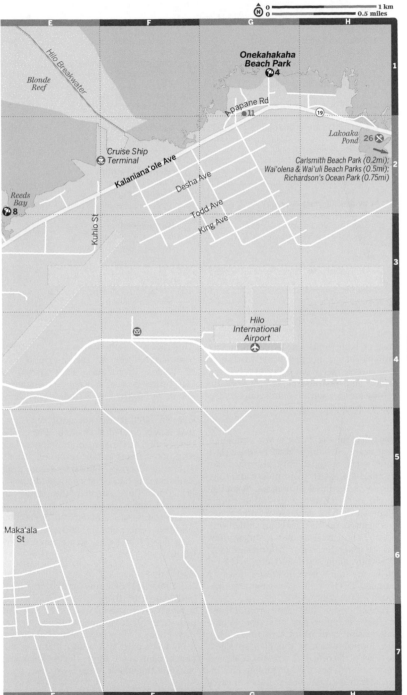

Hilo

work of both professionals and amateurs. Exhibits change monthly, while workshops and classes (such as painting, drawing, ukulele and hula) are ongoing. Check the website for occasional evening concerts featuring top artists.

Kaumana Caves   CAVE

(Map p216; Kaumana Dr) For a raw and somewhat scary adventure, head to these lava caves, which are pitch dark, sharply rocky, dripping wet, low in spots, mossy and thick with ferns. Essential equipment: flashlight (torch) or headlamp with full batteries, hiking shoes with grip, gloves and water, plus helmet and knee pads for added protection. The caves are not a major draw and are generally empty; grounds are lackadaisically maintained and car break-ins can occur. To get here, head 3.5 miles up Kaumana Dr (Hwy 200); the caves are signposted on the right.

Formed by an 1881 flow from Mauna Loa, these caves are part of a vast, 25-mile underground network of lava tubes. They were formed when, as the flow subsided, the edges of the deep lava stream cooled and crusted over. When the hot molten lava inside later drained out, hollow tubes or caves remained.

King Kamehameha Statue   STATUE

(Kamehameha Ave) At the northern end of Wailoa River State Park (p205), a 14ft bronze statue of King Kamehameha stands facing the bay. Sculpted by R Sandrin at the Fracaro Foundry in Vicenza, Italy, in 1963, it was not until June 1997 that it was erected at this site. Princeville Corporation originally commissioned this $125,000 statue for their resort on Kaua'i. But residents opposed the statue since King Kamehameha had never conquered Kaua'i. Princeville thus donated the statue to Hawai'i Island.

The statue, which underwent a $30,000 gold-leaf restoration in 2004, is draped with dozens of lei on Kamehameha Day (p210).

Kalakaua Park   PARK

(136 Kalakaua St) Centrally located, this mini park should be Hilo's 'town square,' but it is mostly green space bypassed by cars and pedestrians. It does come to life on monthly First Fridays, when downtown Hilo throws lively block parties. A bronze statue of the park's namesake, King David Kalakaua, stands in the middle of the lawn.

Hawaii Japanese Center   MUSEUM
(☑808-934-9611; www.hawaiijapanesecenter.com; 751 Kanoelehua Ave; ⊙11am-2pm Wed-Sat; Ⓟ) FREE The Japanese immigrant community has been sizable and influential in Hawai'i, especially in Hilo. Here, learn more about this group through plantation-era artifacts, memorabilia and photos, all in mint condition and neatly organized. Don't miss the eclectic gift shop, which sells vintage dishware, textiles and other gems at reasonable prices.

Additional collections, including rare books, are kept in storage and can be viewed on request.

**Mauna Loa Macadamia
Nut Visitor Center**   FACTORY
(☑888-628-6256, 808-966-8618; www.maunaloa. com; 16-701 Macadamia Rd; ⊙8:30am-5pm) FREE Drive past acres of macadamia nut trees to Hershey-owned Mauna Loa, which offers a self-guided tour of its working factory. Watch the prized mac nut move along the assembly line from cracking and roasting to chocolate dipping and packaging. The gift shop sells the finished product at decent prices, along with mac nut ice cream (single scoop $3.75) on the back patio. Store open daily; factory closed weekends and holidays.

Rainbow Falls   WATERFALL
(Map p216; Waianuenue; Rainbow Dr, off Waianuenue Ave) A regular stop for tour buses, the lookout for this 'instant gratification' cascade is just a few steps from the parking lot. Depending on rainfall, the lovely 80ft waterfall can be a torrent or a trickle. Go in the morning and you'll see rainbows if the sun and mist cooperate. Waianuenue ('rainbow seen in water') is the Hawaiian name for these falls.

To get here, drive up Waianuenue Ave (veer right when it splits into Kaumana Dr) about 1.5 miles from downtown Hilo; follow the signage.

Mokupapapa Discovery Center   MUSEUM
(☑808-933-8180; www.papahanaumokuakea.gov/ education/center.html; 76 Kamehameha Ave; ⊙9am-4pm Tue-Sat) 🖋FREE The Hawaiian archipelago extends far beyond the eight main islands to the Northwestern Hawaiian Islands, forming a long chain of uninhabited islets and atolls containing the healthiest coral reefs in the USA. Learn more about the islands' pristine ecosystems at this compelling museum, which integrates displays on physical science with the Hawaiian creation chant serving as a sonic backdrop, a reminder of the deep cultural folkways that derived from this unique environmental background.

**Wailoa Center & Wailoa River
State Park**   GALLERY
(☑808-933-0416; www.wailoacenter.com; 200 Piopio St; ⊙center 8:30am-4:30pm Mon-Fri, park sunrise-sunset; 🚹) This eclectic, state-run gallery hosts a variety of monthly exhibits. You might find quilts, bonsai, Chinese watercolors or historical photos, all done by locals. Surrounding the center is a low-key park with grassy lawns and charming arc-shaped footbridges crossing the Wailoa River. The main park landmark is a 14ft, Italian-made bronze King Kamehameha Statue. There are also Vietnam War and Shinmachi Tsunami memorials.

Honoli'i Beach Park   BEACH
(Map p216; 180 Kahoa St) Less than 2 miles north of downtown Hilo, this rocky cove is Hilo's best surfing and bodyboarding spot. When the surf's up, it's jammed with locals and not appropriate for novices. Spectators can watch from grassy lawns or the road above. Don't expect sand, swimming or drive-up access. There are daily lifeguards, restrooms, showers and picnic areas.

HILO SIGHTS

ⓘ KING KAMEHAMEHA STATUES: WHICH IS WHICH

Though you may have a feeling of deja vu, Hilo's King Kamehameha statue at Wailoa River State Park is not a copy of the 'identical' statues found in Honolulu and in Kapa'au. The Hilo statue, sculpted in 1963, is larger and the king's face is different. The other two statues date back to the 1880s, and the Honolulu statue is gilded, while the Kapa'au statue is painted. When Hawaii became the 50th US state in 1959, another replica was commissioned and unveiled at the US Capitol in 1969. In addition, the Grand Wailea on Maui has a Kamehameha statue created by the renowned Hawaiian artist Herb Kawainui Kane.

Downtown Hilo

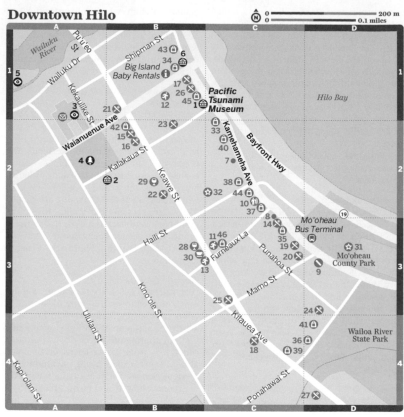

Maui's Canoe   LANDMARK
See the current swirling around a large rock in the upstream Wailuku River? Legend has it that the demigod Maui paddled his canoe with such speed across the ocean that he crash-landed here and the canoe turned to stone. Ever the devoted son, Maui was rushing to save his mother, Hina, from a water monster that was trying to drown her by damming the river and flooding her cave beneath Rainbow Falls.

To get here, go to the Pu'ueo St Bridge, at the northern end of Keawe St just beyond Wailuku Dr.

Tsunami Memorial Clock   MEMORIAL
(Map p202; Kamehameha Ave) This tall green clock is permanently stopped at 1:04, marking the morning of May 23, 1960, when a major tsunami demolished the town. A series of seismic sea waves destroyed hundreds of buildings and killed 61 people. The

longstanding clock had survived the prior 1946 tsunami.

🏃 Activities

While Hilo's coast is lined with reefs rather than sand, its gentle waters are ideal for stand up paddle surfing (SUP) – launch from **Reeds Bay Beach Park** (Map p202; 251 Banyan Dr; 🚻) or Mokuola (Coconut Island; p201). For surfing, head to Honoli'i Beach Park (p205), but only if you're an experienced surfer.

Diving is best on the Kona side but there are decent shore-diving spots in or near Hilo; inquire at Nautilus Dive Center.

★ **Hilo Bayfront Trails**   WALKING
(www.hilobayfronttrails.org) Walk or cycle from downtown Hilo to Banyan Dr along a paved coastal path. While it doesn't overlook the ocean throughout, it's still very scenic. Park at either end, downtown or

Downtown Hilo

Lili'uokalani Park, and enjoy a leisurely loop, stopping for shave ice or lunch along the way.

Orchidland Surfboards SURFING
(☑808-935-1533; www.orchidlandsurf.com; 262 Kamehameha Ave; ⊙9am-5pm Mon-Sat, 10am-3pm Sun) Board rentals, surf gear and advice from owner Stan Lawrence, who opened the Big Island's first surf shop in 1972.

Nautilus Dive Center DIVING
(☑808-935-6939; www.nautilusdivehilo.com; 382 Kamehameha Ave; intro charter dive $85; ⊙9am-5pm Mon-Sat) Hilo's go-to dive shop offers guided dive tours, PADI certification courses and general advice on shore diving.

Mids SURFING
Among Honoli'i Beach's surf breaks, Mids, which breaks right, is recommended for adept visitors only. The left break, called Point, is closer to rocks and usually has bigger waves.

Yoga Shala YOGA
(☑808-443-1979; www.facebook.com/hiloshala; 284 Keawe St; drop-in class $15) Ashtanga yogis can wake early for a morning Mysore practice at this downtown studio. Led classes and bodywork also offered. Check the schedule online.

Rogue SUP WATER SPORTS
(☑808-935-1188; 263 Keawe St; lessons per person $45-65; ⊙9am-5pm Mon-Fri) Specializing in SUP, this shop sell and rents boards. Ask about semi-private and private lessons at Reeds Bay.

Balancing Monkey Yoga Center YOGA
(☑808-633-8555; www.balancingmonkeyyoga. com; 1221 Kilauea Ave, Hilo Shopping Center; drop-in class $10) This small studio offers mostly flow classes. Check the schedule online.

Hilo Municipal Golf Course GOLF
(☑808-959-7711; 340 Haihai St; greens fees Mon-Fri $35, Sat & Sun $40, cart $20) Hilo's main 18-hole course (locally known as 'Muni') offers a well-designed layout, friendly staff, good

clubhouse restaurant and no sand bunkers (thanks to Hilo rain). Morning tee times are favored by the local contingent (mostly avid seniors); call ahead to avoid waiting.

Yoga Centered YOGA
(📞 808-934-7233; www.yogacentered.com; 37 Waianuenue Ave; drop-in class $14) In an attractive space downtown, this studio offers mostly flow classes and a boutique well stocked with quality mats and clothing. Check the schedule online.

👉 Tours

⭐**Hawaii Forest & Trail** HIKING
(📞 808-331-3657; www.hawaii-forest.com; 224 Kamehameha Ave; Mauna Kea summit tour $215; ⊙ 9am-5pm Mon-Fri, to 4pm Sat) Reliable guided-tour company offers island-wide adventures: hiking, ziplining, swimming, birding and more. The Mauna Kea summit tour includes dinner and use of hooded parkas and gloves. This office is the departure point for all Hilo-based tours. Friendly staff can advise on various tours.

Arnott's Mauna Kea Adventures TOURS
(📞 808-339-0921; www.arnottslodge.com; 98 Apapane Rd; tours $180; ⊙ tours Wed-Mon) Arnott's Lodge tours are for budget travelers, not serious stargazers. While safe and reliable, they're also cheaper and leave from Hilo (or you can drive your own car and meet them on Saddle Road for $160). The astronomy is basic, with guides relying on laser pointers (no telescopes). BYO food and warm clothes. Guests staying at **Arnott's Lodge** (📞 808-339-0921; www.arnottslodge.com; 98 Apapane Rd; camping per person $16, dm from $30, r with/without bath $90/70, ste from $100; 🅿 😊 ❄ 🛜) receive a discount.

KapohoKine Adventures ADVENTURE
(Map p202; 📞 808-964-1000; www.kapohokine.com; 93 Banyan Dr, Grand Naniloa Hotel; tours $110-520) Visit the flagship store of this adventure tour company to book tours or shop for gear. Hilo-based tours might involve ziplines, lava hikes, helicopter rides or an exciting (if pricey) combination.

🎓 Courses

Hulakai WATER SPORTS
(📞 808-896-3141; www.hulakai.com; 284 Kamehameha Ave; lesson per 1½hr SUP/surfing $98/150, rental per day SUP/surfboard $70/20; ⊙ 9:30am-5:30pm Mon-Sat, 10am-4pm Sun) Founded by

🏃 City Walk
Historic Downtown Hilo

START MO'OHEAU BANDSTAND
END HILO FARMERS MARKET
LENGTH 1 MILE; HALF DAY

Park your car somewhere along Kamehameha Ave and stop at the historic ❶ **Mo'oheau Bandstand** (p218), c 1905 and a rare survivor of the 1946 tsunami. If you're lucky, the county band will be performing their monthly concert. Next, cross the street toward the Hilo Farmers Market, and continue along Kamehameha Ave to the ❷ **S Hata Building**, a 1912 example of renaissance revival architecture with a distinctive row of arched windows. The US government seized this building from its Japanese owner during WWII. After the war, the owner's daughter bought it back for $100,000.

Along Kamehameha Ave, numerous gift shops vie for attention. Target those that sell locally made items, not imported knockoffs. ❸ **Extreme Exposure Fine Art Gallery** (p218) is ideal for volcano photography. Take note of Haili St for a later visit to the art-deco ❹ **Palace Theater** (p218; 1925), which was the island's first major playhouse, with 'stadium' seating, and still offers great concerts, movies and plays. Continuing along Kam Ave, glance at the art-deco ❺ **SH Kress Company Building**, which was Hilo's branch of the popular five-and-dime store until 1980.

Tour the ❻ **Pacific Tsunami Museum** (p201), which brings to life the two catastrophic tsunami in 1946 and 1960 that permanently changed Hilo's layout and psyche. The museum is located in the old First Hawaiian Bank building, designed by renowned Honolulu architect CW Dickey. Next door, admire the iconic botanical fabrics of the aloha wear at ❼ **Sig Zane** (p219).

Another museum worth a stop is Mokupapapa Discovery Center in the notable ❽ **FW Koehnen Building** (1910), with its eye-catching blue facade with interior koa walls and ohia floors. The museum highlights the Northwestern Hawaiian Islands and their pristine marine environment. Don't miss the ❾ **Locavore Store** (p219), toward the end of the block: all local stuff.

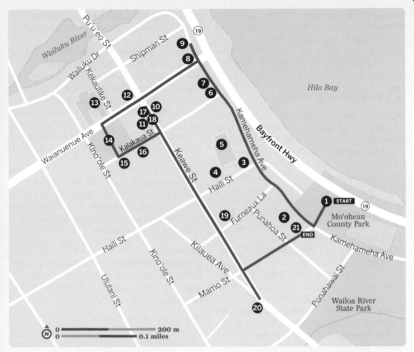

Then head up Waianuenue Ave where, on the left-hand side of the street, you'll pass two wooden buildings typical of early 20th-century Hawai'i: the ⑩ **Burns Building** (1913), which now houses a hostel, and the ⑪ **Pacific Building** (1922). Across the street, the ⑫ **Kaikodo Building** (1908), built with then-novel 'fireproof' steel beams on reinforced concrete, was home to Hilo's first Masonic Lodge. It's now Jackie Rey's Ohana Grill.

Next and most dramatic is the ⑬ **Federal Building** (1919) across Kekaulike St. Designed by architect Henry Whitfield, this stately building is typical of Hilo's early 20th-century government buildings.

Walk through the small but lovely green space of ⑭ **Kalakaua Park** (p204), where a bronze statue of King David Kalakaua (the 'Merrie Monarch') stands in the center. The lily-filled pool honors Korean War veterans, and buried under the grass is a time capsule, sealed on the last total solar eclipse (July 11, 1991), to be opened on the next (May 3, 2106).

Next stop at ⑮ **East Hawai'i Cultural Center/HMOCA** (p201) and check out their current art exhibits. The gallery building (1932), formerly a courthouse and then the county police department headquarters, is now listed

in the National Register of Historic Places. Next door is the notable ⑯ **Hawaiian Telephone Company Building**, which was designed in the 1920s by CW Dickey with Spanish, Italian and Californian mission influences. Note the high-hipped, green tile roof and the brightly colored terracotta tiles set in the building.

Along Keawe St, backtrack half a block to find two gems. ⑰ **Local Antiques & Stuff** (p218) is chock-full of fascinating artifacts and memorabilia from plantation days. Next door, stop for a coffee at longtime ⑱ **Bears' Coffee** (p215).

Turn around and go northwest along Keawe Ave, less bustling than Kamehameha Ave but also offering indie shops worth browsing. An unexpected find is ⑲ **Still Life Books** (p218), a cozy basement space filled with quality secondhand books and LPs. Before heading *makai* (toward the ocean), try the island-grown, island-made chocolate at ⑳ **Hawaiian Crown** (p214).

The ㉑ **Hilo Farmers Market** (p215) is jammed from daybreak on Wednesday and Saturday, when locals and tourists alike meander around a dazzling array of fresh produce, flowers, and other locally made goods. Bring cash and a bag.

a local waterman, Hulakai offers lessons in SUP, surfing and canoeing, plus snorkeling and fishing tours. Kayaks, boards, snorkeling gear and more are available for hire. The original store is located at Shops at Mauna Lani.

✨ Festivals & Events

⭐ **Merrie Monarch Festival**   CULTURAL
(📞808-935-9168; www.merriemonarch.com; Edith Kanaka'ole Tennis Stadium; 3-night admission $25-40; ⊘late Mar/early Apr) The Merrie Monarch Festival swoops into town around Easter and turns laid-back Hilo into *the* place to be. Forget about booking a last-minute room! This sellout three-day hula competition was established in 1964 to honor King David Kalakaua (1836–91), who almost single-handedly revived Hawaiian culture and arts, which had been forbidden by missionaries for 70 years.

Top hula troupes from all the islands vie in *kahiko* (ancient) and *'auana* (modern) categories. *Kahiko* performances are strong and serious, accompanied only by chanting. *'Auana* is closer to the mainstream style, with sinuous arm movements, smiling dancers and melodious accompaniment that includes string instruments. The

---

HILO FOR CHILDREN

Hilo is a family-oriented town, and kids are welcome at most attractions and restaurants. Bear in mind, however, that facilities for diaper (nappy) changing and breastfeeding, as well as high chairs and other special equipment, are available only at major establishments.

Regarding accommodations, many B&Bs and inns don't allow children to stay due to potential noise and damage. Ask when booking to prevent any surprises. Also, if climbing stairs with a stroller is an issue, a hotel with an elevator might be preferable.

For young kids, Hilo's outdoor attractions, such as **Onekahakaha Beach Park** (p200) and **Lili'uokalani Park** (p200), are ideal. Older kids can appreciate the museums, which are brimming with info without being overwhelming: **'Imiloa Astronomy Center of Hawai'i** (p201) is especially geared to curious grade-schoolers.

---

primal chanting, meticulous choreography and traditional costumes are profoundly moving.

The competitions are televised, but to see it live, order tickets by mail on December 1 (no earlier postmarks accepted); follow the detailed website instructions on seating and payment. The 2700 tickets sell out within a month. Book accommodations and organize car rental a year in advance.

Free performances are held earlier in the week at the Afook-Chinen Civic Auditorium.

⭐ **Black & White Night**   FAIR
(www.downtownhilo.com; ⊘5-9pm) Downtown Hilo throws a lively multiblock party on the first Friday of November, with shops open late, live music, and revelers donning their spiffiest black and white.

Aloha First Friday   FAIR
(www.downtownhilo.com; ⊘5-9pm) Restaurants, shops and galleries in downtown Hilo stay open late (later than usual, anyway) on the first Friday each month.

International Festival of the Pacific   CULTURAL
(📞808-934-0177; ⊘Aug) August celebration of the Japanese in Hawaii, featuring a lantern parade and Japanese tea ceremony at Lili'uokalani Park.

Fourth of July   INDEPENDENCE DAY
Entertainment and food all day at Lili'uokalani Park. Fireworks set off from Mokuola (Coconut Island); the best viewing is from the park and along Hilo's bayfront.

Hawai'i County Fair   FAIR
(www.hilojaycees.org; 323 Manono St, Afook-Chinen Civic Auditorium; adult/child $6/2.50; ⊘Sep) Pure nostalgia comes to town for four days in September, with carnival rides, live music, circus shows, games and cotton candy.

King Kamehameha Day Celebration   CULTURAL
(www.kamehamehafestival.org; Mokuola; ⊘Jun 11) King Kamehameha and Hawaiian culture are celebrated on June 11, with traditional hula, music, food and crafts.

May Day Lei Day Festival   CULTURAL
(www.facebook.com/hiloleidayfestival; ⊘May) Beautiful lei displays, demonstrations, live music and hula throughout the month of May.

LEGACY OF TWO TSUNAMIS

Six minutes before 7am on April 1, 1946, an unexpected tsunami walloped Hilo Bay. It had raced across the Pacific from an earthquake epicenter in the Aleutian Islands. Fifty-foot waves jumped the seawall and inundated the town. The waves ripped the first line of buildings from their foundations and propelled them inland, smashing them into the rows behind. As the waves retreated, they sucked splintered debris and a number of people out to sea. By 7am the town was littered with shattered buildings.

Throughout Hawaii the tsunami killed 159 people and caused $25 million in property damage. The hardest hit was Hilo, with 96 fatalities and a demolished 'Little Tokyo' along the bayfront. Shinmachi, which means 'new town' in Japanese, was later rebuilt on the same spot.

Fourteen years later, on May 23, 1960, an earthquake off the coast of Chile triggered a tsunami that sped toward Hilo at 440mph. A series of three waves washed up in succession, each sweeping further into the city. Although tsunami warnings blasted on loudspeakers this time, many people didn't take them seriously.

People along the shore were swept inland, while those higher up were dragged out into the bay. A lucky few managed to grab floating debris and were rescued at sea. In the end, this tsunami caused 61 deaths and property damage of over $20 million. Once more Shinmachi was leveled. But after the second demolition, the bayfront land became parks, while survivors relocated a few miles inland.

✖️ Eating

For its size, Hilo has plenty of eating options. You can eat well even on a budget, especially if you like fresh ahi and other locally caught fish. For an inexpensive, delicious and utterly local meal, try *poke* (cubed raw fish tossed with various flavorings) by the pound or in a ready-to-eat bowl.

Fine dining exists here, although the dress code might be very casual to urbanites. Health foodies can find vegetarian fare, trendy acai bowls, house-made krauts and kombucha on tap. All restaurants are nonsmoking.

Don't miss Hilo's two farmers markets: the downtown market (p215) is a bustling spectacle, with dozens of vendors selling produce and prepared foods, plus clothing and gifts. But beware of non-local goods, from mainland vegetables to cheap crafts made in China. The Kino'ole market (p214) is modest in scale, but staffed by the farmers themselves; everything is locally grown or made.

★**Big Island Candies** SWEETS
(☑800-935-5510, 808-935-8890; www.bigisland candies.com; 585 Hinano St; ◷8:30am-5pm) Once a mom-and-pop shop, this wildly successful confectioner is now a full-fledged destination. In an immaculate showroom-factory, enjoy generous samples, fantastic displays and beautifully packaged candies and cookies. Expect crowds of locals

and Japanese tourists. Don't miss the signature macadamia-nut shortbread.

★**KTA Super Store – Puainako** SUPERMARKET
(☑808-959-9111, pharmacy 808-959-8700; 50 E Puainako St, Puainako Town Center; ◷grocery 5:30am-midnight, pharmacy 8am-7pm Mon-Fri, 9am-7pm Sat) 🍴 An outstanding family-owned company, KTA's flagship store includes a bakery, pharmacy and deli, and a fantastic selection of fresh *poke* (arguably the best in Hilo). Look for the Mountain Apple house label for locally sourced milk, produce and prepared products. Don't miss the takeout bento box meals, which sell out by mid-morning.

Abundant Life Natural Foods MARKET
(☑808-935-7411; www.abundantlifenaturalfoods. com; 292 Kamehameha Ave; ◷8:30am-7pm Mon-Tue & Thu-Fri, 7am-7pm Wed & Sat, 10am-5pm Sun, takeout cafe to 3pm only, closed Sun; 🍴) 🍴 Located downtown, Abundant Life opened in 1977 when only hippies in Hilo ate 'health food.' In addition to a wide variety of groceries, you'll also find natural toiletries, yoga mats and other healthy lifestyle items. A takeout cafe serves prepared meals, smoothies and other standbys.

★**Two Ladies Kitchen** SWEETS $
(☑808-961-4766; 274 Kilauea Ave; 8-piece box $6; ◷10am-5pm Wed-Sat) This hole-in-the-wall is famous statewide for outstanding

JOHN ELK III/ALAMY ©

1. Lyman Museum & Mission House (p200)
This compact building is packed with exhibits on Hawaii's natural and cultural history.

2. Rainbow Falls (p205)
Waianuenue ('rainbow seen in water') is the Hawaiian name for these falls.

3. Richardson's Ocean Park (p200)
This small, black-sand beach is popular for swimming, snorkeling and surfing.

4. Hilo Farmers Market (p215)
A vendor selling fresh-picked coconuts.

ℹ️ OZAKU-YA

Pack a Hilo-style picnic with tasty bites from an *okazu-ya*, akin to Japanese deli. These takeout shops sell dozens of prepared dishes, including *musubi* (rice balls), *maki* (rolled) and *inari* (cone) sushi, chicken long rice (clear noodles), tofu patties, shrimp and vegetable tempura, *nishime* (root-vegetable stew), teriyaki beef, broiled mackerel, Korean or nori (dried seaweed) chicken and countless other foodstuff.

Arrive by mid-morning for a decent selection and bring cash. Vegetarians won't go hungry but *okazu-ya* are geared to meat eaters. Try **Kawamoto Store** (Map p202; 📱808-935-8209; www.kawamotostore.com; 784 Kilauea Ave; per item $1-1.50; ⏰6am-12:30pm Tue-Sun) or **Hilo Lunch Shop** (Map p202; 📱808-935-8273; 421 Kalanikoa St; per item $1-1.50; ⏰5:30am-1pm Tue-Sat).

Japanese *mochi* (sticky rice cake) in both traditional and island-inspired flavors such as *liliko'i* (passion fruit) and *poha* (gooseberry). They're sold in boxes of six to eight pieces. Study the flavor chart on the wall before ordering.

⭐ **Sweet Cane Cafe** HEALTH FOOD $
(📱808-934-0002; www.sweetcanecafe.com; 48 Kamana St; mains $7.50-9, fruit bowls $8-10; ⏰8am-6pm Mon-Sat; 🖊) 🌿 Everything is fresh, locally sourced and vegetarian at this casual cafe. Sandwiches are stuffed with roasted veggies or an ulu jalapeno patty, while the Pesto Zoodles (raw zucchini noodles) are perfectly textured and immersed in succulent mac-nut pesto. Smoothies and acai or pitaya bowls are popular and healthy mini meals. Limited parking.

⭐ **Hawaiian Crown Plantation & Chocolate Factory** SWEETS $
(📱808-319-6158; www.hawaiiancrown.com; 160 Kilauea Ave; chocolates $6.50-8.50; ⏰8:30am-5:30pm Tue-Sat, 11:30am-4pm Sun) 🌿 Locally grown and locally made, these chocolate bars and 'turtles' (up to 80% cocoa) make a perfect gift or treat for yourself. Cacao fans can also buy nibs, either unsweetened or agave sweetened, and learn about this crop from the welcoming proprietor. The shop also offers hot or iced Big Island coffee, satisfying smoothies and healthy acai bowls.

⭐ **Paul's Place** CAFE $
(📱808-280-8646; http://paulsplcafe.wixsite.com/paulsplacecafe; 132 Punahoa St; mains $8-12; ⏰7am-3pm Tue-Sat) In a six-seat dining room, Paul serves exquisite renditions of the classics, including light and crispy Belgian waffles, robust salads and his signature eggs Benedict with smoked salmon, asparagus and a unique sauce. Everything's healthy, served with lots of fresh fruit and veggies. Reservations strongly recommended.

⭐ **Suisan Fish Market** SEAFOOD $
(📱808-935-9349; 93 Lihiwai St; takeout poke $10-12, poke per lb $18; ⏰8am-6pm Mon-Fri, to 4pm Sat, 10am-4pm Sun) For a fantastic variety of freshly made *poke* (sold by the pound), Suisan is a must. Buy a bowl of takeout *poke* and rice and eat outside the shop or across the street at Lili'uokalani Park. Could life be any better?

Conscious Culture Cafe HEALTH FOOD $
(Big Island Booch Kombucha; 📱808-498-4779; www.bigislandbooch.org; 110 Keawe St; mains $9-12; ⏰8am-8pm; 🖊) Keeping the hippie vibe alive downtown, this colorful cafe takes health food up a notch. For breakfast, try the well-stuffed roasted veggie omelet or buckwheat pancakes, moist with apple bananas. Lunch and dinner mains range from mahimahi ceviche tacos to hearty quinoa bowls. Gluten-free and vegan are options. Service could be more attentive.

The cafe's name refers to its house-made cultured products: kimchi, kraut, kombucha and jun (similar to kombucha but sweetened with honey), which can be ordered by the glass or pitcher or to go. The kombucha comes in many flavors, including Super Ginger Tumeric Tonic, which sounds strong but goes down very smoothly.

Sweet Cane By The Bay HEALTH FOOD $
(📱808-657-4198; www.sweetcanecafe.com; 116 Kamehameha Ave; mains $9-11, smoothies $7; ⏰10am-3pm Mon-Sat) The downtown branch of this healthy eatery is compact, with a bright, modern interior. Salads and wraps feature local greens and unique additions such as Kona mango and Puna goat cheese. Thirsty? Get an only-in-Hawaii smoothie made with acai or durian and cacao.

Kino'ole Farmers Market MARKET $
(📱808-557-2780; www.facebook.com/kinoolefarmersmarket; Kino'ole Ave, cnr Kahaopea St; ⏰6-11:30am Sat) 🌿 Hilo's authentic, low-key

Kino'ole farmers market attracts mainly locals and offers 100% locally grown and made products sold by the farmers themselves. The 15 to 20 vendors supply all you need, including fresh produce, baked goods, taro chips, poi (steamed, mashed taro), coffee, plants and flowers. Parking is plentiful.

Miyo's
JAPANESE $

(☏808-935-2273; http://miyosrestaurant.com; 681 Manono St; dinner $11-15; ☺11am-2pm & 5:30-8:30pm Mon-Sat; 🖉🐾) A longtime local favorite, Miyo's is known for delicious home-style Japanese meals and nightly crowds. Try classics such as grilled ahi or *saba* (mackerel), crispy tempura and *tonkatsu* (breaded and fried pork cutlets). Expect a packed, rather noisy, dining room. Reservations are a must.

Hilo Farmers Market
MARKET $

(☏808-933-1000; www.hilofarmersmarket.com; Kamehameha Ave, cnr Mamo St; ☺6am-4pm Wed & Sat) 🌿 Hilo's gathering place is its downtown farmers market, which opened in 1988 with four farmers selling from trucks. Today the market is bustling and attracts sizable crowds. A single pass through the food tent unearths luscious mangoes and papayas but, fair warning, the produce sold here is not 100% locally grown. Ask the seller to be sure.

If you miss Wednesday or Saturday market days, you'll still find a bunch of daily vendors selling produce and flowers.

Cafe 100
LOCAL $

(☏808-935-8683; www.cafe100.com; 969 Kilauea Ave; loco moco $3-5, plate lunches $5-7; ☺6:15am-8:30pm Mon-Thu, to 9pm Fri, to 7:30pm Sat; 🖉🐾) Locals love this drive-in for its satisfying plate lunches and 20 rib-sticking varieties of *loco moco,* including fish and veggie burger options. With a clean seating area and efficient service, this family-owned Hilo icon serves island-style fast food at its finest.

Hilo Bay Sugar Shack
SHAVE ICE $

(☏808-989-2175; 330 Kamehameha Ave; shave ice $2.25-4.75; ☺11am-5pm Mon-Sat) Add a cultural twist to plain shave ice: Filipino 'halo halo' includes coconut milk, purple sweet potato ice cream, agar jellies and avocado. Japanese 'kakigori' features vanilla ice cream, *mochi* (sticky rice cake), strawberry sauce and sweetened azuki beans.

Shave ice syrups are day-glo and sugary: the old-fashioned kind.

Hawaiian Style Cafe
DINER $

(☏808-969-9265; www.facebook.com/hschilo; 681 Manono St; ☺7am-2pm daily, 5-8:30pm Tue-Thu, to 9pm Fri & Sat) Large appetite? Unfazed by meat, gravy and fried food? If yes, come here to fill up on island-style comfort food, surrounded by local families. Breakfast favorites include eggs with *kalua* pig or corned beef hash and frisbee-size pancakes (popular but strangely dry). Go for the generous quantities rather than gourmet quality. Expect long lines during standard mealtimes.

Bears' Coffee
CAFE $

(☏808-935-0708; 106 Keawe St; mains $4-9; ☺6:30am-4pm Mon-Fri, to 1pm Sat, to noon Sun; 📶🖉) A longtime coffee shop with a funky, old-school vibe (and teddy bears lining the walls), Bears is a laid-back spot for cup of joe and eavesdropping on the local bohemian set. Diner-style meals include fluffy souffléd eggs on toast and sprout-filled deli sandwiches.

★ Hilo Bay Cafe
HAWAII REGIONAL CUISINE, SUSHI $$

(☏808-935-4939; www.hilobaycafe.com; 123 Lihiwai St; mains $18-32; ☺11am-9pm Mon-Thu, to 9:30pm Fri & Sat; 🖉) With sweeping bay views and great Hawaii Regional Cuisine, this casually sophisticated restaurant could be stuffy. But it's not. Here you'll find a diverse crowd feasting on an eclectic omnivorous menu, including gourmet versions of comfort food, such as Hamakua mushroom pot pie. The sushi is fresh, with creative rolls and a vibrant sashimi salad featuring generous slabs of ahi.

The ocean-facing bar serves memorable cocktails ($9.50), including a strawberry-guava mojito and GC&T ('C' = cucumber).

BEST POKE
....

KTA Super Store – Puainako (p211)

Suisan Fish Market (p214)

Cousins Seafood & Bento (Map p202; ☏808-969-9900; 14 W Lanikaula St; meals $7-11; ☺6:30am-7:30pm Mon-Fri, to 2pm Sat)

Around Hilo

N 0 ———— 5 km
0 ———— 2.5 miles

island-sourced ingredients and caters to all palates: island tacos stuffed with *kalua* pig, grass-fed beef burger topped with grilled pineapple, and lusciously smooth and rich pumpkin curry. Local art lines the wall; nightly live music features local musicians.

Kanpai
JAPANESE $$

(☎ 808-969-1000; www.facebook.com/kanpais; 190 Keawe St; sushi $7-12, mains $12-18; ☺ 5pm-midnight Mon-Thu, to 1am Fri & Sat) Hip Kanpai looks slick enough for Brooklyn, but it is mellowed with Hilo's small-town camaraderie, easygoing attitude and Pacific fusion soul. The specialties are ramen, sushi and sake. With Japanese and Korean influences, sushi rolls are egregiously experimental, but there's well-cut *nigiri* for traditionalists. Bowls of steaming ramen come spicy and brimming with fresh toppings.

For late-night hanging out, Kanpai serves creative, island-influenced cocktails and good Japanese whiskey.

Jackie Rey's Ohana Grill
HAWAII REGIONAL CUISINE $$

(☎ 808-961-2572; www.jackiereyshilo.com; 64 Keawe St, Kaikodo Bldg; mains $14-30; ☺ 11am-9pm Mon-Fri, 5-9pm Sat & Sun) Located in the historic Kaikodo Building, Jackie Rey's is a 'night out' dining spot, with stylish interior, sweeping bar and slightly overpriced menu. The food is visually appealing and features local ingredients. Among the fresh catch preparations, the Togarashi Mixed Grill combines a succulent scallop, shrimp and veg medley in coconut-lime sauce. Bar service can be hit or miss.

★ Takenoko Sushi
SUSHI $$$

(☎ 808-933-3939; 681 Manono St; nigiri $2.50-8, chef's choice $40; ☺ 11:30am-1:30pm & 5-9pm Thu-Mon) You'll need to reserve a spot at this superb eight-seat sushi bar a year in advance. For the long wait, you're treated to the upper echelon of Japanese cuisine, with top-quality fish (mostly flown fresh from Japan), a spotlessly clean setting, expert sushi chef and gracious service. Each bite is a memorable experience. The three dinner seatings are at 5pm, 7pm and 9pm.

Queen's Court
AMERICAN, HAWAIIAN $$$

(☎ 808-935-9361, 800-367-5004; www.queens courtrestaurant.com; 71 Banyan Dr, Hilo Hawaiian Hotel; breakfast adult/child $23/12, dinner buffet $45, Sunday brunch $33/19; ☺ 6:30am-9:30am

---

HILO EATING

★ Moon & Turtle
HAWAII REGIONAL CUISINE $$

(☎ 808-961-0599; www.facebook.com/moonand turtle; 51 Kalakaua St; tapas $8-22; ☺ 11:30am-2pm & 5:30-9pm Tue-Sat) 🌿 A hit among foodies, this tapas-style restaurant specializes in local seafood, meat and produce prepared in startlingly creative ways. The ever-changing menu is short, but each dish is meticulously sourced and prepared. You'll surely remember (and crave) the smoky sashimi, crispy brussels sprouts and wild boar fried rice. Save some room for the heavenly sweet-tart *liliko'i* (passion fruit) pie.

★ Pineapples
HAWAII REGIONAL CUISINE $$

(☎ 808-238-5324; www.pineappleshilo.com; 332 Keawe St; mains $14-24; ☺ 11am-9:30pm Sun & Tue-Thu, to 10pm Fri & Sat; 🅐) On any given day, Pineapples' open-air dining room is jammed with a convivial crowd, mostly visitors but locals too. The food features

& 5:30-8pm daily, to 9pm Fri-Sun) For big appetites, this longtime hotel restaurant is favored for its all-you-can-eat weekend buffet dinners (seafood on Friday, Hawaiian seafood on Saturday and Sunday). The dining room is conventional, but for its spectacular view of Hilo Bay. Sunday brunch (11am to 2pm) includes seafood, omelets, saimin (local-style noodle soup) and much more. You'll have to roll yourself out of there.

Seaside Restaurant　　　SEAFOOD $$$
(☑ 808-935-8825; www.seasiderestauranthilo.
com; 1790 Kalaniana'ole Ave; meals $26-46; ⊙ 4:30-8:30pm Tue-Thu, to 9pm Fri-Sun) 🌿
Set on a natural Hawaiian fishpond, this multigenerational family restaurant specializes in fresh fish, from locally caught mahimahi to pan-size *aholehole* (flagtail fish). The food is not bad, but for the steep prices, the kitchen could ramp up its game. Still, the Seaside is a real Hilo experience.

🍷 Drinking & Nightlife

Nightlife in Hilo? Well, the town generally shuts down by 10pm and bars are few, but you can increase your options by heading to a restaurant with a bar vibe. For sports bars, consider **Cronies Bar & Grill** (☑ 808-935-5158; 11 Waianuenue Ave; burgers $12-14, mains $20-30; ⊙ 11am-9pm, to 10pm Fri) and **Hilo Burger Joint** (Map p202; ☑ 808-935-8880; www.hiloburgerjoint.com; 776 Kilauea Ave; burgers $12-14; ⊙ 11am-11pm Mon-Sat, to 10pm Sun). For a lively crowd, Pineapples (p216) is always jammed. The sleek bar at Hilo Bay Cafe (p215) has a standout view. And Kanpai (p216) has a trendy urban-hipster feel.

Daytime drinks range from fresh juice to kombucha to local coffee. You'll find the best variety of cafes offering such island drinks downtown.

Wai'oli Lounge & Cafe　　　LOUNGE
(www.queenscourtrestaurant.com/waioli; 71 Banyan Dr, Hilo Hawaiian Hotel; ⊙ 7am-10pm Sat-Thu, to 11:30pm Fri; 🛜) This lounge is mainstream but has good evening entertainment. Try Lito Arkangel's happy hour on Thursday (5:30pm to 8pm) or hear local favorite Darlene Ahuna on Friday (7pm to 9pm). During the day, the space is bright and airy, with a lovely view of Coconut Island (and wi-fi). Food and coffee are average, however.

**Coqui's Hideaway
Sports Bar**　　　SPORTS BAR
(☑ 808-934-7288; www.coquishilo.com; 1550 Kamehameha Ave; cover charge after 8pm $5; ⊙ 3pm-1am Mon & Wed-Sat) With nondescript furnishings and unpretentious staff, Coqui's is the the quintessential untrendy small-town bar. Game rooms offer pool tables, shuffle boards and darts. Karaoke and live music on designated nights; daily happy hour (4:30pm to 7pm). The adjoining diner (6:30am to 2pm) serves decent old-fashioned breakfasts.

Perfect Harmony Tea Room　　　TEAHOUSE
(☑ 808-934-0333; www.perfectharmonyhawaii.
com/tea-room; 276 Keawe St; pot of tea $5-10; ⊙ 10am-5:30pm Sat & Mon-Thu, to 9:30pm Fri) Discover a peaceful tea room hidden in the back of an ethnic clothing boutique. Done in deep colors and Asian motifs, the atmospheric space offers ample seating and a good selection of teas. Prices seem high, but each serving is meant to be savored through multiple infusions. Check the website for occasional Friday night live music.

Hawai'i Nui Brewing　　　BREWERY
(☑ 808-934-8211; www.hawaiinuibrewing.com; 275 E Kawili; ⊙ noon-5pm Mon, Tue & Thu, to 6pm Wed & Fri, to 4pm Sat) This microbrewery has a small tasting room where you can sample excellent craft beer, including brews originated by Mehena Brewing, Hilo's first microbrewer, which it took over in 2009. Mehana's Mauna Kea Pale Ale is the most popular, but don't miss the Hawai'i Nui's Southern Cross, a powerful Belgian ale that gives those Trappist monks a run for their money.

Hilo Town Tavern　　　BAR
(www.hilotavern.com; 168 Keawe St; mains $9-11; ⊙ 11:30am-2am) This super-casual, untrendy tavern has indoor and outdoor stages, a pool hall, lively music and a mixed crowd of locals and tourists. It's among the only spots for local-style bar food, cold beer and nightlife past midnight.

> ### BEST DRINKING & NIGHTLIFE
> •••••••••••••••••••••••••••••
> Kanpai
>
> Cronies Bar & Grill
>
> Pineapples

Bayfront Kava Bar BAR
(☑808-345-1698; www.bayfrontkava.com; 264 Keawe St; cup of kava $5; ⊘4-10pm Mon-Sat) If you're curious about kava ('awa in Hawaiian), try a cup at this minimalist bar. Friendly bar staff serve freshly brewed, locally grown kava root in coconut shells. Get ready for tingling taste buds and a calm buzz. Live music and art exhibitions kick off on a regular basis.

☆ Entertainment

Check venue websites and local newspapers for upcoming shows.

Palace Theater THEATER
(☑808-934-7010; www.hilopalace.com; 38 Haili St; ⊘box office 10am-3pm) This historic theater is Hilo's cultural crown jewel. Its eclectic programming includes art-house and silent films (accompanied by the house organ), music and dance concerts, Broadway musicals and cultural festivals.

Willie K's Gig at the Crown Room LIVE MUSIC
(☑808-969-3333; www.grandnaniloahilo.com/crown-room; 93 Banyan Dr, Grand Naniloa Hotel) A go-to music venue in the '80s, the Crown Room at the Grand Naniloa Hotel was reborn in 2016. Celebrated Maui-based musician Willie K is the headliner, with quarterly shows. Other local musicians perform the rest of the time. Contact the hotel or check listings for details of upcoming shows.

Mo'oheau Bandstand LIVE PERFORMANCE
(parks_recreation@hawaiicounty.gov; 329 Kamehameha Ave) This historic bandstand holds occasional hula shows, band concerts, political rallies and other gatherings. Visit the bandstand's Facebook page or check local newspaper listings for schedules.

BEST SHOPPING

· ·

Extreme Exposure Fine Art Gallery

Local Antiques & Stuff

Basically Books

Locavore Store

Knickknackery

Hilo Guitars & Ukuleles

Stadium Cinemas CINEMA
(☑808-959-4595; 111 E Puainako St, Prince Kuhio Plaza; tickets $6.25-9.50) Typical shopping mall cinema with the usual Hollywood showings.

🔒 Shopping

While locals flock to chain-store-heavy Prince Kuhio Plaza (p220) south of the airport, downtown is far better for unique shops, including a few top-notch antique collections. Be careful to distinguish between products genuinely made in Hawaii and cheap imports.

★Local Antiques & Stuff ANTIQUES
(104 Keawe St; ⊘10:30am-4:30pm Tue-Sat) This teeming display of local artifacts and memorabilia is a must-see. There's something for every budget: retro glass bottles, plantation-era housewares, Japanese kokeshi dolls, vintage aloha shirts, knickknacks galore and valuable koa furniture. A real mom-and-pop operation run by a local couple who amassed their eclectic collection over many years.

★Still Life Books BOOKS
(☑808-756-2919; stillife@bigisland.com; 58 Furneaux Lane; ⊘11am-3pm Tue-Sat) Bibliophiles and audiophiles should set aside ample time to browse this hand-picked inventory of secondhand books and LPs. Expect literature, history, art, travel and philosophy. No potboilers. This cozy basement space is filled with great finds, including the owner, a true book and music aficionado.

★Basically Books BOOKS
(☑808-961-0144; www.basicallybooks.com; 160 Kamehameha Ave; ⊘9am-5pm Mon-Sat, 11am-3:30pm Sun) A browser's paradise, this shop specializes in maps, travel guides and books about Hawaii, including a wide selection for children. Also find gifts, from toys to CDs. Staff are helpful and know their stuff.

★Extreme Exposure Fine Art Gallery PHOTOGRAPHY
(☑808-936-6028; www.extremeexposure.com; 224 Kamehameha Ave; ⊘10am-8pm Mon-Sat, 11am-5pm Sun) At this unpretentious gallery, find excellent nature photography – featuring Hawai'i's wildlife, seascapes, landscapes and lava displays – by photographers Bruce Omori and Tom Kuali'i. There's something

for all budgets, from framed prints to greeting cards.

Most Irresistible
Shop in Hilo GIFTS & SOUVENIRS
(☑808-935-9644; www.facebook.com/mostirresistibleshop; 256 Kamehameha Ave; ⊙9am-6pm Mon-Fri, to 5pm Sat, 10:30am-3:30pm Sun) True to its name, this shop is filled with quality treasures: jewelry, Japanese dishware, children's games and toys, clothing, home textiles, Hello Kitty items and random cute stuff. Staff are friendly and discreet, letting you browse in peace.

Bryan Booth Antiques FURNITURE
(☑808-933-2500; www.bryanboothantiques.com; 94 Ponahawai St; ⊙10am-5pm Mon-Sat) Transporting a rocking chair or dining table home might be a deal breaker. But Bryan Booth's expertly restored wood furniture might convince you otherwise. In his spacious showroom, find exquisite pieces from the late 1800s and early 1900s, along with antique lamps, framed art and china. Expect prices from about $500 to $5000 plus.

Knickknackery – Hilo ANTIQUES
(72 Kapi'olani St; ⊙10am-6pm Tue-Fri, to 1pm Sat) This mesmerizing antiques collection contains carefully selected gems for a range of budgets, such as a 1950s koa wood dresser, a retro Singer sewing machine table, a rare Ni'ihau shell lei, a kitschy Polynesian dancer lamp, or an aloha shirt emblazoned with 'STATEHOOD.' The original store is in Honoka'a.

Grapes: A Wine Store WINE
(☑808-933-1471; www.grapeshawaii.com; 207 Kilauea Ave; ⊙noon-6pm Tue-Sat) This hidden treasure is owned by a true aficionado and packed to the rafters with global stock. Free wine tastings every other Thursday.

Hilo Guitars & Ukuleles MUSIC
(☑808-935-4282; www.hiloguitars.com; 56 Ponahawai St; ⊙10am-5pm Mon-Fri, to 4pm Sat) Find a wide selection of quality ukuleles, from koa or mahogany collectibles to fine entry-level instruments.

Sig Zane Designs CLOTHING
(☑808-935-7077; www.sigzane.com; 122 Kamehameha Ave; ⊙9:30am-5pm Mon-Fri, 9am-4pm Sat) 🖉 Legendary in the hula community, Sig Zane creates iconic custom fabrics, marked by rich colors and graphic prints of Hawaiian flora. You can spot a 'Sig' a mile away.

Hawaiian Force CLOTHING
(☑808-934-7171; www.hawaiianforce.com; 184 Kamehameha Ave; ⊙10am-5pm Mon-Fri, to 4pm Sat) Craig Neff's aloha wear and T-shirts feature bold colors and Hawaiian motifs. While somewhat similar to Sig Zane's modern graphic design, these prints, especially on the T-shirts, make more of a political (and sometimes humorous) statement.

Big Island BookBuyers BOOKS
(☑808-315-5335; www.bigislandbookbuyers.com; 14 Waianuenue Ave; ⊙10am-5pm Mon-Sat) This welcoming, owner-operated secondhand bookstore sells all genres, including Hawaiiana (some new), travel (some new), religion, cookbooks, history, fiction and mass paperbacks.

Mid Pacific Store ANTIQUES
(☑808-895-7377; 76 Kapiolani St; ⊙noon-4:30pm Mon-Fri) Stroll down memory lane at this longtime shop crammed with local antiques, memorabilia and miscellaneous doodads that you now regret discarding.

Locavore Store FOOD
(☑808-965-2372; www.bigislandlocavorestore.com; 60 Kamehameha Ave; ⊙9am-6pm Mon-Fri, to 4pm Sat) In a small yet airy space, this 100% local grocer sells the seasonal produce and handmade goods of 80-plus Big Island farmers and artisans. Prices run on the high side, since they source from small-scale, often organic, suppliers. Find great gifts, including locally made jewelry, toiletries, honey and chocolate.

Big Island Running Co SPORTS & OUTDOORS
(☑808-961-5950; www.bigislandrunningcompany.com; 308 Kamehameha Ave; ⊙10am-5pm Mon-Sat) If you suddenly need new shoes, go to this running specialist for advice on fitting. The selection is limited but includes popular styles of major brands. Pick up a souvenir 'Run Big' or 'Run Aloha' tee or tank! Local running advice is also on offer.

Dragon Mama HOMEWARES
(☑808-934-9081; www.dragonmama.com; 266 Kamehameha Ave; ⊙9am-5pm Mon-Fri, to 4pm Sat) Go home with exquisite bedding custom-made from lovely imported Japanese fabric.

Prince Kuhio Plaza MALL
(☎808-959-3555; www.princekuhioplaza.com; 111 E Puainako St; ⊙10am-8pm Mon-Thu, to 9pm Fri & Sat, to 6pm Sun) Hilo's largest shopping mall includes chain retailers such as Macy's, Sears and American Eagle. There's also a movie theater, indoor playgrounds and video arcades.

Target, Safeway and Walmart are located nearby, but not in the same center.

ⓘ Information

Big Island Baby Rentals (☎808-319-9304; www.bigislandbabyrentals.com; 26b Waianuenue Ave) This Hilo shop can rent out strollers, booster seats, folding chairs and other gear aimed at babies, toddlers and kids.

Bank of Hawaii (Kaiko'o (Hilo) Branch; ☎808-935-9701; www.boh.com; 120 Pauahi St; ⊙8:30am-4pm Mon-Thu, to 6pm Fri) Also with a branch at Kawili St (Waiakea Branch; ☎808-961-0681; www.boh.com; 417 E Kawili St; ⊙8:30am-4pm Mon-Thu, to 6pm Fri).

Downtown Post Office (☎808-933-3014; 154 Waianuenue Ave, Federal Bldg; ⊙9am-4pm Mon-Fri, 12:30-2pm Sat)

First Hawaiian Bank (☎808-969-2211; www.fhb.com; 1205 Kilauea Ave, Hilo Shopping Center; ⊙8:30am-4pm Mon-Thu, to 6pm Fri, 9am-1pm Sat)

Hilo Public Library (☎808-933-8888; www.librarieshawaii.org; 300 Waianuenue Ave; ⊙11am-7pm Tue & Wed, 9am-5pm Thu & Sat, 10am-5pm Fri; ⊛) If you buy a three-month nonresident library card ($10), you can use internet terminals for free and check out books.

Main Post Office (Map p202; ☎808-933-3019; 1299 Kekuanaoa St; ⊙8am-4:30pm Mon-Fri, 9am-12:30pm Sat) Located near Hilo airport.

Police (☎808-935-3311; www.hawaiipolice.com; 349 Kapi'olani St) Call local number for nonemergencies.

DANGERS & ANNOYANCES

While Hilo is relatively safe, the town shuts down at night and it pays to be careful in deserted areas, including downtown.

GAY & LESBIAN TRAVELERS

While Hilo is too small and laid-back to have a gay scene, it's a diverse and accommodating town and gay and lesbian travelers are unlikely to encounter discrimination. That said, Hilo people are low-key and it's probably best not to flaunt sexuality, whether gay or straight.

INTERNET ACCESS

Finding free wi-fi is hit or miss in Hilo, while internet cafes (with computers for rent) are ancient history. In a pinch, drop in to a big-name coffee chain for free wi-fi with a purchase.

MEDICAL SERVICES

Hilo Medical Center is the main hospital and emergency facility in town. For less-critical conditions, you could also try an urgent-care clinic. For prescriptions, there are numerous pharmacies, including those in **KTA Super Store – Puainako** (p211) and large grocery stores.

Hilo Medical Center (☎808-932-3000; www.hilomedicalcenter.org; 1190 Waianuenue Ave; ⊙24hr emergency) The main hospital and emergency facility in town is near Rainbow Falls.

Longs Drugs (☎808-935-3357, pharmacy 808-935-9075; 555 Kilauea Ave; ⊙24hr) General store and pharmacy open 24 hours. Also at Prince Kuhio Plaza (☎808-959-5881, pharmacy 808-959-4508; 111 E Puainako St; ⊙7am-midnight, pharmacy 7am-10pm Mon-Fri, to 7pm Sat, 8am-6pm Sun).

TRAVELERS WITH DISABILITIES

Most museums and indoor attractions are wheelchair accessible, as are **Pana'ewa Rainforest Zoo** (p201) and **Lili'uokalani Park** (p200). Among the beaches, **Onekahakaha Beach Park** (p200) has paved paths and is the easiest to navigate.

While most hotels have elevators, B&Bs and rental houses might require climbing steps so inquire when booking if this would be inconvenient.

HOW HILO GOT ITS NAME

One day King Kamehameha was camped near the mouth of the Wailuku River, which flows from Mauna Kea into into the bay. He commanded his servants to guard his canoe and then left to visit a friend. Hours passed, but the servants dared not leave the canoe unattended. Then one servant had a bright idea to secure the vessel with a rope made by twisting *ti* leaves together.

They left in search of the king. When they found him, he roared, 'Where is my canoe? I ordered you to guard it!' The servants explained how they tied the vessel with twisted *ti* leaves. Satisfied, Kamehameha named the area 'Hilo,' which means 'to twist' in Hawaiian.

ⓘ Getting There & Away

AIR

Hilo International Airport (ITO; Map p202; ☑ 808-961-9300; www.hawaii.gov/ito; 2450 Kekuanaoa St) The Hilo International Airport is located at the northeastern corner of Hilo, less than three miles from downtown. Almost all flights arriving here are interisland, mostly from Honolulu. Rental car booths and taxis are located right outside the baggage-claim area.

CAR

The drive from Hilo to Kailua-Kona (via Waimea) along Hwy 19 is 95 miles and takes about 2½ hours. Driving along Saddle Road can cut travel time by about 15 minutes.

BUS

Hele-On Bus (☑ 808-961-8744; www.hele onbus.org; per trip adult/senior & student $2/1) All buses originate at the Mo'oheau Bus Terminal (☑ 808-961-8343; 329 Kamehameha Ave) in downtown Hilo. From there, buses go around the island, but service is infrequent, sometimes only very early in the morning (for work commuters) or only a few times daily. If you're going to a major destination (such as Kailua-Kona or a South Kohala resort) and are staying within the area, the bus is a feasible option. Check the website for current routes and schedules.

ⓘ Getting Around

BICYCLE

Cycling isn't a major activity in Hilo, and it's primarily for recreation, not for transportation. But Hilo is an eminently cyclable town. **Mid-Pacific Wheels** (☑ 808-935-6211; www. midpacificwheelsllc.com; 1133c Manono St; rental per day road bike $35, mountain bike $25-45; ◷ 9am-6pm Mon-Sat, 11am-5pm Sun) is your best bet for rentals.

BUS

The Hele-On Bus covers much of Hilo, although service is rather infrequent. There are three intra-Hilo routes that cover most of the town: the Keaukaha route includes stops at Hilo Airport, Prince Kuhio Plaza and the beaches.

CAR

Free parking is generally available around town. Downtown street parking is free for two hours (or more, since enforcement is slack); finding a spot is easy except when the Wednesday and Saturday farmers markets are on.

TAXI

The approximate cab fare from the airport to downtown Hilo is $15. If you need to call a taxi try **AA Marshall's Taxi** (☑ 808-936-2654) or **Percy's Taxi** (☑ 808-969-7060).

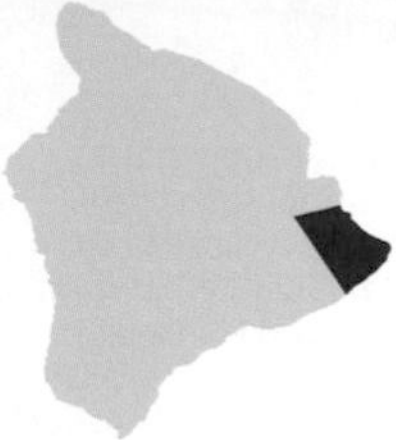

Puna

POP 40,000 / ☎808

Best Places to Eat

➡ Peleʻs Kitchen (p229)

➡ Pahoa Fresh Fish (p229)

➡ Paoloʻs Bistro (p229)

➡ Kaleoʻs Bar & Grill (p229)

Best Scenic Views

➡ Molten lava by land (p232) or by sea (p231)

➡ Marine life in Kapoho Tide Pools (p235)

➡ People-watching at Kehena Beach (p230)

➡ Tree Tunnels along the Red Road (p230)

Why Go?

Hawaiʻi's eastern corner is a challenging place to live. Often drenched by rain, occasionally scorched by lava, and somewhat disconnected from the rest of the island, Puna attracts a unique assortment of free-spirited characters who enjoy living on the edge.

This is the home of hippies, funky artists, alternative healers, Hawaiian sovereignty activists, *pakalolo* (marijuana) growers, organic farmers and off-the-grid survivalists. A nickname for all these folks, which they enthusiastically embrace, is Punatics. Collectively they embody a disconcerting blend of laid-back apathy to the world and intense emotion.

But even if you prefer to keep your mana (spiritual essence) more on the down-low, you'll still find plenty of compelling reasons to explore the land where the sun rises: from warm springs and world-class snorkeling to yoga centers and a couple of fine surf breaks. Go now, before Pele decides it's time to hit the reset button.

When to Go

Apr, May & Sep Crowds and prices dip before and after summer vacation. Mild and sunny days.

Oct & Nov Moderate number of visitors, with decent prices on airfares and accommodations. Expect increased crowds and business closures around Thanksgiving Day.

Dec–Mar & Jun–Aug Accommodations rates double or triple. In Easter, the area around Hilo is jammed during the Merrie Monarch Festival.

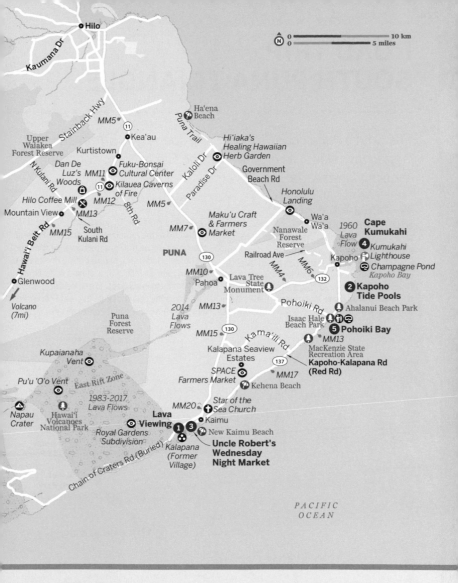

Puna Highlights

1 Lava Viewing (p232) Being hypnotized by Pele's awesome power as she creates the Earth before your very eyes.

2 Kapoho Tide Pools (p235) Chasing schools of fish through an endless maze of ponds and pools.

3 Uncle Robert's Wednesday Night Market (p233) Meeting Puna's cast of characters at a weekly festival of food, friends and fine music.

4 Cape Kumukahi (p234) Feeling one of the world's cleanest breezes blowing across your face at the eastern edge of the island.

5 Pohoiki Bay (p230) Watching local talent tame the ocean at Puna's most happening surf break.

ROAD TRIP: SOUTH PUNA TRIANGLE

● ●

The South Puna coast's incredible scenery is streaked with jagged lava flows, a reminder of the Big Island's constantly evolving landscape.

❶ Pahoa & Lava Tree State Monument

Begin with a hearty breakfast at **Pele's Kitchen** (p229), or an afternoon takeout box of **Pahoa Fresh Fish** (p229; go for the small if you plan on moving later). After that, head east out of town on Hwy 132 toward **Lava Tree State Monument** (p228; Mile 2.5) where a short stroll pays big dividends.

The Drive > At the 'Y' intersection, stay left. (Pohiki Rd to the right is a pleasant narrow-lane alternative route that passes Hawai'i's friendliest hostel, Hedonisia, before hitting the coast.) Just beyond at Mile 3.3, a closed road to the south leads to Puna Geothermal Venture, which harnesses the power of Pele to create clean energy (though not without controversy).

Start Pahoa

End Pahoa

Length 35 miles; 2+ hours

❷ Mile 6.8

As the road curves north, notice Railroad Ave heading left (west). This was the old railway grade for a line connecting the Puna Sugar Company to Hilo. Stretches were improved in 2014 as a way to escape encroaching lava. You'll continue past what remains of Kapoho (consumed by lava) until you reach the four-way intersection at Mile 7.7. Straight ahead offers a 3-mile out-and-back to the **easternmost point** (p234) in Hawaii, and the official public access to **Champagne Pond** (p235).

The Drive > Turn right (south) to continue along the decidedly-not-red Red Road.

❸ Kapoho Tide Pools

The **Kapoho Tide Pools** (p235) are Puna's snorkeling hot spot (literally) and one of the highlights of this drive (although it does require walking half a mile to the ponds).

❹ Ahalanui Beach Park

Continuing south, **Ahalanui Beach Park** (p231) is at Mile 10.5. Even if you're not into the public-pool atmosphere, the rock ledge shore with crashing waves can be photogenic. The turnoff for Puna's surf break and **Isaac Hale Beach Park** (p230) is less than 1 mile further along.

The Drive > Red Road continues through the forested coastline to tree tunnels and the occasional tide pool where kids enjoy splashing around. Just after Mile 15, Kama'ili Rd is another back-road alternative for returning to Pahoa. Look for a cemetery around Mile 15.7 with an ancient heiau hidden behind it.

❺ Kehena Beach & Around

At Mile 16.5, the road crosses the first finger of the 1955 lava flow that originated along a 4-mile rift that crossed Hwy 130. The eruption lasted 88 days and was the first in Lower Puna since 1840. At Mile 18.8 a small parking area and a worn path *makai* (seaward) of the road betray the location of the best patch of sand in Puna: **Kehena Beach** (p230), where anything goes (including clothes).

The Drive > From here it's 1.4 miles to the intersection with Hwy 130.

❻ Chain of Craters Road

Just after you turn north toward Pahoa on Hwy 130, take the sharp left back on the old Chain of Craters Road. Even if you don't have time to hike the 8-mile round trip out to the active lava flow (assuming it's actively flowing), just seeing the scale of the desolation – and the tenacity of the lava-dwellers rebuilding on top of it – gives you a greater appreciation for how precarious life in Puna really is.

❼ Star of the Sea Church

Back on Hwy 130, only a few hundred feet past the Chain of Craters Road junction, look for the turn east to the painted **Star of the Sea Church** (p232), a building worthy of being hauled out of the way of approaching lava as Kalapana was destroyed. Across the way, a small *noni* farm produces one of Puna's miracle elixirs. Enthusiastic claims that extracts can cure everything from coughs and cataracts to cancer have not been substantiated (neither have the warnings that it may cause liver damage).

The Drive > From here, it's a straight shot back to Pahoa and a candlelit dinner for two at Paolo's Bistro or (depending on your company) tacos and beer at Luquin's.

ℹ️ Dangers & Annoyances

Frolicking in tide pools and hot ponds has a potential downside – bacteria, including staphylococcus. In rare cases, infection can lead to necrotizing fasciitis, or flesh-eating disease, contracted by a visitor to Kapoho as recently as 2016.

To minimize risk, go early in the morning when fewer people have entered the pools; go during high tide; and avoid Mondays and post-holidays. Most important, do not enter pools if you have open cuts, and shower immediately after swimming.

ℹ️ Getting There & Away

The **Hele-On Bus** (📞808-961-8744; www.hele onbus.org; per trip adult/senior & student $2/1, 10-ride ticket $15, monthly pass $60) system covers the main corridors connecting much of Puna with Hilo. Getting here from Kona will require a few transfers.

ℹ️ Getting Around

We never recommend hitching. Although it is common practice here, cavalier attitudes toward health, safety and the law warrant a higher-than-usual level of diligence.

We want to love biking here, but are put off by the narrow roads with inconsistent (or non-existent) shoulders and reckless drivers.

Keaʻau

📞808 / POP 2253

Between Hilo and Volcano a series of former sugar plantations and minivillages blend together in a sea of forested sameness. The main town, Keaʻau, is not much more than a cluster of gas stations and stores, including a supermarket. Past Keaʻau toward Pahoa, however, burgeoning residential subdivisions have transformed Puna into sprawling suburbs, with the snarling rush-hour traffic to prove it.

👁️ Sights

⭐ **Haʻena Beach**   BEACH

(Shipman Beach; trailhead at 15-1458 Beach Rd) If you believe paradise is sweetest when earned, trek out to this pristine, postcard-worthy black and white sand beach in a protected cove on the Shipman Estate. Public access is via a 2.5-mile muddy, jungly hike down the Puna Trail that will demand a healthy sacrifice of sweat, tears and possibly (as in our case) blood. For the effort you'll likely have this slice of perfection to yourself.

Best enjoyed at low tide. Trail starts in Hawaiian Paradise Park neighborhood.

There are no facilities at the beach, and nearby buildings and surrounding land are all private property.

Hilo Coffee Mill   FARM

(📞808-968-1333; www.hilocoffeemill.com; 17-995 Hwy 11; ⏰8am-4:30pm Tue, 8am-2pm Thu-Sat) Grab an espresso and a snack while you talk beans with the master roaster at this friendly coffee and tea farm. Free short tours give you a taste of what makes an amazing cup, while longer 90-minute farm excursions (advance bookings, with/without meal $25/20) give a more intimate look at the process. A disc golf course through the plantation provides an engaging way to stretch your legs. Watch for chickens on the 9th. Located roadside between Miles 12 and 13.

Fuku-Bonsai Cultural Center   GARDENS

(📞808-982-9880; www.fukubonsai.com; 17-856 Olaʻa Rd; ⏰8am-4pm Mon-Sat) **FREE** It's as if the ambitions of David Fukumoto have been continually cut back by fate – including an alleged $30 million pesticide disaster – reshaping his dreams into a miniature version of what might have been. The showroom looks half-abandoned, but he is ever optimistic, passionate and eager to display several impressive specimens of the center's commercial focus: the dwarf schefflera indoor bonsai. Turn south off Hwy 11 at Olaʻa Rd between Miles 9 and 10.

👉 Tours

Kilauea Caverns of Fire   TOURS

(📞808-217-2363; www.kilaueacavernsoffire.com; off Volcano Hwy 11, near Kurtistown; tours per person $29-89; ⏰by appointment) These tours through Kazumura Cave (p255) can run a bit large – up to 20 for the one-hour walk and up to eight for the three-hour adventure – but it is a pretty impressive spelunking adventure for all that. The shorter tour is a decent option for families; the minimum age is five years.

🍴 Eating

For groceries, stock up at **Foodland** (📞808-966-9316; 16-586 Old Volcano Rd; ⏰6am-10pm) or **Keaʻau Natural Foods** (📞808-966-8877; 16-586 Old Volcano Rd; ⏰8:30am-8pm Mon-Fri, 8:30am-7pm Sat, 9:30am-5pm Sun), both at Keaʻau Shopping Center. For eating out, you're better off continuing on to Pahoa

THE JUNE 27 LAVA FLOW

On June 27, 2014 Pu'u 'O'o crater began erupting from a new vent on its northeast flank, sending a river of lava crawling across Puna toward Pahoa.

The speed of that river, pouring like slow syrup, meant that daily life was not dramatically impacted, but residents lived with constant, low-level stress, obsessing about where the lava would creep next. While school groups excitedly visited the flow front on field trips, the town anxiously began preparing for the worst.

Fearing the lava would cross Hwy 130 and cut lower Puna off from the rest of the island, the government mobilized the bulldozers. They spent $8 million rebuilding the previously buried Chain of Craters Road to the west, and improved other escape routes along Puna's east coast.

By October, the lava had reached the outskirts of Pahoa, threatening the town's award-winning transfer station and recycling center. The electric company enshrouded utility poles with flame-resistant material and piles of cinders while businesses and residents began evacuating. The final chapter of Pahoa's long history, it seemed, was to be written in liquid stone.

However, in January 2015, after it consumed a house and oozed through the transfer station fence, the lava flow slowed. By March, activity stopped completely – the path of destruction ending just shy of the highway and several businesses.

Life quickly returned to normal (by Pahoa standards), but residents remain acutely aware how lucky they are, and how important it is to celebrate what you have, because Pele might take it away at any moment.

or Volcano where you'll find more creative offerings.

Honi Wai Cafe CAFE $
(☑ 808-966-9645; www.facebook.com/HoniWai; 17-937 Volcano Rd; sandwiches $11-13; ☺10am-6pm Tue-Sat) Grab a fresh hot pastrami sandwich on your way through or enjoy the open dining area – a mix of contemporary chic and country cottage – while you sip a bubble tea and gorge on the Hawaiian nachos topped with fresh *poke* (seasoned cubes of raw fish) and kalua pork. Rotating specials make it worth swinging by on your way back through town too.

Spoonful Cafe THAI $$
(☑ 808-982-8899; 16-569 Old Volcano Rd; mains $11-15; ☺lunch 10am-2pm, dinner 5-9pm; ☎) Of Kea'au's three Asian-inspired restaurants, Spoonful has been consistently the most dependable. Serves standard Thai fare in a comfortable space set away from the main hustle.

🛍 Shopping

Dan DeLuz's Woods ARTS & CRAFTS
(☑ 808-968-6607; 17-4003 Ahuahu Pl, Hwy 11, past Mile 12; ☺10am-5pm Tue-Sat; ☎) Revered master woodworker Dan passed away in 2012, but the grandson he trained carries on the family craft. The shop still has numerous

calabash bowls by the much-loved local talent.

❶ Getting There & Away

Traffic between Kea'au and Hilo is a madhouse during rush hour. Avoid if possible.

The Hele-On Bus (www.heleonbus.org) connects Kea'au to Hilo and Pahoa 11 times Monday to Friday and once Saturday, and five buses travel to Hawai'i Volcanoes National Park Monday to Saturday.

Pahoa

☑ 808 / POP 945

Pahoa sometimes feels like the funky love-child of a Wild West frontier town and a hippie commune. Its ramshackle main street, complete with covered wooden sidewalks and peeling paint, has an unkempt bohemian edge that has captured the heart of many a traveler. Since all roads lead to Pahoa (quite literally), you'll find all types here in the original, eclectic beating heart of Puna.

The main thoroughfare is easily missed if you're bombing down Hwy 130. Take Pahoa Village Rd that splits south from the traffic circle on the north end of town, and reconnects at the Hwy 130 and 132 intersection at the south. Don't miss it.

◉ Sights

★ Maku'u Farmers Market   MARKET
(☑ 808-896-5537; www.facebook.com/makuu
farmersmarket; 15-2131 Pahoa-Kea'au Hwy; parking
$1; ☉ 8am-2pm Sun) Follow the line of cars
turning off Hwy 130 every Sunday morning
for this large, festive and diverse farmers
market. Offerings include psychic readings,
massage, orchids, jewelry, secondhand
goods, and, yes, fruits and vegetables. Enjoy
live music while sampling fresh Hawaiian,
Mexican and Thai grinds by local eateries.
Located *makai* (seaward) between Miles 7
and 8.

Pahoa Transfer Station   VIEWPOINT
(Cemetery Rd) Although the award-winning,
$3.9-million solar-powered transfer station
is a solid waste management marvel, trash-
less travelers flock here to ogle its brush
with obliteration. One arm of the June 27
Lava Flow (p227) threatened the facility
as *pahoehoe* (smooth-flowing lava) oozed
through the fence that was holding the flow
at bay. For residents, the near-apocalyptic
scene is a daily reminder of how close they
came to losing everything. For you, it's a
neat photo op.

Lava Tree State Monument   PARK
(Hwy 132 Mile 2.5; ☉ dawn-dusk) **FREE** An easy
0.6-mile paved loop takes you past ancient
'lava trees,' created in 1790 when *pahoehoe* (smooth-flowing lava) from Kilauea's
East Rift Zone enveloped moisture-laden
ohia before receding, leaving towering im-
pressions of the destroyed tree trunks. The
impressive canopy of non-native albizia
trees formerly growing here amplified the
destruction of Hurricane Iselle as they top-
pled in the high winds, leading to a massive
effort to eradicate invasive species from the
monument.

Also found around here: *Phallus indu-
siatus*, a suggestively shaped stinkhorn
mushroom whose unusual smell is rumored
to elicit certain sensations in some women.

🏃 Activities

★ Jeff Hunt Surfboards   SURFING
(☑ 808-965-2322; www.jeffhuntsurfboards.com;
15-2883 Pahoa Village Rd; rental per day $20;
☉ 10am-5pm Mon-Sat, 11am-3pm Sun) Jeff Hunt
is one of the island's best board shapers, and
at his little hut you can buy one of his boards
(or other makes), talk surfing, accessorize or
rent soft-top boards.

Pahoa Community
Aquatic Center   SWIMMING
(☑ 808-965-2700; 15-2910 Puna Rd; ☉ 9am-
5:45pm Mon-Fri, 9am-4:45pm Sat & Sun) **FREE**
For lap swimming, try this outdoor Olympic-size pool behind the Pahoa Neighborhood Facility. Showers for swimmers only.

🍴 Eating

For such a small town, Pahoa has the best
collection of eateries on this end of the
island.

★ Golden Goat   FUSION $
(☑ 510-883-4783; www.facebook.com/golden
goathawaii; 15-2929 Pahoa Village Rd; mains $6-
8; ☉ 9am-4pm, till later Fri-Sat; ☑) Regular $2
taco specials are a no-brainer, while the
ginger bowls are packed with so much good-
for-you zip you'll feel healthier just ordering
one (and even happier eating it). All that
and smoothies too, served out of a hole in
the wall (OK, it's a window) on the main Pahoa drag.

NOISY NEIGHBORS – COQUI FROGS

Hawaii's most wanted alien is the Puerto Rican coqui frog, only an inch long, but relent-
lessly loud. At sunset, coquis begin their nightly chirping (a two-tone 'ko-kee' call), which
can register between 90 and 100 decibels from 2ft away. Even at a distance, their chorus
maintains 70 decibels, equivalent to a vacuum cleaner.

Coquis accidentally reached the Hawaiian Islands around 1988, and they've proliferated wildly on the Big Island. Around Lava Tree State Monument, densities are the highest in the state, and twice that of their native habitat. Besides causing a nightly racket,
coquis are disrupting the ecosystem by eating the bugs that feed native birds.

However, in what some see as giving up, state and county attention has been shifted
to other invasive species that pose 'significant threat to human health' – which does not
include sleep loss. Although some diligent land owners still patrol their lots with spray
bottles of bleach or citric acid, the coqui is here to stay. Bring ear plugs.

⭐ **Pele's Kitchen** BREAKFAST **$**
(☑ 808-935-0550; www.facebook.com/Peles KitchenRestaurant/; 15-2929 Pahoa Village Rd; mains $5-12; ⏱ 7:30am-noon Tue-Sun; 🖥) Fat pancakes, flavorful scrambles or hearty French toast, all made from scratch. This is breakfast the way it was meant to be. You won't find a more complete collection of local fresh fruit than the Puna Exotic Fruit Sampler. Skip the *loco moco* (but that's kinda true everywhere isn't it?)

Tin Shack Bakery CAFE **$**
(☑ 808-965-9659; www.facebook.com/TinShack Bakery; 15-1500 Akeakamai Loop; mains $4-8; 🖥) Where Puna gets its morning coffee and breakfast bagels. All of Puna. At the same time. Which makes for fascinating people-watching and startlingly educational eavesdropping as you wait for your food. Cookies, cakes, brownies, muffins and pies make great beach snacks.

Pahoa Fresh Fish FISH & CHIPS **$**
(☑ 808-965-8248; 15-2670 Pahoa Village Rd; mains $8-14; ⏱ 9:30am-6:30pm) We're not sure if it serves anything besides fish'n'chips... we've never felt the need to ask. The battered and fried ono and mahimahi are so perfectly crispy, yet juicy, you'll quickly forget about the underwhelming atmosphere and overwhelming use of disposable packaging. Off Hwy 130 at the roundabout.

Ning's Thai Cuisine THAI **$**
(☑ 808-965-7611; www.ningsthaicuisine.com; 15-2955 Pahoa Village Rd; mains $12-16; ⏱ noon-9pm Mon-Sat, 5-9pm Sun; 🖥 ✏) Reliable, above-average Thai food with an emphasis on local, organic ingredients. The green curry is usually top notch, as is the authentic green papaya salad. No alcohol, but you can bring your own.

Sirius Coffee Connection CAFE **$**
(15-2874 Pahoa Village Rd; ⏱ 7am-6pm Mon-Sat, 7am-3pm Sun; 🖥) This simple space offers good coffee, baked treats, wi-fi and computers (30 minutes with/without purchase $2/3).

Island Naturals MARKET **$**
(www.islandnaturals.com; 15-1870 Akeakamai Loop; sandwiches $6-10; ⏱ 7am-8pm Mon-Fri, 7am-7pm Sat & Sun; ✏) Find organic produce, healthy sandwiches, hot mains and the local nouveau hippie crowd.

Paolo's Bistro ITALIAN **$$**
(☑ 808-965-7033; 15-2955 Pahoa Village Rd; mains $14-28; ⏱ 5:30-9pm Tue-Sun) 🍴 The cuisine and atmosphere is in such a different league from anything else in Puna, you'll be excused for thinking you've been transported to Northern Italy. This is Pahoa's best bet for a date night, though come early if you're hoping to sample the night's special, as they frequently run short. Bring your own vino.

Kaleo's Bar & Grill HAWAII REGIONAL **$$**
(☑ 808-965-5600; www.kaleoshawaii.com; 15-2969 Pahoa Village Rd; lunch mains $10-16, dinner mains $12-26; ⏱ 11am-9pm; 🖥) Serving burgers and pizzas and an array of island-fusion fare – such as tempura ahi roll, orzo pasta salad and coconut chicken curry – in a relaxed, family-friendly atmosphere. There's live music most nights, outdoor seating and a consistent local buzz. Reservations recommended on the weekends.

Luquin's Mexican Restaurant MEXICAN **$$**
(☑ 808-965-9990; 15-2942 Pahoa Village Rd; mains $10-19; ⏱ 7am-9pm, breakfast to 11am) If you must have Mexican food in Hawaii, you'll find large portions of generic staples at Luquin's. Pre-load with a few fresh *liliko'i* (passion fruit) margaritas while chatting with the locals at the crowded bar for a perfectly fine evening. These guys do breakfast best; consider starting your day here.

🍷 Drinking & Nightlife

Black Rock Cafe BAR
(15-2872 Pahoa Village Rd; ⏱ 7am-9pm) Half the Black Rock is an average restaurant serving passable burgers and breakfast. The other half is a bar popular with those who are a little more Harley-Davidson than hippie. Not that it gets rough (and hippies do show up too); the Black Rock is just a little salty, smoky and sweaty.

☆ Entertainment

Akebono Theater LIVE MUSIC
(☑ 808-965-9990; 15-2952 Pahoa Village Rd; tickets $10-20) Historic theater hosts occasional live music, film screenings and community events. Located behind Luquin's Mexican Restaurant.

❶ Getting There & Away

Traffic between Hilo and Puna is a nightmare during commuting hours. By all means, avoid driving toward Hilo in the early morning or toward Kea'au and Pahoa in the late afternoon.

Hele-On Bus (www.heleonbus.org) connects Hilo to Kea'au and Pahoa 11 times daily Monday to Friday with three buses continuing south to Kalapana and Kapoho. Reduced service Saturday, and you are on your own Sunday.

Red Road

Although no longer paved with red cinder, winding Hwy 137, aka the Red Road, still provides a colorful journey along Puna's south coast. The swooping drive periodically dips beneath tunnels of monkeypod and mango tree branches before climbing up over the occasional lava flow to provide expansive views along the ragged shoreline.

Connecting the tide pools of Kapoho with the Bohemian enclave of Kalapana, Red Road takes you past Puna's best surf break, isolated forests dotted with hauntingly beautiful cemeteries and heiau, a smattering of yoga retreats, and a secluded black-sand beach.

There are many discreet paths to the water's edge along this road – take one for a private piece of coast, but respect the privacy of local fishermen who might have already staked their claim.

Hwy 137 is also referred to as the Kapoho-Kalapana Road.

⊙ Sights

★ MacKenzie State Recreation Area   PARK

A moody, windswept grove of ironwood trees edge sheer cliffs towering above the ocean. The raw beauty of this powerful landscape makes an unforgettable picnic spot – but has also been the backdrop for supernatural tales and criminal acts. Trails extend either direction from the parking area, and a lava tube 0.1 miles east is an interesting post-lunch adventure. The waves crashing through a hidden sea arch near the tube is a captivating sight.

Swimming is not even tempting, and several fishermen have drowned after being swept off the cliffs by erratic waves. Camping at MacKenzie is no longer allowed; perhaps out of respect for the *huaka'i po*, or 'night marchers,' – groups of chanting warrior spirits that carry torches along the historic King's Road, which passes through here. More likely, the ban is in response to

theft and other crimes that have plagued the isolated park in recent years.

Enter off Hwy 137 between Miles 13 and 14.

Isaac Hale Beach Park   PARK

(Pohoiki; 13-101 Kalapana Kapoho Beach Rd) This rocky beach park is *the* local surf spot serving all of the greater Puna area. Some long-time surfers and bodyboarders regard Pohoiki as the island's top break, despite the omnipresence of sharp *wana* (sea urchins). It is a scenic spot to witness waves pounding local talent, especially on the crowded weekends. Waters are generally too rough for swimming, but you'll find plenty of local children splashing around the boat ramp to the right of the parking lot.

A well-worn path heading west beyond the boat ramp leads to a small, somewhat scummy, natural hot pond.

The camping area to your left as you enter the park consists of a pristine lawn, with picnic tables, barbecues, and bathrooms with flush toilets and drinking water. The night security guard will check your permits – which is a good thing as the place can occasionally collect a rowdy crowd of loiterers. Lava boat tours leave from the parking lot. Turn *makai* (seaward) around Mile 11.5 off Hwy 137.

Kehena Beach   BEACH

(Hwy 137, Mile 19) If any place captures the vibe of Puna, it's this beautiful black-sand beach tucked beneath a cliff where all walks of life – hippies, Hawaiians, gays, families, seniors, tourists – do their own uninhibited things. Expect nudity and *pakalolo* (marijuana), though nobody cares if you don't participate. Think twice about swimming; the surf is treacherous and drownings happen. To get here, turn into a small parking area at Mile 19 and look for the steep path leading down to the beach.

Sunday sees a drum circle providing a constant rhythm for dancers, fire spinners, jugglers and hoopers.

Come early on a weekday to avoid the crowds, and be aware that nudity is illegal on all Hawaiian beaches. Don't leave valuables in your car.

🏃 Activities

★ Pohoiki Bay   SURFING

(Isaac Hale Beach Park) Most newcomers will want to paddle around the pier by the boatramp and work the left break of First Bay while figuring out the hierarchy. Things get decidedly more touch-and-go (and less socially forgiving) at the busy middle of Second Bay, and you better know what you're doing before heading beyond: if Third Bay is on, it's big.

Shacks & Bowls   SURFING

(Isaac Hale Beach Park) To the left of Isaac Hale Beach Park's parking lot at the end of the road wait the twin breaks of Shacks and Bowls: solid choices for goofy riders. Enter the water in front of the staffed lifeguard stand to catch the rip-tide out, but cut a hard left or you're likely to end up around the point in Pohoiki Bay...or beyond.

Ahalanui Beach Park   SWIMMING

(⊘ 7am-7pm) Crowds flock to the large, spring-fed thermal pool deep enough for swimming, populated by tropical fish and protected from the surf by a concrete sea wall. Temperatures average around 90°F (32°C), but drop with the incoming tide. Unfortunately cleanliness also ebbs and flows, and entering the untreated water if you have open sores can lead to bacterial infection. The park gates are never locked; come early or late for more serene soaking. There are picnic tables, portable toilets and a lifeguard daily.

Don't leave valuables in your car.

☞ Tours

Moku Nui Lava Tours   BOATING

(☑ 808-938-1493; www.mnlavatour.com; per person $195) For a more personal lava-watching experience, join Kanoa aboard his 25ft cata-

maran. With a maximum of six passengers, everyone gets a clear view from their swivel chairs during the entire 30 minutes at the ocean entry. Those seats aren't covered, however, so bring a rain jacket and waterproof bag for your camera. Departs from Isaac Hale Beach Park.

Lava Ocean Tours   BOATING

(☑ 808-966-4200; www.seelava.com; adult/child from $180/145) The high-riding, 49-passenger *Lavaone* gets you close enough to feel the lava's heat – assuming it's flowing. Well-narrated tours motor from Isaac Hale Beach Park to the sea entry near Kalapana. Operators try to give every covered seat a clear view while zig-zagging in front of the lava for 30 minutes. Twilight tours are otherworldly. Warning: you may get seasick.

❶ Getting There & Away

Hele-On Bus (www.heleonbus.org) runs the length of Hwy 137 traveling from Kapoho toward Kalapana three times Monday to Friday and twice Saturday.

Kalapana Area

Once a close-knit fishing village near Kaimu Beach (the island's most famous black-sand beach), Kalapana was erased from the map in 1990 by Kilauea's Pu'u 'O'o-Kupaianaha eruption. The lava consumed nearly everything – save for the Star of the Sea Church (which the community moved in the nick of time) and Uncle Robert's family

---

GEOTHERMAL ENERGY HEADACHE

Geothermal energy sounds ideal: dependable, emission-free energy from water heated deep below the surface. Puna Geothermal Venture (PGV) thought the same thing and built a facility just outside of Pahoa in 1993. The problem is that PGV's hot water comes with a non-optional extra: hydrogen sulfide (H_2S), a poison that can cause irritation, eye damage, pulmonary edema and even death. The plant's closed loop returns the water to the ground, but a series of accidental leaks have many locals steaming mad.

Some residents are calling for a health-effects study and tighter safety regulations, while others want the plant shut down entirely. In the latter camp, a group of vocal Hawaiians believe that the operation violates the fire goddess Pele, and is an insult to their religion – though others see it as a benevolent gift from the goddess. Many in all camps vehemently oppose fracking to increase output, though it's not clear that is even an option in Puna.

As the debate rages, the plant hums along off Hwy 132 (closed to visitors), while Hawaii continues to burn 10 million barrels of oil each year for electricity (13 times more than than the average for all other states), emitting 7 million tons of carbon dioxide and other harmful gases. In 2015 Hawaii committed to producing 100% renewable energy by 2045.

compound (which now hosts a near continual celebration of life). Other less fortunate Hawaiians shrugged off the disaster, commenting that Pele has every right to take back the land she gave them.

The lava flow has moved to the west (for now), and while more tenacious residents rebuild on the practically still-steaming rocks, hikers flood by for a chance to see the Earth's creation firsthand. A parking and information area at the end of Hwy 130 points you toward the lava.

◉ Sights

★ **Lava Viewing Area**   VIEWPOINT
(www.hawaiicounty.gov/lava-viewing/; end of Hwy 130; ◷3-9pm) Pele (the goddess of fire) is fickle. She may treat you to a primordial fireworks display of molten rock exploding in the waves or show you nothing at all. Keep expectations in check. When flows are consistent, Civil Defense sets up an information center, recently located at the end of Hwy 130. Although you can hike to the lava at any time, the parking lot is staffed by informative personnel and emergency services between 3pm and 9pm.

At the time of research, it was a 4-mile one-way hike down the gravel emergency road to view the ocean entry, and another 1 to 3 miles over warm lava rock to find surface breakouts. Enterprising locals rent bicycles ($10 per hour) in varying stages of repair.

Dress appropriately, bring plenty of water and a light, and respect private property. If venturing near an active flow, remember that what looks like solid rock may be just a thin crust over a nasty mistake.

New Kaimu Beach   BEACH
(southwest end of Hwy 137) Kaimu was the most beautiful black-sand beach in Hawaii until the 1990 lava flow that consumed Kalapana torched its stately palms and filled the bay with *pahoehoe* (smooth-flowing lava). Now, a 0.3-mile walk along a red-cinder path takes you to a tiny cove where black sand accumulates and dissipates as nearby lava flows battle the forces of erosion. Residents have planted hundreds of palm seedlings in hopes of returning the land to its former glory. Swimming is unwise.

On your walk out, look for the Hawaii Star Visitors Sanctuary, the world's second official UFO landing pad, dedicated in 2014. The founders hope that the piles of rocks and small shrines will entice extraterrestrials to land here and establish diplomatic relations with the peaceful Kingdom of Hawai'i.

Star of the Sea Church   CHURCH
(◷9am-4pm) Known locally as the 'Painted Church,' this historic Catholic chapel is noted for its collection of murals including a simple trompe l'oeil cathedral behind the altar. Built in 1928 in Kalapana, it was nearly consumed by advancing lava in May of 1990. Residents scrambled through the night to load the church onto a truck and clear the highway of low branches and power lines to move it to safety. It is now located off Hwy 130 at Mile 20.

THE FATE OF KALAPANA
....

When the lava flow creeping up on Kalapana in 1986 abruptly stopped after consuming only 14 houses, the residents – guardians of its famous palm-lined Kaimu black-sand beach and multiple cultural sites – let out a collective sigh of relief. But what seemed like providence turned out to be only a stay of execution. By late 1990 they would all be homeless.

The eruption began in 1983 when Kilauea started releasing pressure at a vent in the East Rift Zone later named Pu'u 'O'o (p249). Initially the flows followed natural contours, which led them into the sparsely populated Royal Gardens Subdivision on the hillside below.

However, in 1986 the eruption shifted east to Kupaianaha vent, and flows began consuming new territory. As lava tubes became blocked, breakouts sent fingers in new directions, fanning out in an unpredictable Pascal's triangle of obliteration that kept residents on high alert. Then, in May of 1990, the volcano pointed all of its energy directly at Kalapana. By the time the Kupaianaha flow stopped in early 1991, it had claimed 180 homes, a park visitor center and multiple archaeological sites, and entirely filled in Kaimu Bay, covering its beach.

The murals depict a blend of Catholic and Native Hawaiian history and mythology.

Beyond its interior decorating, the church is also noted for a cursory connection to the first priest in Kalapana, Father Damien, whose legendary work on Moloka'i with leprosy patients combined with his posthumous miracles led to his canonization in 1990. Find him depicted here in stained glass.

🐾 Tours

Consult current lava reports thoroughly before risking buyer's remorse. For much of the latest flow cycle, you could reach the ocean entry via a 4-mile walk on a gravel road followed by less than 0.1 miles to the viewpoint – hardly guide-worthy.

Surface breakouts are another story, however, and could be at the road's edge, or a dangerous 6-mile trek over breakable crust. In the latter case, a guide is a wise investment.

★ **Native Guide Hawaii**   HIKING
(☑ 808-982-7575; www.nativeguidehawaii.com; tour per person incl lunch $150-300) 🖉 For the personal touch, Native Hawaiian and cultural practitioner Warren Costa offers customized all-day tours that reveal gems you wouldn't find on your own. The per-person price drops to $150 for parties of two or more.

★ **Hawaii Outdoor Guides**   HIKING
(☑ 808-937-5472; www.hawaiioutdoorguides.com; tour per person incl transportation $179) Top-notch Kona outfit now does lava hikes. Price includes transportation from Hilo or Kona.

Volcano Discovery Hawai'i   TOURS
(Volcano Adventures; www.volcanodiscovery.com/tours/hawaii.html; 7-day tour per person $2950) For those interested in a 'deep dive' into Hawai'i's volcanoes, these week-long tours explore current eruptions and historic flows. Led by geologists and customized for your group's particular interests.

Kalapana Cultural Tours   HIKING
(☑ 808-345-4964;www.kalapanaculturaltours.com; tour per person $150) A small army of young, eager guides provides a solid choice for lava hikes and boat tours. The company is owned by a local Hawaiian family, and tours can be booked in Kaimu. Just confirm they've reached their minimum number of participants.

🍴 Eating

The Hot Dog Guy   FAST FOOD $
(www.facebook.com/thehotdoguy.pahoahi; Kalapana lava viewing, Hwy 130; hotdog $2-7; ⊙daily, weather permitting) Jesse 'the hot dog guy' serves bison, reindeer or all-beef hotdogs and brats, cooked any way you like 'em out of his tiny cart. Given his mobility, he occasionally migrates. Check his Facebook page for latest whereabouts.

★ **Uncle Robert's Wednesday Night Market**   MARKET
(Ho'olaule'a Market; ⊙5-9pm Wed) *The* place to be on a Wednesday night is the late Uncle Robert's family compound where a significant percentage of the population turns out to live aloha. Local live music gets you dancing, while artisans and farm-fresh food aplenty keep you satiated. Park close for a fee ($2) or down the road for free. Some of the mainstay eateries are open daily.

Uncle's Kaimū Farmers Market   MARKET
(⊙8am-noon Sat) A more subdued affair than the Wednesday night festivities at the same place. Stock up on local produce.

🍷 Drinking & Nightlife

Uncle Robert's Awa Bar   BAR
(end of Hwy 137; ⊙1-6pm Sun-Mon, 3-9pm Tue-Fri, 9am-9pm Sat) After walking out to New Kaimu Beach, shade up with a cup of *'awa* (kava), a muscle-relaxing drink used in many traditional ceremonies that will help slow your internal clock to Puna time. There are usually a few local characters talking story or watching the world do whatever it does here at the end of the road.

ℹ️ Getting There & Away

From Pahoa, Hele-On Bus (www.heleonbus.org) services run clockwise around Hwys 132, 137 and 130, passing here three times Monday to Friday and twice Saturday.

PUNA KAPOHO AREA

Kapoho Area

Aside from hosting some of the Big Island's best snorkeling, this forgotten corner of Puna consists of little more than scattered farms and a few gated communities.

The small village of Kapoho occupied the **Four Corners** area (where Hwy 132 meets Red Road) until January, 1960, when a 0.5-mile-long curtain of fiery lava began spewing out of a nearby sugarcane field. The main flow of *pahoehoe* (smooth-flowing lava) ran toward the ocean, but an offshoot of *'a'a* (rough, crumbly lava) crept toward the town, burying orchid farms in its path. Two weeks later Kapoho's nearly 100 homes and businesses were buried.

From Four Corners, a detour east to Cape Kumukahi is a low-commitment side-trip to Hawaii's easternmost point, while heading north on the unpaved Government Beach Road will take you through the Puna that time forgot.

◉ Sights

★ **Cape Kumukahi**   VIEWPOINT
(end of Hwy 132) As the distinguished easternmost point of the island, Kumukahi ('first beginnings') holds a revered place in Hawaiian lore. The **Kings Pillars** (piles of rock barely distinguishable from natural lava) mark the solstices, passing the sun between them. Pele's shark brother Kamohoali'i lives offshore, guarding the gourd that holds the waters of life. Some say Pele started her journey here, poking holes along the Eastern Rift Zone as she journeyed to Kilauea.

Captain Cook almost lost everything when a violent storm threatened to run him aground as he rounded Cape Kumukahi. A lucky last-minute wind-shift blew him to safety and back on route toward his unlucky fate.

From Kumukahi Lighthouse, it's a rough, ankle-twisting 0.25-mile walk along vanishing trails to the shore. You won't find much to mark this place's significance except for a powerful sense of peace, and the freshest breeze on the planet. The air arrives here after weeks at sea – untarnished by human activity – where it is sampled regularly by scientists studying atmospheric carbon and pollution levels.

Kumukahi Lighthouse   LIGHTHOUSE
(end of Hwy 132) When the lava flow of January 1960 approached Cape Kumukahi, it parted around the 1.7 million candlepower lighthouse – the strongest in Hawaii at the time. Old-timers say Pele avoided the structure after the light's keeper offered her a meal. Others say she spared the beacon because of its benevolent role in saving lives. Whatever the reason, the now-automated skeleton tower light still stands 1.6 miles east of the Four Corners at the end of the smooth unpaved road.

🏃 Activities

★ **Kapoho Tide Pools**   SNORKELING

(Wai'ōpae Tide Pools Marine Life Conservation District; suggested donation $3; ⊙7am-7pm) The best snorkeling on the Big Island's windward side is in this sprawling network of tide pools. Here Kapoho's lava-rock coast is a mosaic of protected, shallow, interconnected pools, some heated, containing a rich variety of sea life. You can pool-hop for hours, tracking saddle wrasses, Moorish idols, butterfly fish, sea cucumbers and much more. Coral gardens can be found in farther out pools; sea turtles like the warm pocket to the south and octopuses are known to visit.

Wear reef shoes to avoid cutting your feet on the lava rock, and remember to keep your distance from sea turtles: 50yd in water and 20ft on land.

From Hwy 137, turn on Kapoho Kai Dr just over 1 mile south of Four Corners. Park at the intersection with Kikiao St on the south side, and walk the remaining 0.5 miles through the neighborhood (follow the paint markings).

Champagne Pond   SNORKELING

(Laimana Rd, Kapoho Bay) At the northern corner of Kapoho Bay, volcanically heated water bubbles between a bevy of vacation homes bristling with 'No trespassing' signs. The small protected pool is open to the ocean whose cold water sinks, giving the pond a split personality. It's a fine place to snorkel with kids, and turtles visit, though less frequently of late. The gravelly beach is good for combing.

Unquestioned public access is via a 1.3-mile high-clearance 4WD road over sharp *'a'a* (rough, jagged type of lava) from Kumukahi Lighthouse (p234).

Turn *makai* (seaward) 0.1 miles before the lighthouse, then take the first major right. If your vehicle can clear the loose, steep, potholed crux 0.2 miles in, you'll be fine the rest of the way. If not, it's still a beautiful – if hot – walk. Bring water.

OFF THE BEATEN TRACK

GOVERNMENT BEACH ROAD

Down the dusty bends of Government Beach Rd you'll find ancient mango groves draped with vines and birds-nest ferns, historic rock walls and occasional pockets of off-the-grid settlements where long-time Puna locals move when they need to get away from it all.

The empty stretches of jagged East Puna Coast found in **Nanawale Forest Reserve** are great places for a picnic, while watching the waves crash at **Honolulu Landing** – a once-protected bay used for loading ships offshore that is now unapproachable by boat – reminds you how ephemeral the coastline can be.

The road has been improved in recent years as locals demanded more escape routes from encroaching lava, but the unpaved surface can challenge low-slung cars and will stop any vehicle after a rainstorm.

Some visitors park outside the Kapoho Beach Community gates on Kapoho Beach Rd off Hwy 137 and walk 0.6 miles to a signed access point off Laimana Rd. This route utilizes private neighborhood roadways and passes 'No trespassing' signs, so we cannot recommend it.

🍴 Eating

Cajun Paradise Farms   CAJUN $

(☑808-756-1199; www.facebook.com/pg/Cajun Paradise; 14-4488 Pahoa-Kapoho Rd; ⊙9am-4pm Thu-Sun) Smoothies, coffee and daily light snacks served with a generous helping of Cajun aloha (it's a thing; here anyway).

❶ Getting There & Away

Hele-On Bus (www.heleonbus.org) service runs clockwise around Hwys 132, 137 and 130, passing here three times Monday to Friday and twice Saturday on the way to Isaac Hale Beach Park (Pohoiki).

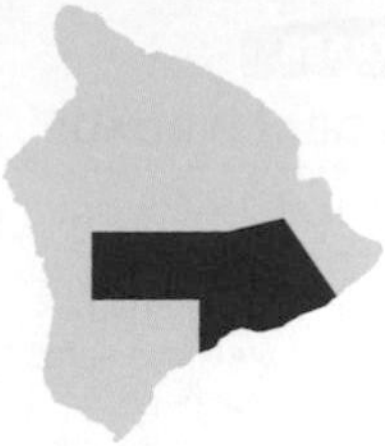

Hawai'i Volcanoes National Park

📑 808

Best Places to Eat

➡ 'Ōhelo Café (p257)

➡ The Rim Restaurant (p253)

➡ Thai Thai Restaurant (p256)

➡ Kilauea Lodge Restaurant (p257)

Best Volcanic Resources

➡ USGS Hawaiian Volcano Observatory (http://hvo.wr.usgs.gov)

➡ Hawai'i County Civil Defense (www.hawaii county.gov/civil-defense)

➡ Trail & Road Closures (www.nps.gov/havo/closed_areas.htm)

➡ Air Quality (www.hawaii so2network.com)

Why Go?

From the often-snowy summit of Mauna Loa, the world's most massive volcano, to the boiling coast where lava pours into the sea, Hawai'i Volcanoes National Park is a micro-continent of thriving rainforests, volcano-induced deserts, mountain meadows, coastal plains and geological marvels in between.

At the heart of it all is Kilauea – the earth's youngest and most active shield volcano. Since 1983 Kilauea's East Rift Zone has been erupting almost nonstop from the Pu'u 'O'o vent, adding nearly 500 acres of new land to the island.

The national park staff excel at managing this chaotic landscape. Their education programs deftly blend modern science with ancient beliefs and customs, and their outreach feels boundless. Ample interpretive signs, unusually inform-ative trail guides, a slew of well-thought-out ranger-led hikes, living history programs and a weekly lecture series all provide visitors with a solid connection to the park and the people of Hawai'i.

When to Go

Jun–Aug The summer Hawai'i Volcanoes National Park Cultural Festival is crowded, but for good reasons: free park entrance and ample activities for the whole family.

Aug & Sep Clouds and rain are a fact of life (this is a rainforest after all) but August and September tend to have more clear days on average.

Eruptions Volcanoes don't follow schedules; try to keep yours flexible enough to take advantage of short-notice lava-viewing opportunities.

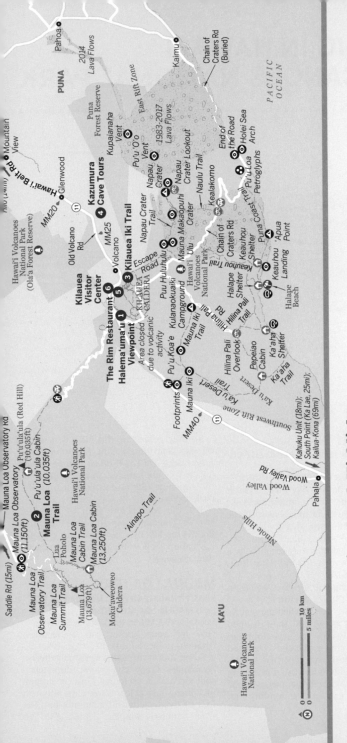

Hawai'i Volcanoes National Park Highlights

1 Halema'uma'u Viewpoint (p244) Looking into the glowing heart of the earth and paying respects to Pele.

2 Mauna Loa Trail (p238) Summiting the sculpted rock flanks of the world's largest above-water volcano.

3 Kilauea Iki Trail (p238) Imagining the rolling chaotic waves of lava that flooded this crater floor not too long ago.

4 Kazumura Cave Tours (p255) Exploring the surprisingly beautiful plumbing of a volcano while hoping it doesn't decide to flush you out.

5 The Rim Restaurant (p253) Watching the sun set over a steaming post-apocalyptic landscape while sharing drinks or a meal.

6 Kilauea Visitor Center (p244) Trying to find a question the rangers haven't been asked, and don't know the answer to.

HIKING IN HAWAI'I VOLCANOES NATIONAL PARK

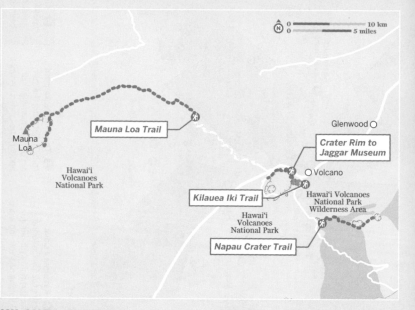

KILAUEA IKI TRAIL

START/END KILAUEA IKI PARKING LOT ON CRATER RIM DR
LENGTH 4.5 MILES RETURN, 2–3 HOURS

If you can only do one day hike, make it this one. Do the loop counterclockwise through an astounding microcosm of the park that descends through fairy-tale ohia forests to a mile-wide, still-steaming lava lake that was filled relatively recently by a fiery fountain spewing 403 million gallons of lava per second.

Kilauea Iki erupted for five weeks at the end of 1959, filling the crater with several meters of lava that washed against its walls like ocean waves and then drained back into the fissure. The lava fountain that formed the cinder pile above reached 1900ft, the highest ever recorded in Hawaii. This awesome sight turned terrifying when boulders blocked the passage like your thumb on a garden hose, sending a jet of lava shooting across the crater toward crowds of visitors.

To fully appreciate this hike, first watch the excellent vintage film, *Eruption of Kilauea 1959–1960 at Kilauea Visitor Center* (or on YouTube), then grab a very informative brochure ($2, or download it from the park's website).

Hit the trail before 8am to beat the crowds. The faint footpath across the crater floor is marked by *ahu* (stone cairns) to aid navigation. Follow them; the crust can be thin elsewhere.

MAUNA LOA TRAIL

START TRAILHEAD (END MAUNA LOA RD)
END MAUNA LOA SUMMIT
LENGTH 19.6 MILES RETURN, 3–5 DAYS

One for your bucket list: a relentless (though nontechnical) 19.6-mile hike ascending 7000ft through surprisingly diverse lavascapes. Enjoy epic views, unmatched solitude and a profound sense of accomplishment. Take at least three days, although four or five is better for a summit bid. Get your required camping permit ($10 per

The raw power of creation is a consistent presence across the Big Island, but here, the primal energy of the land seems to literally bubble just beneath the surface.

group) from the **Backcountry Office** (p252) a day before you start.

The first day climbs 3400ft over 7.5 miles of ancient *pahoehoe* (smooth-flowing lava) and collapsed lava tubes to Pu'u'ula'ula (Red Hill) where a historic cabin with bunkbeds (bring your own bedding) gets you out of the elements. Collected rainwater is usually available, but treat before drinking. Fill everything before bed; the spigot often freezes, and you'll want an early start in the morning.

The next day, tackle the grueling, but sublimely rewarding, 11.6-mile march up another 3200ft to the Mauna Loa Cabin (13,250ft, also with bunkbeds and untreated water). Lava flows seemingly pour out of red, serrated fissures to cover technicolored cinder fields. This marvelous dreamscape can also become a nightmare if you lose the trail – easy to do when the *ahu* (stone cairns used to mark a trail) disappear in rain, fog or snow. It is impossible to distinguish between solid rock and thin crust over a bottomless lava tube.

Note that the actual summit (13,677ft) is on the other side of Moku'aweoweo Caldera from the cabin. The trail splits at Mile 9.5, and while some hikers do the additional 5.2-mile round-trip Summit Trail on their way to the cabin, most elect to tackle their 16.8-mile day on the way down. Or better yet, spend two nights on top of the world. Of course, there's the option of summiting via the **Mauna Loa Observatory Trail**, but that's cheating.

Be prepared for severe winter conditions year-round. You'll be on rock the entire time – don't underestimate what that does to your joints.

CRATER RIM TO JAGGAR MUSEUM

START KILAUEA VISITOR CENTER
END VOLCANO HOUSE
LENGTH 5 MILES ROUND TRIP, 2½ HOURS

Rather than deadhead to Jaggar Museum to check Halema'uma'u Crater off your Hawai'i to-do list, consider getting to know Kilauea first. Explore a few short trails along the crater's rim to learn the lay of the land and understand Pele before banging on her door at the park's drawcard sight.

Start at **Kilauea Visitor Center** (p244); this often-overlooked resource provides vital information for your visit.

After you have a good grasp of the park's natural history, head right (west) out of the center toward the end of the bus parking lot. Tucked back along the service road is the **Volcano Art Gallery** (p248) housed in the historic **1877 Volcano House**. This is the building that housed Mark Twain, Robert Louis Stevenson and Louis Pasteur during their separate visits to Kilauea. It now houses rotating exhibits of park-inspired art.

HOW-TO HIKING TIPS

➡ Be prepared for changing weather: a sunny stroll can turn cold and wet in an instant.

➡ This is a surprisingly dry area and dehydration comes easily. No drinking water is available, except possibly at primitive campgrounds (where it must be treated before drinking), so pack at least three quarts of water per person per day.

➡ Campfires are prohibited.

➡ A compass and binoculars are handy: mist or vog (volcanic fog) can impede navigation.

➡ All overnight hikes require a $10 permit, available in person only one day in advance from the **Backcountry Office** (p252). One permit covers up to 12 people for seven nights. Be sure to download the park's backcountry trip planner covering potential hazards with safety tips and advice for protecting wildlife and archaeological sites.

➡ If you prefer to join a group, the nonprofit **Friends of Hawai'i Volcanoes National Park** (p252) leads weekend hikes and field trips.

OTHER HIKES IN THE HAWAI'I VOLCANOES NATIONAL PARK

Under 5 Miles

➡ **Mauna Iki Trail** For solitude in a mesmerizing lava landscape, head 2 miles across the Ka'u Desert to our favorite viewpoint: the barren summit of Mauna Iki (3032ft).

➡ **Pu'u Huluhulu Trail** (Mauna Ulu Eruption Trail; www.nps.gov/havo/planyourvisit/upload/mauna_ulu_trail_guide-1.pdf) Technically just the first part of the **Napau Crater Trail** (p247), this mellower 3-mile hike starts with a close-up inspection of the multicolored 1969 fissure eruption that destroyed Chain of Craters before the road reached its 10th birthday. The trail ends atop Pu'u Huluhulu (shaggy hill).

➡ **Keanakako'i Trail** This short, 1-mile section of the Crater Rim Trail takes you from the Devastation Trail parking to the eastern closure at **Keanakako'i Crater**. Before lava covered the floor of the crater in 1877, ancient Hawaiians mined dense basalt here that was good for making adz (ax-like tools used for cutting and shaping wood).

➡ **Kipuka Puaulu** (Bird Park; www.nps.gov/havo/planyourvisit/hike_day_kipukapuaulu.htm; 🚹) A shady, 1.2-mile hike easy enough for young kids loops through a rainforest *kipuka* (oasis) that has rebounded after years of intensive grazing turned it into a grassland. Now, thanks to fencing and aggressive restoration this parcel is a haven for birds and bird-watchers.

➡ **Devastation Trail** When Kilauea Iki erupted in 1959, wind-born spatter toasted the rainforest to the south. The resultant wasteland is now slowly being repopulated with stalwart ohia trees, ferns and 'ohelo shrubs. This trail is only 0.5 miles long, paved and wheelchair-accessible, but offers fantastic views of distant Mauna Loa looming behind Kilauea caldera.

10+ Miles

➡ **'Ainapo Trail** (☎808-928-8403) This 10.2-mile trail was part of the route used by ancient Hawaiians to leave offerings at Mauna Loa's summit. Its 7600ft climb is so challenging that when geologist Dr Jaggar hiked it to observe eruptions in 1914, he immediately began lobbying for a new route – hence the Mauna Loa Trail. Access 'Ainapo (Darkened Land) via private land with advance permission.

➡ **Ka'u Desert Trail** This 12.1-mile trek from Mauna Iki to Hilina Pali Overlook crosses plenty of twisted lava and soft sand before traversing the grassy scrub high above the coastal plain. Overnight at **Pepeiao Cabin** or descend to **Ka'aha Shelter** on the coast. Both have water catchments (treat before drinking). Ongoing eruptions keep the trail closed between Jaggar Museum and Mauna Iki.

Head back toward the main Crater Rim Dr, and look for signs for **Sulphur Banks Trail** (p248) which parallels the road. Follow it for approximately 0.2 miles through the trees to a boardwalk across a depression filled with colorful rocks emitting the stench of rotten eggs: SO_2.

The trail continues east, exiting a small copse of trees into a steaming meadow and, just beyond, the parking for the **steam vents**. Continue across the road.

At the intersection with the **'Iliahi and Crater Rim Trails**, turn right toward the appropriately named **Steaming Bluff** (p248). The cracks in the earth here emit more steam and less of the pungent SO_2 – though a close inspection of the guard rails suggests the gas is still fairly corrosive.

Between the wisps of steam (or blinding pillows depending on the weather) you'll get your first full view of **Kilauea Caldera** (p245), one of the world's most active volcanoes. At various times throughout history lava has filled this entire caldera.

To your left (east) look for the thin fin of forested land with a pile of cinders peaking up from behind. This is **Byron Ledge**, and behind it is **Pu'u Pua'i** (p249), one result of a record-setting lava fountain that erupted in 1959, filling **Kilauea Iki** (p249) crater on the other side of the ledge.

To the right (west) you may be able to see Jaggar Museum and the Hawaiian Volcano Observatory perched atop sacred cliffs: head that direction on Crater Rim Trail, which for the most part provides unobstructed views of Kilauea.

At about Mile 2.6 you'll arrive at **Jaggar Museum** (p246) with displays on the geology and mythology of Kilauea. The **front porch** (p244) is currently as close as you are allowed to get to the lava lake at Halemaʻumaʻu, which is still about a mile away (tip: it feels much closer after dark).

After paying your respects to Pele, return the way you came – the trail is closed beyond this point. When you get back to Steaming Bluffs, stay on Crater Rim Trail which takes you 0.8 miles back to the start.

Or, for bonus points, take the lower ʻIliahi Trail across to the **Halemaʻumaʻu Trail** which descends 1 mile through the ohia and tree fern forests to the bottom of Kilauea Caldera. Return the same way, or continue another 2.2 miles to return along **Waldron Ledge**. This makes for a tiring, but complete exploration of the summit crater.

Whichever you choose, finish with drinks at **Uncle George's Lounge** (p253).

NAPAU CRATER TRAIL

START MAUNA ULU TRAILHEAD
END NAPAU CRATER
LENGTH 6.5 MILES ONE WAY; TWO HOURS

At the Mauna Ulu Trailhead registration box, look across the road for a trail heading south through the vegetation. This 0.5-mile add-on loop explores the sensuous ramparts of the **1969 fissure** which kicked off the five-year eruption of Mauna Ulu.

From the fissure, the trail rounds the end of the forest, crossing the the **old Chain of Craters Road** (built 1960, buried 1969) before passing through two *kipuka* (oasis) besieged by an impressive army of **lava trees**.

At Mile 1.5, a side trail takes you 100ft up the side of **Puʻu Huluhulu**, a 500-year-old cone that used to be the tallest point around – until Mauna Ulu (Growing Mountain) took over. A spur trail climbs 100ft to spectacular views.

From here, Napau Crater Trail continues across fields of psychedelic *pahoehoe* (smooth-flowing lava) around Mauna Ulu's north flank, gradually summiting **ʻAlae Lava Shield** (p249), which used to be a crater, at Mile 2.7.

Descend 300ft over 2 miles toward the **Kane Nui o Hamo** shield, which formed 400 to 750 years ago but is still torn open by a steaming red fissure. At its base is the mile-long **Makaopuhi Crater** (p247). The trail skirts to the south.

Naulu Trail intersects at Mile 4.7, but continue straight through a muddy fern forest past the rock walls of the **Old Pulu Factory** (p249), which ravaged the forest for 20 years while they harvested tree ferns.

The trail ends abruptly at Mile 6.5 on the very sheer edge of **Napau Crater** (watch your step) from where you can see **Puʻu ʻOʻo** (p249) puffing away across the lavascape being buzzed by tour helicopters.

On the return, consider the Naulu Trail, which is only 3.4 miles down (800ft) to the road instead of 4.2 miles back up (300ft) to your car. Naulu follows the route of the old **Chain of Craters Road**, which occasionally makes a post-apocalyptic appearance between fingers of lava.

PUNA COAST TRAILS

Experience secluded snorkeling, white-sand beaches, soaring cliffs and savagely beautiful landscapes on these remote backcountry trails. This is the wilder side of Hawaiʻi Volcanoes, and all of the approaches – the Hilina Pali, Keauhou, Kaʻu Desert and Puna Coast Trails – are hot, steep and strenuous. Carry lots of extra water, and remember: what hikes down, must climb back up.

Pick up your required overnight hiking permit ($10 per group) at the **Backcountry Office** (p252), where rangers have information on current trail closures and conditions, and just as importantly, water-catchment levels at primitive backcountry shelters and campgrounds.

With swimming, snorkeling, white sand and coconut trees, Halape is the most popular overnight destination, followed by Keauhou. Endangered hawksbill sea turtles nest all along the coast here; travel responsibly and stay at least 50yd away in water and 20ft on land.

The easiest route to the coast is the gently sloping Keauhou Trail (7 miles one-way). Exit via the Puna Coast Trail (10 miles) to avoid the 2700ft climb. The shortest route to Kaʻaha is via the Hilina Pali Trail (3.6 miles one-way), which continues to Halape (8 miles). It begins with a brutal cliff descent from **Hilina Pali Overlook** (p247), dropping 1500ft in 2.2 miles of switchbacks. For a true epic, head to the far west on the Kaʻaha Trail and climb up to the Kaʻu Desert Trail – but bring plenty of water.

ROAD TRIP: CHAIN OF CRATERS ROAD

This is it: possibly the most scenic road trip on an island packed with really scenic road trips. Heading south from Crater Rim Dr, paved Chain of Craters Road winds almost 19 miles and 3700ft down the southern slopes of Kilauea, ending abruptly at rivers of lava making their way to the coast. Drive slowly, especially in foggy or rainy conditions, and watch out for endangered nene (Hawaiian goose).

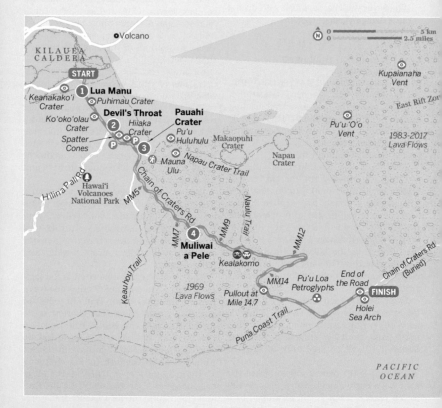

Start Devastation Trail Parking

End Holei Sea Arch

Length 19 miles; 1½ to 5 hours

❶ Lua Manu & Nearby Craters

First up is Lua Manu (Bird Crater; Mile 0.4), one in a series of pit craters which form when lava in an underground reservoir vacates, leaving a hollow chamber to collapse in on itself; ie there's no eruption. The lava on the northwest edge didn't come out of, but rather poured into, the crater during the 1974 eruption of Keanakako'i. The next two pit craters (Puhimau, and Ko'oko'olau) are similar, but forested and not quite as photogenic (though good for bird-watching).

The Drive > At Mile 2.2, the single-lane Hilina Pali Rd (18 miles round trip) turns off to the right. It's an interesting side trip following fault scarps to the fringes of the Ka'u Desert before descending to the top of Hilina Pali (windy cliff). Back at Chain of Craters, continue a mere 250ft to a small, unsanctioned pulloff barely wide enough for a car.

❷ Devil's Throat

A faint path heading northwest along a crack in the earth leads to a pit crater ominously named **Devil's Throat**. In 1920 the hole was narrow enough for a horse to jump across, now it's over 100ft wide with sheer vertical walls. Keep a firm grip on children.

The Drive > Just beyond, the road cuts through a pair of spatter cones at Mile 2.4, answering your burning questions about what they look like on the inside (spoiler alert: they look like rock).

❸ Pauahi Crater

At Pauahi Crater (Pauahi translates to 'destroyed by fire'; Mile 3.2) note the reddish spatter ramparts just behind the overlook which filled the bottom of the crater in 1973. After the eruption, the lava drained, leaving just a bathtub ring. The large, likely steaming, rocky cone directly east is **Mauna Ulu** (p249), which completely erased the original Chain of Craters Road during its brief life. Just north is the 500-year-old forested Pu'u Huluhulu (Shaggy Hill). **Napau Crater Trail** (p247) (trailhead at Mile 3.7) winds between the two.

The Drive > As you approach Mile 4, look for interesting formations in the 1969 lava flow, including a lava arch (sometimes formed around trees) and lava balls (cooling lava that rolls along the edges of a flow building like snowballs).

❹ Muliwai a Pele

Shortly beyond this point, the road traverses sprawling fields of barren nothingness, courtesy of Mauna Ulu. At the **Muliwai a Pele** (River of Pele) overlook (Mile 7.5) you can see *'a'a* (rough, jagged lava) abutting *pahoehoe* (smooth-flowing lava) and where a lava river flowed down the mountainside. If the top of this river had cooled over forming a crust, we'd be looking at a lava tube instead.

From this point on, the road begins regressively descending a series of *pali* (cliffs). Get the big picture at Kealakomo picnic tables, possibly the windiest place in the park to have lunch.

Below the switchbacks, watch for some particularly nice *pahoehoe* drips above the road (Mile 13.5), and then see what happens when that nice *pahoehoe* drips across the road (Mile 14). Take in the whole man-versus-nature scene from the pullout at Mile 14.7: imagine the smoking red lava pouring down the *pali,* consuming the road, then imagine the bulldozers scraping in a new road after the lava cooled.

The Drive > A trail to sacred Pu'u Loa Petroglyphs peels off east at Mile 16.3, while the Puna Coast Trail heads west. Continuing on the road, it's an easy 2.5 miles along the craggy coast to the Holei Sea Arch.

ⓘ Getting There & Away

The park is 30 miles (45 minutes) from Hilo and 95 miles (2¾ hours) from Kailua-Kona via Hwy 11. The turnoffs for Volcano village are a couple miles east of the main park entrance. Hwy 11 is prone to flooding, washouts and closures during rainstorms. Periods of drought may close Mauna Loa Rd and Hilina Pali Rd due to wildfire hazards.

The public **Hele-On Bus** (☑ 808-961-8744; www.heleonbus.org; adult one-way $2) departs fives times Monday through Saturday (no service Sunday) from Hilo, arriving at the park visitor center ($5 surcharge) about 1¼ hours later. One bus continues to Ka'u. There is no public transportation once you get inside the park, and hitchhiking is illegal in all national parks.

Cyclists are permitted on paved roads, and a handful of dirt ones, including the Escape Rd but not on any trails – pavement or no.

Hawai'i Volcanoes National Park

This vast and varied park can fill as many days as you give it, particularly if you enjoy hiking. Or you can drive it all in one long 66-mile round-trip journey that takes you down Chain of Craters Road to the suitably named End of the Road and back up (with a detour to Hilina Pali) ending at Jaggar Museum for a sunset viewing of Halema'uma'u. Even less time? Stick to Crater Rim Dr, where many of the key sites are located. In any case, start at the informative Kilauea Visitor Center, just past the entrance, on your right.

◉ Sights

★ Hawai'i Volcanoes National Park   PARK

(☑ 808-985-6000; www.nps.gov/havo; 7-day entry per car $10; ♿) Even among Hawaii's many wonders, this national park stands out. Its two active volcanoes testify to the ongoing birth of the islands: quiet Mauna Loa (13,677ft) sprawling above, its unassuming mass downplaying its height, and young Kilauea (4091ft), one of the world's most active volcanoes, providing near-continual sources of awe. With luck, you'll witness the primal power of molten earth boiling into the sea. But the park contains much more: overwhelming lava deserts, steaming craters, lava tubes and ancient rainforests.

For hikers, the possibilities are endless.

★ Halema'uma'u Viewpoint   VIEWPOINT

(Crater Rim Dr) The original Halema'uma'u Overlook off Crater Rim Dr has been closed since 2008 due to volcanic activity and the very real threat of death (ie don't even think about sneaking out there). Fortunately, the next-closest view from the Jaggar Museum patio is also extraordinary. There's absolutely nothing like watching a gaping crater full of roiling hot lava send a billowing column of steam into the sky – especially after dark when the flickering spotlights of creation set everything aglow.

Halema'uma'u is really a crater within the crater of Kilauea Caldera. The name means 'house of the 'ama'u fern,' though ancient songs also refer to it as Halemaumau without the 'okina (glottal stops), or 'house of eternal fire.'

About 3000ft across and almost 300ft deep, today this house spews a constant column of volcanic ash and gases like sulfur dioxide, which along with Pu'u 'O'o vent creates the vog that can carpet the island.

How active Kilauea Volcano will be when you visit is subject to the whims of Pele, the Hawaiian goddess of fire and volcanoes who makes her home here, so set expectations low, and hope to be pleasantly surprised. Best viewing is on a clear night after sunset, though a break in thunderclouds can create an otherworldly frame for Pele's fire. There's never a wrong time to visit.

★ Pu'u Loa Petroglyphs   ARCHAEOLOGICAL SITE

(Mile 16.4, Chain of Craters Rd) The gentle, 1.3-mile round-trip to Pu'u Loa (roughly, 'hill of long life') leads to one of Hawai'i's largest concentrations of ancient petroglyphs, some over 800 years old. Here Hawaiians chiseled more than 23,000 drawings into *pahoehoe* (smooth-flowing lava) with adz tools quarried from Keanakako'i (p171). Stay on the boardwalk – not all petroglyphs are obvious, and you might damage some if you walk over the rocks. The trailhead parking is signed between Miles 16 and 17 on Chain of Craters Road.

★ Kilauea Visitor Center & Museum   MUSEUM

(☑ 808-985-6000; www.nps.gov/havo; Crater Rim Dr; ⊙ 9am-5pm, film screenings hourly 9am-4pm; ♿) ⊘ Stop here first. Extraordinarily helpful (and remarkably patient) rangers and volunteers can advise you about volcanic activity, air quality, road closures, hiking-trail conditions and how best to spend however much time you have. Interactive museum exhibits are small but family friendly, and will teach even science-savvy adults about the park's delicate ecosystem and Hawaiian heritage. All of the rotating movies are excellent. Pick up fun junior ranger program activity books for your kids before leaving.

Check the outdoor signboards by the entrance for upcoming daily and evening talks, ranger-led hikes and other activities guaranteed to enhance your visit. A well-stocked nonprofit bookstore inside the center sells souvenirs, rain ponchos, walking sticks and flashlights. Wheelchairs are free to borrow. There are also restrooms, a pay phone, and a place to fill up your water bottles.

★ **Kilauea Iki Overlook** VIEWPOINT
(Crater Rim Dr) When 'Little Kilauea' burst open in a fiery inferno in November 1959, it filled the crater with a roiling lake of molten rock fed by a 1900ft fountain that lit up the night sky with 2 million gushing tons of lava per hour at its peak. The lake took over 30 years to completely solidify.

From the overlook, you can view the steaming mile-wide crater and wonder whether the trail traversing the middle is as astonishing as it looks. (It is.)

Kilauea VOLCANO
Kilauea volcano lies at the center of activity in Hawai'i Volcanoes National Park. The unassuming bump on Mauna Loa's southeast flank would be easily overlooked if not for its massive steaming crater and a boiling lava cauldron in Halema'uma'u. Researchers initially thought it was just a vent of Mauna Loa, but later discovered a separate lava system – a particularly active system that first broke the earth's surface as early as 600,000 years ago, and has been erupting continuously since 1983.

Mauna Loa VOLCANO
The world's largest subaerial (above water) volcano, Mauna Loa (Long Mountain) is so massive that you feel its presence more than see it. Even when it doesn't have its head in the clouds, it's impossible to pick out its summit (13,680ft) – the curse of a shield volcano which builds slowly from lava oozing down its flanks. Its bulk makes up half the Island of Hawai'i, stretching over 60 miles long and covering an area of 2035 sq miles.

Mauna Loa is so heavy that it has actually compressed the earth's crust underneath it, essentially sitting in the bottom of a 26,000ft (5-mile) deep bowl in the ocean floor. This means that from its true base to the summit, the volcano is 56,000ft (10.6 miles) tall.

Unlike most volcanoes, Mauna Loa does not sit on the intersection of two tectonic plates, but rather gets its eruptive inclinations from a stationary 'hot spot' below the crust: a mass of magma pushing upwards as the plate moves over it. Since 1843 (when we really started keeping track of these things) Mauna Loa has erupted 33 times, usually starting with activity at the summit caldera before letting off pressure at its flanks along the rift zones. Its 1868 eruption (p252) caused the largest earthquake recorded in Hawaii.

Mauna Loa's 4-mile by 1.5-mile summit crater, Moku'aweoweo (literally 'fish section,' likely referring to the red flesh of the 'aweoweo fish), formed around 750 years ago when the magma vacated the summit through a vent near modern-day Kulani Prison.

Due to the frequent eruptions and its relatively high elevation, not much lives on top of Mauna Loa, save some moss in damp lava tubes and a few insects. The area above 10,000ft is appropriately called the 'alpine stone desert,' and much of it is periglacial (shaped by freeze-thaw processes).

Native Hawaiians believe the mountain is sacred, and throughout history holy men would make treks to the summit via the 'Ainapo Trail (p240) to set offerings at the caldera. The first European to reach the

HAWAI'I VOLCANOES NATIONAL PARK

I BRAKE FOR NENE

When reports come in that a nene goose has been hit by a car, park biologists spring into action, setting up signs and roadblocks. They aren't preserving the area for some zoological CSI, but rather trying to prevent further carnage. Nene bond for life and sometimes when one is killed the other will linger in the area, returning to the spot they last saw their missing partner. Don't destroy families; slow down.

Kilauea Caldera, Crater Rim Drive & Volcano

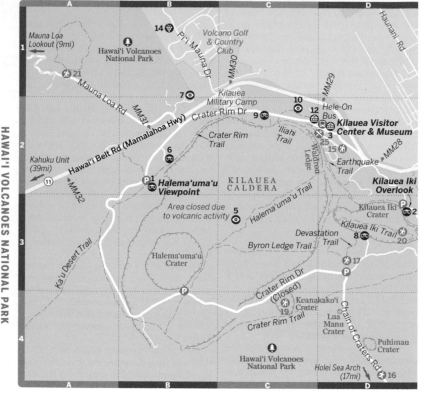

summit, Archibald Menzies, did so on his third attempt in 1794. His barometric measurements of the elevation (13,635ft) were surprisingly accurate.

Jaggar Museum
MUSEUM

(☎808-985-6051; Crater Rim Dr; ⊙10am-8pm daily; ⏩) There's plenty packed into this small one-room geology museum including real-time seismographs and tiltmeters recording earthquakes inside the park (and under your feet). Other exhibits introduce Hawaiian gods and goddesses and give a short history of the neighboring Hawai'i Volcano Observatory (closed to visitors), founded by famed vulcanologist Dr Thomas A Jaggar. Park rangers frequently give geology talks inside the museum, while throngs of visitors pack the porch outside for the best view of the lava lake in Halemaʻumaʻu Crater.

Footprints
HISTORIC SITE

A short, 0.8-mile walk down the Mauna Iki trail from the Kaʻu Desert trailhead on Hwy 11 brings you to a field of scattered footprints preserved in fragile sediment and continually being revealed and reburied by windblown sand. A few are protected under a roof; enjoy these rather than risk destroying others by tromping off the trail.

In 1782, Kamehameha killed his cousin. Kiwalaʻo had just become the new ruler of Hawaiʻi Island, but Kamehameha was having none of it and summarily defeated him at the Battle of Mokuohai. Keoua (Kiwalaʻo's half-brother) wanted to settle the score – which is how he and his army came to be marching through the Kaʻu Desert during a particularly nasty eruption remembered as Keonehelelei (the falling sands).

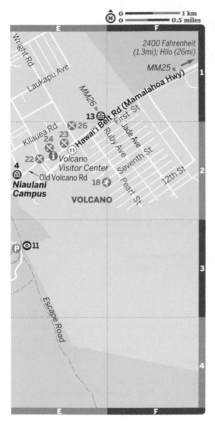

Ka'u Desert
AREA

Although the Kilauea rain shadow keeps this area relatively dry, it's not a true desert; but what rain does fall is highly acidic from the upwind eruptions. While that's hard on the plant life, it does maintain a rugged and starkly memorable landscape pocked with cinder cones and craters draped with drifts of shimmering Pele's hair (long strands of volcanic glass threads). Whet your appetite with the low-commitment hike to Footprints before tackling the **Mauna Iki** (p240) or **Ka'u Desert Trails** (p240).

Makaopuhi Crater
VOLCANO

This jaw-dropping, mile-long crater is the largest in the East Rift Zone. Although once accessible by road, it's now 5 miles along the **Napau Crater Trail**, or a grueling 2 miles up the Naulu Trail.

Mauna Loa Lookout
VIEWPOINT

(Mauna Loa Rd) A narrow, winding and pot-holed drive along lonely Mauna Loa Rd passes heavily forested *kipuka* (oases) as you come ever closer to the world's most massive active volcano. At the end of the road lies epic Mauna Loa Lookout (6662ft), a protected cluster of endangered *'ahina-hina* (Mauna Loa silversword) plants, and the start of the challenging and rewarding Mauna Loa Trail (p238). For best views, wander a short way east down the trail for vistas that encompass smoking Kilauea far below.

Hilina Pali Overlook
VIEWPOINT

(Hilina Pali Rd) This serenely beautiful over-look looms 1700ft above the coastal flats of Hilina Slump: a semidetached landmass sinking 4in each year, and which may be primed for cataclysmic collapse. The last minor drop – 11ft during the 1975 earth-quake – sent a tsunami to lap at Califor-nia's coast. If the whole thing were to break free, it could trigger 1000ft waves that would annihilate Pacific civilization; though some scientists believe debris piles from previous slumps may hold Hilina in place.

Turn west off Chain of Craters Road, 2 miles past the Crater Rim intersection and follow the one-lane paved road to the end. Drive carefully – this is nene country, and your eyes will likely be popping at the end-less volcanic wastelands and spectacular views of Mauna Loa. After 4 miles, you'll pass **Kulanaokuaiki Campground** (www.nps.gov/havo/planyourvisit/camp.htm; Hilina Pali

Despite days of offerings to appease Pele, Kilauea belched a massive cloud of steam, hot sand, suffocating gas, rocks and ash that swept across the Ka'u Desert on hurricane-force winds. Two-thirds of Ke-oua's warriors were caught in the sticky wet hell-storm. As they gasped for breath, stum-bling to their deaths, their feet left ghostly footprints in the muck. That muck dried, preserving the gory moment for all eternity. Or at least that's how famed geologist Dr Jaggar imagined it.

While hundreds, if not thousands of war-riors did die in that blast, new evidence suggests the footprints likely don't belong to them. Pyroclastic surges like that were ap-parently a regular part of Kilauea's cycle be-tween 1500 and 1790. The footprints – which include those of women and children – are more likely records of normal life persever-ing in this harsh landscape.

Kilauea Caldera, Crater Rim Drive & Volcano

Rd) FREE at the end of the still-active Koa'e fault zone.

From the road's end, you may be tempted to hit the **Hilina Pali Trail**, but the shoreline isn't as close as it looks, and the 'up' is leagues harder than the 'down.' However, prepared hikers can thread together a few sublime backcountry loops in this little-explored corner of the park.

Sulphur Banks   AREA
(Ha'akulamanu; off Crater Rim Dr) A wooden boardwalk weaves between misty, rocky vents stained chartreuse, yellow, orange and other psychedelic colors by tons of sulfur-infused steam rising from deep within the earth. Once frequented by rare birds (hence the Hawaiian name, Ha'akulamanu), invasive plants and other changes to the environment have made it less hospitable to nene and *kolea* (Pacific golden plover). The easy 0.7-mile one-way trail connects to Crater Rim Dr near the parking lot for Steaming Bluff. Wheelchair-accessible.

Steam Vents & Steaming Bluff   VIEWPOINT
(Crater Rim Dr) Creating impressive billowing plumes in the cool early morning, these vents make a convenient drive-up photo op. Hot rocks below the surface boil rainwater as it percolates down, producing the steam. While the vents at the parking area are perfectly fine, even more evocative is Steaming Bluff, found along a short walk out to the rim. Here, curtains of steam frame the cliffs above a post-apocalyptic view, giving you the distinct feeling that something BIG happened here.

Volcano Art Center   GALLERY
(☏ 808-967-7565; www.volcanoartcenter.org; Crater Rim Dr; ☉9am-5pm) ✐ Near the visitor center, this sharp local art gallery spotlights museum-quality pottery, paintings, woodwork, sculpture, jewelry, Hawaiian quilts and more in a series of rotating exhibits. The nonprofit shop, housed in the historic 1877 Volcano House hotel, is worth a visit just to admire its construction. Ask about upcoming art classes and cultural workshops, including the **Aloha Fridays** weekly immersive experiences (11am to 1pm Friday).

Thurston Lava Tube   CAVE
(Nahuku; off Crater Rim Dr; ⊕) On Kilauea's eastern side, Crater Rim Dr passes through a rainforest thick with tree ferns and ohia trees to the overflowing parking lot for ever-popular Thurston Lava Tube. A 0.3-mile loop walk starts in an ohia forest filled with birdsong before heading underground through a gigantic (but short) artificially lit lava tube. It's a favorite with tour groups, so come early or late to avoid the crowd. For a more memorable experience, visit the glowing maw after dark.

Mauna Ulu LANDMARK

(off Chain of Craters Rd) In 1969, eruptions from Kilauea's East Rift Zone began building a new lava shield, Mauna Ulu (Growing Mountain). By the time the flow stopped in 1974, it had covered 10,000 acres of park and added 200 acres of new coastal land. It also buried a 6-mile section of the original Chain of Craters Road in lava up to 300ft deep. Today the signed turnoff for Mauna Ulu is 3.5 miles down Chain of Craters Road.

'Alae Lava Shield LANDMARK

The once-awesome 'Alae crater did not go easily. The Mauna Ulu eruption had just filled the 1440ft-wide and 540ft-deep crater with a lake of molten lava when a rift opened on the crater's floor. Thirteen million cubic yards of lava – almost four times the volume of the Great Pyramid of Giza – drained back into the earth in only 30 minutes. The victory was short-lived, however, as Mauna Ulu eventually filled the crater again, leaving nothing but this small pit crater which formed as the lava lake cooled and collapsed inward.

Old Pulu Factory HISTORIC SITE

Ancient Hawaiians used *pulu,* the golden, silky fibers found at the base of *hapu'u* (tree fern) fiddleheads, to dress wounds and embalm the dead. In the 1860s entrepreneurs collected tons of *pulu* to stuff pillows and mattresses. A factory employing 50 to 75 people was establised to harvest, process and export the fibers. It closed in 1880, and not much remains but the rock walls of three structures occasionally liberated from the jungle by park rangers. It's 6 miles down the Naupu Crater Trail.

Pu'u 'O'o VOLCANO

While Halema'uma'u gets featured in the most Hawai'i volcanoes selfies, Pu'u 'O'o vent is doing the majority of Kilauea's dirty work. It is the longest-lasting and most voluminous of the volcano's eruptions, oozing an estimated 80 to 160 million gallons of lava per day, or 120 to 240 Olympic-sized swimming pools' worth. Hiking to Pu'u 'O'o is prohibited; be wary of any guide who tells you otherwise.

Lava Tree Molds AREA

(off Mauna Loa Rd) Near the start of Mauna Loa Rd, there's a turnoff to some neglected lava tree molds – deep wells that formed when lava flows engulfed the rainforest and hardened around the waterlogged trees instead of burning them upon contact. As the trees disintegrated, they left holes where the trunks once stood. Some are now sprouting new trees, but most are collecting trash.

Pu'u Pua'i Overlook VIEWPOINT

Pu'u Pua'i (Gushing Hill) formed when cinder and ash spewing from the 1959 Kilauea Iki fountain was carried southwest on the wind, piling on the rim and devastating the forest behind it. For a better perspective, consider hiking the Kilauea Iki Trail (www.nps.gov/havo/planyourvisit/brochures.htm), which you can see on the crater floor far below.

Kilauea Overlook VIEWPOINT

(Crater Rim Dr) A pause-worthy panorama, most remarkable for the 6-ton volcanic bomb sitting defiantly on the rim daring you to take eruptions lightly. Frustratingly, there is no view from the covered picnic tables, but there is shelter from wind and rain.

End of the Road LANDMARK

(Chain of Craters Rd) Quite. The road ends where the lava says it ends, having consumed this coastal section of Chain of Craters Road repeatedly since 1969. Currently there is a small ranger shack and pit toilets at the turnaround. Parking is limited to the shoulders as you approach, and fills up in the evening with lava-hunters. Come early or you could add another mile to your already 4-plus-mile hike out to the flow.

Kealakomo VIEWPOINT

(Chain of Craters Rd) About halfway along Chain of Craters Road is this coastal lookout (elevation 2000ft), with picnic tables and commanding views. That inky black snake's tongue licking the shoreline is from the 1969 Mauna Ulu eruption that obliterated the original Chain of Craters Road. Just beyond it is Apua Point, accessible via the Puna Coast trails. Below Kealakomo (entrance path), the road descends in long, sweeping switchbacks, some cut deeply through lava flows.

Holei Sea Arch LANDMARK

Constantly brutalized by unrelenting surf, the coastal section of Chain of Craters Road has sharply eroded lava-rock *pali* (cliffs). Visible from near the road's end, this ephemeral high rock arch is a dramatic

1. Thurston Lava Tube (p248)
Take an underground stroll through this gigantic, glowing cavern.

2. Lava flow entering the ocean
Molten lava pouring into the sea is a fantastic spectacle.

3. Lava field
Plants slowly recolonise the stark lava deserts.

4. Pu'u 'O'o (p249)
The longest-lasting and most voluminous of Kilauea's eruptions.

landmark carved by crashing waves; the same waves that will destroy it entirely within a few hundred years. Go now.

🏃 Activites

Hiking

For detailed information on hiking in the Hawai'i Volcanoes National Park, see p238.

Backcountry Office HIKING, BACKPACKING
(☑808-985-6178; Crater Rim Dr, Visitor Emergency Operations Center (VEOC); ◷8am-4pm) All overnight hikes in Hawai'i Volcanoes National Park require a $10 permit good for 12 people for up to seven nights. Get it in person up to one day ahead from this office.

Other Activities

Chain of Craters Road SCENIC DRIVE
Chain of Craters Road winds 20 miles and 3700ft down the southern slopes of Kilauea Volcano, ending abruptly at the East Rift Zone on the Puna Coast. This scenic drive (p242) takes in an impressive array of sights along the paved two-lane road.

USGS Hawaiian Volcano Observatory VOLUNTEERING
(HVO; http://hvo.wr.usgs.gov/volunteer) 🍃 Full-time volunteers help monitor the Big Island's volcanoes; minimum three-month commitment, apply in advance.

Stewardship at the Summit VOLUNTEERING
(www.nps.gov/havo/planyourvisit/summit_steward ship.htm; Kilauea Visitor Center; ◷9am-noon) **FREE** Weekly volunteer projects spend the morning tackling invasive plants like Hima-layan ginger *(Heydechium gardnerianum)*. Hiking is required, but reservations are not. Check with Kilauea Visitor Center (p244) for details.

👉 Tours

Friends of Hawai'i Volcanoes National Park TOURS
(☑808-985-7373; www.fhvnp.org; annual membership adult/student/family $30/15/45) Leads weekend **Sunday Walks in the Park** and organizes volunteer activities. Its incredibly popular **Puapo'o Lava Tube Tour** (adult/child $30/25, first Wednesday and third Saturday of the month) sells out almost immediately upon being posted (six weeks in advance). Plan ahead.

For a deeper dive into the natural history of the rainforest and lava tubes, try the six-hour **Wild Caves Exploration Institute** (adult/child age 7–12 with lunch $200/100, every other Wednesday and Saturday).

Hawaiian Walkways HIKING
(☑808-322-2255; www.gowaipio.com; adult/child $190/99) Hit two of the park's iconic craters while hiking 7 miles with a certified guide. Speaks Japanese.

Volcano Bike Tours CYCLING
(☑808-934-9199; www.bikevolcano.com; tours $110-134) If you're really into fresh air, try these informative guided cycling tours of the park. The three- to five-hour trips are mostly downhill (ie not much exercise) along Crater Rim Dr and Chain of Craters Road at a casual pace, rain or shine.

1868 EARTHQUAKE

'The crust of the earth rose and sunk like the sea in a storm...The streams ran mud, the earth was rent in thousands of places...and multitudes of people were prostrated by the shocks,' TM Coan wrote in *Scribner's Weekly* about what is still the largest earthquake in Hawai'i Island's recorded history.

After several days of near continual tremors and an eruption on Mauna Loa's summit, on April 2, 1868 the southeast flank of the island slipped toward the ocean, causing a 7.9 magnitude earthquake. The quake flattened every building in Ka'u and triggered a 50ft tsunami that swept several coastal fishing villages out to sea and killed at least 46 people. A massive mudslide near Wood Valley, 1 mile wide and up to 90ft deep, slid 1000ft down and 3 miles seaward, burying 30 people, their homes and countless livestock.

Aftershocks from the quake continued until April 7, when a 2-mile-long crack opened along Mauna Loa's Southwest Rift Zone, releasing a series of fissure eruptions. Lava poured down the mountainside, reaching the ocean 10 miles away in less than three hours.

OFF THE BEATEN TRACK

VIEWING LAVA UP CLOSE

Lucky travelers may be able to view liquid rock making the 6.4-mile journey from the Pu'u O'o Vent to the ocean: a journey of pure creation, and sometimes destruction. If the show is really on, there will be surface flows, lava 'skylights' and flaming trees. When the flow mellows or changes course, you may be able to see a steam plume during the day, or an unearthly red glow after dark – even more ominous when it's coming from a crack between your feet.

Where the lava will be flowing when you visit and whether or not you can reach it are impossible to predict. Ask at the Kilauea Visitor Center, call the park or check the NPS website (www.nps.gov/havo) for updates, but know that sometimes it can be an arduous 10-mile round-trip hike or more from the end of Chain of Craters Road. Staying informed about the flow helps manage expectations (especially those of kids).

Lava entering the ocean is wondrous but extremely dangerous. The explosive clash between seawater and 2100°F lava can spray scalding water and poisonous steam hundreds of feet into the air and throw flaming lava chunks well inland. Unstable ledges of lava crust (called lava benches) sometimes collapse without warning. Several observers have been injured, some fatally, over the past decade. Stay well inland from the lava flow and heed all official warnings.

It may be easier to hike to the flow from the other side at the county-run lava viewing area (p232) at the end of Hwy 130 in Puna. There, locals often rent time-saving bicycles, and guides are plentiful.

No matter where you begin, bring a flashlight and plenty of water, and plan to stick around after sunset.

★✱ Festivals & Events

★ **Hawai'i Volcanoes National Park Cultural Festival**   CULTURE, ARTS
(www.nps.gov/havo/planyourvisit/events.htm; 🚻) FREE This annual cultural festival held in the summer, usually some time between May and August, celebrates traditional Hawaiian arts, crafts, music and hula with demonstrations and hands-on exhibits. Park entrance is free during events.

★ **After Dark in the Park**   LECTURE SERIES
(www.nps.gov/havo/planyourvisit/events_adip. htm; Kilauea Visitor Center; suggested donation $2; ⊙7pm Tue) Experts in science, conservation, art or history unlock the mysteries of the park in this award-winning lecture series. In our experience, they're so fascinating we would go even if there was more of a night-life around here.

Hula Arts at Kilauea   ARTS, CULTURE
(www.volcanoartcenter.org; 🚻) 🍴 A free series of outdoor *kahiko* (ancient) hula performances happens near the Volcano Art Center (p248) on one Saturday morning each month.

✖ Eating

★ **The Rim Restaurant**   HAWAII REGIONAL $$$
(www.hawaiivolcanohouse.com/dining; Crater Rim Dr, Volcano House; breakfast buffet adult/child $20/10, lunch mains $14-20, dinner mains $20-40; ⊙7-10am, 11am-2pm & 5:30-8:30pm) The better-than-average modern cuisine crafted from local ingredients may be overpriced for the quality, but you come here for the ambience. Call ahead to reserve a table by the floor-to-ceiling windows that afford absolutely staggering volcano views at sunset. The well-stocked breakfast buffet will power you through all but the longest hikes.

🍺 Drinking & Nightlife

Uncle George's Lounge   BAR
(Crater Rim Dr, Volcano House; mains $14-20; ⊙11am-9:30pm) The small bar serves The Rim's lunch menu (and its view) all day long. Favorite Volcano House hack: when it's crowded, get your food and drinks 'to go' and occupy the lounge chairs between the two restaurants for a quieter, more relaxed scene.

'OHI'A LEHUA

'Ohi'a was a bird catcher, an important person responsible for gathering the colorful feathers that adorned the cloaks of the *ali'i* (noble rulers). Pele, the goddess of fire, awoke to find 'Ohi'a trekking across her mountainside, and promptly fell in love with him. When 'Ohi'a refused her advances because he was engaged to Lehua, Pele grew angry, and trapped his feet in lava and turned him into a tree. A distraught Lehua begged the other gods to change him back; but Pele's magic was too great. The best they could do was turn her into a flower and attach her to the tree so they could be together. It is said that if you separate the lovers by picking a flower, the heavens will cry in the form of rain.

The ubiquitous fuzzy-flowered *'ohi'a lehua (Metrosideros polymorpha)* is one of the first plants to recolonize fresh lava fields. Regardless of whether this is the ultimate act of revenge by two lovers undoing Pele's work, it is an impressive and important feat that involves sending roots hundreds of feet through the tiniest pores and cracks to find water. These forest-defining trees live 200 to 1500 years and are highly adaptable, growing from the ocean to the tree line as shrubs or towering trees depending on the environment. They have long been a cornerstone of Hawai'i's forests and culture. And they are under attack.

As early as 2010, ohia began dying from an invasive fungal infection that enters through wounds on the tree and chokes off its flow of water and nutrients. Once a tree shows signs of infection, it's usually dead within a few weeks; thus the name ROD: Rapid Ohia Death. The disease is spreading across the island at an alarming rate, and there currently is no cure. By the end of 2016, over 47,000 acres were affected.

The State of Hawaii has placed a quarantine on the island. It's now illegal to make lei from the flowers. In some areas, you may be asked to spray your shoes with alcohol to help prevent the spread. It's uncertain if any of this will help, or if the composition of Hawai'i's forests will be reshaped permanently.

☆ Entertainment

Nā Leo Manu　　　TRADITIONAL MUSIC
(www.nps.gov/havo/planyourvisit/cultural-programs.htm; Kilauea Visitor Center; ⊘ 6pm, 3rd Wed of the month) **FREE** As part of the park's ongoing celebration of Hawaiian culture and history, the monthly Nā Leo Manu concerts bring talent from across the islands for an evening of music, singing, dancing and storytelling. Check the website for exact dates and times.

❶ Information

The park is open 24 hours a day, except when eruption activity and volcanic gases necessitate temporary closures. For current lava flows, and trail, road and campground status, check the website or call ahead.

The park's main entrance sits at almost 4000ft, with varying elevation and climates inside the park boundaries. Chilly rain, wind, fog and vog typify the fickle weather, which can go from hot and dry to a soaking downpour in a flash. Near Kilauea Caldera, temperatures average 15°F cooler than in Kona, so bring a rain jacket and pants, especially if visiting at night.

DANGERS & ANNOYANCES

Although few people have died due to violently explosive eruptions at Kilauea, come prepared if you plan to walk about or hike: bring sturdy shoes or boots, long pants, a hat, sunscreen, water (and snacks), and a flashlight with extra batteries. For more information see the Visitor Center's excellent safety film.

Lava

Even cooled hard lava can be dangerous. Uneven and brittle surfaces made of glass-sharp rocks can give way over unseen hollows and lava tubes while the edges of craters and rifts crumble easily. Deep earth cracks may be hidden by plants. When hiking, abrasions, deep cuts and broken limbs are all possible. In short, it's critical that you stay on marked trails and heed warning signs. Blazing paths into unknown terrain can damage fragile areas, lead to injuries and leave tracks that encourage others to follow.

Vog & Sulfuric Fumes

Another major, constant concern is air quality. Halema'uma'u and Pu'u 'O'o belch thousands of tons of deadly sulfur dioxide daily. Where lava meets the sea it creates a 'steam plume,' as sulfuric and hydrochloric acid mixes with airborne silica (or glass particles). All this combines to create 'vog' which, depending on the winds, can settle over the park. People with respiratory and heart conditions, pregnant women, infants and young children should take care when visiting.

Dehydration

Vast areas of the park qualify as desert, and dehydration is common. Carrying three quarts of water per person is the standard advice, but bring more and keep a gallon in the trunk: you'll drink it.

Volcano

🕿 808 / POP 2231

The primal power of Hawai'i's volcanoes attracts the eccentric, the adventuresome and the counter-cultural. That demographic, plus an assortment of park rangers, conservationists and creative types all live on Pele's doorstep in the misty rainforest village of Volcano. It's easy to miss, tucked away in the oppressively green tree fern and ohia thicket, but its location makes it an ideal base for exploring Hawai'i Volcanoes National Park. Just remember where you parked your car it may be overgrown by morning.

◎ Sights

★ **Niaulani Campus** GALLERY
(Volcano Art Center; 🕿 808-967-8222; www.volcano artcenter.org; 19-4074 Old Volcano Rd; ⊗ 9am-5pm Mon-Fri) On the edge of an old-grown ohia forest, this campus of the main Volcano Art Center (p248) gallery in Hawai'i Volcanoes National Park showcases spillover and related exhibits unencumbered by the park's thematic requirements. The regular schedule of creative workshops, native culture classes, yoga, music and performance art adds depth to your stay in this otherwise sleepy town.

2400 Fahrenheit GALLERY
(🕿 808-985-8667; www.2400f.com; 11-3200 Old Volcano Rd; ⊗10am-4pm Thu-Mon) Michael and Misato Mortara form hot glass into sculptures and vessels as complex and beautiful as the Big Island. Visit in the morning, or just after lunch for your best chance of seeing the action. Turn off Hwy 11 at Old Volcano Rd and follow it 0.5 miles to the end.

Volcano Garden Arts GALLERY
(🕿 808-985-8979; www.volcanogardenarts.com; 19-3834 Old Volcano Rd; ⊗10am-4pm Tue-Sun) Do your Big Island art shopping at this gallery and studio in the fern forest. Walls

and tables overflow with paintings, handicrafts and jewelry produced by dozens of regional creatives. The space is surrounded by quiet gardens backed by Café Ono (p256). Feeling inspired? Rent the small **cottage** (🕿 808-985-8979, 808-967-7261; www.volcanoar tistcottage.com; 19-3834 Old Volcano Rd; cottage incl breakfast $129; 🕿) out back to embark on your own artistic journey.

🏃 Activities

Hale Ho'ōla SPA
(🕿 808-756-2421; www.halehoola.net; 11-3913 7th St; treatments $35-160; ⊗ by appointment only) This professional Hawaiian massage center offers a full menu of body and skin treatments: a blissful complement to a long day's hike. Combines indigenous ingredients, traditional methods and holistic spirituality for therapeutic ends, and offers authentic massage like *lomilomi*. Located in the wing of a private home in the fern forest. Appointments required.

☞ Tours

★ **Kazumura Cave Tours** TOURS
(🕿 808-967-7208; www.kazumuracave.com; off Volcano Hwy, past Mile 22; from $30; ⊗ Mon-Sat by appointment) After learning his property straddled **Kazumura Cave** – the world's longest lava tube – Harry Schick tirelessly worked to become an expert on this geologic phenomenon. Although 20 years of tours has made his delivery a bit rote, the abundant information and unique sights still make for a fascinating adventure. The recommended four-hour tour ($50) culminates with the appropriately named Wow Formation.

Hawaii Photo Retreat WALKING, PHOTOGRAPHY
(🕿 808-985-7487; www.hawaiiphotoretreat.com; 1-5 day tours $495/day; ⊗ by reservation) Trying to capture the Big Island's big beauty on camera can leave even the most seriously aspiring photographers frustrated. Let professional shooters and Volcano residents Ken and Mary Goodrich help you get it all in perspective with personalized instruction from the field to the digital darkroom. Transportation and food not included.

Niaulani Rain Forest Tour WALKING
(🕿 808-967-8222; www.volcanoartcenter.org; 19-4074 Old Volcano Rd, Volcano Art Center; ⊗ 9:30am Mon; 🚼) 🎟 FREE Join an hour-long, easy nature walk through Volcano's rainforest. Guides cover the ecological importance of

KILAUEA'S RECENT ERUPTIONS

In 2008 Halema'uma'u, located within the larger Kilauea Caldera, renewed its activity, becoming a burbling cauldron of lava in the corner of a sea of destruction. The lake of fire turned the clouds of steam molten red at night, drawing people from far and wide. In traditional Hawaiian spirituality, this is the home of the goddess Pele – a woman not known for her even temperament.

Although Hawai'i's shield volcanoes typically lack the explosive nature of other volcanoes (lava mostly just oozes down the mountain toward the ocean) Pele does occasionally send up dramatic geysers of fire.

However, Ka wahine 'ai honua ('the earth-eating woman,' as Pele is known) exacts a price for this entertainment. Since 1983, this side of the island has been remade several times over. Lava blocked the coastal road to Puna in 1988, and covered the village of Kalapana in 1990. Flows then crept further west, engulfing Kamoamoa Beach in 1994, later claiming an additional mile of road and most of Wahaula Heiau. In 2008, the Thanksgiving Eve breakout sent lava back through Kalapana, and in 2014, Pu'u 'O'o's eruption knocked on the door of Pahoa, Puna's main center of population. There is truly no telling how (or even if) lava will be flowing by the time you read this.

old-growth koa and ohia forests, traditional Hawaiian uses of plants, and the key role of birds. The walk is free, but donations are appreciated. Call to ask about forest restoration volunteer workdays.

⭐ Festivals & Events

Volcano Village Artists Hui   ART
(www.volcanovillageartistshui.com; ⊙ late Nov) 🏵
FREE Tour pottery, fiber work, wood sculpture, ceramics, woodblock prints, glass blowing and photography studios over a three-day weekend in late November. There's no better time to visit Volcano.

🍴 Eating

⭐ Volcano Farmers Market   MARKET $
(www.thecoopercenter.org; 19-4030 Wright Rd, Cooper Community Center; ⊙6-10am Sun; 🅟)
🏵 The whole community comes out to this weekly market to buy farm-fresh produce, flowers, local crafts and more.

Eagle's Lighthouse Café   SANDWICHES $
(☑808-985-8587; www.eagleslighthouse.com; 19-4005 Haunani Rd; mains $5-11; ⊙7am-5pm Mon-Sat; 🕸🍴) Fresh and hearty sandwiches, salads and grab-and-go wraps are served out of a small kitchen fronted by picnic tables serenaded by nonstop contemporary Christian music. The breakfast bowl is a filling prehike option, though the croissant sandwich likely won't power you through to lunch on its own. Daily hot lunch specials are hit-or-miss.

Tuk Tuk Thai Truck   THAI $
(☑808-747-3041; www.tuk-tukthaifood.com; 19-4030 Wright Rd, Cooper Community Center; mains $10-13; ⊙11am-6pm Tue-Sat; 🍴) Heaping piles of pad thai and a veritable river of savory curry pour out of this local's favorite lunch spot. Seating is limited to a nearby picnic table, so take it with you to one of the park's scenic overlooks – if you can resist the aroma that long. (We couldn't.)

⭐ Thai Thai Restaurant   THAI $$
(☑808-967-7969; 19-4084 Old Volcano Rd; mains $15-26; ⊙11:30am-9pm; 🍴) Authentically flavored and well portioned if somewhat overpriced (and splitting a plate will cost you a $6 surcharge). The chefs recognize that good Thai food doesn't have to set your tongue on fire – unless you are into that. We are fans of the rich and peanutty Special Curry, and the tom yum soup. It can get crowded; think dinner reservations.

Café Ono   CAFE $$
(☑808-985-8979; www.cafeono.net; 19-3834 Old Volcano Rd, Volcano Garden Arts; mains $14-16; ⊙11am-3pm Tue-Sun; 🕸🍴🌱) 🏵 Lunch on organic vegetarian and vegan comfort foods like salads, sandwiches and pasta in the sun room behind the art gallery (p255), or in the garden around a somewhat disheveled fish pond. The hot dishes may not all be prepared to order, but they've got enough home-style goodness to survive the rigorous microwaving. Coffee and dessert served 10am to 4pm.

Lava Rock Café   DINER $$

(☑808-967-8526; 19-3972 Old Volcano Rd; mains breakfast & lunch $7-11, dinner $12-24; ⊙7:30am-9pm Tue-Sat, closes 4pm Sun & 5pm Mon; ☎️🚻) This roadhouse joint is nearly always jumping. Even though the stick-to-your-ribs menu of burgers, seafood and pasta is nearly all forgettable, the cold beer on tap and a casual atmosphere means you'll likely meet local characters, making it a fine place to unwind in the evening.

★'Ōhelo Café   MODERN AMERICAN $$$

(☑808-339-7865; www.ohelocafe.com; 19-4005 Haunani Rd, cnr Old Volcano Rd; pizza $12-15, mains $21-40; ⊙11:30am-2:30pm & 5:30-9:30pm, closed 1st Tue of the month) Finally, foodies have a reason to linger in Volcano. Combining local flavors with international flare, the portions here may be small, but the execution is spot on. Don't miss the cauliflower appetizer, and the thin-crust margherita pizza makes a fine lunch. Dinner reservations are wise, especially if you can nab a seat at the Chef's Table and watch the action.

Kilauea Lodge Restaurant   INTERNATIONAL $$$

(☑808-967-7366; www.kilauealodge.com; 19-3948 Old Volcano Rd; mains breakfast & lunch $10-14, dinner $25-40; ⊙7:30am-2pm & 5-9:30pm; ☎️) Volcano's venerable kitchen offers an eclectic mix of fresh local seafood, steak, pasta and European classics like duck à l'orange. Hardwood floors, a huge stone fireplace and impeccable service make the venue date-worthy, but the food frequently falls short of its aspirations. Breakfast is a solid bet, however.

❶ Information

Volcano Visitor Center (19-4084 Old Volcano Rd; ⊙usually 7am-7pm) Unstaffed tourist information kiosk with brochures aplenty. Next door is a coin laundromat, ATM and hardware store selling some camping gear.

❶ Getting There & Away

The main drag and most businesses are along Old Volcano Rd which parallels Hwy 11 just *mauka* (inland) between Miles 26 and 27.5.

Five daily (none Sunday) Hele-On Bus (www.heleonbus.org) services travel to and from Hilo, with one continuing on to Ka'u.

Ka'u

📞 808 / POP 8540

Best Places to Eat

➡ Mehe's Ka'u Bar & Grill (p269)

➡ Hana Hou Restaurant (p266)

➡ DJ's Pizza and Bakeshop (p269)

➡ Punalu'u Bake Shop (p266)

Best Places to Stroll

➡ On the mesmerizing black sand of Punalu'u Beach Park (p265)

➡ Along the restless shores of Ka Lae (p267)

➡ Through the diverse landscapes of the Kahuku Unit (p260)

Why Go?

Much of Ka'u, the southernmost district in Hawai'i, feels comfortably stuck in the mid 20th-century. Large ranches and macadamia nut plantations abut forested highlands teeming with deer, goat and mouflon sheep. Below, old plantation towns fringe a sparse wind-swept coastal zone along the deep blue Pacific – the longest uninhabited coastline on the island.

We'll be frank: this isn't where you go for tons of warm aloha or, at least, not the openly given sort you find in more touristed areas. Here, locals fiercely protect their rural, stay-away-from-it-all culture: quashing coastal resorts, lobbying for protected land, pioneering off-the-grid living, and speaking lots of pidgin.

That being said, with the right attitude and sense of adventure, time spent in Ka'u will add a welcome dash of intrigue to any itinerary.

When to Go

Apr–Jun Although the dry parts of Ka'u get less than 30in of rain per year, this is the time to maximize your clear skies.

May The Ka'u Coffee Festival livens things up a bit in Pahala in the middle of the month.

Jul 'Ohi'a lehua trees can flower year round, but are most abundant during late spring through early summer – great times to visit the Kahuku Unit.

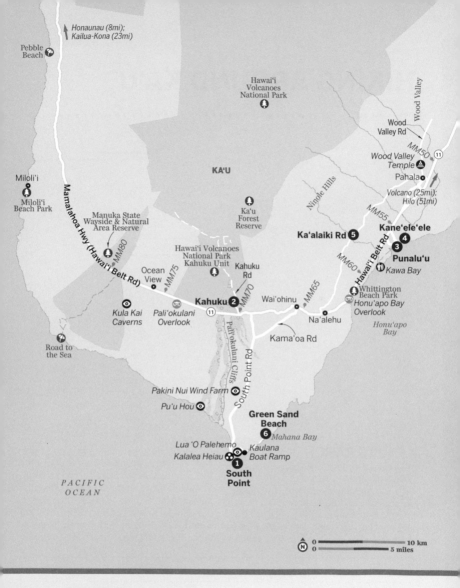

Ka'u Highlights

❶ South Point (p267)
Plunging off the edge of the earth into crystal-blue waters teeming with fish.

❷ Kahuku (p270) Exploring Ka'u's rich cultural heritage and astounding ecological diversity on an excellent ranger-led hike.

❸ Punalu'u (p265)
Digging your toes into inky black sands at a respectful distance from nesting sea turtles.

❹ Kane'ele'ele (p265)
Following in the footsteps of ancient Hawaiians on the 'Trail by the Sea' past ancient heiau with controversial histories.

❺ Ka'alaiki Road (p266)
Cruising along Ka'u's pastoral back road where time passes at its own pace.

❻ Green Sand Beach (p267) Being sandblasted as you bounce along the vacant grassland in the back of a rusty old pickup truck.

HIKING AROUND KAʻU

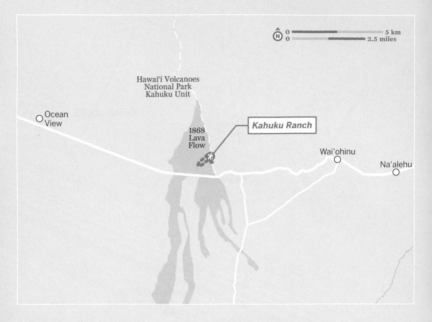

KAHUKU RANCH

START/END PUʻU O LOKUANA TRAILHEAD
LENGTH 2 MILES; 1 HOUR

This leg-stretching glimpse into Kaʻu's past starts by walking between a row of old-growth **native ohia trees** (*Metrosideros polymorpha*) on your left, and **invasive christmasberry** (*Schinus terebinthifolia*) crowding out other plants on your right. Near the **old ranch gate** a stressed-out ohia has sent out **aerial roots** to collect additional moisture from the air – a coping mechanism.

Kahuku's grazing history began in 1793 when King Kamehameha received a gift of 12 Texas longhorn cattle. He promptly

---

SHORT HIKES IN THE KAHUKU UNIT

Glover Trail The highlight of the 3-mile Glover Trail loop is standing at the edge of a huge forested pit crater, a deep bowl full of trees looking like the entrance to the underworld. The lower trailhead is about 3 miles beyond the Upper Palm trailhead (4WD recommended). After 2.2 miles, the trail returns to the road 0.8 miles beyond your car.

Palm Trail This 1.8-mile ramble (plus 0.8-mile return along the road) traverses pasture land with lonely views over rolling hills and swishy tall grass prairie. Highlights include ranching-era infrastructure, native forest remnants and striking volcanic features along a fissure from Mauna Loa's 1868 eruption. It's the park's only trail that allows mountain biking, best enjoyed in a counter-clockwise direction to maximize the mildly technical descent.

The Big Island doesn't lack for wild spaces, but there's something about the lonely coastline and gale-driven, lonely hinterlands of Ka'u that sets the area apart as particularly untamed.

Ohia trees, Kahuku Ranch

declared them sacred, which meant they quickly multiplied, running rampant throughout the land eating everything they could reach. Later landowners experimented with other animals like goats and mouflon sheep which continue that destructive legacy today.

Cross the main road, and follow the ranch road across the **1868 lava flow** that spared the pasture ahead, forming a *kipuka* (area of older land surrounded by new lava). Although now hidden below a dense mat of non-native pasture grass, satellite images reveal an extensive **network of rows and mounds** where ancient Hawaiians grew *'uala* (sweet potato) and *kalo* (taro).

Exit the *kipuka* and enter Captain Robert Brown's nightmare. Having just started ranching at Kahuku less than three years before, Captain Brown was reluctant to vacate when a series of earthquakes dev-

astated surrounding communities in 1868. On the night of April 7, however, the **fissure eruption** here began gushing lava above his home, forcing his family to flee for higher ground. There they watched their house and 300 head of trapped cattle be incinerated.

Continue up the lava flow and along the **historic airstrip** that once serviced the ranch lands. Cross the main road again to **Pu'u o Lokuana** (p270) cinder cone. As you stand on the summit looking up the mountain, try to imagine the surrounding hillsides covered in forest – how it looked before humans harvested koa trees for canoes and sandalwood for market, then cleared the rest for pasture.

Return to the Pu'u o Lokuana Trailhead via the switchbacks on the cone's south face – or channel your inner child and somersault down the soft grass.

ROAD TRIP: SOUTH POINT ROAD

It's worth making this trip for the bracing sea air and clifftop views alone (and the wind turbines, for the renewable energy nerds). But it also comes with bragging rights: you've gone as far south as is possible before you fall off the edge of the U.S.

① Pali'okulani Overlook

The best place to start your journey down South Point Rd is actually 5 miles west on Hwy 11 at this **overlook** (p268). There you have a commanding view of the escarpment that forms the southernmost tip of Hawai'i running from highway to sea, reaching an average height of 400ft.

Pali'okulani (*pali* means 'cliff') was formed when the land west of the Kahuku fault either slid into the ocean, or possibly just sunk in place (geologists disagree). If you're coming from the Hilo side, consider making the detour.

The Drive > Start your odometer where South Point Rd turns off Hwy 11 in a semiforested

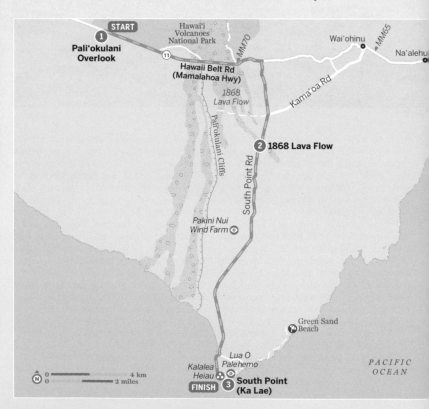

Start Pali'okulani Overlook, Hwy 11, Mile 69.5

End Boat Hoist Parking

Length 12 miles; at least 1 hour

Ka Lae (p267)

area where residents continue a long tradition of agriculture. Things begin to open up at about Mile 3.

② 1868 Lava Flow

At the site of this lava flow, the Swedish Space Corporation's satellite tracking station comes into view, as do acres of grassy plain stretching out below. Much of this is homestead land promised to Hawaiian families by the Department of Hawaiian Home Lands. But decades of administrative and funding issues have delayed infrastructure improvements, leaving the area mostly vacant.

At Mile 4.8, the rusty carcasses of 37 windmills from the failed Kamaoa wind farm lie next to their foundations under the smug shadow of the Pakini Nui wind farm on the horizon – which produces 2.3 times as much power as Kamaoa did, but with only 14 turbines.

The Drive > Continue on to the fork in the road at Mile 10: the road left heads toward the parking for Green Sand Beach, while the road right heads toward the most southern place in the US, Ka Lae.

③ South Point (Ka Lae)

Welcome to **Ka Lae** (p267)! Heading right, park on the asphalt above the **boat hoist**, and take a stroll out to **Kalalea Heiau** (p268) and **Lua 'O Palehemo** before taking the obligatory selfie at the very bottom of the US – it will create great symmetry hanging next to your selfie from Barrow, AK (better get on that).

❶ Getting There & Away

While the **Hele-On Bus** (☑ 808-961-8744; www.heleonbus.org; adult one-way $2, 10-ride ticket $15, monthly pass $60) does circumnavigate the island, around here the schedules are infrequent and inconvenient for visitors.

A standard car will get you most places you want to go, but 4WD expands your exploration options considerably.

Pahala

☑ 808 / POP 1356

Pahala's quiet streets are mostly lined with unrestored early-20th-century plantation houses occupied by unemployed early-20th-century plantation workers. While Hawaii's sugar boom was coming to an end, the lands around here still managed to produce record yields – but that only helped for so long. In the mid-1990s, forced to choose between pay cuts or the mill closing, the workers chose the latter. Many left, some stayed, and a few manage to eke out a living growing coffee and macadamia nuts.

Pahala dozes just inland from Hwy 11, south of Mile 51. The unhurried town center, with a gas station, a bank and a post office (but no dining options), is at the corner of Kamani and Pikake Sts.

◉ Sights

★ Ka'u Coffee Mill   FARM
(☑ 808-928-0550; www.kaucoffeemill.com; 96-2694 Wood Valley Rd; ⊙ 8:30am-4:30pm) 🚗 This down-to-earth, hydro-powered coffee farm roasts its own award-winning beans – which some connoisseurs rate as highly as Kona coffee. Taste a variety of brews at the gift shop located on-site in a sea of verdant hills. Free, informative coffee tours at 10am, noon and 2pm take you through the process from field to cup.

From Hwy 11, follow Kamani St inland, turn right onto Pikake St, then continue on Wood Valley Rd for about 2 miles.

Wood Valley Temple   TEMPLE
(Nechung Dorje Drayang Ling; ☑ 808-928-8539; www.nechung.org; Wood Valley Rd; requested donation $5; ⊙ usually 10am-5pm) Its official name, which translates to 'Immutable Island of Melodious Sound,' perfectly captures the valley's wind and birdsong. Just outside Pahala, you can't miss the splash of color of this Tibetan Buddhist temple

juxtaposed against its green, 25-acre forested retreat center. Visitors are welcome to join daily chanting and meditation sessions (9am and 6pm Monday to Saturday, or 10am Sunday), or to just visit the temple and gift shop. A meditative **guesthouse** (☑ 808-928-8539; www.nechung.org; Wood Valley Rd; s $65-85, d $95; 🖥) lets you stay a few nights.

After starting life as Nichiren Mission in 1902, the temple was rebuilt in 1925 and then abandoned when the sugar mill closed. It reopened in the 1970s, and was visited by the Dalai Lama in 1994.

Turn off Hwy 11 onto Kamani St, then right into Pikake St, which becomes Wood Valley Rd; the retreat is about 5 miles inland.

✪ Festivals & Events

Ka'u Coffee Festival   CULTURAL
(www.kaucoffeefestival.com) In mid-May, Pahala wakes up with a strong brew of music, coffee, hula, coffee-farm and mill tours, farm-to-fork food, more coffee and even stargazing.

❶ Information

Ka'u Hospital (☑ 808-932-4200; www.kauhospital.org; 1 Kamani St; ⊙ 24hr emergency) The rural health clinic is your only 24-hour emergency hospital option between Kona and Hilo.

❶ Getting There & Away

Hele-On Bus (www.heleonbus.org) schedules three trips daily (one Sunday) to Kona and one trip daily (except Sunday) to Volcano and Hilo. If you arrive on a bike and have the legs for it, Wood Valley Rd is a pleasant ramble.

Punalu'u

Historically a major Hawaiian settlement, Punalu'u is now an uninhabited black-sand beach flanked by temple ruins. The area is known for its sea turtles who manage to do OK despite the throngs of visitors. Remember to stay 50yd away from turtles in water and 20ft on land.

In recent history, the bay was besieged by Sea Mountain, a fish hook–shaped golf course with a small condo complex dangling like bait to entice investors. However, local opposition has successfully prevented further development, citing threats to both cultural and environmental resources.

⊙ Sights

★ Punalu'u Beach Park   BEACH
(Black Sand Beach) Beyond the nearly omni-present green sea turtles basking in the sun, or the rare hawksbill turtles that lay their eggs here (be careful where you walk), this windswept beach is famous for its black sand: pulverized basalt from Mauna Loa eruptions that absorb and reflect the sunlight in a mesmerizing scene fringed by stately palm trees. The rough, cold waters and undertows frequently make swimming undesirable, but a lifeguard is posted and when it's calm, snorkeling is a treat.

★ Kane'ele'ele Heiau   TEMPLE
(Punalu'u Nui) Also referred to as Punalu'u Nui, 800-year-old Kane'ele'ele Heiau was the region's *luakani*, or place of human sacrifice. A large flat stone below the southwest corner of the temple walls is believed to have served this purpose, while a pit full of bones discovered during construction of nearby sugar warehouses appears to confirm it. Reach the heiau by following a short steep trail up Kahiolo Point above the warehouse foundations.

Look for a path heading east from the heiau paved with smooth gray stones set to ease the journey of barefoot warriors over the *'a'a* (rough, jagged lava). This section of the 175-mile Ala Kahakai (p127; Trail by the Sea) National Historic Trail is well preserved and provides a great day hike east to Kamehame Beach (3 miles), a turtle nesting site protected by the Nature Conservancy, or southwest to Kawa Bay (2.7 miles).

Kawa Bay   BEACH
(⊙ 6am-6pm) In the past a flash-point for coastal-access and land-rights issues, Kawa Bay is now a quiet, pebbly cove. It's bounded by a creek and cliff-top heiau on one side, and **Ka'alaiki**, the island's second-largest freshwater spring system and fishpond estuary, on the other. It's a peaceful place to picnic, and some locals do surf, but beware: there are strong currents and sharks. Park at the yellow gate at Mile 58.5 on Hwy 11 and walk 0.5 miles down the track to the cove.

Henry Opukahaia Chapel   CHURCH
(⊙ service Sun) A small rock chapel and cemetery above the bay is dedicated to Punalu'u resident, Henry Opukaha'ia. Several years after watching his parents get killed in a war between rival chiefs, he boarded a ship for Boston. Although he never returned to Hawaii (he died of typhus at age 26), his conversion to Christianity and desire to take it back home inspired the first wave of missionaries to the islands.

✦ Activities

Kawa Bay   SURFING
(Windmills; Kawa Bay) Surf breaks are hard to come by in Ka'u, making Kawa Bay (sometimes called Windmills) the local go-to. Go with a local. Or channel Nu'uanupa'ahu, the Ka'u chief who honed his legendary surfing skills here; skills which allowed him to survive shark attacks and win the respect of his rival, Kalaniopu'u (though the latter did later die from his wounds).

⊙ Getting There & Away

One Hele-On Bus (www.heleonbus.org) from Hilo drops you at the beach, while the three buses daily from Kona leave you to walk the one mile from Hwy 11.

Na'alehu
📞 808 / POP 866

Tiny Na'alehu is the southernmost town in the USA – a title it milks for all it's worth. Although the name means 'Volcanic Ashes', Na'alehu is a greenscape filled with sprawling trees and pastel-colored plantation houses that give it a lost-in-time rural feel. This is underscored by the beautiful, but boarded-up, **Na'alehu Theatre**, a 1940s movie house along the main road. The town serves as central Ka'u's commercial center (such as it is) with a minimarket, hardware store, laundromat, library, playground, post office, gas station and ATM.

Just west, the town of **Wai'ohinu** ('Sparkling Water'; population 230) occupies the hillside between Miles 65 and 66 on Hwy 11. The town was briefly the county seat of Hawai'i Island in 1900, but now is known mostly for the Mark Twain Monkeypod Tree and the quiet lifestyle so cherished by its quiet inhabitants.

⊙ Sights

Mark Twain Monkeypod Tree   HISTORIC SITE
In 1866 Mark Twain wrote in yet another long letter home that in Wai'ohinu, 'trees and flowers flourish luxuriantly, and three of those trees – two mangoes and

an orange – will live in my memory as the greenest, freshest and most beautiful I ever saw.' A tree conspicuously absent from his travelogues, however, is the Monkeypod he supposedly planted. Nevertheless, legend has it that plant it he did. Here. Find the sign marking the spot *mauka* (inland) of Hwy 11 near Wai'ohinu city park.

A hurricane claimed that original tree in 1956, and the stately specimen now sprawling over the highway is what resprouted from its roots.

Honu'apo Bay Overlook   VIEWPOINT
For killer coastal views, pause at the scenic lookout above Honu'apo Bay northeast of Na'alehu. This sweep of shoreline and scrub is part of the longest stretch of undeveloped coastline in Hawaii, and land trusts and the county continue to purchase large sections to keep it that way. On a clear day, you may be able to see Kilauea's Halema'uma'u crater steaming silently above the Ka'u Desert ramping up to the horizon.

Whittington Beach Park   BEACH
(Hwy 11, Mile 60.6) North of Na'alehu, this small park has tide pools, an ancient Hawaiian fishpond frequented by birds, and the photographic ruins of a historic pier. There's no beach despite the name, and swimming is limited to the estuaries, but hawksbill sea turtles frequent. Facilities include restrooms, outdoor showers and picnic pavilions, but no drinking water. Camping by advance county permit only.

✖ Eating

★ Hana Hou Restaurant   DINER $
(☎808-929-9717; www.naalehurestaurant.com; 95-1148 Na'alehu Spur Rd; mains $8-16; ☺8am-7pm Sun-Thu, till 8pm Fri & Sat; 🛜) Hana Hou embodies all the glory and nostalgia of a 1940s family diner – because it was, and still is, one. The menu is filled with local takes on good ol' American comfort food. Come for the peppered mahimahi, but stay for the homemade pies. (We recommend the roasted macadamia nut cream pie.) Sandwiches and wraps are great for picnicking.

Punalu'u Bake Shop   BAKERY $
(☎808-929-7343; www.bakeshophawaii.com; 95-5642 Hwy 11; baked goods $3-8, mains $6-10; ☺9am-5pm) The US's southernmost bakery is squarely on the tour bus circuit and usually crowded – for good reason. If you want to try the Portuguese fried sweet pastry called a *malasada* (you do) get here early. Bonus: clean restrooms, a picnic area outside, and all manner of kitschy Hawaiiana in the gift shop.

Ka'u Farmers Market   MARKET $
(☺7am-noon Wed & Sat) A small farmers market sets up in front of Ace Hardware twice weekly. Grab some fresh fruit on your way through town.

DON'T MISS

KA'ALAIKI ROAD
....

Hit the high road between Pahala and Na'alehu for an elevated look at central Ka'u's even quieter pastoral side. Freshly paved Ka'alaiki Rd (also called Old Cane Haul Rd) crosses rocky cascades between verdant hills with commanding sea views. You'll find coffee farms, macadamia nut plantations, and even eucalyptus forests: one failed attempt at creating a post-sugar economy. Best of all, except for the occasional work truck, you'll likely have it to yourself.

The most striking feature along this route is the **Ninole Hills**, geologic oddities that have puzzled scientists for their relatively old age – which you can see by the gulches and creeks not normally found in younger, porous lava rock. Recent studies of the gravity around here (apparently denser rocks have more gravitational pull) have determined that the 125,000-year-old hills once made up the Southwest Rift Zone. It later shifted several miles northwest, possibly when the Kona slumps released pressure on that side. But while this may mean eruptions are less likely here, landslides like the mile-wide 1868 event (p252) are still a very real threat.

To find the road, turn at Punalu'u Bakeshop in Na'alehu. In Pahala make your way to the northwest edge of town and follow the road out, taking a left at the first three-way intersection.

Shaka Restaurant AMERICAN $$

(☑808-929-7404; 95-5673 Mamalahoa Hwy; mains breakfast & lunch $8-15, dinner $12-22; ☺7am-9pm) Capitalizing on its position as the southernmost place in the USA to get your buzz on, this sports bar excels at the sports, the bar, and the fascinating conversations with local characters. The food on the other hand is just OK, cleanliness questionable, and service hit or miss. Although, they do whip up a surprisingly tasty *loco moco* (dish of rice, fried egg and hamburger patty topped with gravy or other condiments).

Drinking & Nightlife

Flyin' Hawaiian Coffee COFFEE

(☑808-640-4712; www.flyinhawaiiancoffee.com; 95-5668 Mamalahoa Hwy; drinks $3-5; ☺8am-4:30pm Mon, Wed, Sat) Find this coffee truck bathed in a little ray of sunshine on the front lawn of the United Methodist Church three days a week, serving 100% Ka'u coffee in a variety of hyper-caffeinating forms.

Getting There & Away

Hele-On Bus (www.heleonbus.org) sends three coaches daily (one Sunday) from Kona, and one daily (none Sunday) from Hilo.

South Point (Ka Lae)

The southernmost tip of the Big Island, and of the USA, Ka Lae ('the Point') appropriately feels like the end of the earth. The first Polynesian sailors likely made landfall here, and archaeologists suggest it was consistently occupied ever since. Today, however, it's a mostly vacant landscape with a rare green sand beach on one end, and a lofty cliff taunting your inner daredevil on the other.

Sights

★Ka Lae AREA

(South Point Complex; South Point Rd) Ka Lae, the southernmost point of Hawai'i Island, feels palpably unwelcoming, yet hauntingly peaceful. It is mostly an empty grassland fringed by restless rocky shores all scoured by relentless wind. Standing near the actual point, you can imagine the ancient Polynesians landing here, fighting violent surf after months at sea to arrive at...this. But, despite the challenges, early Hawaiians made South Point their home, their

legacy found in rock walls, mooring holes and burial sites scattered throughout the area.

One of the things that kept people here is the confluence of ocean currents just offshore which make South Point one of Hawai'i's most bountiful fishing grounds. It's also one of the most dangerous: the Hala'ea current doesn't hit land again until Antarctica. It was named after a greedy chief who regularly confiscated other people's hard-earned catches. A group of fed-up fishermen decided to answer his demands by simultaneously filling his canoe with every last fish. His boat capsized and the chief was carried away by the current to face his watery judgment.

On land, keep an eye out for the endangered *'ohai* shrub, a member of the pea family. Its oval leaf clusters smell like tangerines and its flowers are often used to make leis.

★Green Sand Beach BEACH

(Papakolea Beach) This legendary beach on Mahana Bay isn't really *that* green, but it is a rare and beautiful sight. Its color comes from crystals of olivine, the mineral found in the semiprecious gemstone known as peridot. Olivine is created in high-heat environments – like during the formation of stars or volcanic eruptions. This batch comes from the latter, and is what's left behind as waves erode the littoral cone looming above the cove. Swimming is only advisable on the very few exceptionally calm days.

To get here take the left (east) fork of South Point Rd some 10 miles from Hwy 11 to the old barracks. Park here (don't leave any valuables in your car) and hike the dusty, windy, hot 2.5 miles to Mahana Bay. Start by heading south to the **Kaulana boat ramp** then veer left (east) following the coastline. The unceasing winds will sandblast your face the entire way making the trip feel twice as far as it is. Bring lots of water.

Alternatively, you can support the local economy by bouncing along in the back of one of the dilapidated 4WD pickups that usually cluster at the barracks offering rides for cash (one way/round trip $10/15) – an adventure in itself.

Whether you arrive on foot or off-road vehicle, you'll have to scramble down the cliff to the beach, which is becoming a major tourist attraction despite the difficult access. Go early, late or when it's overcast to beat the crowds.

Kalalea Heiau
TEMPLE

Testament to the area's important fishing grounds, this ancient temple and shrine is where Hawaiians left offerings in return for a bountiful catch. Some still do today, although their angling methods have changed. Look for salt pans in the area: depressions carved in the rocks where fishermen would evaporate ocean water then use the remaining salt to cure their catch.

🍷 Drinking & Nightlife

Ka Lae Coffee
COFFEE

(📞208-964-3604; kalaecoffeekau@yahoo.com; 94-2166 South Point Rd; ⊗8am-5pm; 📶) Tucked behind a family home and fronting a greenhouse bursting with orchids, the US's southernmost coffee shop is a relaxed place to rejuvenate after a morning at South Point. Yoga classes (by donation) happen among the blossoms every Sunday at 9am, and some Wednesdays.

🛍 Shopping

Paradise Meadows Orchard & Bee Farm
COFFEE

(📞808-929-9148; www.paradisemeadows.com; 93-2199 South Point Rd; ⊗9am-5:30pm) This small farm stand packs a lot in, offering samples of locally produced coffee, honey and mac nuts (though the chocolate is by Guittard). Its crystallized *'ohi'a lehua* honey should be adopted as the official flavor of Hawai'i. Try to coax a tour of the aquaponics greenhouse out of a busy staffer for an interesting look at engineered sustainability.

Ocean View & Around

Ah, Ocean View. Yes, given that it's plastered to the side of scrubby lava flows, nearly every lot in this 10,000-acre subdivision does have a view of the ocean – so what if it's 5 to 10 miles away and several thousand feet down? Of course that lot probably also has views of a neighbor's school bus, yurt or junkyard bristling with 'Stay Away' signs.

For some, this is a rugged, wild place with land 'priced right' for hearty individuals looking for a fresh start. For others, this is a raw, rough scene where land is cheap for a reason. The people who move here either have an acute sense of adventure or greatly value their privacy. Or both.

The best beaches below the subdivision are on private property at the end of gated 4WD roads, leaving the Road to the Sea your only real option for exploring the desolate coast.

◎ Sights

★ Pali'okulani Overlook
VIEWPOINT

Be sure to get your bearings at the Hwy 11 viewpoint perched on a 1907 lava flow. Commanding views take in Pali'okulani, the ragged cliff edge jutting out in front of South Point which protects eastern Ka'u from Mauna Loa's Southwest Rift Zone lava flows. The fault extends far out to sea where the underwater cliffs eventually reach almost 1 mile high. Recent submarine geology expeditions to these *pali* (cliffs) have determined Mauna Loa has been active for at least 650,000 years.

Road to the Sea
AREA

(Humuhumu Point) This high-clearance 4WD road crosses enough *'a'a* (rough, jagged lava) to shake your fillings loose. However, once only for adventurers, these remote black-and-green-sand beaches with looming cliffs and cinder cones are no longer human-free pockets. You may find, after all the trouble of getting here, that the sea is too rough to swim and the beach too windy to enjoy. Even so, this trip into the volcanic 'great beyond' is enjoyable for the scenery alone.

To find the Road to the Sea, turn *makai* (seaward) off Hwy 11 at the row of mailboxes between Miles 79 and 80 (look for the old 'Taki Mama' sign painted on a surfboard). From there it's 6 miles of rudimentary, seemingly never-ending lava which most high-clearance vehicles can handle, but you'll want 4WD at Mile 3.1 where the road drops off a lava bench. It takes about 45 minutes or so to reach the first green-sand beach, depending on how rough you like your ride.

Another 0.5 miles to the east (hike it unless you have a rock-crawler) an incongruous tree provides shade over a bleached coral beach. To the west, a series of littoral cones (mounds of tephra formed as hot lava explosively boils in to the ocean), coves and fishponds provide unending coastal exploration. To get here, head back inland to the yellow gate (now on your left) – which we are assured is for emergency closures only, not to limit access.

Less than 1 mile beyond the gate, you'll reach a red *pu'u* (hill) hiding the crescent green-, black- and white-sand beach where sea turtles frequently nest. The historic **Ala Kahakai National Historic Trail** continues west to **Awili point**, one of a scarce handful of places in Hawaii where the Olive Ridley sea turtle (*Lepidochelys olivacea*) has nested, and the site of a record-setting *ulua* (giant trevally fish) take: 23 in one night.

Bring as much water as you can carry, because it can be a mercilessly hot and shadeless walk in any direction. Every direction recommended.

Manuka State Wayside & Natural Area Reserve PARK
(http://dlnr.hawaii.gov/dsp/parks/hawaii/manuka-state-wayside/; Hwy 11, Mile 81.2) `FREE` This 13-acre reserve offers a pleasant 2-mile nature trail through transitional forest to a volcanic crater. Following the uneven lava rock path, and assisted by an interpretive trail guide, you'll identify 30 species of plants, find historic agricultural sites, and explore old lava flows – although some of the interpretive signs have wandered off in recent years. Bring bug repellent.

👉 Tours

⭐ **Kula Kai Caverns** TOURS
(☎808-929-9725; www.kulakaicaverns.com; 92-8864 Lauhala Dr; tours adult/child 6-12yr from $20/10) Polished underground tours are led by conservationists who emphasize respectful stewardship of these 'living museums.' The geologically interesting caves are accessible to casual visitors during a basic hour-long tour which explores a short, lighted cave section. Enthusiastic guides present Hawai'i's cavern-oriented cultural and ecological history. There's also a longer 'crawling' tour ($60) and a two-hour extended twilight tour ($95). Group sizes are kept small, usually with a two- or four-person minimum. Reservations are required.

🍴 Eating

Ocean View Market SUPERMARKET
(Hwy 11, Ocean View Town Center; ⊙6am-9pm) By the post office and an auto-parts store, this community grocery store sells hot food and sandwiches and a decent variety of goods and fresh produce, especially considering how far out this spot is located.

LO'IHI SEAMOUNT

The Hawaiian Islands' youngest volcano is still well below the ocean and likely won't make its fiery debut for another 10,000 years or more, if at all. It has been growing at an average rate of 0.1ft per year over its 400,000 year life span. Although an eruption caused a swarm of over 4,000 earthquakes in 1996 (three of which rattled the residents of Ka'u), lately Loi'hi has been relatively quiet, and its summit is still 3200ft below sea level.

A 2014 expedition to map and study Loi'hi sampled unique iron-eating bacterial mats found at the base of the mountain – a crushing 3 miles under the ocean.

⭐ **Mehe's Ka'u Bar & Grill** AMERICAN $
(☎808-929-7200; 92-8754 Hawaii Blvd; mains $8-13; ⊙lunch 11am-3:30pm, dinner 5-9pm, bar 10am-10pm, till 2am Fri) In an area with few options, Mehe's is a surprisingly good one. Friendly staff serve burgers, sandwiches and a rotating selection of daily specials to local characters and visitors alike while the horseshoe bar buzzes with the latest Ocean View gossip. Karaoke is the most 'happening' thing between Kona and Hilo on a Friday night.

Ka-Lae Garden THAI $
(☎808-494-7688; www.kalaegarden.com; 92-8395 Mamalahoa Hwy; mains $10-12; ⊙11am-7pm Wed-Sun) The dishes served in this tiny restaurant are made-to-order with fresh ingredients, some of which are grown in the organic herb garden behind the building. Skip the pad Thai and tuck into a steaming bowl of Panang curry with a side of crisp green papaya salad.

DJ's Pizza and Bakeshop PIZZA $$
(☎808-929-9800; www.djspizzabakeshop.com; 92-8674 Lotus Blossom Lane; pizza slice $3, full pizza $16-23, sandwiches $11; ⊙10:30am-8pm Mon-Sat; 🖉) The pizza is only above-average, however, the gluten-free crust and vegan meatball sandwich are a welcome find in the area. Come here to satisfy your sweet treat cravings with custom-baked pies and cakes made with advance notice (worth the wait).

ℹ Getting There & Away

Hele-On Bus (www.heleonbus.org) runs three times daily (one Sunday) to Kona, and one daily (none Sunday) to Volcano and Hilo. Given the overlap, there are three or four daily buses heading as far as Pahala.

Kahuku Unit

In 2003, the Hawai'i Volcanoes National Park and the Nature Conservancy jointly bought historic Kahuku Ranch in the biggest conservation land purchase in the state's history. This deal added a whopping 116,000 acres to the park, increasing its size by over 50%.

Kahuku is part of Hawai'i's largest traditional *ahupua'a* (land division). Sacred bird catchers once scoured the upper forests to make the yellow and red *'ahu 'ula* (royal feather cloaks) while the lowlands were important farming grounds. It was also the epicenter for Hawai'i's ranching heritage, which haphazardly started with King Kamehameha I, and was formalized under Captain Robert Brown. It continued through several owners (and their neighbors) until the National Park Service finally took over.

Today, the Kahuku Unit remains a largely wild, undeveloped and under-visited playground for history buffs and nature lovers.

◉ Sights

Kahuku Unit's four hiking trails that lead through green pastures to volcanic cinder cones, lava tree molds, rainforests and lava flows come alive during the excellent ranger-guided hikes (offered some weekends; advance reservations not usually required), but you are welcome to enjoy them by yourself on any weekend (Friday to Sunday). Double-check opening hours at Kilauea Visitor Center before making the trip, as the park keeps expanding them. The entrance is 4 miles west of Wai'ohinu *mauka* (inland) off Hwy 11 at Mile 70.5.

For a self-guided walking tour through Kahuku Ranch, see p260.

Pu'u o Lokuana   HISTORIC SITE

High points like this red cinder cone make great lookouts no matter whether you're Kamehameha keeping an eye out for rival chief Keoua in the 1780s, Captain Brown watching lava consume your house in 1868, or the US Army scanning for Japanese ships and planes using secret new RADAR technology in 1942. In the last case, the looking-out happened below ground where 'scope dopes' analyzed blips transmitted from the tower above to monitoring rooms carved into the cone's core.

The concrete blocks of the radar tower were set aside as the ranch mined the top 100ft of cinder to pave area roads.

ℹ Getting There & Away

Although part of Hawai'i Volcanoes National Park, the Kahuku Unit is 42 miles southwest on Hwy 11 from the main park entrance.

Unfortunately, the Hele-On Bus schedule makes visiting via public transportation impractical.

Understand Hawai'i, the Big Island

Hawai'i, the Big Island Today

Aloha 'aina – 'love of the land' in Hawaiian – is a traditional Hawaiian attitude that now resonates with many. Hawai'i residents, whether kama'aina (born and raised here) or transplants, and visitors too, value the island. But due to divergent interpretations, islanders sometimes clash. Major issues on Hawai'i include tourism and the economy, post-sugar agriculture and Native Hawaiian rights.

Best on Film

Song of South Kona (1986) Miloli'i, the 'last Hawaiian fishing village,' and its people are revealed in this evocative documentary.

Black Widow (1987) Location buffs will appreciate the scenes in Hilo's Kaikodo Building in the movie's climax.

The Descendants (2011) Glimpse contemporary island life of a well-to-do Honolulu family.

Best in Print

Wild Meat and the Bully Burgers (Lois-Ann Yamanaka; 1996) Growing up local in 1970s Hilo, told with raw emotion in pidgin.

Pele, the Fire Goddess (Pua Kanaka'ole Kanahele and Dietrich Varez; 1991) Legend of Pele retold by a renowned *kumu* hula (hula teacher) and strikingly illustrated.

Kapoho: Memoir of a Modern Pompeii (Frances Kakugawa; 2011) Memories of Kapoho, demolished by lava when the author was 18.

Best in Music

Lei Pua Kenikeni (Mark Yamanaka; 2010) Falsetto vocalist with Japanese heritage and Hawaiian soul.

Hear (Brittni Paiva; 2005) This then-teenage prodigy plays ukulele, bass, guitar and keyboards.

Memories of You (Diana Aki; 1990) The 'songbird of Miloli'i' epitomizes the Hawaiian falsetto style.

Economic Recovery

Since the 1960s, Hawai'i's economy has rested primarily on tourism, an industry blamed for burdening infrastructure and natural resources, increasing traffic and disturbing residential neighborhoods. Tourism is subject to national economic trends. The 2008 recession hammered the influx of visitors for over five years: in 2013, Hawai'i saw 1.3 million visitors, down 25% from its 2007 peak of 1.6 million. But by 2016, Hawai'i's visitor counts recovered to 1.5 million. Even a dengue fever outbreak from late 2015 to early 2016 didn't deter travelers.

In another positive sign for tourism, Hawaiian Airlines launched a thrice-weekly Kona–Japan route in 2016. Japan Airlines had cut its route to Kona International Airport in 2010 – a blow, considering Japan's steady tourist stream. (Direct flights between Hilo and the mainland are still limited to one Los Angeles route.)

On the ground, Airbnb has proliferated across the island, creating a huge new pool of accommodations. While popular with travelers, some hotels and B&Bs complain about financial disparity. With their official permits, they pay higher property taxes in addition to business income taxes. Airbnb hosts? Maybe, maybe not.

During the recession, the island's overall unemployment rate hovered around 10% and home prices dropped, especially in Puna. By mid 2016, however, unemployment was down to 4%, slightly higher than the statewide 3.2% rate, but lower than the nationwide average of 4.5%.

Sustainable Agriculture

The end of Hawai'i's sugar industry in the mid 1990s came at a somewhat fortuitous time. By the early 2000s, a locavore movement was sprouting, in tandem with widespread interest in all things 'gourmet.' Who's not a foodie nowadays? The average person recognized the benefits of locally sourced, small-scale, organic, top-quality food.

Hawai'i's agriculture successfully diversified into signature coffee, papayas, macadamia nuts and orchids – as well as aquaculture and boutique crops from mushrooms to tea to, yes, medical marijuana. Meanwhile, the Big Island still has the largest cattle operation, Parker Ranch, and the only two remaining dairy cattle farms statewide.

To be sustainable, however, local agriculture must be an everyday experience. 'Eat local' is still a catchphrase and not reality, with 85% to 90% of food still imported. Simply put, locals must produce – and eat – more local food, which can cost significantly more than mass-produced imports.

Since the late 2000s, 'agritourism' has blossomed on Hawai'i Island, with many working farms now welcoming visitors. Farmers have established successful collaborations with restaurants, chefs, grocery and retail stores and even the solar energy industry. Hawai'i County is the only county statewide with a specific ordinance recognizing agritourism, which is not embraced by all. Some warn that farmers might focus more on profitable tourist enterprises than on actual farming – and affect their rural neighbors' lifestyles and property taxes.

Development vs Culture

Island land use will always be controversial, as the government, private owners and the general public often have competing interests. Prime coastal properties owned by the state or county are sometimes converted to beach parks – a recent example is Kekaha Kai State Park. But the latest scuffle involves Mauna Kea and the Thirty Meter Telescope (TMT) that was approved by the state in 2013.

In October 2014 and throughout 2015, protestors successfully blocked not only physical access to the summit, but also further development of the gigantic telescope. The original 'Save Mauna Kea' movement was soon embraced by other activists, including GMO (genetically modified organism) opponents, native sovereignty fighters and general environmentalists – and became a remarkable grassroots success story. Some officials want the summit area to continue as an observatory site, but also to become a park – to return the land to the people and to stop the impasse.

Such protests about the *'aina* reflect today's chapter in the Hawaiian Renaissance that commenced in the 1970s, a rebirth of Native Hawaiian cultural, artistic and linguistic traditions.

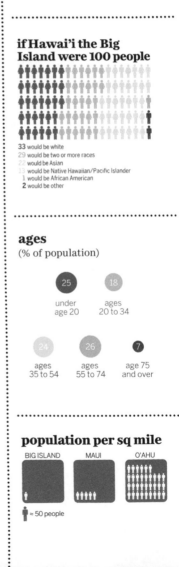

POPULATION: **196,430**

AREA: **4028 SQ MI**

CURRENCY: **US DOLLAR ($)**

GDP: **GROSS BUSINESS RECEIPTS: $4887 MILLION**

TIME: **HAWAII-ALEUTIAN STANDARD TIME (GMT/ UTC MINUS 10 HOURS)**

if Hawai'i the Big Island were 100 people

33 would be white
29 would be two or more races
22 would be Asian
13 would be Native Hawaiian/Pacific Islander
1 would be African American
2 would be other

ages
(% of population)

25 under age 20

18 ages 20 to 34

24 ages 35 to 54

26 ages 55 to 74

7 age 75 and over

population per sq mile

BIG ISLAND   MAUI   O'AHU

= 50 people

History

Hawaii's discovery is one of humanity's great epic tales, starting with ancient Polynesians who first found their way to these tiny islands. Almost a millennium passed before Western explorers, whalers and missionaries arrived. In the tumultuous 19th century, a global melting pot of immigrants came to work on Hawaii's plantations before the kingdom founded by Kamehameha the Great was overthrown, making way for US annexation.

Polynesian Migrations

The earliest settlers to Hawaii were Polynesians, long believed to have arrived from the Marqueses Islands between AD 300 and 600. Another wave arrived from Tahiti around AD 1000, and they apparently conquered the original settlers and settled in significant numbers across the major islands. They landed at Ka Lae, the southernmost point of Hawai'i, where adzes, fishhooks, pendants and ruins of heiau (temples) have been found.

Polynesians journeyed back and forth between Hawaii and Tahiti, proving that their ability to navigate across 2000-plus miles was no fluke. They were highly skilled seafarers, crossing open ocean in double-hulled canoes not with maps but the sun, stars, wind and waves to guide them. They brought over two dozen food plants (now known as 'canoe plants'), including taro, sweet potato, sugarcane and coconut, along with chickens, pigs and dogs.

Ancient Hawai'i

When for unknown reasons the trans-Pacific canoe voyages stopped around AD 1500, ancient Hawaiian culture evolved in isolation, but with similarities to cultures throughout Polynesia. Hawaiian society was highly stratified, ruled by a chiefly class called *ali'i* whose power derived from their ancestry: they were believed to be descended from the gods. In ancient Hawai'i, clan loyalty trumped individuality, elaborate traditions of gifting and feasting conferred prestige, and a pantheon of shape-shifting gods animated the natural world.

Ancient Hawaiian Sites

....

Halema'uma'u, Hawai'i Volcanoes National Park

....

Pu'uhonua O Honaunau National Historical Park, Honaunau

....

Puako Petroglyph Preserve, Puako

....

Pu'ukohola Heiau National Historic Site, Kawaihae

....

Ka Lae, South Point

....

Keanakako'i & Lake Wai'au, Mauna Kea

TIMELINE

30 million BC	AD 300–600	1000–1300
The first Hawaiian island, Kure, rises from the sea, where the Big Island is today. Borne by wind, wing and wave, plants, insects and birds colonize the new land.	The first wave of Polynesians, most likely from the Marquesas Islands, voyage by canoe to the Hawaiian Islands.	Sailing from Tahiti, a second wave of Polynesians arrives. Their tools are made of stone, shell and bone.

VOYAGING BY THE STARS

Can humans sail 2400 miles, from Hawaii to Tahiti, without radar, compass, satellites or sextant? In 1976, a Hawaiian group sailed from O'ahu in a double-hulled wooden canoe called *Hokule'a* ('Star of Gladness') – to reenact the ancient Polynesian voyaging of their ancestors.

The Polynesian Voyaging Society, which launched the project, needed a navigator who still possessed knowledge of traditional wayfaring – and they found one in Micronesian master navigator, Mau Piailug. He knew how to guide a vessel using horizon or zenith stars (which always rose over known islands), ocean currents, winds, landmarks and time. (The trick is to hold the canoe still in relation to the stars while the island sails toward you.)

Academic skeptics had long questioned whether early Hawaiian settlers could have journeyed back and forth across such vast distances. After 33 days at sea, the crew of the *Hokule'a* achieved the so-called impossible by reaching Tahiti. This historic achievement helped spark a revival of interest in Hawaii's Polynesian cultural heritage.

Since its 1976 voyage, the *Hokule'a* has made 10 more trans-oceanic voyages, sailing throughout Polynesia and to the US mainland, Canada, Micronesia and Japan. Its latest voyage, which began in 2014, will circumnavigate the globe, visiting over 26 countries and traveling more than 45,000 nautical miles before returning to Hawaii in 2017. Learn more at www.hokulea.com.

Ranking just below *ali'i*, kahuna (experts or masters) included priests, healers and skilled craftspeople like canoe makers. The largest class was the *maka'ainana* (commoners), who could live wherever they pleased, but who were obligated to support the *ali'i* through taxes paid in kind with food, goods and physical labor. The lowest *kaua* (outcast or untouchable) class was shunned and did not mix with the other classes, except as slaves or human sacrificial victims.

Captain Cook & Western Contact

On January 18, 1778, British naval explorer Captain James Cook accidentally sailed into the main Hawaiian Islands chain while searching for the fabled Northwest Passage. Ending several hundred years of cultural isolation, his arrival irrevocably altered the course of Hawaiian history. When Cook dropped anchor off O'ahu to barter for fresh water and food, as he had elsewhere in the Pacific, Hawaiians knew absolutely nothing of Europeans, nor of the metals, guns and diseases their ships carried.

When Cook returned to the islands almost a year later, he sailed around before eventually anchoring at Kealakekua Bay in South Kona. Cook's ships were greeted by a thousand canoes, and Hawaiian chiefs

1778–79	1791	1793	1810
Captain Cook, the first foreigner known to reach the islands, visits Hawai'i twice. On his second visit, a conflict over a stolen boat leads to his death in Kealakekua.	Kamehameha I establishes Pu'ukohola Heiau in his quest to rule first Hawai'i and then the other major islands.	Cattle arrive on Hawai'i as a gift from British Captain George Vancouver to Kamehameha I.	Kamehameha I unites the major Hawaiian Islands into one sovereign kingdom. His royal court moves from Lahaina, Maui, to Honolulu, O'ahu.

HAWAIIAN DEATH PENALTY

In ancient Hawai'i, a strict code – called the *kapu* (taboo) system – governed every aspect of daily life. It prohibited *ali'i* (royalty) from mingling with commoners and men from eating with women; it kept women from eating pork or entering *luakini* heiau (sacrificial temples). It determined whom they married and when they fished or harvested crops. Penalties for transgressions often meant death.

Although fiercely uncompromising, ancient society was also forgiving at times. Anyone who had broken *kapu* or been defeated in battle could avoid the death penalty by fleeing to a *pu'uhona* (place of refuge). At the heiau (temple), a kahuna (priest) would perform purification rituals, lasting a few hours up to several days. Absolved of their transgressions, *kapu* breakers were free to return home in safety. In South Kona, Pu'uhonua o Honaunau National Historical Park is a vivid example of such a refuge.

and priests honored him. Cook had landed during the makahiki festival, a time of celebration in honor of the god Lono, and some have hypothesized that the Hawaiians mistook Cook for the god.

Cook set sail some weeks later, but storms forced him to turn back. By then the makahiki had ended, and suspicion replaced welcome. A series of minor conflicts provoked a skirmish between Cook and the local chief, Kalaniopu'u. When Cook fatally shot a Hawaiian man, he was immediately mobbed and killed on February 14, 1779.

Once 'discovered,' the Hawaiian Islands became a prime Pacific way-station for traders, who would buy furs in the Pacific Northwest and stop here for supplies and fragrant *'iliahi* (sandalwood), then a valuable commodity in China. By the 1840s, Hawaii also became the whaling capital of the Pacific, with over 700 whaling ships stopping at Hawaiian ports annually. The main commodity in the islands was salt – happened to be useful for curing hides. For Hawaiian chiefs, the main items of interest were firearms, which the Europeans willingly traded.

> When Kamehameha the Great died, two loyal chiefs buried him in a secret place to prevent rivals from stealing his bones, which were believed to hold great *mana* (spiritual power or essence). That place remains a secret today.

Kamehameha the Great

Kamehameha ('Lonely One') was born in the Big Island's North Kohala district around 1753. Belonging to the *ali'i* (royalty) class, he became a strong warrior under the guidance of his powerful uncle, Chief Kalaniopu'u. As a young man, Kamehameha was present with his uncle at Kealakekua Bay when Captain Cook was killed in 1779.

At the time, the major islands of Hawai'i, Kaua'i, Maui and O'ahu were independently ruled. Kamehameha I took control of Kona and Kohala by 1782, but fought inconclusively for eight years to rule all of Hawai'i. When a kahuna advised him to build a *luakini* heiau (sacrificial temple)

1820	1826	1848	1863
The first Christian missionaries to the Hawaiian Islands land at Kailua-Kona.	Missionaries formulate an alphabet for the Hawaiian language and set up the first printing press.	King Kamehameha III institutes the Great Mahele, a land redistribution act. Two years later, further legislation allows commoners and foreigners to own land for the first time.	Kohala Sugar Company, the island's first sugar plantation, is established.

to appease the war god Kuka'ilimoku, the result was Pu'ukohola Heiau, built in less than a year in Kawaihae. In 1791 he killed a rival cousin to become *ali'i* of Hawai'i.

Kamehameha then began a monumental campaign to conquer the other major islands. In 1810, after gaining control of Maui, O'ahu and Kaua'i, Kamehameha became the first *mo'i* (king) of the Kingdom of Hawai'i, named after his birthplace. Kamehameha was a shrewd politician, a savvy businessman and a singular leader who reigned over the most peaceful era in Hawaiian history.

While Kamehameha I absorbed foreign influences, he fastidiously honored traditional culture, despite simmering doubts among his people about the justice of the *kapu* system. When he died at his home in Kailua-Kona in 1819, his son, 22-year-old Liholiho (Kamehameha II), joined the changing tide. In a shocking act of repudiation, Liholiho, egged on by his father's favorite wife, Queen Ka'ahumanu, broke the *kapu* against men and women eating together and ordered many heiau (temples) and *ki'i* (deity images) destroyed. Hawaiian society plunged into chaos.

Christian Missionaries & Hawaiian Converts

Hawai'i's first Protestant missionaries chanced upon a fortuitous time and place to arrive. American Congregationalists from Boston landed at Kailua Bay on April 19, 1820, less than a year after Kamehameha I died. As Hawai'i's ancient religion had just been abolished, missionaries found a receptive audience. Because the missionaries' god was clearly powerful, Christianity attracted Hawaiian converts, notably Queen Ka'ahumanu.

Another novel concept that attracted interest was literacy. Ancient Hawaiians had no written language; they preserved their mythology through lengthy oral epics, recited word for word by trained kahuna. The missionaries established a Hawaiian alphabet using Roman letters and Hawaiians, accustomed to prodigious feats of memory, rapidly learned to read and write. By the mid 1850s, Hawai'i had a literacy rate higher than the US rate.

Eventually, missionaries banned the Hawaiian language in schools in order to distance Hawaiians from their 'hedonistic' cultural roots. They abolished public nudity, polygamy (which was accepted and even necessary in the isolated islands), and 'lewd' hula dancing and chants and songs that honored 'heathen' gods.

Many missionaries became influential royal advisors and received large tracts of land in return, prompting them to leave the church altogether and turn their land into sugar plantations. It is often said that the missionaries came to do good – and did very well.

History Museums

Hawaii Plantation Museum, Papaikou

Lyman Museum & Mission House, Hilo

Pacific Tsunami Museum, Hilo

Hulihe'e Palace, Kailua-Kona

'Imiloa Astronomy Center of Hawai'i, Hilo

Laupahoehoe Train Museum, Laupahoehoe

Hawaii Japanese Center, Hilo

HISTORY CHRISTIAN MISSIONARIES & HAWAIIAN CONVERTS

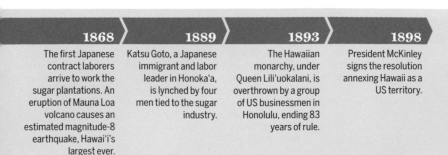

1868	1889	1893	1898
The first Japanese contract laborers arrive to work the sugar plantations. An eruption of Mauna Loa volcano causes an estimated magnitude-8 earthquake, Hawai'i's largest ever.	Katsu Goto, a Japanese immigrant and labor leader in Honoka'a, is lynched by four men tied to the sugar industry.	The Hawaiian monarchy, under Queen Lili'uokalani, is overthrown by a group of US businessmen in Honolulu, ending 83 years of rule.	President McKinley signs the resolution annexing Hawaii as a US territory.

The Great Mahele

Traditionally, no Hawaiian owned land. Instead the *ali'i* constituted an absolute monarchy and managed the *'aina* in stewardship for all. This didn't sit well with resident US expatriates, who considered voting and land ownership to be fundamental rights.

In 1840 King Kamehameha III (Kauikeaouli) tried to modernize the Hawaiian political system by promulgating Hawai'i's first constitution, which established a constitutional monarchy with limited citizen representation. Then, instigated by foreigners, he passed a series of revolutionary land reform acts beginning with the Great Mahele ('Great Division') of 1848.

The Great Mahele was intended to create a nation of small freeholder farmers, but it was a disaster for Hawaiians. Unused to the concept of private land ownership, many Hawaiians simply failed to do the paperwork to claim property titles or, if they did, impulsively cashed out, selling their land to acquisitive foreigners.

Within 30 to 40 years, foreigners owned fully three-quarters of the kingdom, and Hawaiians – who had already relinquished so much of their traditional culture so quickly during the 19th century – lost their sacred connection to the land.

> Born and raised on a farm, Gerald Kinro brings personal insight into *A Cup of Aloha*, an oral-history portrait of Kona's coffee industry.

King Sugar & the Plantation Era

Ko (sugarcane) was a 'canoe plant,' introduced by the first Polynesians. In the 1830s, foreigners realized Hawai'i was ideal for growing sugarcane and promptly established small plantations using low-cost Hawaiian labor. Due to introduced diseases including typhoid, influenza, smallpox and syphilis, however, the Hawaiian population had precipitously declined. By some estimates around 800,000 indigenous people lived on the islands before Western contact. By 1860 Hawaiians numbered fewer than 70,000.

To fill the labor shortage, plantation workers were imported from overseas. First, beginning in the 1850s, came Chinese laborers and soon after Japanese and Portuguese immigrants. After the US annexed Hawaii in 1898, Puerto Ricans, Koreans and Filipinos arrived. These diverse immigrant groups transformed Hawai'i into the multiethnic, multicultural society it is today.

During California's Gold Rush and later the US Civil War, Hawai'i's sugar exports to the mainland soared. As late as 1960, 'King Sugar' remained the state's largest industry. Due to cheaper labor and production costs abroad, however, the 1960s marked a turning point. On Hawai'i, smaller companies along the sugar-dominated Hamakua Coast began consolidating in the 1970s. Hamakua Sugar Company still had some 800

> Five holding companies, known as the Big Five, dominated the sugar industry: Castle & Cooke, Alexander & Baldwin, C Brewer & Co, American Factors and Theo H Davies & Co. Today only Alexander & Baldwin remains. Now diversified into other holdings, it's still powerful and the fifth-largest landowner statewide.

1916	1921	1946	1959
Hawai'i Volcanoes National Park is established.	The Hawaiian Homes Commission Act sets aside 200,000 acres for homesteading by Hawaiians with 50% or more Native Hawaiian blood, granting 99-year leases costing $1 a year.	Hawaii's most destructive tsunami, generated by an Alaskan earthquake, kills 122 people on Hawai'i Island.	Hawaii becomes the 50th US state. Hawaii's Daniel Inouye, a decorated WWII vet, is the first Japanese American elected to the US Congress.

CATTLE & PANIOLOS

In 1793, Captain George Vancouver gave King Kamehameha a few cattle, a gift that would irrevocably affect Hawai'i's economy and ecology. Aided by a 10-year *kapu* on cattle (which was not lifted until 1830), the original small herd proliferated into a dangerous nuisance. Wild cattle destroyed crops and houses, and they attacked people. In 1832, Kamehameha III sought help from California cowboys.

Three Spanish-Mexican *vaquero* (cowboys) moved to Hawai'i and began breaking in horses and rounding up hordes of cattle. They became known as *paniolo* (a corruption of *espanol*, Spanish, the language that they spoke), a term still used to refer to island cowboys. Hawaiians were quick to learn and excel in horsemanship and roping. The oldest and largest ranch across Hawaii is Parker Ranch (p158), established in Waimea by John Palmer Parker, a sailor from Massachusetts.

workers in the 1980s, but it closed in 1993. Ka'u Sugar Company, the last on the island, closed in 1996.

Hawaiian Kingdom Overthrown

King David Kalakaua, who reigned from 1874 to 1891, fought to restore Hawaiian culture, arts and indigenous pride. He composed 'Hawai'i Pono'i,' the state song today. In 1887, a secret antimonarchy organization, headed mostly by Americans, forced Kalakaua to sign a new constitution under the threat of violence. The 'Bayonet Constitution' reduced the king to a figurehead. It also limited voting rights, effectively disenfranchising all but wealthy, mostly white businessmen and landowners. Soon the US got its base at Pearl Harbor, and foreigners consolidated their power.

When Kalakaua died, his sister Lili'uokalani ascended the throne and tried to restore the monarchy. On January 17, 1893, a 'Committee of Safety,' composed mostly of haole (Caucasian) American residents and supported by US Minister John Stevens and a contingent of US marines and sailors, forcibly arrested her and took over Honolulu's 'Iolani Palace in a tense but bloodless coup d'état.

The 50th State

After the short-lived Republic of Hawai'i was annexed as a US territory in 1898, the road to statehood was long and bumpy. The islands presented new issues: distance from the mainland, strong labor unions and a huge non-white population. But a series of significant events paved the way.

In 1936 Pan American Airways began regular commercial flights from the US mainland to Hawaii, launching the transpacific air age and mass tourism. Wireless telegraph service, followed by telephone service,

In ancient Hawai'i, each island was divided into *moku* (districts), wedge-shaped regions running from the mountains to the sea. *Moku* were subdivided into smaller, similarly wedge-shaped, self-sustaining *ahupua'a*. For example, Kona is a *moku* containing Honaunau, an *ahupua'a*.

1960	1971	1983	1993
A tsunami generated off South America destroys over 100 buildings and kills 61 people in Hilo.	Hilo's Merrie Monarch Festival holds its first hula competition, highlighting a cultural renaissance.	Kilauea volcano begins an eruption cycle now the longest in recorded history. Lava flows eventually destroy the entire village of Kalapana, residential subdivisions and a coastal road.	Federal 'Apology Bill' acknowledges the US government's role in the kingdom's illegal takeover a century ago.

For an encyclopedia-like resource on Hawaiian history, visit www.hawaii-history.org for a handy timeline and informative summaries on ancient and modern Hawaii.

A 2010 study using high-precision radiocarbon dating of samples discovered that Hawaiian migrations occurred between AD 1190 and 1290 – much more recently and rapidly than commonly believed.

between Hawaii and the mainland alleviated doubts about long-distance communication. Most important, WWII proved the strategic military role of O'ahu's Pearl Harbor and the Hawaiian Islands generally.

While Southern conservatives, both Democrat and Republic, remained wary of the islands' multicultural melting pot, Hawaii became the 50th US state in 1959. More than 90% of island residents voting for statehood. After statehood, tourism exploded, thanks to the advent of jet airplanes and the commercializing of Hawaii (think tiki craze, *Blue Hawaii*, aloha shirts and Waikiki). Hotel construction boomed, and the architecturally acclaimed Mauna Kea Beach Hotel opened in 1965, setting the gold standard for archetypal beach resorts. By 1970 tourism would add $1 billion annually to state coffers. By then, sugar and pineapple plantations were struggling, and tourism was Hawaii's obvious replacement industry.

Native Hawaiian Renaissance

In 1976, the homegrown Polynesian Voyaging Society built and sailed *Hokule'a* – a replica of a traditional Polynesian double-hulled canoe – from O'ahu to Tahiti and back. Suddenly traditional Hawaiian culture garnered widespread attention. The same year, a small grassroots group, Protect Kaho'olawe 'Ohana (PKO), began illegally occupying Kaho'olawe, an island taken by the US government during WWII and used as a practice bombing site; it was returned to the state in 1994.

After the state held its landmark Constitutional Convention in 1978, public schools were mandated to teach Hawaiian language, and Hawaiian-immersion charter schools proliferated. Hawaiian became an official state language (in addition to English). Local residents – of all ethnicities – showed new interest in Hawaiian culture, especially hula and music.

Small but vocal contingents of political activists began pushing for some measure of Hawaiian sovereignty, from complete secession from the USA to a nation-within-a-nation model. Today the US federal government still has not acknowledged Native Hawaiians as an indigenous people, however.

2000	2006	2008	2013
US Senator Daniel Akaka first introduces the Native Hawaiian Government Reorganization Act (the 'Akaka Bill'), asking for federal recognition of Native Hawaiians as indigenous people.	Papahanuamokuakea Marine National Monument, protecting the remote Northwestern Hawaiian Islands, is established. Designated a World Heritage Site in 2010; expanded in geographical area in 2016.	O'ahu-born Barack Obama becomes the first African American US President; he is reelected in 2012. In both races, he wins over 70% of the Hawaii vote.	Hawai'i County Bill 113 was passed, keeping biotech companies out and prohibiting farmers from growing GMO crops (exemption granted for papayas).

People of the Big Island

Mention Hawai'i and you might start fantasizing about sandy beaches, swaying palms and blazing sunsets. But the heart of the Big Island is found elsewhere: in its diverse people. Whether residents are Native Hawaiian, *kama'aina* or transplanted from afar, they're united by small-town values, respect for multicultural traditions, interracial tolerance and enthusiastic pursuit of 'the good life.'

Big Island Identity

First-timers to the Big Island might be surprised at its 'normalcy.' With shopping malls, SUVs and big-name coffee chains and groceries, the island has many commonalities with Anytown, USA. Underneath the veneer of consumer culture and the tourist machine, however, is a different world, defined by – and proud of – its otherness, its geographic remoteness and its unique blend of Polynesian, Asian and Western traditions.

East vs West Hawai'i

While Honolulu folk view Hilo, the capital town, as 'country' or even da boonies (the boondocks), everything's relative. Here, Hilo is 'town,' where people wear unwrinkled aloha shirts and wristwatches, work in government offices, sleep early and lead ordinary lives. In Hilo, people go way back; locals are likely to bump into high school classmates around town and, upon meeting another local, they're likely to discover a network of mutual acquaintances and connections. With the highest statewide percentage of Japanese Americans (33%), Hilo's plantation roots are clear.

In contrast, Kailua-Kona has become the island's economical powerhouse and tourist hub. (In 2014, visitor arrivals at Kona international airport numbered 1.2 million, more than twice the half-million arrivals at Hilo airport.) It's busy and 'haole-fied,' with a 48% white population due to an influx of transplants. It's less of a tight community, unless you're already locally rooted. Traffic along the Queen Ka'ahumanu Hwy is a nightmare, and Kailua residents often gripe about the county's short-sightedness in improving Kona's jammed roads when Hilo is sitting pretty with a well-planned system.

The differences between Hilo and Kailua-Kona spread into adjacent east-west regions. While mainlanders might consider the cross-island distance moderate (or even rather short), Big Islanders are typically rooted to their locality. Some folks can barely recall the last time they visited the other side of the island (much less truly remote Ka'u).

Being Local

The Big Island personality is informal, unpretentious and sincere – the best of small-town attributes. Locals embrace their longstanding connections, often maintaining friendships with high-school classmates and invariably bumping into familiar faces whenever they step out. As a rule,

ISLAND ETIQUETTE

→ Don't be pushy and 'no make waves' (don't make a scene). Common courtesy is highly rated here.

→ Don't try to speak pidgin.

→ Try to correctly pronounce Hawaiian place names and words. Even if you fail, the attempt is appreciated.

→ Don't overdress, but don neat, casual sportswear.

→ Remove your shoes before entering homes, including B&Bs.

→ Don't collect or even move stones, coral or any natural object. Treat ancient Hawaiian sacred sites (essentially all of nature) with respect.

→ Ask permission before picking flowers or fruit on private property.

→ Give a *shaka* (Hawaii's hand-greeting sign) if another driver lets you merge.

→ Tread lightly at 'locals only' beaches.

→ Don't freak out at every gecko and cockroach. It's the tropics. There are critters.

loud assertiveness is considered unseemly. It's better to avoid embarrassing confrontations and to 'save face' by keeping quiet.

Politically, the majority are moderate Democrats, often voting along party, racial, ethnic, seniority and local/nonlocal lines. Most locals are not overtly political, and the most vocal, liberal and passionate speakers at community meetings are typically brash mainland transplants pushing for environmental conservation, sustainability, slow growth and non-GMO food. 'Loudmouth haole,' locals might think. But younger Native Hawaiians have recently made headlines in their successful grassroots efforts to stop further telescope development on Mauna Kea.

Locals generally support progressive trends, keeping with the Hawaiian concept of *aloha 'aina* (love of the land). But they are less averse to big-box chain stores and mass-produced packaged goods. While big-name grocery stores might be anathema to politically left-leaning mainlanders, budget-minded locals just trying to get by welcome the discounts and variety. And despite guzzling expensive gas, a monster-size pickup truck remains the status-symbol vehicle for many locals.

Lifestyle

The typical Hawai'i lifestyle is changing with the influence of newcomers and less-traditional younger generations, but Big Islanders generally center their lives around family. The workday starts and ends early; even workaholics tend to be backyard gardeners, surfers or golfers. Not surprisingly, Hawaii residents have the longest life expectancy in the US: 81.3 years.

Regional differences can be stark. For example, Puna is teeming with off-the-grid types who grow their own food and live in makeshift shelters, eschewing creature comforts like hot showers. In Hilo and Kona, choosing such a lifestyle is practically unheard of (or regarded as far-out hippie culture). In Hawai'i's major towns, locals tend toward the conventional 'American dream,' meaning marriage, kids, a comfortable home and stable employment. Among locals, there can be pressure to conform – to take over the family restaurant or dental practice. There's a strong sense of family loyalty, legacy and continuity here.

Mainland transplants typically arrive with more money and different dreams – a second career running a B&B or a coffee plantation, carefree retirement or youthful experimentation. Here on Hawai'i, mainlanders feel free to be unconventional, and they often take risks or try novel ventures that might deter locals.

O'ahu and Maui expats constitute a newer wave of transplants. While Hilo has long been viewed as a rainy backwoods, older generations now say, 'Hilo still feels like old Hawaii.' Hawai'i real estate remains the most affordable statewide, while urban problems from traffic to crime remain tolerable. High density is still quite unknown here, making it ideal for 'gentleman farmers' and anyone seeking wide open spaces.

Family

'Ohana (family) extends beyond bloodlines to close friends, co-workers, classmates and teammates. To possess the *'ohana* spirit means you are welcoming and generous, as a family should be.

Hanai (adopted or foster) children are common in Hawaiian families, which are typically close-knit beyond the nuclear family. Indeed, people often refer to a 'calabash cousin,' meaning a close friend akin to a cousin but not a blood relation.

Locals also refer to 'uncle' or 'aunty' regardless of family connection. The person might be a beloved public figure (eg Aunty Genoa Keawe) or simply a next-door neighbor. Either way, the moniker connotes affection and respect.

Multiculturalism

Today's immigrants to the Big Island are overwhelmingly white, so the island's diversity stems from historical plantation-era ethnic groups: Native Hawaiians, Japanese, Filipino, Portuguese and Chinese. It's a unique mix that's markedly different from mainland diversity, as it lacks the significant African American and Latino populations.

Among the oldest generation of locals (now in their 70s to 90s), plantation-era stereotypes still inform social hierarchies and alliances. During plantation days, whites were the wealthy plantation owners, and their legendary surnames remain household names (eg Parker Ranch, Lyman Museum). Their ingrained privilege is one reason why subtle suspicion, even resentment, toward haole still lingers.

But in a growing generational divide, Hawaii's youth often dismiss the old distinctions even as they continue to speak pidgin. Due to intermarriage, you cannot always assume a person's race or ethnicity by surname. It's not uncommon nowadays to meet locals who can rattle off four or five different ethnicities in their ancestry – Hawaiian, Chinese, Portuguese, Filipino and Caucasian, for example. Generally, locals feel most bonded with other locals. While tourists and transplants are usually welcomed with aloha, they must earn the trust of locals by being *pono* (respectful).

Besides, no ethnic group has ever kept exclusive for long on Hawai'i. Instead different groups have always freely adopted and shared cultural customs. Look around: people of all colors dance hula and play ukulele, pop firecrackers on New Year's Eve, display *maneki-neko* (Japanese lucky cat), remove shoes indoors and give the *shaka* wave.

Population

Hilo remains the island's largest town with 45,400 residents, followed by Kailua-Kona at 12,700. But the island's growth resembles suburban sprawl, so regional numbers are more revealing. If you look at the Kona region, its population of almost 48,000 rivals the Hilo region's 53,000.

In 2010, Hawai'i's population totaled 185,000, led by rampant growth in Puna's extensive grid of subdivisions. In two decades, from 1990 to 2010, Puna's population more than doubled, from 21,000 to 45,000.

WHO'S WHO?

Haole White or Caucasian person (except local Portuguese), further defined as 'mainland haole' or 'local haole.' It can be insulting or playful, depending on the context.

Hapa Person of mixed ancestry; *hapa* is Hawaiian for 'half.' A common racial designation is *hapa haole* (part white and part other, such as Hawaiian, Asian etc).

Hawaiian Person of Native Hawaiian ancestry. It's a faux pas to call any Hawai'i resident 'Hawaiian' (as you would a Californian or a Texan), thus semantically ignoring the islands' indigenous people.

Kama'aina Person who is native to a particular place; literally 'child of the land.' The term connotes deep connection to a place; a Hilo native is a *kama'aina* of Hilo, not of Kona. In a commercial context, *kama'aina* discounts apply to any resident of Hawaii (ie anyone with a Hawaii driver's license).

Local Person who grew up in Hawaii. Locals who move away can retain their local 'cred.' But transplant residents never become local, no matter how long they live in Hawaii. To call a transplant 'almost local' is a compliment, despite its insider-outsider attitude.

Malihini Person who's just moved to Hawaii; 'newcomer.'

Transplant Person who moved to the islands as an adult.

Commuter traffic between Puna and Hilo has become a vexing problem – a half-hour drive can easily top an hour.

In the Big Island's ethnic mix, there's no majority. Haole (whites) constitute the largest ethnic group at 33%, an ever-rising percentage. People of two or more races (including part-Hawaiians) constitute the second-largest group at 29%, followed by Filipinos at almost 11% and Japanese at 8%. Hawaiians (not including part-Hawaiians) and other Pacific Islanders constitute 13% of the population.

The number of 'pure' Hawaiians has dropped steadily ever since Captain Cook's arrival, and while a sizable number identify themselves as Hawaiian or part-Hawaiian, experts estimate the number of pure Hawaiians to be under 5000 nationwide.

Note that regions greatly vary in ethnic composition. In Hilo, 38% of the population is mixed race, 22% is Japanese, 18% is white and 10% is Native Hawaiian. But in Kailua-Kona the population is 35% white, 23% mixed race, 20% Native Hawaiian and 4% Japanese.

Religion

Although Hawaiians abandoned their ancient religion for Christianity soon after King Kamehameha I died, religious traditions survived underground. Today you'll glimpse them in public ceremonies, such as when a kahuna (priest) blesses the land during a groundbreaking. Many ancient historical sites – *pu'uhonua* (places of refuge), heiau (temples) and petroglyph fields – are also religious sites, chosen for the mana (spiritual essence) of the land. Certain natural landmarks, such as Halema'uma'u Crater and Mauna Kea, are still considered sacred.

Many residents do not claim adherence to a particular faith, and the religious milieu is tolerant rather than dogmatic. Roman Catholicism has the largest number of adherents, due to a significant Filipino population, followed by Mormonism, which has attracted many South Pacific converts. Mainstream Protestant Christianity is struggling with declining membership, while evangelical churches are burgeoning. Buddhism is prevalent among Japanese residents, and their temples are important community centers.

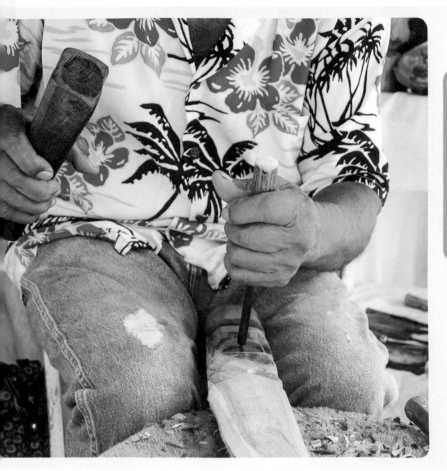

Hawaiian Arts & Crafts

E komo mai (welcome) to these unique Polynesian islands, where storytelling and slack key guitar are among the sounds of everyday life. Contemporary Hawaii is a vibrant mix of multicultural traditions, with the state capital of Honolulu standing at the crossroads of East and West. Underneath it all beats a Hawaiian heart, pounding with an ongoing revival of Hawaii's indigenous language, artisanal crafts, music and the hula.

Island Music

Hawaiian music is rooted in ancient chants. Foreign missionaries and sugar-plantation workers introduced new melodies and instruments, which were incorporated and adapted to create a unique local musical style. *Leo ki'eki'e* (falsetto, or 'high voice') vocals, sometimes just referred

Above Traditional Hawaiian woodworking

to as soprano for women, employs a signature *ha'i* (vocal break, or split-note) style, with a singer moving abruptly from one register to another.

But if you tune your rental-car radio to today's island radio stations, you'll hear everything from US mainland hip-hop beats, country-and-western tunes and Asian pop hits to reggae-inspired 'Jawaiian' grooves. A few Hawaii-born singer-songwriters, most famously Jack Johnson, have achieved international stardom. To discover new hit-makers, check out this year's winners of the Na Hoku Hanohano Awards (www.nahokuhanohano.org), Hawaii's version of the Grammies.

Steel Guitar, Ukulele & Slack Key

Spanish and Mexican cowboys introduced the guitar to Hawaiians in the 1830s. Fifty years later, O'ahu-born high-school student Joseph Kekuku started experimenting with playing a guitar flat on his lap while sliding a pocket knife or comb across the strings. His invention, the Hawaiian steel guitar *(kika kila),* lifts the strings off the fretboard using a movable steel slide, creating a signature smooth sound.

Heard all across the islands is the ukulele, derived from the *braguinha,* a Portuguese stringed instrument that was introduced to Hawaii in 1879. Ukulele means 'jumping flea' in Hawaiian, referring to the way players' deft fingers swiftly move around the strings. The ukulele is enjoying a revival as a young generation of virtuosos emerges, including Nick Acosta, who plays with just one hand, and genre-bending rockers led by Jake Shimabukuro, whose album *Peace Love Ukulele* (2011) reached number one on Billboard's world music chart.

Both the ukulele and the steel guitar contributed to the lighthearted *hapa haole* (Hawaiian music with predominantly English lyrics) popularized in the islands after the 1930s, of which 'My Little Grass Shack' and 'Lovely Hula Hands' are classic examples. For better or for worse, *hapa haole* songs became instantly recognizable as 'Hawaiian' thanks to Hollywood movies and the classic *Hawaii Calls* radio show, which broadcast worldwide from the banyan-tree courtyard of Waikiki's Moana hotel from 1935 until 1975.

Since the mid-20th century, the Hawaiian steel guitar has usually been played with slack key *(ki ho'alu)* tunings, in which the thumb plays the bass and rhythm chords, while the fingers play the melody and improvisations, in a picked style. Traditionally, slack key tunings were closely guarded secrets among *'ohana* (extended family and friends).

Hula

Ancient Stories

In ancient Hawai'i, hula sometimes was a solemn ritual, in which *mele* (songs, chants) were an offering to the gods or celebrated the accomplishments of *ali'i* (chiefs). At other times hula was lighthearted entertainment, in which chief and *kama'aina* (commoner) danced together, including at annual festivals such as the makahiki held during harvest season. Most importantly, hula embodied the community – telling stories of and celebrating itself.

Browse classic and contemporary Hawaiian recordings online – including those by Na Hoku Hanohano Award–winning musicians – at Mountain Apple Company (www. mountainapplecompany.com) and Mele (www. mele.com).

To find out more about slack key guitar, visit George Winston's Dancing Cat music label website (www. dancingcat.com) to listen to sound clips, browse bios of celebrated island guitarists and download a free ebook.

MUSIC FESTIVALS

For the most bang for your buck, go to a music festival, such as the **Waimea Ukulele & Slack Key Guitar Institute Concert** (p159; November), **Laupahoehoe Music Festival** (p192; April) or **Hawai'i Volcanoes National Park Cultural Festival** (p253; summer). Also check venues that bring in local talent: **Kahilu Theatre** (p161; Waimea), **Palace Theater** (p218; Hilo) and **Honoka'a People's Theatre** (p188). In Hilo, **Willie K's Gig at the Crown Room** (p218) features worthy acts, and occasionally Willie himself.

Ukuleles for sale in a market

Traditionally, dancers trained rigorously in *halau* (schools) under a *kumu* (teacher), so their hand gestures, facial expressions and synchronized movements were exact. In a culture without written language, chants were important, giving meaning to the movements and preserving Hawaii's oral history, anything from creation stories about gods to royal genealogies. Songs often contained *kaona* (hidden meanings), which could be spiritual, but also slyly amorous, even sexual.

> Can't resist the rhythms of the hula? Look for low-cost (or even free) introductory dance lessons at resort hotels, shopping malls and local community centers and colleges. No grass skirt required!

Celebrating Hula

Renowned *kumu* hula 'Iolani Luahine and Edith Kanaka'ole established a strong hula legacy on Hawai'i. Today Hilo hosts the celebrated and competitive Merrie Monarch Festival (p210) around Easter, while the smaller, community-spirited 'Iolani Luahine Hula Festival takes place in Keauhou in late January. Another competition, Moku O Keawe (p137), comes to Waikoloa in early November. Don't miss the year-round outdoor hula performances (p253) at Hawai'i Volcanoes National Park.

Traditional Crafts

Traditional Hawaiian crafts have become so popular with tourists that cheap imitation imports from factories across the Pacific and Asia have flooded island stores. Shop carefully, buy local and expect to pay more for high-quality handmade pieces, for example, at Volcano Art Center (p248); Kimura Lauhala Shop (p103) and Ipu Hale Gallery (p103) in Holualoa; Gallery of Great Things (p161) in Waimea; and Waipi'o Valley Artworks (p190) in Kukuihaele.

Woodworking

Ancient Hawaiians were expert woodworkers, carving canoes out of logs and hand-turning lustrous bowls from a variety of beautifully

Lauhala weaving

grained tropical hardwoods, such as koa and milo. *Ipu* (gourds) were also dried and used as containers and as drums for hula. Contemporary woodworkers take native woods to craft traditional bowls, exquisite furniture, jewelry and free-form sculptures. Traditionally, Hawaiian wooden bowls are not decorated or ornate, but are shaped to bring out the natural beauty of the wood. The thinner and lighter the bowl, the finer the artistry and greater the value – and the price. Don't be fooled into buying cheaper monkeypod bowls imported from the Philippines.

Fabric Arts

Lauhala weaving and the making of *kapa* (pounded-bark cloth) for clothing and artworks are two ancient Hawaiian crafts.

Traditionally *lauhala* served as floor mats, canoe sails, protective capes and more. Weaving the *lau* (leaves) of the *hala* (pandanus) tree is the easier part, while preparing the leaves, which have razor-sharp spines, is messy work. Today the most common *lauhala* items are hats, placemats and baskets. Most are mass-produced, but you can find handmade beauties at specialty stores like the Big Island's Kimura Lauhala Shop (p103) near Kailua-Kona.

Making *kapa* (called *tapa* elsewhere in Polynesia) is no less laborious. First, seashells are used to scrape away the rough outer bark of the *wauke* (paper mulberry) tree. Strips of softer inner bark are cut (traditionally with shark's teeth) and pounded with mallets until thin and pliable, and further softened by being soaked in water to let them ferment between beatings. Softened bark strips are then layered atop one another and pounded together in a process called felting. Large sheets of finished *kapa* are colorfully dyed with plant materials and stamped or painted by hand with geometric patterns before being scented with flowers or oils.

Hawaii has been the home of many modern painters, and scores of visiting artists have drawn inspiration from the islands' rich cultural heritage and landscapes. *Encounters with Paradise: Views of Hawaii and Its People, 1778– 1941,* by David Forbes, is a vivid art-history tour.

TRAVEL & LEARN

Explore Hawaiian language, art, music and dance at a variety of cultural classes, workshops and lessons held all over the island, including at beach resorts and hotels. Check calendar listings in newspapers and visit the following venues: Volcano Art Center (p248) in Volcano; Society for Kona's Education & Art (p113) in Honaunau; Donkey Mill Art Center (p102) in Holualoa; and East Hawai'i Cultural Center/HMOCA (p201) in Hilo.

In ancient times, *kapa* was worn as everyday clothing by both sexes, and used as blankets for everything from swaddling newborns to burying the dead. Today authentic handmade Hawaiian *kapa* cloth is rarely seen outside of museums, fine-art galleries and private collections.

Kapa Hawaii (www.kapahawaii.com) celebrates the art of *kapa* with photo essays, news about workshops and events, and how-to tips for making, displaying and caring for this handmade fabric.

Island Writings
From Outside & Inside

Until the late 1970s, Hawaii's literature was dominated by nonlocal Western writers observing these exotic-seeming islands from the outside. Globetrotters such as Mark Twain and Isabella Bird wrote the earliest travelogues about the islands. Best-selling modern titles include James Michener's historical saga, *Hawaii* (1959), and Paul Theroux's caustically humorous *Hotel Honolulu* (2001). More recently, Hawaii-centered historical fiction written by nonresidents includes *The Last Aloha* (2009), by Gaellen Quinn, and *Bird of Another Heaven* (2007), by James Houston.

Meanwhile, locally born contemporary writers have created an authentic literature of Hawaii that evokes island life from the inside. Leading this movement has been Bamboo Ridge Press (www.bamboo ridge.com), which for almost four decades has published new local fiction and poetry in an annual journal and has launched the careers of many contemporary writers in Hawaii. The University of Hawai'i Press (www.uhpress.hawaii.edu) and Bishop Museum Press (www.bishop museum.org) have also made space for local writers to air their voices, especially with insightful nonfiction writings about Hawaiian culture, history, nature and art.

Pidgin Beyond Plantations

In 1975, *All I Asking for Is My Body*, by Milton Murayama, vividly captured sugar plantation life for Japanese *nisei* (second-generation immigrants) around WWII. Murayama's use of pidgin opened the door to an explosion of vernacular literature. Lois-Ann Yamanaka has won widespread acclaim for her poetry (*Saturday Night at the Pahala Theatre*, 1993) and stories (*Wild Meat and the Bully Burgers*, 1996), in which pidgin embodies her characters like a second skin.

More than a pidgin dictionary, *Pidgin to Da Max*, by Douglas Simonson (aka Peppo), Pat Sasaki and Ken Sakata, is a side-splitting primer on local life that has knocked around forever because it (and its sequels) are so funny.

Indeed, redeeming pidgin – long dismissed by academics and disparaged by the upper class – has been a cultural and political cause for some. The hilarious stories (*Da Word*, 2001) and essays (*Living Pidgin*, 2002) of Lee Tonouchi, a prolific writer and playwright whose nickname is 'Da Pidgin Guerrilla,' argue that pidgin is not only essential to understanding local culture, but is also a legitimate language. Another great introduction to pidgin is *Growing Up Local* (1998), an anthology of poetry and prose published by Bamboo Ridge Press.

Volcano Legends

On Hawai'i, the omnipresence of Pele, the volcano goddess, has inspired vivid storytelling of myths and legends. Recommended books include the following:

➜ *Pele*, written and illustrated by Herb Kawainui Kane.

➜ *Powerstones: Letters to a Goddess*, by Linda Ching and Robin Stephens.

➜ *The Legends and Myths of Hawai'i*, by King David Kalakaua.

➜ *Madame Pele: True Encounters with Hawai'i's Fire Goddess*, compiled by Rick Carroll.

➜ *Hawai'i Island Legends: Pikoi, Pele and Others*, compiled by Mary Kawena Pukui.

➜ *Hawaiian Mythology*, by Martha Beckwith.

Hawaii on Screen

Nothing has cemented the paradisaical fantasy of Hawaii in the popular imagination as firmly as Hollywood. Southern California's 'dream factory' continues to peddle variations on a South Seas genre that first swept movie theaters in the 1930s. Whether the mood is silly or serious, whether Hawaii is used as a setting or a stand-in for someplace else, the story's familiar tropes rarely change, often romantically glossing over the islands' history of colonization.

Hawaiian Folktales, Proverbs & Poetry

Folktales of Hawai'i, illustrated by Sig Zane

'Olelo No'eau, illustrated by Dietrich Varez

Hānau ka Ua: Hawaiian Rain Names

Obake Files, by Glen Grant

Hollywood arrived in Hawaii in 1913, more than a decade after Thomas Edison first journeyed here to make movies that you can still watch today at Lahaina's **Wo Hing Museum** (www.lahainarestoration.org/wo-hing-museum; 858 Front St; adult/child $7/free, incl admission to Baldwin House; ⊙10am-4pm) on Maui. By 1939, dozens of Hollywood movies had been shot in Hawaii, including the musical comedy *Waikiki Wedding* (1937), in which Bing Crosby crooned the Oscar-winning song 'Sweet Leilani.' Later favorites include the WWII–themed drama *From Here to Eternity* (1953), the musical *South Pacific* (1958), and Elvis Presley's goofy postwar *Blue Hawaii* (1961). Today, Hawaii actively encourages and supports a lucrative film industry by maintaining state-of-the-art production facilities and providing tax incentives. Hundreds of feature films have been shot in the state, including box-office hits *Raiders of the Lost Ark* (1981), *Jurassic Park* (1993), *Pearl Harbor* (2001), *50 First Dates* (2004), *Pirates of the Caribbean: On Stranger Tides* (2011), *The Hunger Games: Catching Fire* (2013) and *Jurassic World* (2015).

Hawaii has hosted dozens of TV series since 1968, when the original *Hawaii Five-O*, an edgy cop drama unsentimentally depicting Honolulu's gritty side, debuted. In 2010 *Hawaii Five-O* was rebooted as a prime-time drama, filmed on O'ahu. That island also served as the location for the hit series *Lost,* which, like *Gilligan's Island* (the pilot of which was filmed on Kaua'i), is about a group of island castaways trying to get home. To find *Lost* filming locations, visit www.lostvirtualtour.com.

For a complete filmography and a list of hundreds of TV episodes filmed here, including what's currently being shot around the islands, check the Hawaii Film Office website, http://filmoffice.hawaii.gov.

Lei

Greetings. Love. Honor. Respect. Peace. Celebration. Spirituality. Good luck. Farewell. A Hawaiian lei – a handcrafted garland of fresh tropical flowers – can signify all of these meanings and many more. Lei-making may be Hawaii's most sensuous and transitory art form. Fragrant and ephemeral, lei embody the beauty of nature and the embrace of 'ohana (extended family and friends) and the community, freely given and freely shared.

The Art of the Lei

In choosing their materials, lei makers express emotions and tell a story, since flowers and other plants may embody Hawaiian places and myths. Traditional lei makers may use feathers, nuts, shells, seeds, seaweed, vines, leaves and fruit, in addition to more familiar fragrant flowers. The most common methods of making lei are by knotting, braiding, winding, stringing or sewing the raw natural materials together.

Above Making fresh flower lei by hand

Worn daily, lei were integral to ancient Hawaiian society. In the islands' Polynesian past, they were part of sacred hula dances and given as special gifts to loved ones, as healing medicine to the sick and as offerings to the gods, all practices that continue today. So powerful a symbol were they that on ancient Hawaii's battlefields, a lei could bring peace to warring armies.

Today, locals wear lei for special events, such as weddings, birthdays, anniversaries and graduations. It's no longer common to make one's own lei, unless you belong to a hula *halau* (school). For ceremonial hula, performers are often required to make their own lei, even gathering raw materials by hand.

Does an airport lei greeting to surprise your *ipo* (sweetheart) sound like fun? Several companies offer this service, including Greeters of Hawaii (www.greetersof hawaii.com), which has been in the business of giving aloha since 1957.

Modern Celebrations

For visitors to Hawaii, the tradition of giving and receiving lei dates back to 19th-century steamships that brought the first tourists to the islands. Later, disembarking cruise-ship passengers were greeted by vendors who would toss garlands around the necks of *malihini* (newcomers).

In 1927, the poet Don Blanding and Honolulu journalist Grace Tower Warren called for making May 1 a holiday to honor lei. Every year, Lei Day is still celebrated across the islands with Hawaiian music, hula dancing, parades, and lei-making workshops and contests.

The tradition of giving a kiss with a lei began during WWII, allegedly when a hula dancer at a USO club was dared by her friends to give a military serviceman a peck on the cheek when offering him a flower lei.

Lei: Dos & Don'ts

➡ Do not wear a lei hanging directly down around your neck. Instead, drape a closed (circular) lei over your shoulders, making sure equal lengths are hanging over your front and back.

➡ When presenting a lei, bow your head slightly and raise the lei above your heart. Do not drape it with your own hands over the head of the recipient because this isn't respectful; let them do it themselves.

ISLAND LEI TRADITIONS

Lei are a universal language in Hawaii, but some special lei evoke a particular island.

Hawai'i, the Big Island Lei made from lehua, the pom-pom flowers of the ohia plant, are most often red or pink. According to legend, the first lei was made of lehua and given by Hi'iaka, goddess of healing, to her sister Pele, goddess of fire and volcanoes.

O'ahu The yellow-orange *'ilima* is the island's official flower, and a symbol of Laka, the Hawaiian goddess of hula dancing. Once favored by royalty, an *'ilima* lei may be made of up to a thousand small blossoms strung together.

Maui The *lokelani* (pink damask rose, or 'rose of heaven') is a soft, velvety and aromatic flower. It was imported by 19th-century Christian missionaries for their gardens in Lahaina. Today it's Maui's official flower, the only exotic flora so recognized in Hawaii.

Lana'i A yellowish-orange vine, *kauna'oa* is traditionally gathered from the island's windward shores, then twisted into a lei. One traditional Hawaiian chant sings of this plant growing on Lana'i like a feathered cape lying on a strong chief's shoulders.

Moloka'i *Kukui* (candlenut) lei are either made from the laboriously polished, dark-brown nuts of Hawaii's state tree (in which case, they're usually worn by men) or the tree's white blossoms, which are Moloka'i's official flower.

Kaua'i On the 'Garden Island,' leathery, anise-scented *mokihana* berries are often woven with strands of glossy, green maile vines. *Mokihana* trees thrive on the rain-soaked western slopes of Mt Wai'ale'ale.

Plumeria lei

➡ Don't give a closed lei to a pregnant woman for it may bring bad luck; choose an open (untied) lei or *haku* (head) lei instead.

➡ Resist the temptation to wear a lei intended for someone else. That's bad luck. Never refuse a lei, and do not take one off in the presence of the giver.

➡ When you stop wearing your lei, don't throw it away. Untie the string, remove the bow and return the lei's natural elements to the earth (eg scatter flowers in the ocean, bury seeds or nuts).

Shopping for Lei

A typical Hawaiian lei costs anywhere from $10 for a single strand of orchids or plumeria to thousands of dollars for a 100% genuine Ni'ihau shell lei necklace. Beware that some *kukui* (candlenut) and puka shell lei are just cheap (even plastic) imports.

When shopping for a lei, ask the florist or shopkeeper for advice about what the most appropriate lei for the occasion is (eg for a bride, pick a string of pearl-like *pikake* jasmine flowers), and indicate if you're giving the lei to a man or a woman.

If you want to buy a lei to wear, try farmers markets, florists and also supermarkets, such as the KTA Super Store (p211), which always stocks fresh vanda orchid and other flower lei. Most locals wear lei only for special events, such as weddings and public ceremonies. To see master-crafted specimens, visit the island during the Merrie Monarch Festival (p210) in Hilo or on May Day Lei Day (p210).

On O'ahu, it's a tradition for passengers to throw their lei into the sea as their departing ship passes Diamond Head. If the flowers of their lei float back toward the beach, it's said that they'll return to Hawaii someday.

Landscapes & Wildlife

Calling this island big is no misnomer: Hawai'i claims twice as much land as the other Hawaiian Islands combined, and with distinct ecological zones ranging from rainforests to desert and shoreline to alpine, it houses a dizzying array of plants and animals. Stewardship of these natural resources is a traditional Hawaiian value, reflected in *aloha 'aina* – love and respect for the land. But that sentiment struggles against a constant onslaught of invasive species, changing global climate and increasing population pressures.

Wildlife

Above A nene (native Hawaiian goose)

Born of barren lava flows, the Hawaiian Islands were originally populated by the plants and animals that could traverse the Pacific – such as seeds clinging to a bird's feather, insects burrowed in a piece of driftwood or fern spores that floated thousands of miles through the air. The process of populating the island took millions of years, with each new recruit arriving tens to hundreds of thousands of years after the last.

Once here, plants and animals gradually adapted to the environment, slowly evolving into new forms and new species. Over 90% of Hawaii's flora and fauna is endemic (ie unique to the islands), and many have lost the defenses they once needed to survive in their more competitive homes. This is one reason they fare so poorly against the onslaught of invasive species and human-caused environmental changes.

Each new predator, insect or disease that arrives here finds an ecosystem not used to being confronted with new predators, insects or diseases – and the results have been disastrous. Hawaii is now home to 39% of the US' endangered species. As the 'extinction capital of the world,' at least 271 species of Hawaiian plant, insect, bird and snail have already disappeared entirely – and more are on their way out.

Animals

Only two mammals made it to Hawaii on their own, and both are now endangered. The Hawaiian hoary bat once occupied forests throughout the archipelago, but due to habitat loss is now only found on Hawai'i and Kaua'i. The Hawaiian monk seal population is declining at about 4% annually, and even if that number can be stabilized, they'll never be entirely in the clear due to environmental and human threats.

On the plus side, up to 10,000 migrating North Pacific humpback whales travel to Hawaiian waters for calving each winter, after an international ban on commercial whaling brought that number up from 4000 in the late 1990s. Other whales (such as blue and fin whales) also pass through. By federal law, you may not get within 100yd of any whale in Hawaiian waters.

Show-stealing spinner dolphins, named for their acrobatic leaps above water, are big business for Hawai'i tour operators. But these nocturnal feeders come into sheltered bays during the day to rest, and disturbance by swimmers and unethical boat captains disrupt their natural cycles. The issue has become such a problem that in 2016 the National Oceanic & Atmospheric Administration proposed making the current guideline – to stay at least 50yd away – into a federal law.

Endangered *honu* (green sea turtles), hawksbill and leatherback turtles also swim in Hawai'i's waters and bask on sunny beaches where they lay their eggs in the warm sand. Keep back at least 20ft on land as startled turtles may abandon their nesting and drop their eggs in the ocean. Stay 50yd away in the water.

Hawai'i's coral reefs teem with over 500 tropical fish species, including bright yellow tangs, striped butterflyfish and Moorish Idols, silver needlefish and neon-colored wrasse, which change sex (and color) as they mature. Stay off the reef, and watch your flippers as they can easily damage the fragile coral. Avoid using sunscreen in sensitive tidal areas, as the chemicals can poison the reef. Even better: wear long sleeves.

Hawaii's endemic birds are often spectacular examples of adaptive radiation: its 110 endemic species likely evolved from only 30 immigrants. However, two-thirds are already extinct due to predatory feral animals (like mongoose and pig) and diseases introduced by non-native birds. Avian malaria has decimated populations at lower elevations as rising global temperatures increase the numbers of mosquitoes. Avian pox is also a growing threat.

There has been one small success story in the world of endemics: the endangered nene (Hawaiian goose), Hawaii's official state bird. These descendants of Canada geese who were likely blown off course 500,000 years ago are making a comeback. Conservation and breeding efforts in Hawai'i Volcanoes National Park alone increased numbers from 30 individuals in 1932 to around 250 today. Watch for them on the roadways, and be aware that a man was fined $10,000 in 2016 for intentionally killing a nene.

Plants

Extravagantly diverse flora occupies every island niche. But what you'll see today is not what the first Hawaiians saw when they arrived here. Over half of the native forests have already disappeared, mainly due to logging, agriculture and invasive plants. Most commercial 'Hawaiian' agricultural products are exotic imports – including papayas, pineapples, mangoes, macadamia nuts and coffee.

Of course, the first Polynesian settlers began that import frenzy, bringing boatloads of useful plants with them including breadfruit (food), pandanus (food and fiber), hau (fiber and construction), sugarcane (food) and *kukui* (candlenut trees; oil, spice and tattoos).

Things really got out of hand, however, with the introduction of grazing animals like cows, pigs, sheep and goats. These walking lawnmowers ate many plants to the brink of extinction – from the endangered Mauna Kea silversword that flowers once in its life high up on the mountainsides, to the endangered *'ohai* that once occupied coastal dunes in abundance. Ranching decimated forests: animals consumed the understory while *paniolo* (Hawaiian cowboys) cleared the overstory.

On the slopes of Mauna Kea, distinctive flora include the yellow-flowered *mamane* tree and tiny-leafed *pukiawe* shrub with its red, pink and white berries. Back down by the beach, native coastal plants to look for include: *'ilima,* its delicate orange-yellow flowers often strung into lei; pink-flowering *pohuehue* (beach morning-glory) with its dark green, glossy leaves; and *naupaka* shrubs, whose pinkish-white flowers look as if they've been torn in half (by a broken-hearted lover, according to Hawaiian legend).

Out on lava flows, look for low-lying shrubs bursting with *'ohelo* berries, emerald-green *hapu'u* (tree ferns) and fuzzy-blossomed ohia trees. The latter is an important early colonizer of new lava, providing shade and creating soil for other species to follow. Sadly, however, the future of the ohia is uncertain with the spread of Rapid Ohia Death (ROD), a fungal disease that has now affected 47,000 acres of the Big Island's forests. There is no known cure, meaning the vegetated face of Hawai'i may be changed forever.

In densely populated areas such as Kailua-Kona, you'll notice many of the non-native ornamental flowering plants commonly grown in other tropical places around the world (bird of paradise, blood-red anthurium, orchids etc). Some of these are nonthreatening, but many can be invasive, spreading on their own accord and causing damage to native ecosystems. Being able to differentiate the two – while appreciating both – is another step toward understanding and loving this tropical paradise.

National, State & County Parks

About 13% of the Big Island is protected as national, state or county parks, with additional land set aside as preserves and botanical gardens. Refuges, such as the Hakalau Forest National Wildlife Refuge, due east of Mauna Kea, also provide protection for natural resources.

Hawai'i Volcanoes National Park has been on a decades-long mission to restore and protect the island's native biota. A key piece of that involved removing goats and other grazers while fencing off much of the park's borders. An additional 5-mile cat-proof fence was erected in 2016 to protect the Hawaiian petrel from marauding feral kitties.

Some of the most idyllic Hawai'i beaches are protected as parklands, including Hapuna Beach and Kekaha Kai State Park – a beach explorer's

Native coastal plant *naupaka*

dream. Head to the Hamakua Coast ('the wet side') for lush forest walks at Kalopa State Recreation Area and Akaka Falls State Park where the drawcard sight is a 420ft waterfall. Over two-dozen county beach parks ring the island as well, offering terrific snorkeling, camping and, of course, chillin'.

Meanwhile, a visit to Kaloko-Honokohau National Historic Park or Pu'ukohola Heiau National Historic Site will illustrate that the Ancient Hawaiians were skilled agronomists and fishermen, as well as devout in their beliefs.

The Land

Hawai'i's varied landscape, weather and elevation supports an impressive range of the earth's ecosystems. As storms roll in from the east, they saturate the east coast before hitting the massive bulks of Mauna Loa and Mauna Kea. These mountains effectively shelter the west regions of the island, creating dry coastal zones and even an arid desert zone in the northwest. While Hilo is being ravaged by a tropical storm, you may not even feel a whisper of wind in Kona.

Lowland and montane rainforests creep up the sides of the mountains while the upper reaches of the saddle between Mauna Loa and Mauna Kea is largely a grassy shrub-land – a result of both altitude and the rain shadow effect. Above the saddle, subalpine and alpine extremes rule the day, and areas of permafrost have even been found on Mauna Kea's summit.

But, while all of this is subtly fascinating, the most obvious forces shaping the land and its inhabitants are the volcanic flows. These have consistently hit the reset button during Hawai'i's formation and evolution, carving up the land into a mosaic of barren rock, pioneer forests and old-growth *kipuka* (forest oasis).

Hawai'i's Volcanoes

Science, mythology, nature and culture all mix dramatically on the Big Island. Geologic forces and Pele, goddess of fire and volcanoes, conspire to create a powerfully majestic and ever-changing landscape that defines the people, plants and animals that call Hawai'i home.

The Hawaiian Islands were all created by a rising column of molten rock – a 'hot spot' – under the Pacific Plate. As the plate moves northwest a few inches each year, magma pierces upward through its crust, occasionally reaching the surface to create volcanoes. This process has been ongoing for 70 million years, building a chain of over 80 volcanoes that stretches from the Aleutian Trench near Alaska through the Midway Islands before ending here.

The Big Island is made up of five or seven volcanoes – depending on whether you count the two hiding underwater. These differ from volcanoes found along tectonic plate boundaries, which tend be formed by sticky, explosive lava. Hot-spot eruptions typically have higher basalt content, making the lava flow more like a liquid. Eruption after effusive eruption sends the molten rock pouring across great distances to slowly build up layer after layer of rock. This process creates the gently sloped shield volcanoes of Hawaii, exemplified by the rounded mass of Mauna Loa.

This is not to say shield volcanoes don't have their explosive side, as Kilauea reminded onlookers and scientists in 2008 when it belched a pyroclastic cloud of ash, steam and rocks over the rim of its crater. These occasional, violent eruptions occur when the lava typically found bubbling at the surface retreats below the water table. If the caldera collapses in, rocks and rubble may trap subterranean steam until it builds enough pressure to pop the cork.

Hawai'i's volcanoes also produce impressive fissure and fountain eruptions. The former occurs when the ground splits open to release a curtain of fire spitting skyward. The latter forms at a single point of origin, like the 1959 Mauna Iki eruption that shot a geyser of lava almost 2000ft into the air.

Eruptions and lava flows pose a continual threat to Big Island residents, and the unstable new earth those flows create are also a source of near-daily earthquakes. On rare, but catastrophic occasions, large chunks of Hawai'i island have calved off and slid toward the sea, sending devastating tsunami across the Pacific Ocean – affecting shorelines from Japan to California.

Geologically speaking, Hawai'i is a young, dynamic island. Its recent history is recorded in hardened lava flows pierced by steam and sulfur vents. But that history is still being written. If Pele is feeling frisky, you might witness creation itself: a lava flow exploding clouds of billowing steam and shattered rock as it adds new land to Hawai'i's shoreline.

Survival Guide

Directory A–Z

Climate

Kailua-Kona

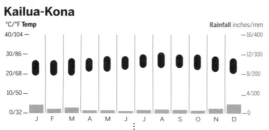

Customs Regulations

Non-US citizens and permanent residents may import the following duty-free:

➜ 1L of liquor (if you're over 21 years old)

➜ 200 cigarettes (one carton) or 100 non-Cuban cigars (if you're over 18)

➜ $100 worth of gifts

Hawaii has stringent restrictions against importing any fresh fruits and plants. Because Hawaii is a rabies-free state, the pet quarantine laws are draconian.

Before leaving Hawaii, make sure any fresh flowers or produce has been commercially packaged and approved for travel.

Discount Cards

Children, students, seniors, state residents and active and retired military personnel usually receive discounts at museums and attractions. All but children need to present valid ID proving their status.

Food & Drink

Meals are early and start on the dot in Hawaii: typically 6am breakfast, noon lunch and 6pm dinner. Dress codes are relaxed ('island casual'), with no jackets or ties normally required. Men can get away with an aloha shirt and neat khaki or golf shorts at most resort restaurants.

➜ **Hawaii Seafood** (www. hawaii-seafood.org) Info on local seafood, including sustainability information.

➜ **Edible Hawaiian Islands** (http://ediblehi.com) An excellent print and web resource on locally sourced food in the state.

➜ **Slow Food Hawaii** (www. slowfoodhawaii.com) Recipes and information on locally sourced food and festivals.

Electricity

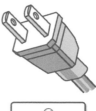

Type A
120V/60Hz

Type B
120V/60Hz

Health

Before You Go
HEALTH INSURANCE
No matter how long or short your trip, make sure you have adequate travel insurance, purchased before departure. At a minimum, you need coverage for medical emergencies and treatment, including hospital stays and an emergency flight home if necessary. Medical treatment in the USA is of the highest caliber, but the expense could bankrupt you.

WEBSITES
➡ **Hawaii State Department of Health** (http://health. hawaii.gov) General healthcare information in the state.

➡ **Hawaii Medical Service Association** (https://hmsa. com/search/provider) Physician finder.

In Hawai'i, the Big Island
AVAILABILITY & COST OF HEALTH CARE
There are good medical clinics on all four 'sides' (north, south, east and west) of the Big Island. As is the case anywhere in the USA, the quality of health care is high – and so is the price. Be sure to purchase travel insurance before you visit.

ENVIRONMENTAL HAZARDS
The greatest environmental hazard on the Big Island is the water that surrounds it. Hawaii suffers from one of the highest rates of drownings in the country, and on the Big Island, many beaches don't have lifeguards. Always be aware of the tides and currents, and if you're not a confident swimmer, stay close to shore.

The other hazard particular to the Big Island is lava. Obviously lava should be given a wide berth. Don't poke it with a stick (yes, there is a tour company

that does this). Don't get too close to the flow. And be aware that the gases that arise from a lava flow can be as dangerous as the flow itself.

INFECTIOUS DISEASES
As of 2016, the Hawaii state Department of Health confirmed the presence of dengue fever on the Big Island. The few cases that have been reported are isolated, and the state has implemented strict control protocols whenever a case has been found. The best means of preventing dengue are basic mosquito control tactics that you should practice in any case – wearing bug repellent and light-colored clothes (trousers and long-sleeved shirts), keeping windows and screen doors shut etc.

TAP WATER
The tap water on the Big Island is generally fine to drink.

TRADITIONAL MEDICINE
Throughout the island you will see businesses offering traditional Hawaiian massages (known as *lomilomi*), hot stone treatments, ayurvedic programs and a host of other traditional and New Age medicinal services. While we can't speak to the scientific benefits of these services, we sure felt great after a massage.

European sailors remarked extensively on the general health of the Native Hawaiians they encountered.

The indigenous population, then and now, believed in living a life defined by *pono*, a complicated term that means 'righteousness', which can extend beyond good moral living to a lifestyle we would recognize as healthy: a balanced diet and regular amounts of exercise, via labor and sport.

Internet Access
➡ Wi-fi is now available at almost all accommodations; it's usually free at B&Bs, condos and vacation rentals.

➡ Bigger towns have at least one coffee shop offering free wi-fi.

Legal Matters
If you are arrested, you have the right to an attorney; if you can't afford one, a public defender will be provided free. The **Hawaii State Bar Association** (☎808-537-1868; https://hsba.org) makes attorney referrals.

In addition to Hawaii's road rules (p308), be mindful of the following laws:

➡ Bars, clubs and liquor stores may require photo ID to prove you're of legal age (21 years) to buy alcohol. You must be 18 years old to buy tobacco.

➡ Drinking alcohol anywhere other than at a private residence, hotel room or licensed premises (eg bar, restaurant) is illegal, which puts beach parks off-limits.

EATING PRICE RANGES
The following price ranges refer to an average main course at dinner in a restaurant (lunch is usually much cheaper) or a set meal at a casual takeout eatery. Unless otherwise stated, taxes and tip are not included.

$ less than $15

$$ $15 to $25

$$$ more than $25

→ Possessing marijuana or nonprescription narcotics, hitchhiking and public nudity are all illegal in Hawaii.

→ Smoking is generally prohibited in all public spaces, including airports, bars, restaurants and businesses.

LGBTIQ+ Travelers

The state of Hawaii has strong minority protections and a constitutional guarantee of privacy that extends to sexual behavior between consenting adults. Locals tend to be private about their personal lives, so you will not see much public hand-holding or open displays of affection. Everyday LGBTQ life is low-key, and there's not much of a 'scene' to speak of – with a few exceptions it's more about picnics and potlucks, not nightclubs.

Money

Credit cards are widely accepted by most businesses (except some lodgings) and often required for reservations. Traveler's checks (US dollars) are occasionally used.

ATMs & Eftpos

→ ATMs are available in all major towns and 24/7 at most banks, convenience stores, shopping centers and airports.

→ Expect a minimum surcharge of $2.25 per transaction, plus any fees charged by your home bank.

→ Most ATMs are connected to international networks (eg Plus, Cirrus) and offer decent exchange rates.

→ Hawaii's two largest banks are Bank of Hawaii (www.boh.com) and First Hawaiian Bank (www.fhb.com).

Checks

Out-of-state personal checks are generally not accepted, except at some privately owned lodgings (eg B&Bs, condos, vacation rentals).

Credit & Debit Cards

Major credit cards are widely accepted. Typically they're required for car rentals, hotel reservations, buying tickets etc. B&Bs, condos and vacation rentals may refuse credit cards or add a 3% surcharge.

Taxes & Refunds

A 4% state sales tax is tacked onto virtually everything, including meals, groceries and car rentals (which also entail additional state and local taxes). Lodging taxes total 13.25%.

Tipping

Tipping is *not* optional; only withhold tips in cases of outrageously bad service.

→ **Airport skycaps & hotel porters** $2 to $3 per bag, minimum per cart $5.

→ **Bartenders** 15% to 20% per round, minimum $1 per drink.

→ **Housekeeping** $2 to $5 per night, left under card provided; more if you're messy.

→ **Parking valets** At least $2 when handed back your car's keys.

→ **Restaurant servers & room service** 15% for substandard service, 20% for good service, unless a gratuity is already charged.

→ **Taxi drivers** 15% of metered fare, rounded up to next dollar.

Traveler's Checks

Rather archaic nowadays, traveler's checks in US dollars are still accepted like cash at bigger tourist-oriented businesses in Hawaii, such as resort hotels. Smaller businesses like grocery stores usually refuse them.

Opening Hours

Banks 8:30am–4pm Monday–Friday, some to 6pm Friday; 9am–noon or 1pm Saturday.

Bars & clubs Noon–midnight daily, some to 2am Friday and Saturday. Bars may close early if business is slow.

Businesses (general) & government offices 8:30am–4:30pm Monday–Friday, some post offices also 9am–noon Saturday.

Restaurants Breakfast 6–10am, lunch 11:30am–2pm, dinner 5–9:30pm. Smaller restaurants may have more flexible hours.

Shops 9am–5pm Monday–Saturday, some also noon to 5pm Sunday; major shopping areas and malls keep extended hours.

Post

The US Postal Service delivers mail to and from Hawaii.

ETIQUETTE

Hawaiians are friendly folk, but also protective of their land and culture.

→ **Kapu** A '*Kapu*' sign means off-limits or forbidden – respect these restrictions at all times.

→ **Island time** While Hawaiians are sensitive to tourist sensibilities, they tend to operate on a more casual time schedule.

→ **Dress code** People certainly wear sandals to business meetings, but on the flip side, they also dress up for church and a nice meal.

Service is reliable, but slower than within the continental USA. First-class airmail between Hawaii and the mainland usually takes three to four days

Public Holidays

On the following national holidays, banks, schools and government offices (including post offices) close, and museums, transportation and other services operate on a Sunday schedule. Holidays falling on a weekend are usually observed the following Monday.

New Year's Day January 1

Martin Luther King Jr Day Third Monday in January

Presidents' Day Third Monday in February

Prince Kuhio Day March 26

Good Friday Friday before Easter Sunday (in March or April)

Memorial Day Last Monday in May

King Kamehameha Day June 11

Independence Day July 4

Statehood Day Third Friday in August

Labor Day First Monday in September

Columbus Day Second Monday in October

Veterans Day November 11

Thanksgiving Fourth Thursday in November

Christmas Day December 25

Telephone

Cell Phones

International travelers need a multiband GSM phone to make calls in the USA. Popping in a US prepaid rechargeable SIM card is usually cheaper than using your home network. SIM cards are available at telecommunications and electronics stores, which also sell inexpensive prepaid phones, including some airtime.

PRACTICALITIES

Newspapers Major dailies include the Hawaii Tribune-Herald, West Hawaii Today and Honolulu Star-Advertiser.

Radio About 25 FM and five AM radio stations; National Public Radio (NPR) is at the lower end of the FM dial.

TV & DVD All major US TV networks and cable channels; DVDs coded region 1 (US and Canada only).

Weights & measures Imperial system (except 1 US gallon = 3.79L)

Among US cell-phone service providers, Verizon has the most extensive network; AT&T and Sprint get decent reception. Coverage is good in bigger towns but spotty or nonexistent in rural areas.

Dialing Codes

➜ All Hawaii phone numbers consist of a three-digit area code (808) followed by a seven-digit local number.

➜ To call long-distance from one island to another, dial 1 + 808 + local number.

➜ Always dial 1 before toll-free numbers (800, 888 etc). Some toll-free numbers only work within Hawaii or from the US mainland and Canada.

➜ To call Canada from Hawaii, dial 1 + area code + local number (note international rates still apply).

➜ For all other international calls from Hawaii, dial 011 + country code + area code + local number.

➜ To call Hawaii from abroad, the international country code for the USA is 1.

Pay Phones & Phonecards

➜ Pay phones are a dying breed, though they are occasionally found at shopping centers, hotels, beaches, parks and other public places.

➜ Some pay phones are coin-operated (local calls usually cost 50¢), while others

---

only accept credit cards or phonecards.

➜ Private prepaid phonecards are available from convenience stores, supermarkets, pharmacies etc.

Time

➜ Hawaii-Aleutian Standard Time is GMT/UTC minus 10 hours. Hawaii doesn't observe Daylight Saving Time.

➜ In midwinter, the sun rises around 7am and sets around 6pm. In midsummer, it rises before 6am and sets after 7pm.

➜ During standard time (winter), Hawaii time differs from Los Angeles by two hours, from New York by five hours, from London by 10 hours, from Tokyo by 19 hours and from Sydney by 21 hours. During daylight saving time (summer), the difference is one hour more for countries that observe it.

➜ Upon arrival, set your internal clock to 'Island time,' meaning slow down!

Toilets

➜ Be careful where you relieve yourself outside. if you're by private property or land marked 'Kapu', you might seriously piss off a local (no pun intended).

➜ Beach parks tend to have free facilities; some are

surprisingly clean, some, not so much.

➡ In more rustic eco-retreats, waste is often turned into fertilizer.

Tourist Information

➡ **Go Hawaii** (www.gohawaii.com/big-island/) Official tourism portal for the Big Island.

➡ **Big Island Now** (www.bigislandnow.com) Updated news site on Big Island tourism.

➡ **Kona 123** (www.kona123.com) Big Island tourism information curated by locals.

➡ **Kona Web** (www.konaweb.com) Maintains an exhaustive events calendar for the island.

➡ **Hawaii Department of Land & Natural Resources** (☑808-961-9540; http://camping.ehawaii.gov/camping; Room 204, 75 Aupuni St, Hilo; ⊙8am-3:30pm Mon-Fri) Advance state park camping permits are required. Nonresident fees are $18 per campsite for up to six people ($3 for each additional person), $50 per A-frame shelter and $80 to $90 per cabin.

Travelers with Disabilities

Major hotels are equipped with elevators, phones with TDD (telecommunications device for the deaf) and wheelchair-accessible rooms (which must be reserved in advance); most B&Bs and small hotels are probably not.

Guide and service dogs are not subject to the general quarantine rules for pets if they meet the Department of Agriculture's minimum requirements (see http://hdoa.hawaii.gov/ai/aqs/guide-service-dogs for details). All animals must enter the state at Honolulu International Airport.

Wheelchair-accessible vans can be rented from **Wheelchair Getaways** (☑800-638-1912; www.wheelchairgetaways.com). Car-rental agencies may offer hand-controlled vehicles; reserve them well in advance. If you have a disability parking placard from home, bring it with you. Pu'uhonua O Hōnaunau National Historical Park and Hawai'i Volcanoes National Park lend wheelchairs free of charge.

For Hawaii-specific info on airports, all-terrain beach wheelchairs, transportation, medical and other support services, visit the **Disability & Communication Access Board** (☑808-586-8121; http://health.hawaii.gov/dcab/) website. **Access Aloha Travel** (☑808-545-1143, 800-480-1143; www.accessalohatravel.com) is a full-service local travel agency.

Visas

Generally not required for Canadians or for citizens of Visa Waiver Program countries for stays of 90 days or less with ESTA pre-approval.

Visitor Visa

Double-check current visa and passport requirements *before* coming to the USA. See the 'Visas' section of the US Department of State website (http://travel.state.gov) and the Travel section of the US Customs & Border Protection website (www.cbp.gov).

Currently under the US Visa Waiver Program (VWP) visas are not required for citizens of 37 countries for stays up to 90 days (no extensions) if they register online at least 72 hours before arrival with the Electronic System for Travel Authorization, which costs $14. Canadian visitors are generally admitted visa-free for stays up to 182 days.

Upon arrival, the Department of Homeland Security (www.dhs.gov) requires that almost all foreign visitors (currently excluding most Canadian citizens) have their digital photograph taken and electronic (inkless) fingerprints scanned; the process typically takes less than a minute.

Work

➡ US citizens can legally work in Hawaii. Short-term employment will probably mean entry-level jobs in the service industry.

➡ There are many work-for-food-and-board style internships offered at permaculture farms, which are thick on the ground in areas like Puna and South Kona.

➡ Specific outdoor skills (eg scuba diving) might land you a job with an activity outfit.

➡ Check the listings in newspaper classifieds and websites like Craigslist, which maintains an active Big Island page.

Transportation

GETTING THERE & AWAY

Virtually all visitors arrive on the Big Island by air, mostly from Honolulu International Airport on O'ahu. Travelers must then catch an inter-island flight to one of the Big Island's two primary airports, Kona International Airport at Keahole or Hilo International Airport. Flights and tours can be booked online at lonelyplanet.com/bookings.

Arriving on the Big Island

Car rental booths for major agencies line the road outside the arrivals area at both airports. Taxis are curbside. Shuttle-bus services typically cost as much as taxis.

Hilo International Airport (ITO; ☑808-961-9300; www.hawaii.gov/ito; 2450 Kekuanaoa St) The approximate taxi fare from the airport to downtown is $20. Shuttle-bus services typically cost as much as taxis.

Kona International Airport (KOA; ☑808-327-9520; http://hawaii.gov/koa; 73-200 Kupipi St) From the airport to Kailua-Kona a taxi costs $30 and to Waikoloa it's $55.

Speedi Shuttle (☑808-329-5433, 877-242-5777; www.speedishuttle.com; airport transfer Kailua Kona shared/private $32/124, Mauna Lani $59/186; ☺9am-last flight) will get you to destinations up and down the Kona Coast; it costs $34/100 for a shared/private shuttle to Kailua-Kona and $55/170 to the Waikoloa resort area. Book in advance.

Air

All checked and carry-on bags leaving the Big Island for the US mainland must be inspected by a US Department of Agriculture (USDA) x-ray machine at the airport.

International Airports

Interisland flights from to the Big Island arrive at either Kona International Airport or Hilo International Airport. Only a few direct flights arrive from the US mainland, Canada and Japan, and virtually all arrive in Kona.

Kona International Airport at Keahole (KOA; ☑808-327-9520; http://hawaii.gov/koa; 73-200 Kupipi St) Mostly interisland and some US mainland and Canada flights arrive at Hawai'i's main airport, 7 miles northwest of Kailua-Kona on Hwy 19.

Hilo International Airport (ITO; ☑808-961-9300; www.hawaii.gov/ito; 2450 Kekuanaoa St) All flights to Hilo's airport are interisland (mostly from Honolulu) except one from Los Angeles.

CLIMATE CHANGE & TRAVEL

Every form of transportation that relies on carbon-based fuel generates CO_2, the main cause of human-induced climate change. Modern travel is dependent on airplanes, which might use less fuel per mile per person than most cars but travel much greater distances. The altitude at which aircraft emit gases (including CO_2) and particles also contributes to their climate change impact. Many websites offer 'carbon calculators' that allow people to estimate the carbon emissions generated by their journey and, for those who wish to do so, to offset the impact of the greenhouse gases emitted with contributions to portfolios of climate-friendly initiatives throughout the world. Lonely Planet offsets the carbon footprint of all staff and author travel.

Airlines Flying to & from the Big Island

A few major carriers fly directly from the US mainland, Canada and Japan to Kona: Air Canada, Alaska Airlines, American Airlines, Delta Air Lines, Hawaiian Airlines, United Airlines and WestJet. Hilo has only one direct flight by United Airlines from Los Angeles.

Tickets

Fares for direct flights from the US mainland and Canada are extremely variable, depending on season, day of the week and demand. In general, return fares from the US mainland to Hawai'i cost from $400 (in low season from the West Coast) to $800 or more in high season from the East Coast.

Package tours, which often include airfare, hotel and car, offer bargains for couples who would stay at affiliated hotels anyway; single travelers don't benefit as much because rates are based on double occupancy. **Pleasant Holidays** (☑800-742-9244; www.pleasantholidays.com) offers competitive vacation packages from the US mainland.

Sea

Most cruises around the Hawaiian Islands have ports of call in Hilo and in Kona. Cruises range from seven-day whirlwind hops to 49-day marathons.

Major cruise lines include the following:

Holland America (☑877-932-4259; www.hollandamerica.com) Departures from San Diego and Vancouver, British Columbia.

Princess Cruises (☑800-774-6237; www.princess.com) Departures from Los Angeles, San Francisco, Vancouver, Auckland and Sydney.

Royal Caribbean (☑866-562-7625; www.royalcaribbean.com) Departures from Honolulu and Vancouver.

Norwegian Cruise Lines (☑866-234-7350; www.ncl.com) Departures from Honolulu, Seattle and Vancouver.

GETTING AROUND

Renting a car is the only way to explore all of the Big Island. The island is divided into six districts: Kona, Kohala, Waimea, Hilo, Puna and Ka'u. The Hawai'i Belt Rd circles the island, connecting the main towns and sights. A 4WD vehicle will be handy for off-the-beaten-track adventures, but for basic sightseeing it's unnecessary. Public transit by bus is available, but service is limited and you'll probably find it way too time-consuming.

Air

Airlines Flying to & from the Big Island

The main interisland carrier, **Hawaiian Airlines** (HA; ☑800-367-5320; www.hawaiianairlines.com), flies frequently into Kona and Hilo airports in jet planes. With its impressive on-time record, Hawaiian Airlines is a reliable choice.

Two smaller, commuter-oriented airlines, **Mokulele Airlines** (☑866-260-7070; www.mokuleleairlines.com) and **Island Air** (☑800-388-1105; www.islandair.com), fly turboprop planes into Kona and also Waimea. Smaller turboprop planes fly so low that their flights almost double as sightseeing excursions. One drawback (besides the noise): carry-on baggage limits are stricter.

Hawaiian Airlines Flies numerous routes from Honolulu, Maui and Kaua'i to Kona and Hilo. Flying to a Neighbor Island, including Moloka'i and Lana'i, often requires changing planes in Honolulu.

Island Air Flies turboprop planes from Honolulu to Kona six times daily.

Mokulele Airlines Flies turboprop planes to Kona from Honolulu (three to five times daily), from Kahului, Maui (10 to 14 times daily), from Kapalua, Maui (two to three times daily) and from Ho'olehua, Moloka'i (two to five times daily). There's also less-frequent service to Waimea.

Tickets

Interisland airfares vary wildly; expect to pay from $80 to $180 one way. Round-trip fares are typically double the one-way fare. While it's possible to walk up and catch an interisland flight, especially to Honolulu, the fare will be steep. Generally, the earlier you book, the cheaper the fare.

Car & Motorcycle

For more on driving in the Big Island, see p32.

To circumnavigate the island on the 225-mile Hawai'i Belt Rd (Hwys 19 and 11), you'll need at least five hours.

From Hilo

TO	DISTANCE (MILES)	TIME (HR)
Hawai'i Volcanoes National Park	30	¾
Hawi	76	1¾
Honoka'a	41	1
Kailua-Kona	86	2
Na'alehu	66	1½
Pahoa	20	½
Waikoloa	72	1¾
Waimea	55	1¼
Waipi'o Lookout	50	1¼

From Kailua-Kona

TO	DISTANCE (MILES)	TIME (HR)
Hawai'i Volcanoes National Park	98	2¼
Hawi	53	1¼
Hilo	86	2
Honoka'a	53	1¼
Na'alehu	59	1½
Pahoa	102	2¼
Waikoloa	26	¾
Waimea	40	1
Waipi'o Lookout	63	1½

Automobile Associations

American Automobile Association (AAA; ☑800-736-2886, roadside assistance 800-222-4357; www.hawaii.aaa.com) Members are entitled to discounts on select car rentals, hotels and attractions, plus free road maps and travel-agency services. AAA has agreements with automobile associations in other countries (for example, CAA in Canada). Bring your membership card from home.

Driver's License

➡ US citizens can legally drive in the state of Hawaii with a valid driver's license from another state if they are at least 18 years old. Likewise, international visitors can legally drive in Hawaii with a valid driver's license from their home country if they are at least 18 years old.

➡ Car-rental agencies will generally accept foreign driver's licenses written in English and containing a photo. Otherwise you must present an International Driving Permit issued by your home country in addition to your foreign driver's license.

Insurance

➡ Required by law, liability insurance covers any people or property that you might hit. For damage to the rental vehicle, a collision damage waiver (CDW) costs an extra $15 to $20 per day.

➡ If you decline CDW, you will be held liable for any damages up to the full value of the car.

➡ Even with CDW, you might be required to pay the first $100 to $500 for repairs; some agencies will also charge you for the rental cost of the car during the time it takes to be repaired.

➡ If you have vehicle insurance at home, it might cover damages to rental cars; confirm with your insurance agent before your trip.

➡ Some credit card companies offer reimbursement coverage for collision damages if you rent the car with their cards; check your credit card benefits.

➡ Most credit card coverage is invalid for rental over 15 days or for 'exotic' vehicles, such as convertibles and 4WDs.

Maps

Highly recommended is the *Environmental Designs Hawai'i Map,* which contains insets of towns, plus info on geology, culture, rainfall and place names. If you're island hopping, pick up the durable, waterproof *National Geographic Hawai'i Adventure Travel Map,* which indicates roads, landmarks and elevation for the major Hawaiian Islands.

Other options include the *James Bier Map of Hawai'i: The Big Island,* an excellent topo map with geographical details such as lava flows by date. The colorful, waterproof *Franko's Hawaii (Big Island) Guide Map* highlights ocean sports and marine life. For longer trips, invest in the comprehensive *Ready Mapbook* road atlases, one covering East Hawai'i and one covering West Hawai'i.

Motorcycle & Moped

➡ Moped rentals cost from $50/250 per day/week; motorcycle rentals start around $100 per day, depending on the make and model. A sizable credit card deposit is usually necessary. Most rental agencies are located in Kailua-Kona.

➡ You can legally drive a moped in Hawaii with a valid driver's license issued by your home state or country. Motorcyclists need a valid US state motorcycle license or specially endorsed International Driving Permit.

➡ The minimum age for renting a moped is 16 years; for a motorcycle it's 21.

➡ State law requires mopeds to be ridden only by one person and prohibits their use on sidewalks and freeways. Mopeds must always be driven in single file at speeds not exceeding 30mph.

➡ Helmets are not legally required for those 18 years or older, but rental agencies often lend them for free – use 'em.

➡ Riding on the rainy windward side of Hawai'i will necessitate four-weather gear.

Rental

RENTAL AGENCIES

For information on rental agencies in the Big Island, see p32.

RATES & RESERVATIONS

➡ The daily rate for renting a small car usually ranges from $35 to $75, while typical weekly rates go from $175 to $300; taxes, fees and surcharges can easily add $10 or more per day. SUVs, vans and convertibles are much pricier than standard models.

➡ Rental rates usually include unlimited mileage.

➡ Always reserve in advance online, then recheck periodically for lower rates.

Most agencies don't charge a penalty if you cancel at the last moment.

➜ Reserve child-safety seats (about $10 per day, $50 per rental) when booking.

Road Conditions & Hazards

➜ Everyday hazards include drunk drivers and speeding along the highway. In rural areas, look out for livestock and wildlife.

➜ Roads and bridges can flood during rainstorms, especially in Hilo, Puna and Ka'u. Watch out for muddy, rocky landslides by gulches along the Hamakua Coast.

➜ Driving off-road or to Mauna Kea's summit is risky for standard cars (and for novice 4WD drivers). In such remote areas, you'll be miles from any help.

➜ On narrow, unpaved or potholed roads, locals may hog both lanes and drive over the middle stripe until an oncoming car approaches.

➜ In hyphenated addresses, such as 75-2345 Kuakini Hwy, the first part of the number identifies the tax zone and section, while the second part identifies the street address. If numbers suddenly jump unsequentially, you've just entered a new zone, that's all.

Road Rules

Slow, courteous driving is the rule on the Big Island. Generally speaking, locals don't honk (except in an emergency) or tailgate, and they let other drivers pass and merge. Do the same and you might receive an appreciative *shaka* (local-style hand wave) from other drivers.

➜ Drive on the right-hand side of the road.

➜ Talking or texting on handheld devices (eg cell phones) while driving is illegal.

➜ Driving with a blood alcohol level of 0.08% or higher or when impaired by drugs (even if legally prescribed) is illegal.

➜ It's illegal to carry open containers of alcohol (even if they're empty) inside a vehicle; unless they're full and still sealed, store them in the trunk.

➜ Seat belts are required for drivers, front-seat passengers and anyone aged under 18 years.

➜ Child safety seats are required for children aged three and under. Those aged four to seven must sit in a booster seat unless they are 4ft 9in tall, in which case they must use a lap-only seat belt in the back seat.

➜ Speed limits are posted and enforced.

➜ Turning right at a red light is permitted unless a sign prohibits it, but local drivers often wait for the green light.

➜ At four-way stop signs, cars proceed in order of arrival. If two cars arrive simultaneously, the one on the right has the right of way. When in doubt, let others go first.

➜ When emergency vehicles (ie police, fire or ambulance) approach from either direction, carefully pull over to the side of the road.

A DRIVER'S PARADISE

Not only a tropical paradise, the Big Island is also a driver's paradise. From the top of Mauna Kea to miles of coastline, from lush rainforests to lava deserts, you can navigate through staggering scenery on nicely paved roads with very few people on them. Explore the island's greatest drives:

Kohala Mountain Road (Hwy 250) An exhilarating trip down the spine of the Kohala Peninsula.

Hamakua Coast (Hwy 19) Twist and turn across deep tropical valleys plunging toward the ocean.

Pohoiki and Kapoho Roads These adjacent Puna roads are like a jaunt into the Platonic ideal of jungle.

Napo'opo'o Road In South Kona, this road traverses the wet jungle mountain slope to the savannah bottomlands.

Saddle Road (Hwy 200) Drive between the world's two highest peaks.

Kawaihae to Hawi (Hwy 270) Ring the surreal, windswept hills of North Kohala.

Hilina Pali Road Coast beneath a big sky through the volcanic wastes of Hawai'i Volcanoes National Park.

Ka'alaiki Road Only Ka'u locals know about this freshly paved jaunt amid green hills and distant sea.

Old Mamalahoa Hwy A winding journey through the backcountry of Ahualoa.

Bicycle

For more information on bicycle travel in the Big Island, see p33.

Road Rules

➡ Bicyclists are generally required to follow the same state laws and road rules (p308) as applicable to cars.

➡ State law requires all cyclists under age 16 to wear helmets.

➡ For more bicycling information, including downloadable cycling maps, search the website of the Hawaii Department of Transportation (http://hidot.hawaii.gov/highways).

Transporting Bicycles

➡ Bicyclists are generally required to follow the same state laws and road rules (p308) as applicable to cars.

➡ State law requires all cyclists under age 16 to wear helmets.

➡ For more bicycling information, including downloadable cycling maps, search the website of the Hawaii Department of Transportation (http://hidot.hawaii.gov/highways).

Bus

The island-wide **Hele-On Bus** (⌨808-961-8744; www.heleonbus.org; per trip adult/senior & student $2/1, 10-ride ticket $15, monthly pass $60) will get you to major destinations on the Big Island, but service is limited, especially on Sunday and holidays. Always check the website for current routes, schedules and fares. Most buses originate from the Mo'oheau Bus Terminal in downtown Hilo.

A one-way adult fare includes a free two-hour transfer. You cannot board with a surfboard or boogie board; luggage, backpacks, skateboards and bicycles are charged $1 each. Children under four years old ride free with fare-paying passenger.

Behind the Scenes

SEND US YOUR FEEDBACK

We love to hear from travelers – your comments keep us on our toes and help make our books better. Our well-traveled team reads every word on what you loved or loathed about this book. Although we cannot reply individually to your submissions, we always guarantee that your feedback goes straight to the appropriate authors, in time for the next edition. Each person who sends us information is thanked in the next edition – the most useful submissions are rewarded with a selection of digital PDF chapters.

Visit **lonelyplanet.com/contact** to submit your updates and suggestions or to ask for help. Our award-winning website also features inspirational travel stories, news and discussions.

Note: We may edit, reproduce and incorporate your comments in Lonely Planet products such as guidebooks, websites and digital products, so let us know if you don't want your comments reproduced or your name acknowledged. For a copy of our privacy policy visit lonelyplanet.com/privacy.

WRITER THANKS

Adam Karlin

Mahalo: Alayna Kilkuskie, my best Big Island contact and lobster night diving partner; Alexander for putting me on this assignment, co-authors Luci and Loren for all their help, and of course, the usual cast of Hawaii characters who make the Big Island one of my favorite places on Earth. And finally, and as always: Rachel and Sanda, for coming out and reminding me paradise is better with family.

Loren Bell

The biggest *mahalo* are reserved for the forces that created this adventurer's playground – be it Pele or geophysical processes, or both – and the stewards who protect it. The intense beauty of Hawai'i is well reflected in the many people who helped me along the way. But the one who deserves highest praise is Kari. Having you by my side is the best part of all of this – even if it sometimes seems I'm too busy to notice. I always notice.

Luci Yamamoto

Mahalo to Alex Howard for an opportunity to explore my home island again. To island residents, both locals and transplants, thanks for talking story and sharing your lives with me. To David Bock, Derek Kurisu and Bobby Camara, I appreciate your singular insights about Hawai'i. Most of all, endless thanks to my parents, wonderful assistants and true *kama'aina*.

ACKNOWLEDGEMENTS

Climate map data adapted from Peel MC, Finlayson BL & McMahon TA (2007) 'Updated World Map of the Köppen-Geiger Climate Classification', Hydrology and Earth System Sciences, 11, 163344.
Cover photograph: Mauna Kea Observatory, Michele Falzone/AWL ©

THIS BOOK

This 4th edition of Lonely Planet's *Hawai'i, the Big Island* guidebook was researched and written by Loren Bell, Adam Karlin and Luci Yamamoto. The previous edition was written by Sara Benson and Luci Yamamoto. This guidebook was produced by the following:

Destination Editor Alexander Howard
Product Editors Vicky Smith, Kirsten Rawlings
Senior Cartographer Corey Hutchison
Book Designers Gwen Cotter, Clara Monitto
Assisting Editors Imogen Bannister, Pete Cruttenden, Samantha Forge, Gabrielle Innes, Anne Mulvaney, Fionnuala Twomey

Assisting Cartographer Valentina Kremenchutskaya
Cover Researcher Naomi Parker

Thanks to Hannah Cartmel, Brendan Dempsey-Spencer, Sasha Drew, Shona Gray, Alison Lyall, Wayne Murphy, Catherine Naghten, Claire Naylor, Karyn Noble, Darren O'Connell, Anthony Phelan, Martine Power, Roberta Snijders, Luna Soo, Tony Wheeler and Tracy Whitmey

Index

NOTES

Map Legend

Sights
- 🏖 Beach
- 🐦 Bird Sanctuary
- 🔵 Buddhist
- 🏰 Castle/Palace
- ✝ Christian
- 卍 Confucian
- 🕉 Hindu
- ☪ Islamic
- ✡ Jain
- ✡ Jewish
- ❶ Monument
- 🏛 Museum/Gallery/Historic Building
- ☢ Ruin
- ⛩ Shinto
- ☬ Sikh
- ☯ Taoist
- 🍷 Winery/Vineyard
- 🐾 Zoo/Wildlife Sanctuary
- ⊙ Other Sight

Activities, Courses & Tours
- © Bodysurfing
- 🔵 Diving
- 🔵 Canoeing/Kayaking
- • Course/Tour
- 🔵 Sento Hot Baths/Onsen
- 🔵 Skiing
- 🔵 Snorkeling
- 🔵 Surfing
- 🔵 Swimming/Pool
- 🔵 Walking
- 🔵 Windsurfing
- ➕ Other Activity

Sleeping
- 🛏 Sleeping
- 🔺 Camping

Eating
- 🔵 Eating

Drinking & Nightlife
- 🔵 Drinking & Nightlife
- 🔵 Cafe

Entertainment
- 🔵 Entertainment

Shopping
- 🔵 Shopping

Information
- 💲 Bank
- 🔵 Embassy/Consulate
- ➕ Hospital/Medical
- @ Internet
- 🔵 Police
- 🔵 Post Office
- 🔵 Telephone
- 🔵 Toilet
- ❶ Tourist Information
- • Other Information

Geographic
- 🏖 Beach
- ⋈ Gate
- 🔵 Hut/Shelter
- 🔵 Lighthouse
- 🔵 Lookout
- ▲ Mountain/Volcano
- 🔵 Oasis
- ❶ Park
-)(Pass
- 🔵 Picnic Area
- 🔵 Waterfall

Population
- ✪ Capital (National)
- ◉ Capital (State/Province)
- ● City/Large Town
- ● Town/Village

Transport
- 🔵 Airport
- Ⓑ BART station
- ⊗ Border crossing
- 🔵 Boston T station
- 🔵 Bus
- ⋯🔵⋯ Cable car/Funicular
- ⊸🔵⊸ Cycling
- ⊸🔵⊸ Ferry
- Ⓜ Metro/Muni station
- ⊸🔵⊸ Monorail
- Ⓟ Parking
- 🔵 Petrol station
- Ⓢ Subway/SkyTrain station
- 🔵 Taxi
- ⊶🔵⊶ Train station/Railway
- ⊸🔵⊸ Tram
- Ⓤ Underground station
- • Other Transport

Note: Not all symbols displayed above appear on the maps in this book

Routes

- Tollway
- Freeway
- Primary
- Secondary
- Tertiary
- Lane
- Unsealed road
- Road under construction
- Plaza/Mall
- Steps
- Tunnel
- Pedestrian overpass
- Walking Tour
- Walking Tour detour
- Path/Walking Trail

Boundaries
- International
- State/Province
- Disputed
- Regional/Suburb
- Marine Park
- Cliff
- Wall

Hydrography
- River, Creek
- Intermittent River
- Canal
- Water
- Dry/Salt/Intermittent Lake
- Reef

Areas
- Airport/Runway
- Beach/Desert
- Cemetery (Christian)
- Cemetery (Other)
- Glacier
- Mudflat
- Park/Forest
- Sight (Building)
- Sportsground
- Swamp/Mangrove

OUR STORY

A beat-up old car, a few dollars in the pocket and a sense of adventure. In 1972 that's all Tony and Maureen Wheeler needed for the trip of a lifetime – across Europe and Asia overland to Australia. It took several months, and at the end – broke but inspired – they sat at their kitchen table writing and stapling together their first travel guide, *Across Asia on the Cheap*. Within a week they'd sold 1500 copies. Lonely Planet was born.

Today, Lonely Planet has offices in Franklin, London, Melbourne, Oakland, Dublin, Beijing and Delhi, with more than 600 staff and writers. We share Tony's belief that 'a great guidebook should do three things: inform, educate and amuse'.

OUR WRITERS

Adam Karlin

Kailua-Kona & the Kona Coast, Kohala & Waimea Adam is a Lonely Planet author based out of wherever he is. Born in Washington DC and raised in the rural Maryland tidewater, he has been exploring the world and writing about it since he was 17. It's a blessedly interesting way to live one's life. Also, it's good fun.

Loren Bell

Hawai'i Volcanoes National Park, Ka'u, Mauna Kea & Saddle Road, Puna When Loren first backpacked through Europe, he was in the backpack. That memorable experience corrupted his 6-month-old brain, ensuring he would never be happy sitting still. His penchant for peregrination has taken him from training dogsled teams in the Tetons to chasing gibbons in the jungles of Borneo – with only brief pauses for silly 'responsible' things like earning degrees. When he's not demystifying destinations for Lonely Planet, Loren writes about science and conservation news. He base-camps in the Rocky Mountains where he probably spends too much time on his mountain bike and skis.

Luci Yamamoto

Hamakua Coast, Hilo A fourth-generation native of Hawai'i, Luci is unfazed by rain, pidgin and long Hawaiian words. When she left law to be a writer, she heard the old adage: write what you know. For Lonely Planet she thus targeted the Hawaiian Islands. To her surprise, her *kama'aina* background was only a launchpad – and she discovered extraordinary new people and places on her home island. Currently a writer, editor, Iyengar yoga teacher, and blogger (www.yogaspy.com) in Vancouver, she regularly returns to Hawai'i and recharges her local 'cred.' Even more than papayas and *poke,* she loves the Big Island's aloha spirit.

Published by Lonely Planet Global Limited
CRN 554153
4th edition – Sep 2017
ISBN 978 1 78657 705 4
© Lonely Planet 2017   Photographs © as indicated 2017
10 9 8 7 6 5 4 3 2 1
Printed in China